The Psychology of Social and Cultural Diversity

Social Issues and Interventions

This edited series of books examines the psychological study of social problems and interventions. Each volume draws together newly commissioned chapters by experts in social psychology and related disciplines in order to provide a multifaceted analysis of a particular contemporary social issue. Utilizing both case studies and theory, this series presents readers with a comprehensive examination of complex social problems while concurrently advancing research in the field. Editors have been chosen for their expertise of the featured subjects, rendering Social Issues and Interventions an urgent and groundbreaking collection for scholars everywhere.

Series editor: Marilynn B. Brewer

Explaining the Breakdown of Ethnic Relations: Why Neighbors Kill
Edited by Victoria Esses & Richard Vernon

Improving Intergroup Relations: Building on the Legacy of Thomas F. Pettigrew
Edited by Ulrich Wagner, Linda Tropp, Gillian Finchilescu, and Colin Tredoux.

The Psychology of Social and Cultural Diversity
Edited by Richard J. Crisp

The Psychology of Social and Cultural Diversity

Edited by

Richard J. Crisp

A John Wiley & Sons, Ltd., Publication

This edition first published 2010
© 2010 Blackwell Publishing Limited

Blackwell Publishing was acquired by John Wiley & Sons in February 2007. Blackwell's publishing program has been merged with Wiley's global Scientific, Technical, and Medical business to form Wiley-Blackwell.

Registered Office
John Wiley & Sons Ltd, The Atrium, Southern Gate, Chichester, West Sussex, PO19 8SQ, United Kingdom

Editorial Offices
350 Main Street, Malden, MA 02148-5020, USA
9600 Garsington Road, Oxford, OX4 2DQ, UK
The Atrium, Southern Gate, Chichester, West Sussex, PO19 8SQ, UK

For details of our global editorial offices, for customer services, and for information about how to apply for permission to reuse the copyright material in this book please see our website at www.wiley.com/wiley-blackwell.

The right of Richard J. Crisp to be identified as the author of this work has been asserted in accordance with the UK Copyright, Designs and Patents Act 1988.

Wiley also publishes its books in a variety of electronic formats. Some content that appears in print may not be available in electronic books.

Designations used by companies to distinguish their products are often claimed as trademarks. All brand names and product names used in this book are trade names, service marks, trademarks or registered trademarks of their respective owners. The publisher is not associated with any product or vendor mentioned in this book. This publication is designed to provide accurate and authoritative information in regard to the subject matter covered. It is sold on the understanding that the publisher is not engaged in rendering professional services. If professional advice or other expert assistance is required, the services of a competent professional should be sought.

Library of Congress Cataloging-in-Publication Data

Crisp, Richard J., 1973-
 The psychology of social and cultural diversity / Richard J. Crisp.
  p. cm.– (Social issues and interventions)
 Includes bibliographical references and index.
 ISBN 978-1-4051-9562-1 (hardcover : alk. paper) – ISBN 978-1-4051-9561-4
(pbk. : alk. paper) 1. Social groups. 2. Categorization (Psychology) 3. Group identity.
4. Cultural pluralism. I. Title.
 HM716.C75 2010
 305.8009'051–dc22

                                                                2010003119

A catalogue record for this book is available from the British Library.

Set in 10.5/12.5pt Galliard by Thomson, Noida, India

01   2010

Contents

Notes on Contributors

Christopher L. Aberson, Humboldt State University

Catherine E. Amiot, Université du Québec à Montréal

Verónica Benet-Martínez, University of California, Riverside

Marilynn B. Brewer, University of New South Wales

Lindsey Cameron, University of Kent

Chi-Yue Chiu, Nanynang Technological University

Richard J. Crisp, University of Kent

Wendy P. van Ginkel, Erasmus University Rotterdam

Miles Hewstone, University of Oxford

Geoffrey C. Ho, University of California, Los Angeles

Ying-yi Hong, Nanynang Technological University

Karen A. Jehn, University of Melbourne

Daan van Knippenberg, Erasmus University Rotterdam

Norman Miller, University of Southern California

Angela-MinhTu D. Nguyen, University of California, Riverside

Sun No, Macalester College

Floor A. Rink, University of Groningen

Roxane de la Sablonnière , Université de Montréal

Diana T. Sanchez, Rutgers University

Katharina Schmid, University of Oxford

Margaret Shih, University of California, Los Angeles

Marija Spanovic, University of Southern California

Douglas Stenstrom, California State University, Los Angeles

Carmit T. Tadmor, Tel-Aviv University

Rhiannon N. Turner, University of Leeds

Maykel Verkuyten, Utrecht University

Sven Waldzus, ISCTE-Lisbon University Institute

Series Preface

The series of volumes on *Social Issues and Interventions* represents a joint effort of the Society for the Psychological Study of Social Issues (SPSSI) and Wiley-Blackwell, launched in 2006. Consistent with SPSSI's dual mission of encouraging systematic research on current social issues and bringing the findings of social psychological research to bear on public policy, the goal of the series is to help fill the gap between basic research on social issues and translation into social policy and program interventions. Each book in the series is an edited volume devoted to a specific social issue-relevant theme, covering related theory, research, and application.

Editors and contributors to each volume are experts in social psychology and related disciplines in order to provide a multifaceted analysis of a particular contemporary social issue. Utilizing both case studies and theory, this series is intended to present readers with a comprehensive examination of complex social problems while concurrently advancing research in the field.

As the third volume in the series, *The Psychology of Social and Cultural Diversity* fulfills the purposes envisioned for this venture, bringing together multiple perspectives to focus on a compelling and critically important social issue. The unprecedented degree of cultural, religious, and ideological diversity now existing within, as well as between, nation-states constitutes a unique challenge of the twenty-first century. Although managing the consequences of diversity has political, economic, and institutional aspects, the psychological challenges of living in a complex multicultural world are particularly profound. Realizing the benefits of diversity without the costs of conflict or alienation will require new forms of social identity, new ways of thinking about differences, and new psychological adaptations to embrace change and

complexity. The 14 chapters in this volume address these psychological dimensions of managing diversity with research-based insights that
should be of interest and relevance to social scientists and policy makers
alike. The message that comes through from the collective works is that
the problems are complex but the promise of diversity can and will be
realized.

Marilynn B. Brewer
Series Editor

1

Introduction

Richard J. Crisp

Diversity has become the defining characteristic of our social and cultural worlds. We are now constantly confronted with a multitude of ways in which we can define ourselves, and categorize others. Ethnicity, nationality, gender, religion, occupation, politics—our social and cultural worlds are increasingly, and unassailably, multifaceted. Since the mid-1950s we have seen unprecedented intercultural exchange, and the geographical boundaries that previously divided cultures have been slowly but surely eroded. In the United States, for example, 33.5 million people (12% of the population) were born overseas (US Census Bureau, 2004), and in the United Kingdom it is 4.9 million (8.3% of the population) (National Statistics, 2001). We no longer live in the provincial, homogenized worlds that characterized much of human history; we live in worlds defined by diversity.

As a consequence, diversity is arguably *the* most persistently debated characteristic of modern societies. The nature of a world in which traditional social, cultural, and geographic boundaries have given way to increasingly complex representations of identity creates new questions and new demands for social scientists and policymakers alike. Understanding the psychology of social and cultural diversity is critical to how we answer these questions, and meet these demands. This book is all about the multifaceted nature of modern society and, in particular, the psychological and behavioral consequences of increasing social and cultural diversity. The book brings together scholars from a wide range of perspectives to offer, for the first time, an integrated volume that explores the psychological implications and applications of this timely social issue. The contributors provide cutting-edge analyses and discussions of theory and research as well as directly addressing policy implications and prospective interventions.

The chapters are organized into six thematic groupings that high-light the range of perspectives that characterize the field: *social identity, culture, intergroup attitudes, intergroup relations, group processes,* and *interventions*. As well as illustrating how social and cultural diversity is an important focus in all of these domains, these groupings provide the basis for drawing parallels in theory and research that crosscut these boundaries. A summary and introduction to what you will find in these chapters is outlined below.

Part I: Social Identity

The three chapters in Part I focus on how diversity can define social identity and, in particular, antecedents, processes, and consequences of possessing multiple identities for social behavior. In Chapter 2: *Social Identity Complexity and Acceptance of Diversity* Marilynn Brewer discusses recent research developing the concept of social identity complexity. The notion of identity is central to social and cultural psychology, and social identity complexity is an approach that incorporates an understanding of our evolving societies with these perspectives. Brewer argues that in large and complex societies people are differentiated along many meaningful dimensions, including gender, age, religion, ethnicity, and political ideology. Furthermore, such categorizations are crosscutting so that people can share a common ingroup membership on one dimension but be different along others. Social identity complexity conceptualizes the way in which this complex and differentiated social structure is reflected in individuals' representations of their own identity. In this chapter Brewer outlines theory and empirical support for the idea that social identity complexity can promote generalized tolerance and acceptance of diversity for individuals, groups, and society at large.

Building on the idea that social and cultural diversity can have a considerable impact on self-construal, in Chapter 3: *Facilitating the Development and Integration of Multiple Social Identities: The Case of Immigrants in Québec* Catherine Amiot and Roxane de la Sablonnière outline their model of social identity development that focuses specifically on how individuals integrate multiple identities into their self-concept. Their model draws conceptual links between social psychological theories (i.e., social identity theory, self-categorization theory) and developmental principles to outline the factors that facilitate identity integration. In particular, they argue that the integration of multiple social identities should be facilitated when membership of multiple groups is meaningful to the individual, and those groups support, recognize, and value the contribution made by their individual members. They discuss factors that may inhibit this integration process (threat, status, and power differentials) and apply their model to the case of immigration in Québec.

In Chapter 4: *Costs and Benefits of Switching among Multiple Social Identities* Margaret Shih, Diana Sanchez, and Geoffrey Ho discuss research that has revealed considerable benefits of possessing multiple identities for psychological health. This research has shown how diversity that defines the self (for instance, regarding being both a woman and Asian as central to one's identity) can afford a psychological buffer against negative life events. They discuss research showing that people with accessible multiple identities can identify flexibly with one or other of these identities depending on factors such as individual differences, motivations, and social context, and how this flexible self-construal may afford an adaptive and effective psychological buffer against negative life events, enhancing well-being and promoting positive adjustment outcomes.

Part II: Culture

The chapters in Part II continue to examine the implications of possessing multiple identities for the self-concept, but from the perspective of cross-cultural psychology. In Chapter 5: *Multicultural Identity: What It Is and Why It Matters* Angela-MinhTu D. Nguyen and Verónica Benet-Martínez outline theory and research on biculturalism, and in particular, the concept of bicultural identity integration. Being bicultural (e.g., Chinese Americans who maintain both their Chinese cultural identity as well as identifying with American culture) has been found to have unique and positive impacts on a range of cognitions and behavior. Nguyen and Benet-Martínez define biculturalism, its components, and related constructs (e.g., acculturation strategies) and go on to compare the different ways of measuring it (e.g., unidimensional versus bidimensional models). They focus in particular on bicultural identity integration and discuss the impacts of differing degrees of integration on a range of cognitions and behaviors.

In Chapter 6: *What I Know in My Mind and Where My Heart Belongs: Multicultural Identity Negotiation and its Cognitive Consequences* Carmit Tadmor, Sun No, Ying-yi Hong, and Chi-yue Chiu outline an integrative model of the development and cognitive consequences of possessing a multicultural identity (that is, defining one's identity in terms of more than one culture). The authors argue that developing a multicultural identity involves integrating ideas and practices from different cultures, processes that have a significant and lasting impact on cognitive functioning. In particular, such experiences can lead to greater cognitive flexibility, through the process of cultural frame-switching, and the authors illustrate how this can be demonstrated in disparate domains such as creative performance. The authors discuss the model's implications for immigration policies and the development of multicultural competence.

Part III: Intergroup Attitudes

While Parts I and II focus on examining how diversity defines identity, the chapters in Part III move on to consider how exposure to social and cultural diversity impacts attitudes toward *others*. While these chapters broadly shift to exploring the implications of perceiving, rather than possessing, multiple identities, the work discussed draws upon key themes that have been developed in the previous chapters (such as the psychological and behavioral benefits of diversity, and the psychological processes that are engaged to deal with a world characterized by diversity).

The first chapter in Part III illustrates how researchers have examined multicultural diversity from two vantage points—not only the effects on the individual who is defined by multiple identities but also the effects of diversity on perceivers. In Chapter 7: *Multiculturalism and Tolerance: An Intergroup Perspective* Maykel Verkuyten examines key questions faced by multicultural societies, including: "Should Sikhs be allowed to wear a turban rather than a helmet on construction sites or a crash helmet when riding a motorcycle?," "Should Muslim teachers refuse to shake hands with children's parents of the opposite sex?," and "Should civil servants be allowed to wear a headscarf or students wear a burqa or a niqab?" Verkuyten examines multiculturalism and tolerance as they relate to social and cultural diversity, exploring the interaction between salient policies of multiculturalism versus assimilation and psychological processes, and the notion that multicultural policies should involve active support for cultural difference.

In Chapter 8: *Diversity Experiences and Intergroup Attitudes* Christopher Aberson explores the impact of diversity experiences and beliefs on intergroup attitudes. This work illustrates how it is not only important to experience diversity *per se*, but that there are a number of conditions that are critical to ensure that diversity is experienced in the *right way,* and that such experiences are valued, and have an impact on individuals' broader ideological orientations. He first examines the impacts of diverse educational and work experiences, with a special focus on interventions designed to promote positive experiences and attitudes. He then discusses research on diversity-valuing attitudes and their relationship to more positive intergroup attitudes, focusing on research that has illuminated the psychological mechanisms that mediate the relationship between attitudes and experience. The chapter ends with a discussion of the implications of this work for social policies such as affirmative action, as well as suggestions for future research.

Part IV: Intergroup Relations

Chapters 7 and 8 introduced the idea that exposure to social and cultural diversity can have significant implications not only for the self, but for how individuals perceive and evaluate others. The two chapters in this section develop this idea in their discussions of the impact of exposure to diversity on intergroup relations. In particular, these chapters have developed laboratory-based analogues of the categorization processes that defined exposure to diversity. This has allowed an examination of the basic cognitive, motivational, affective, and ideological processes that underlie reactions to diversity and differentiation. As these authors illustrate, lessons learned in the laboratory can then usefully inform and instruct the ways in which policymakers should implement strategies for improving intergroup relations.

In Chapter 9: *The Effects of Crossed Categorizations in Intergroup Interaction* Norman Miller, Marija Spanovic, and Douglas Stenstrom discuss research into the impacts of crossed categorization on intergroup bias. The crossed categorization paradigm is a precise experimental analogue of the relationship between the self and others in socially diverse contexts. The authors illustrate how crossed categorization is a structural feature of societies and human relations that has a significant impact on how we perceive, understand, and relate to others. They use the crossed categorization paradigm to answer questions such as: "How do people process, integrate, and categorize others in the face of complex social and cultural diversity?," "What occurs when one category dominates the intergroup setting?," and "How do affective and cognitive processes influence the categorization process?" They argue that at the heart of crossed categorization research is the ability to model real-world situations wherein individuals are routinely faced with multiple salient categorizations.

In Chapter 10: *Complexity of Superordinate Self-categories and Ingroup Projection* Sven Waldzus discusses how diversity impacts on processes described by the ingroup projection model. This model is a psychological account of how social groups are evaluated within the context of a common frame of comparison. In other words, it provides a framework for understanding how high-status and/or majority groups can psychologically exclude minority groups. According to the model, ingroup members tend to project their group's characteristics (e.g., White) on to the superordinate group prototype (e.g., British), providing a basis for discriminating against other (typically minority) groups (e.g., Asian), because they then deviate from the ingroup norm (which has been defined by the dominant majority group). Waldzus describes research that has examined whether it is possible to reduce ingroup projection by encouraging more complex (diverse) representations of superordinate categories, and the potential benefits of highlighting diversity for social relations that are defined by differing status.

Part V: Group Processes

Continuing with the theme developed in Parts III and IV, that exposure to social and cultural diversity can have an impact on attitudes and behaviors toward others, and developing the idea that diversity can be represented by social categories that either reinforce or crosscut existing differences, the next two chapters examine the effects of diversity on performance in work groups and organizations. In Chapter 11: *The Categorization-Elaboration Model of Work Group Diversity: Wielding the Double-Edged Sword* Daan van Knippenberg and Wendy van Ginkel outline how work group diversity affects group functioning and performance. In particular, they describe the Categorization-Elaboration Model, a model that can account for diverging outcomes observed in several decades of research on work group diversity. The model accounts for how diversity can both disrupt group performance by forming "faultlines" along converging bases for group differentiation but, under the right conditions, can also stimulate elaborative processing of task-relevant information leading to facilitated group performance. The authors discuss empirical evidence in support of the model, from experimental and field research, and its implications for the management of diversity, focusing on a variety of factors including team composition, leadership, training, and development.

In Chapter 12: *Divided We Fall, or United We Stand? How Identity Processes Affect Faultline Perceptions and the Functioning of*

Diverse Teams Floor Rink and Karen Jehn further discuss the implications of faultlines in work groups, using the social identity and self-categorization perspectives. They argue that identity processes determine whether diversity faultlines will result in a negative or positive impact on work teams. Drawing on research using the common ingroup identity model that shows how subgroup identification moderates reactions to weakened group boundaries, the authors discuss a number of practical ways in which groups and organizations can deal with diversity that is perceived as threatening, and illustrate the value in combining research in social categorization, intergroup relations, and group productivity.

Part VI: Interventions

In Part VI two chapters describe how research on diversity is being harnessed to develop interventions for promoting tolerance, improving intergroup relations, and enhancing well-being and psychological health. In Chapter 13: *Combined Effects of Intergroup Contact and Multiple Categorization: Consequences for Intergroup Attitudes in Diverse Social Contexts* Katharina Schmid and Miles Hewstone combine some of the concepts already discussed in this volume in their research, showing how intergroup contact can lead to more differentiated perceptions of outgroups via enhanced social identity complexity. Drawing on research into crossed categorization, they examine the combined effects of intergroup contact and multiple categorization processes on perceived differences and intergroup bias in socially and culturally diverse contexts.

Finally, in Chapter 14: *The Application of Diversity-based Interventions to Policy and Practice* Lindsey Cameron and Rhiannon Turner discuss the prospects for application of psychological interventions based on diversity research to educational contexts. They illustrate how the school environment provides the most likely context within which children will come into contact with others from different ethnic or racial backgrounds. However, they point to evidence that shows how children typically choose friends from within their own ethnic or racial group rather than spontaneously developing cross-group friendships. They show how encouraging, in particular, intervention strategies that encourage cross-group friendship may be one of the most effective methods by which the opportunity for diverse contact experiences can be harnessed, leading to reduced prejudice in both children and adults.

References

National Statistics (2001). *People and migration: Foreign-born*. Retrieved December 1, 2009, from http://www.statistics.gov.uk/cci/nugget.asp?id= 1312.

US Census Bureau (2004). *Foreign-Born Population of the United States: Current Population Survey*. Retrieved December 1, 2009, from http://www.census.gov/prod/2004pubs/p20-551.pdf.

Part I

Social Identity

2

Social Identity Complexity and Acceptance of Diversity

Marilynn B. Brewer

In social psychology, much of the research on social identity and inter-group relations has been dominated by the power of social category distinctions to produce us–them thinking, with associated ingroup biases, intergroup discrimination, and hostility (Brewer, 1979; Tajfel, 1978, 1981). And, indeed, salient ingroup–outgroup differentiation has been found to underlie a wide range of group behavior, from discriminatory allocations in the laboratory to protracted intergroup conflicts where national identities are at stake (Bar-Tal, 2007; Kelman, 1999). Such research has led many in social psychology to assume that strong ingroup identification and outgroup prejudice and hostility are one and the same. However, as Amin Maalouf points out in his book *In the Name of Identity* (1996/2003), it is not group identity per se that has such negative consequences for intergroup behavior, but rather the focus on a *singular* identity that reduces the complexity of individual attachments and affiliations to a single, central us–them distinction.

A dominant ingroup–outgroup distinction may arise under condi-tions of novelty or uncertainty where one dimension of group identity is made highly salient, as it is in some laboratory settings (e.g., Mullin & Hogg, 1998; Tajfel et al., 1971), or in the real world, under conditions of intense conflict where a particular group identity is under chronic threat or attack. But in the modern, complex social world, such singular ingroup–outgroup differentiations (dramatic and powerful as they may be) may be more the exception than the rule.

In a large and complex society, persons are differentiated or subdi-vided along many meaningful social dimensions, including gender and sexual orientation, life stage (e.g., student, worker, retiree), economic sector (e.g., technology, service, academic, professional), religion, ethnicity, political ideology, and recreational preferences. Each of these divisions provides a basis for shared identity and group membership that may become an important source of social identification. Further, most of these differentiations are crosscutting in the sense that individuals may share a common ingroup membership on one dimension but belong to different categories on another dimension. Hence, having multiple group memberships has the potential to reduce the likelihood that one's social world can be reduced to a single ingroup–outgroup distinction.

The present chapter will review the concept of *social identity complexity* and discuss how an individual's cognitive representation of his or her own ingroups can impact inclusiveness of social identity and intergroup attitudes. The general idea is that individuals in complex societies have multiple ingroup memberships that are, objectively, crosscutting categories. However, membership in such crosscutting groups may not in itself be sufficient to reduce ingroup bias and intergroup discrimination. Rather, it is the subjective representation of identity complexity that matters for intergroup attitudes. In the following sections I will review the theory underlying social identity complexity and then empirical research on measuring identity complexity and its relationship to intergroup attitudes, tolerance, and acceptance of diversity. Finally, I will consider the policy implications of this program of research for multicultural societies.

Crosscutting Identities: Objective vs. Subjective Representations

The idea that crosscutting social categorizations reduce the propensity for intergroup conflict has a long history in the social sciences. Anthropologists (e.g., Gluckman, 1955; Murphy, 1957), sociologists (e.g., Blau, 1977; Coser, 1956), political scientists (e.g., Almond & Verba, 1963; Lipset, 1959), and social psychologists (e.g., Brewer, 2000; Crisp & Hewstone, 1999, 2007) have all postulated that the existence of orthogonal, crosscutting social differentiations reduces the likelihood of intrasocietal cleavages and internal conflict (see LeVine & Campbell, 1972, Chapter 4). Coser (1956) hypothesized, for instance:

> In flexible social structures, multiple conflicts crisscross each other and thereby prevent basic cleavages along one axis. The multiple group affiliations of individuals makes them participate in various group conflicts so that their total personalities are not involved in any single one of them. Thus

segmental participation in a multiplicity of conflicts constitutes a balancing mechanism within the structure.

(pp. 153–154)

Similarly, Lipset (1959) identified role differentiation and crosscutting ties as essential structural preconditions for the development of stable democracies.

From a social psychological perspective, the question to be asked is whether ingroup bias and intergroup discrimination based on a particular ingroup–outgroup distinction are reduced when another crosscutting ingroup–outgroup category distinction is introduced. There are a number of theoretical reasons why multiple crosscutting social identities might reduce discrimination along any one dimension.

First, crosscutting distinctions make social categorization more complex and reduce the magnitude of ingroup–outgroup differentiations. According to social categorization theory (Deschamps & Doise, 1978; Vanbeselaere, 1991), processes of intracategory assimilation and intercategory contrast counteract each other when categories are crosscutting. Thus, the effects of category accentuation are reduced or eliminated, and differences between groups are minimized (or no greater than perceived differences within groups). This undermines the cognitive basis of ingroup bias.

Second, partially overlapping group memberships reduce the evaluative significance for the self of intergroup comparisons (Brown & Turner, 1979), thereby undermining the motivational base for intergroup discrimination (Vanbeselaere, 1991).

Third, multiple group memberships reduce the importance of any one social identity for satisfying an individual's need for belonging and self-definition (Brewer, 1991), again reducing the motivational base for ingroup bias.

Finally, principles of cognitive balance (Heider, 1958; Newcomb, 1963) are also brought into play when ingroups and outgroups have overlapping membership. When another person is an ingroup member on one category dimension but belongs to an outgroup in another categorization, cognitive inconsistency is introduced if that individual is evaluated positively as an ingroup member but is also associated with others who are evaluated negatively as outgroup members. In an effort to resolve such inconsistencies, interpersonal balance processes should lead to greater positivity toward the outgroup based on overlapping memberships.

Of these theoretical mechanisms underlying effects of cross-categorization, the concepts of social differentiation and decategorization have received the lion's share of research attention (Crisp &

Hewstone, 2007). Much of the social psychological literature on the effects of multiple categorization (including many of the chapters in the present volume) focuses on perception of *other* persons (for reviews, see Crisp & Hewstone, 1999, 2007; Urban & Miller, 1998; Miller, Spanovic, & Stenstrom, this volume). When research participants are presented with information about another person or group of people who share their ingroup membership on one dimension but belong to an outgroup on another dimension, it has been found that perceivers sometimes evaluate others on the basis of one dominant categorization and ignore or even inhibit alternative categorizations (e.g., Macrae, Bodenhausen, & Milne, 1995; Rothbart & John, 1985), sometimes evaluate others on the basis of an additive combination of the different category memberships (e.g., Brown & Turner, 1979; Hewstone, Islam, & Judd, 1993), and sometimes create a compound category with emergent properties that are not predicted from the contributing categories considered separately (e.g., Brewer, 1988; Kunda, Miller, & Claire, 1990).

One thing that has not always been taken into account in trying to explain these variations in perceptions of others is the way that the perceiver represents his or her *own* multiple category identities. For instance, how a person who is both White and Christian responds to another individual who is Black and Christian may well depend on how the perceiver defines his or her racial and religious identities as ingroups. Understanding the structure of multiple social identities is important because representations of one's ingroups have effects not only on the self-concept but also on the nature of relationships between self and others.

Importantly, the actual complexity of multiple, partially overlapping group memberships may or may not be reflected in the individual's *subjective* representation of his or her multiple identities. For instance, a woman who is both White and Christian may think of her religious ingroup as composed primarily of white people, even though, objectively, there are many nonwhite Christians. Conversely, she may think of her racial ingroup as largely Christian, despite the fact that there are many whites who embrace other religions. By reducing the subjective inclusiveness of both ingroups to their overlapping memberships, the individual maintains a relatively simplified identity structure. Importantly, all of the factors that would mitigate intergroup bias when categories are crossed would operate to *enhance* bias if two different bases of categorization are convergent (i.e., ingroup–outgroup distinctions on one category overlap perfectly with ingroup–outgroup distinctions on a second category, as when distinctions based on ethnicity and religion are correspondent) (Arcuri,

1982). Thus, the implications of multiple ingroup identities depend not only on the objective structure of category membership but on whether the crosscutting structure is mapped onto the individual's subjective representation of his/her social identities.

Social Identity Complexity Theory

Roccas and Brewer (2002) introduced the concept of *social identity complexity* to represent the subjective structure of multiple group identities. The idea behind the social identity complexity construct is that it is not only how many social groups an individual identifies with that matters but, more importantly, how those different identities are subjectively combined to determine the overall inclusiveness of the individual's ingroup memberships.

Roccas and Brewer (2002) identified four different patterns that capture the ways any two or more crosscutting group memberships could be subjectively combined to define an individual's resultant ingroup. One way that an individual can achieve simultaneous recognition of more than one social identity and yet maintain a single ingroup representation is to define the ingroup as the *intersection* of multiple group memberships. For instance, a female lawyer can define her primary social identity in terms of the compound combination of *both* sex and profession, an identity shared only with other women lawyers. In this representation, the compound category is a single, unique social identity with properties that make it distinct from either of the larger categories from which it is derived.

A second pattern for coping with multiple group memberships is *dominance*, where the individual adopts one primary group identification to which all other potential group identities are subordinated. In this model, the ingroup is defined as those who share membership in this primary ingroup category; alternative social identities are *embedded* within the primary group identification (as sources of intragroup variation), but not extended to those outside that ingroup. For instance, a female lawyer who assigns primacy to her professional identity regards all lawyers as fellow ingroup members. Being a woman (or sailor, or Yale Law School graduate, etc.) is a characteristic that describes what *kind* of a lawyer she is, what makes her more or less similar to others in her ingroup category (and to the category prototype), but her social identity is not extended to women or Yale graduates as a whole.

A third pattern is that of *compartmentalization*, in which different identity groups are isolated rather than combined. With compartmentalization, social identities are context- or situation-specific. In certain

Table 2.1 Alternative Patterns of Combination of Two Ingroups (Arrayed in Accord with Complexity Components)

Low complexity			*High complexity*
Intersection	*Dominance*	*Compartmentalization*	*Merger*
Only those who share both category memberships are recognized as ingroup members	One group identity defines ingroup membership; other identities are viewed as subgroups	Group membership identities are activated separately in different contexts	Others sharing either or both group memberships are simultaneously recognized as ingroup members
No differentiation of separate ingroups	Low differentiation, low integration	High differentiation, low integration	High differentiation, high integration

contexts, one group membership becomes the primary basis of social identity whereas other group identities become primary in different contexts. At the office, for instance, one's professional identity may be the only relevant basis for ingroup–outgroup distinctions; shared identities based on sex, ethnicity, religion, or recreational group memberships are irrelevant and not activated in this setting. Back home, however, religious affiliation or cultural group membership may become the most important basis for shared identity and the social self. With this mode of identity structure, multiple ingroup identities are maintained as a whole, but the individual does not activate these social identities simultaneously and hence acknowledges only one ingroup at a time.

The final pattern for representation of multiple social group identities is *merger*, in which crosscutting group memberships are simultaneously recognized and embraced in their most inclusive form. In this mode, ingroup identification is extended to others who share *any* of one's important social category memberships—the ingroup is the *sum* of one's combined group identifications. For our female lawyer, her identification with women as a social group crosses the boundary of lawyer and non-lawyer, while her identification with lawyers crosses the sex divide, and both identity groups are important and salient across situations. With the merger pattern, the individual recognizes that each of his/her group memberships incorporates a different set of people as ingroup members and the combined representation is the *sum* of all of these group identities—more inclusive than any one ingroup identity considered alone.

Adopting Tetlock's (1983) definition of cognitive complexity as characterized by both *differentiation* and *integration* of potentially conflicting beliefs and values, Roccas and Brewer argued that these four patterns could be arrayed along a dimension of complexity and inclusiveness, defined by intersection at one extreme (low complexity) and merger at the other (high complexity). Intersection is the least complex form because it reduces multiple, potentially diverse group identities to a single, highly exclusive social identity. Dominance is also on the low-complexity end of the continuum, since it suppresses inconsistencies within a single ingroup–outgroup dimension. Compartmentalization represents the next level of complexity in that separate identities are acknowledged and differentiated, but without any attempt at reconciliation. Merger represents the highest level of complexity because it preserves both differentiation and integration in an inclusive social identity.

Table 2.1 provides a summary of the hypothesized patterns of ingroup combination, ordered in terms of the social identity complexity dimension.

Measuring Social Identity Complexity: Perceived Membership Overlap

In considering how to operationalize the social identity complexity construct, Roccas and Brewer (2002) noted that one way to think about the different patterns of ingroup combination is in terms of the perceived overlap in the *composition* of group memberships. Some persons may perceive the different groups to which they belong as containing the same members. The groups "Catholic" and "Italian" could serve as an example: Although these two groups do not objectively share all of their members (many Italians are not Catholic, and many Catholics are not Italian), some people may perceive them as highly overlapping: When they think about Italians they think about Catholics, and persons of different religious faith are not considered "real" Italians. High perceived overlap in group memberships implies that the different ingroups are actually conceived as a single convergent social identity. In this case, the subjective boundaries of both ingroups are defined in such a way that they contain only those who share the other identity as well. On the other hand, when overlapping membership between various ingroups is perceived to be relatively small, the boundaries of each ingroup are defined in such a way that they include members who do *not* share the other identities. In this case, the combined group identities are larger and more inclusive than any of the ingroups alone. In sum, the more a person perceives the groups to which he belongs as sharing the same members, the less complex is his social identity.

To measure individual differences in perceived overlap of their ingroup memberships, we first elicit information from respondents to identify their three or four most important group memberships across different domains (e.g., religion, ethnicity, occupation, political organizations, sports). We then ask them a set of questions regarding their subjective impression of the extent of overlap in membership between all possible pairings of their ingroups, in each direction of comparison (e.g., Of persons who are Catholic, how many are also university students? Of persons who are university students, how many are also Catholic?). Judgments are made on a 10-point scale, where 1 = very few, 5 = about half, and 10 = all. An index of *overlap complexity* is created by calculating the mean rating of proportion of overlap between ingroups, where high values indicated greater overlap and less complexity in the representation of multiple identities.

Preliminary studies using this method for assessing social identity complexity suggested that the measure has reasonable construct validity

(Roccas & Brewer, 2002). Individual differences in overlap complexity, for example, proved to be significantly correlated with associated values from the Schwartz (1992, 1994) value inventory. From responses to the Schwartz inventory, we focused on four value indices that reflected the two dimensions (openness vs. conservatism; power vs. universalism) we had predicted to be related to social identity complexity. Openness was computed as the average importance placed on creativity, freedom, independent, curious, choosing own goals, daring, a varied life, and an exciting life. Conservatism was defined as the average of humble, accepting my portion in life, devout, respect for tradition, moderate, politeness, obedient, self-discipline, honoring parents and elders, family security, national security, social order, clean, and reciprocation of favors. Power was an index based on the importance of social power, authority, wealth, and preserving my public image, and universalism was derived from ratings of broadminded, wisdom, social justice, equality, a world at peace, a world of beauty, unity with nature, and protecting the environment.

We expected power and conservatism to be negatively related to social identity complexity because they are associated with high need for structure and consistency. Conversely, we expected that openness and universalism would be positive related to the complexity index. Results of the correlational study supported those expectations. Scores on the overlap complexity measures were higher (lower complexity) for persons who ascribe relatively high importance to conservatism values and/or to power. Conversely, importance of openness to change and universalism values were associated with lower overlap scores (higher social identity complexity).

Motives Underlying Social Identity Complexity

Like Tetlock (1983, 1986), we assume that greater levels of integrative complexity require effort-demanding cognitive strategies and resources. Social identity complexity is the product of a process of recognizing and interpreting information about one's own ingroups. Having a complex social identity is dependent on two conditions: first, awareness of more than one ingroup categorization, and second, recognition that the multiple ingroup categories do not converge. Reconciling the incongruences that are implied by this nonconvergence requires cognitive resources. Thus, like other forms of integrative complexity (Tetlock, Skitka, & Boettger, 1989; Woike & Aronoff,

1992), social identity complexity is subject to situational and motivational determinants as well as individual differences in cognitive style (Schroder, Driver, & Streufert, 1967). Some individuals may be chronically high in social identity complexity. For such persons, integrative complexity in thinking about multiple ingroup identities may become automatized, requiring relatively little conscious effort or cognitive resources. In most cases, however, social identity complexity can be expected to vary as a function of the individual's current motivation to think about his or her multiple ingroup identities and available cognitive resources to merge these identities in an inclusive manner.

More specifically, social identity complexity will be affected by stable individual differences in the motivation to attend to complex information. Consistent with this prediction, we have found that scores on the overlap complexity measure are significantly correlated with individual differences in *need for cognition* (Miller, Brewer, & Arbuckle, 2009). Conversely, social identity complexity should be negatively related to intolerance of ambiguity or uncertainty. A complex social identity lessens the possibility of obtaining firm and unequivocal answers that pertain to group membership of self and of others. When there is low overlap between ingroups, another individual may be simultaneously an ingroup member and an outgroup member. Consequently, there is no definite answer to questions such as "is this person one of 'us' or one of 'them?'" Therefore, it is likely that individuals with high need for closure prefer to perceive their ingroups as similar to each other and as sharing their members, and are thus likely to have relatively low social identity complexity.

In addition, social identity complexity will be affected by situational factors that temporarily affect attentional resources, or *cognitive load*. Situational demands that place a heavy load on attention capacities, such as performing multiple tasks concurrently, usually have detrimental effects on information processing, retrieval, and analysis (e.g. Conway, Carroll, Pushkar, & Arbuckle, 1996; Osterhouse & Brock, 1970; Petty, Wells, & Brock, 1976). Individuals are not constantly aware of all their group memberships: Usually they are most aware of the categories that render the social context subjectively most meaningful—the social categories in which there is most similarity within groups and maximum distinctiveness between groups (Oakes & Turner, 1990; Turner, Hogg, Oakes, Reicher, & Wetherell, 1987). Moreover, it is likely that the overlap between ingroups is more chronically accessible than nonoverlap because individuals are usually surrounded by others who share their same ingroups. Thus, the awareness of complex social identities may require greater cognitive effort and attention than more simple ingroup representations. Consistent with this reasoning, Miller et al. (2009) found that manipulating demand for cognitive elaboration influenced participants' responses on the overlap complexity measure. Participants who were told to think carefully about their responses generated significantly lower overlap ratings than participants who were told to respond quickly, "off the top of their heads."

As a consequence of the cognitive effort associated with overlap complexity, cognitive overload may affect the accessibility of information that contributes to a complex social identity (simultaneous awareness of multiple ingroups, and awareness of nonoverlap between them) more than the accessibility of information pertaining to simple social identity (awareness of only one ingroup or perception that all ingroups overlap extensively), resulting in a temporary reduction of social identity complexity.

A similar line of reasoning applies to the effects of acute stress on social identity complexity. Considerable research indicates that anxious people appear to have diminished cognitive resources (for a review see Wegner & Wenzlaff, 1996). Anxiety is especially detrimental to performance on effortful tasks, but has little effect on easy tasks or automatic ones (Eysenck, 1992; Kahneman, 1973). In addition, extensive research indicates that stress causes the narrowing of attentional focus (e.g. Neufeld & McCarty, 1994; Steblay, 1992). Under stress, individuals often focus on the central features of stimuli and neglect peripheral characteristics. This could affect social identity complexity in that individuals under stress will tend to perceive their groups as largely overlapping and largely similar. These predictions are specific to negative moods that deplete cognitive processing.

Results from preliminary studies conducted in Israel (Roccas & Brewer, 2002) supported this relationship between stress-related moods and social identity complexity. Respondents in one study completed a mood checklist, which was administered before the complexity measure. The mood checklist consisted of 15 mood states that tapped four types of mood: stress (e.g., worried, agitated), cheerful (e.g., happy, joyful), calm (e.g., calm, relaxed), and sad (e.g., sad, disappointed). Participants were instructed to check all the items that reflected their current mood. We calculated the correlation between social identity complexity scores and the presence of stress-related mood and found that overlap complexity was significantly correlated with stress-related mood in the expected direction. That is, individuals who were experiencing stress had higher social identity complexity scores (lower complexity) than individuals who were not experiencing such emotions. Consistent with the hypothesis that mood effects on social identity complexity would be specific to stress-related affect, the correlations between the other three mood indices and the index of complexity were all nonsignificant.

Experiential Bases of Social Identity Complexity

Most of the time, individuals are surrounded by others who are similar to themselves (Kelley & Evans, 1995). We are first exposed to our family members, who naturally have the same race, religion, and socioeconomic status as ourselves. Youngsters go to school with children who live in the same neighborhood, and consequently homogeneity of the immediate social environment is maintained, albeit to a lesser degree. The immediate social environment within which most people are socialized is objectively less complex than the society as a whole. Thus, the local social structure encourages the perception of relatively high similarity and overlap between ingroups, leading to a relatively simple social identity. To develop a complex social identity, special conditions are necessary—conditions that enhance the simultaneous awareness of more than one ingroup and the awareness that these ingroups overlap only partially.

The most obvious factor that may affect social identity complexity is the actual complexity of the experienced social environment. Social environments that are ethnically and religiously diverse, in which different bases for ingroup–outgroup distinctions are crosscutting rather than convergent, confront the individual with knowledge about the differences in meaning and composition of different social categorizations (see Amiot & de la Sablonnière, this volume). Consistent with this, Miller et al. (2009) found that racial diversity of participants' neighborhoods was a significant predictor of overlap complexity scores (see also Schmid & Hewstone, this volume). Note, however, that living in a diverse, multicultural society may not always be sufficient to provide the conditions for complex identity formation. There are a number of contextual factors that may moderate the direct relationship between complexity and diversity of the social environment and development of a complex social identity.

Living in a multicultural society may enhance awareness that social categorization based on ethnic heritage and social categorization based on national citizenship do not completely overlap and hence raises social identity complexity, including the possible development of complex bicultural identity (see Tadmor, Hong, Chiu, & No, this volume and Nguyen & Benet-Martínez, this volume), but the impact of a multicultural environment may be experienced differently for different participants, depending on their actual exposure to diversity. In addition, the effects of a multicultural society on social identity complexity are likely to depend on the extent to which the society is stratified along ethnic lines and on prevailing norms concerning multiculturalism.

Living in a stratified society, especially when there is a high degree of congruence between status and ethnic group membership, may reduce experienced complexity even when the society is multicultural. In a society in which members of different religious or ethnic groups engage in different occupations, for example, there is high objective overlap between the occupational and the ethnic group, and thus, low social identity complexity can be expected. Moreover, in stratified societies, primary groups are usually composed of individuals who are members of the same ethnic group or social class, and thus contact with individuals who could be simultaneously ingroup and outgroup members is minimal (Kelley & Evans, 1995; Massey & Denton, 1989).

Furthermore, the effect of living in a multicultural society on social identity complexity is also likely to be moderated by societal norms concerning multiculturalism. When people of many cultural backgrounds live together, the cultural groups they form are often not equal in power. Accordingly, some groups are dominant, and their ideology may have extensive influence both on the actual diversity and on the perception of diversity of the whole society. Some dominant groups are explicitly assimilationist, and hold an ideology that promotes a single culture in the nation, while others are integrationist and explicitly encourage the maintenance of the cultural heritage of nondominant groups (Berry, 1997). It is likely that integrationist ideology enhances the social identity complexity of members of the dominant group, because it encourages the various ethnocultural groups to express their diversity, and raise its salience. Thus, when integrationist norms prevail, members of the dominant group are more likely to be aware of nonoverlap between their ethnic or racial group and the other groups to which they belong.

Social Identity Complexity and Intergroup Relations

Social identity complexity is based on chronic awareness of cross-categorization in one's own social group memberships and those of others. A simple social identity is likely to be accompanied by the perception that any individual who is an outgroup member on one dimension is also an outgroup member on all others. In contrast, if an individual is aware that one of his ingroups only partly overlaps with any other of his ingroups, then we assume that he is also aware that some of his ingroup members have crossed group memberships: they are ingroup members on one dimension, but are simultaneously outgroup members on others. Making salient that an outgroup member on one category dimension is an ingroup member on another decreases bias by comparison with instances where the latter information is not available (Gaertner, Dovidio, Anastasio, Bachman, & Rust, 1993). We suggest that this effect of social identity complexity can be extended to a tolerance and acceptance of outgroups in general.

Overlap Complexity and Tolerance: Empirical Evidence

Two preliminary studies reported by Roccas and Brewer (2002) provided initial support for the idea that social identity complexity would be associated with tolerance for diversity and acceptance of outgroups. In the first study, American college students completed the overlap complexity measure and then an additional section at the end of their questionnaires in which they rated (on a 7-point scale of feelings of closeness) a series of target persons described by category memberships. Tolerance for outgroup members was computed by averaging the responses to three targets. One of the targets was a member of an outgroup defined by race, one was a member of an outgroup defined by religion, and one was a member of an outgroup defined both by race and religion. (The descriptions were tailored for each participant according to his or her own race and religion.) As expected, closeness toward outgroup members was higher for persons who had lower scores (higher complexity) on the overlap measure ($r = -.32$, $p = .01$), and this relationship between overlap complexity and tolerance was significant even when controlling for personal values.

In a follow-up study conducted in Israel, respondents reported their readiness to engage in social contact with recent immigrants from the former Soviet Union. We asked the students about the acceptability of contact with outgroup members (on a 5-point scale of readiness) in six domains: intermittent social relations, next-door neighbor, guest at one's home, intimate friend, having a child play together, and having a child marry a recent immigrant. As expected, overlap complexity was significantly related to readiness to engage in social contact with outgroup members, such that lower overlap scores predicted higher readiness (and lower social distance).

After the initial publication of the theory, two larger-scale studies of the relationship between individual differences in overlap complexity and tolerance were undertaken—one a telephone survey of Ohio residents, the other a computerized questionnaire study among college students. Brewer and Pierce (2005) assessed the relationship between social identity complexity and tolerance in a large-sample mail and phone survey of adults from Ohio. In this study, a mail survey was used to identify potential participants for a phone survey and to obtain a listing of group memberships from each respondent. These group memberships were then used to construct a personalized phone interview for each respondent contacted. Specifically, three of the participant's own identified ingroup memberships across different crosscutting domains, along with the ingroup "American," were used when asking each respondent about the extent of the overlap between memberships in these groups. The phone interview also elicited responses to items measuring attitudes toward affirmative action and multiculturalism, as well as emotional distance from outgroups as measured by "feeling thermometer" questions. These variables were then tested for a relationship to the overlap measure of social identity complexity.

The results confirmed that social identity complexity was associated with both tolerance-related policy preferences and affect toward outgroups. The mean overlap score across four ingroups was significantly correlated with attitudes toward affirmative action, multiculturalism, and affect toward outgroups after controlling for age, education, and ideology. That is, holding the number and diversity of ingroups constant, individual differences in the subjective representation of these multiple group memberships proved to be a significant predictor of intergroup attitudes. This finding seems particularly compelling when it is noted that the overlap scores computed in this study did not include the participants' racial and ethnic group memberships, but were based on categories such as church membership, occupational category, and sports fanships. The subjective representation of these non-ethnic groups was nonetheless related to tolerance of ethnic outgroups in the manner predicted by Roccas and Brewer (2002).

Miller et al. (2009) developed a computerized version of the ingroup elicitation questionnaire and overlap measure in order to replicate and extend the Brewer and Pierce study with a sample of college students. One purpose of this follow-up study was to determine whether we could rule out other correlated dispositional variables as the source of any relationship between membership overlap scores and intergroup attitudes. Although Brewer and Pierce (2005) found that the relationship was significant when controlling for political ideology, the role of various measures of cognitive style as a potential correlate of social

Table 2.2 Correlates of Individual Differences in Overlap Complexity

	1	2	3	4	5	6	7
1 SIC overlap	—						
2 Tolerance of ambiguity	.00	—					
3 Closemindedness	.18*	-.05	—				
4 Need for cognition	-.23**	-.03	-.40**	—			
5 Liberalism	-.15*	.22*	-.07	.09	—		
6 Affective distance to outgroups	.20*	.06	.12	-.15*	-.15*	—	
7 Race-related attitudes	-.32**	-.07	-.15*	.14*	.25**	-.26*	—
8 Implicit prejudice	.35**	ns	ns	-.16*	-.04	.56**	-.28*

*p < .05;
**p < .01.

identity complexity had yet to be examined. Another purpose of the computerized study was to extend the range of racial attitude measures associated with social identity complexity to include performance on an implicit measure of racial prejudice.

Participants (white college students) completed the computerized social identity complexity measure and demographic questions including a one-item measure of liberalism-conservatism, followed by the 18-item need for cognition scale (Cacioppo, Petty, & Kao, 1984) and the discomfort with ambiguity and closemindedness subscales of the need for closure scale (Webster & Kruglanski, 1994). Feeling thermometers for racial/ethnic groups were utilized to measure affect toward outgroups, and a series of items were presented to measure attitudes regarding race-related issues. Finally, respondents went on to complete a version of the Affect Misattribution Procedure (Payne, Cheng, Govorun, & Stewart, 2005), designed to measure implicit affective reactions to black and white faces.

Table 2.2 (adapted from Miller et al., 2009) displays the bivariate correlations obtained among social identity complexity, need for cognition, need for closure, ideology, interracial affective distance, and race-related attitudes. Replicating previous findings, the overlap measure of social identity complexity was significantly correlated with liberalism, such that those with lower perceived overlap (higher social identity complexity) were ideologically more liberal than those with high overlap scores. Contrary to expectations, intolerance for ambiguity did not prove to be significantly related to the overlap scores. However, closemindedness and need for cognition were significantly correlated in the expected direction; those with lower perceived overlap were higher in need for cognition and lower in closemindedness than those with higher overlap scores. When all three cognitive style measures were entered simultaneously in a linear regression to predict overlap scores, only need for cognition remained significant.

Replicating findings reported by Brewer and Pierce (2005), overlap complexity was a significant predictor of explicit affect toward racial outgroups and race-related attitudes. Importantly, it was also correlated with the implicit measure of racial prejudice, which is closely related to the affective component of intergroup attitudes. This is interesting because it suggests that social identity complexity is not simply a "cold cognition" way of viewing the social world. The inclusiveness of one's own ingroups, as reflected in overlap complexity, clearly has affective consequences. Individuals high on social identity complexity are less likely to differentiate affectively between members of their own ethnic ingroup and members of other ethnic groups.

As expected, need for cognition and liberalism was also related to the measures of racial attitudes, thus raising our second question of whether the relationship between social identity complexity and tolerance is accounted for by these prior individual difference variables. Simultaneous regression was used to assess the contribution of membership overlap scores as a predictor of interracial affect, race-related attitudes, and implicit prejudice, controlling for need for cognition and liberalism-conservatism. The overlap complexity measure remained a significant predictor of all the tolerance measures. Further, need for cognition no longer had a significant influence on either interracial affect or race-related attitudes when controlling for political ideology and social identity complexity overlap scores. These results suggest that social identity complexity has a more proximal relationship to our racial tolerance measures (both explicit and implicit), consistent with an account where need for cognition and other cognitive style variables are potential antecedents of social identity complexity, but not direct determinants of intergroup attitudes. It is of particular interest that it was the positive need for cognition that proved to be most strongly associated with perceived overlap, rather than measures of resistance to cognitive complexity or ambiguity. Although this needs to be explored further, it does suggest that it is the active *seeking* of cognitive stimulation and experience that promotes the more complex representation of one's multiple, crosscutting social identities.

Implications for Pluralistic Societies and Public Policy

The research thus far on social identity complexity as an individual difference variable suggests that how individuals represent and experience their own multiple ingroup identities has significant implications for their functioning in a pluralistic society. Going beyond the individual difference approach, however, what we need now is more understanding of what institutional arrangements, social policies, and ideologies promote complex rather than simple social identities. Pluralistic societies provide the *potential* for complex multiple identities, but segregated living arrangements, discriminatory practices in legal, political, and economic arenas, and political power-mongering can all reduce the actualization of that potential.

Currently, the debate about how to manage cultural diversity in pluralistic societies is cast as a conflict between assimilationist "color-blind" ideology on the one hand, and "multicultural" ideology on the other (Correll, Park, & Smith, 2008; Richeson & Nussbaum, 2004; Wolsko,

Park, Judd, & Wittenbrink, 2000). But there is an alternative to representing assimilationism and multiculturalism as two extremes along a single bipolar continuum. The key is to capitalize more effectively on our capacity for multiple social identities. All individuals have multicultural heritage, and all of us are capable of juggling multiple identities across a lifetime (Seelye & Wasilewski, 1996). The question is, do all members of a society have equal access to participation in multiple, crosscutting identity groups?

In pluralistic societies where one cultural group is a dominant majority and others are minority and/or newcomers, it is relatively easy for members of the majority group to enter new identity groups (e.g., occupational identities, political organizations) and to move effortlessly across different ingroup identities in different domains of life. Members of distinctive minority groups, however, by virtue of self-categorization or categorization by others, are vulnerable to single dominant group identity where alternative sources of social identity (religion, politics, occupation) converge with or are subordinated to their ethnic/cultural group membership.

Policymakers don't often think of themselves as dictating social identities, but structural arrangements and legal institutions can greatly influence how identities are defined and whether lines of social differentiation in a society are experienced as crosscutting or convergent. Situations in which social differentiations based on ethnicity, gender, age, religion, occupation, political power, and economic roles are all crosscutting require patterns of interdependence and accommodation that promote integration and complex social identities. Situations in which distinctions based on gender, ethnicity, class, and power are convergent set the stage for division along a single societal faultline.

Although multiculturalism as an ideology of mutual respect and recognition of cultural diversity is consistent with liberal democracy (see Verkuyten, this volume), multiculturalism as public policy needs to be approached cautiously. In many cases, policymakers may be applying multicultural concepts in ways that may well cause much more harm than good in the long run. The perils appear when multiculturalism is understood to mean the preservation of existing category distinctions which are then transported into legal policies and institutions in ways that require codifying what constitute culture groups and protected cultural practices and heritage, and then institutionalize these as the basis for allocation of political power and resources. We need to be sensitive to the potential for public policy to influence or constrain social identities. Institutionalizing cultural differences in the political arena reduces opportunities for adopting crosscutting identities. Such policies of necessity privilege particular lines of differentiation among society members that correspond to ethnic groups and encourage monolithic, essentialized perceptions of cultural groups. Reified groups become the faultline for conflict and separatism. In addition, because cultural identities are usually ascribed rather than achieved social group memberships, individuals are pigeonholed by accident of birth into political units. What we need are policies that facilitate rather than create barriers to cross-category participation. What we should advocate is not a world in which group distinctions and cultural differences are denied or suppressed, but one in which meaningful social identities are compatible so that one's ethnic or cultural identity does not limit access to other social identities.

References

Almond, G. A., & Verba, S. (1963). *The civic culture: Political attitudes in five nations.* Princeton, NJ: Princeton University Press.

Arcuri, L. (1982). Three patterns of social categorization in attribution memory. *European Journal of Social Psychology, 12,* 271–282.

Bar-Tal, D. (2007). Sociopsychological foundations of intractable conflicts. *American Behavioral Scientist, 50,* 1430–1453.

Berry, J. W. (1997). Immigration, acculturation and adaptation. *Applied Psychology: An International Review, 46,* 5–68.

Blau, P. M. (1977). *Inequality and heterogeneity.* New York: The Free Press.

Brewer, M. B. (1979). Ingroup bias in the minimal intergroup situation: A cognitive-motivational analysis. *Psychological Bulletin, 86,* 307–324.

Brewer, M. B. (1988). A dual process model of impression formation. In R. Wyer & T. Srull (Eds.), *Advances in social cognition* (Vol. 1, pp. 1–36). Hillsdale, NJ: Erlbaum.

Brewer, M. B. (1991). The social self: On being the same and different at the same time. *Personality and Social Psychology Bulletin, 17,* 475–482.

Brewer, M. B. (2000). Reducing prejudice through cross-categorization: Effects of multiple social identities. In S. Oskamp (Ed.), *Claremont Symposium on Applied Social Psychology: Reducing prejudice and discrimination* (pp. 165–183). Thousand Oaks, CA: Sage.

Brewer, M. B., & Pierce, K. P. (2005). Social identity complexity and outgroup tolerance. *Personality and Social Psychology Bulletin, 31,* 428–437.

Brown, R., & Turner, J. C. (1979). The criss-cross categorization effect in intergroup discrimination. *British Journal of Social Psychology, 18,* 371–383.

Cacioppo, J. T., Petty, R. E., & Kao, C. F. (1984). The efficient assessment of "need for cognition." *Journal of Personality Assessment, 48,* 306–307.

Conway, M., Carroll, J. M., Pushkar, D., & Arbuckle, T. (1996). Anticipated interaction, individual differences in attentional resources, and elaboration of behavior. *Social Cognition, 14*, 338–366.

Correll, J., Park, B., & Smith, J. A. (2008). Colorblind and multicultural prejudice reduction strategies in high-conflict situations. *Group Process and Intergroup Relations, 11*, 471–492.

Coser, L. A. (1956). *The functions of social conflict*. New York: Free Press.

Crisp, R. J., & Hewstone, M. (1999). Differential evaluation of crossed category groups: Patterns, processes, and reducing intergroup bias. *Group Processes and Intergroup Relations, 2*, 1–27.

Crisp, R. J., & Hewstone, M. (2007). Multiple social categorization. In M. Zanna (Ed.), *Advances in experimental social psychology* (Vol. 39, pp. 163–254). Orlando, FL: Academic Press.

Deschamps, J.-C., & Doise, W. (1978). Crossed category membership in intergroup relations. In H. Tajfel (Ed.), *Differentiation between social groups: Studies in the social psychology of intergroup relations* (pp. 141–158). London: Academic Press.

Eysenck, M. W. (1992). *Anxiety: The cognitive perspective*. Hillsdale, NJ: Erlbaum.

Gaertner, S. L., Dovidio, J., Anastasio, P., Bachman, B., & Rust, M. (1993). The common ingroup identity model: Recategorization and the reduction of ingroup bias. In W. Stroebe & M. Hewstone (Eds.), *European review of social psychology* (Vol. 4, pp. 1–26). London: Wiley.

Gluckman (1955). *Customs and conflict in Africa*. London: Blackwell.

Heider, F. (1958). *The psychology of interpersonal relations*. New York: Wiley.

Hewstone, M., Islam, M. R., & Judd, C. M. (1993). Models of crossed categorization and intergroup relations. *Journal of Personality and Social Psychology, 64*, 779–793.

Kahneman, D. (1973). *Attention and effort*. Englewood Cliffs, NJ: Prentice Hall.

Kelley, J., & Evans, M. D. (1995). Class and class conflict in six western nations. *American Sociological Review, 60*, 157–178.

Kelman, H. C. (1999). *Transforming the relationship between former enemies: A social-psychological analysis*. In R. L. Rothstein (Ed.), *After the peace: Resistance and reconciliation* (pp. 193–205). Boulder, CO and London: Lynne Rienner.

Kunda, Z., Miller, D. T., & Claire, T. (1990). Combining social concepts: The role of causal reasoning. *Cognitive Science, 14*, 551–577.

LeVine, R. A., & Campbell, D. T. (1972). *Ethnocentrism: Theories of conflict, ethnic attitudes and group behavior*. New York: Wiley.

Lipset, S. M. (1959). Some social requisites of democracy: Economic development and political legitimacy. *American Political Science Review, 53*, 69–105.

Maalouf, A. (1996/2003). *In the name of identity*. New York: Penguin Books.

Macrae, C. N., Bodenhausen, G. V., & Milne, A. B. (1995). The dissection of selection in person perception: Inhibitory processes in social stereotyping. *Journal of Personality and Social Psychology, 69*, 397–407.

Massey, D. S., & Denton, N. A. (1989). Hypersegregation in U.S. Metropolitan areas: Black and Hispanic segregation along five dimensions. *Demography, 26*, 373–91.

Miller, K. P., Brewer, M. B., & Arbuckle, N. L. (2009). Social identity complexity: Its correlates and antecedents. *Group Processes and Intergroup Relations, 12*, 79–94.

Mullin, B.-A., & Hogg, M. A. (1998). Dimensions of subjective uncertainty in social identification and minimal intergroup discrimination. *British Journal of Social Psychology, 37*, 345–365.

Murphy, R. F. (1957). Intergroup hostility and social cohesion. *American Anthropologist, 59*, 1018–1035.

Neufeld, R. W. J., & McCarty, T. S. (1994). A formal analysis of stressor and stress-proneness effects on simple information processing. *British Journal of Mathematical and Statistical Psychology, 47*, 193–226.

Newcomb, T. (1963). Stabilities underlying changes in interpersonal attraction. *Journal of Abnormal and Social Psychology, 66*, 376–386.

Oakes, P. J., & Turner, J. C. (1990). Is limited information processing the cause of social stereotyping? In W. Stroebe & M. Hewstone (Eds.), *European review of social psychology* (Vol. 1, pp. 111–135). London: Wiley.

Osterhouse, R. A., & Brock, T. C. (1970). Distraction increases yielding to propaganda by inhibiting counterarguing. *Journal of Personality and Social Psychology, 15*, 344–358.

Payne, B. K., Cheng, C. M., Govorun, O., & Stewart, B. D. (2005). An inkblot for attitudes: Affect misattribution as implicit measurement. *Journal of Personality and Social Psychology, 89*, 277–293.

Petty, R. E., Wells, G. L., & Brock, T. C. (1976). Distraction can enhance or reduce yielding to propaganda: Thought disruption versus effort justification. *Journal of Personality and Social Psychology, 34*, 874–884.

Richeson, J. A., & Nussbaum, R. J. (2004). The impact of multiculturalism versus color-blindness on racial bias. *Journal of Experimental Social Psychology, 40*, 417–423.

Roccas, S., & Brewer, M. B. (2002). Social identity complexity. *Personality and Social Psychology Review, 6*, 88–106.

Rothbart, M., & John, O. (1985). Social categorization and behavioral episodes: A cognitive analysis of the effects of intergroup contact. *Journal of Social Issues, 41*(3), 81–104.

Schroder, H. M., Driver, M. J., & Streufert, S. (1967). *Human information processing.* New York: Holt, Rinehart & Winston.

Schwartz, S. H. (1992). Universals in the content and structure of values: Theoretical advances and empirical tests in 20 countries. In M. Zanna (Ed.), *Advances in experimental social psychology* (Vol. 25, pp. 1–65). San Diego, CA: Academic Press.

Schwartz, S. H. (1994). Are there universal aspects in the content and structure of values? *Journal of Social Issues, 50,* 19–45.

Seelye, H. N., & Wasilewski, J. H. (1996). *Between cultures: Developing self-identity in a world of diversity.* Lincolnwood, IL: NTC Publishing.

Steblay, N. M. (1992). A meta-analytic review of the weapon focus effect. *Law and Human Behavior, 16,* 413–424.

Tajfel, H. (Ed.) (1978). *Differentiation between social groups: Studies in the social psychology of intergroup relations.* London: Academic Press.

Tajfel, H. (1981). *Human groups and social categories.* Cambridge, UK: Cambridge University Press.

Tajfel, H., Billig, M., Bundy, R., & Flament, C. (1971). Social categorization and intergroup behaviour. *European Journal of Social Psychology, 1,* 149–178.

Tetlock, P. E. (1983). Accountability and complexity of thought. *Journal of Personality and Social Psychology, 45,* 74–83.

Tetlock, P. E. (1986). A value pluralism model of ideological reasoning. *Journal of Personality and Social Psychology, 50,* 819–827.

Tetlock, P. E., Skitka, L., & Boettger, R. (1989). Social and cognitive strategies of coping with accountability: Conformity, complexity, and bolstering. *Journal of Personality and Social Psychology, 57,* 632–641.

Turner, J. C., Hogg, M. A., Oakes, P. J., Reicher, S. D., & Wetherell, M. S. (1987). *Rediscovering the social group: A self-categorization theory.* Oxford, UK: Basil Blackwell.

Urban, L. M., & Miller, N. (1998). A theoretical analysis of crossed categorization effects: A meta-analysis. *Journal of Personality and Social Psychology, 74,* 894–908.

Vanbeselaere, N. (1991). The different effects of simple and crossed categorizations: A result of the category differentiation process or of differential category salience? In W. Stroebe & M. Hewstone (Eds.), *European review of social psychology* (Vol. 2, pp. 247–278). Chichester, UK: Wiley.

Webster, D. M., & Kruglanski, A. W. (1994). Individual differences in need for cognitive closure. *Journal of Personality and Social Psychology, 67,* 1049–62.

Wegner, D. M., & Wenzlaff, R. M. (1996). Mental control. In T. Higgins & A. Kruglanski (Eds.), *Social psychology: Handbook of basic principles* (pp. 466–492). New York: Guilford Press.

Woike, B. A., & Aronoff, J. (1992). Antecedents of complex social cognitions. *Journal of Personality and Social Psychology, 63,* 97–104.

Wolsko, C., Park, B., Judd, C., & Wittenbrink, B. (2000). Framing interethnic ideology: Effects of multicultural and color-blind perspectives on judgments of groups and individuals. *Journal of Personality and Social Psychology, 78,* 635–654.

3

Facilitating the Development and Integration of Multiple Social Identities

The Case of Immigrants in Québec

Catherine E. Amiot and Roxane de la Sablonnière

How do people entering a new social group come to endorse this group's values, norms, and behaviors and, more symbolically, this group's identity? How can we facilitate the transition of new group members into their new group setting, for example as individuals migrate to a new country or join a new work organization? Adopting a social psychological perspective, our aim is to provide an overview of some factors that come into play as individuals join new social groups and come to develop a sense of attachment, pride, and identification to this setting—in other words, how they come to endorse a new social identity.

A multitude of situations require that individuals develop ties to new social groups over their life span. For instance, joining a new school or work organization are common yet important developmental transitions (Eccles & Midgley, 1990; Fisher, 1986; Moreland & Levine, 2001). Dramatic social changes such as those triggered by political instability and the reorganization of economic systems also require individuals undergoing such changes to revise their value system and adhere to new lifestyles and everyday routines. In this chapter, we focus on immigration as an important social change that triggers the need—among both immigrants and members of host communities[1]—to adapt to this change and develop and integrate a new cultural identity into one's sense of self. To address the issue of how new cultural identities become integrated, we first discuss the importance of this worldwide phenomenon and its impacts. We then describe a model of social identity development and integration (Amiot, de la Sablonnière, Terry, & Smith, 2007) and apply some of its basic tenets to policy design and intervention in the realm of immigration.

Throughout this chapter, the particular case of Québec will be highlighted and discussed. Québec is a principally French-speaking Canadian province that presents interesting identity and intergroup dynamics. Given their geopolitical situation as the only French-speaking majority in North America, French-speaking Québécois have developed an avid desire to protect and preserve their cultural and linguistic distinctiveness. This desire is currently particularly strong given the recent massive increase in immigration in Québec (i.e., to compensate for low birthrates and an aging population; Institut de la statistique du Québec, 2000, 2007) and the predominance and vitality of the English language worldwide. Because Québec is far from being the only place in the world facing the challenge of dealing with increased immigration and issues of cultural and linguistic diversity and distinctiveness, let us now turn to an overview of the importance of immigration worldwide.

Immigration and the Integration of a New Cultural Identity into the Self

Immigration is on the rise internationally. According to the United Nations, the number of individuals who do not live in their country of origin more than doubled between 1975 and 2002. Specifically, approximately 175 million people were living outside their country of birth in 2002 (United Nations, 2002). In the United States, immigrants represented 0.8% of the population in 1990, whereas they made up 10.1% of the population in 2000 (Perry & Mackun, 2001). Canada's immigrant population in 1996 already comprised a large percentage of the general population (i.e., 17.4%). In 2006, this percentage rose to 19.8% (Statistics Canada, 2007), and demography experts predict that in 2017, immigrants will make up 22.2% of the total Canadian population (Statistics Canada, 2005).

The province of Québec is experiencing a dramatic increase in immigration, which is radically transforming its cultural and social profile. For instance, 32,500 immigrants were welcomed in 2000 compared to 48,000 in 2007. From 1999 to 2001, more than 60% of the population increase in Québec was due to immigration. Immigrants from visible minority groups (i.e., non-European countries) are also on the increase. For example, in 1995, only 15% of immigrants to Québec came from Africa, while in 2008, this percentage rose to 29.8% (Ministère de l'immigration et des communautés culturelles, 2000, 2009). Immigrants to Québec also have increasingly diverse religious backgrounds. The percentage of Québec residents of Roman Catholic faith (i.e., the religion of the original European settlers and of the majority of Québécois) increased by 1.3% between 1999 and 2001, whereas residents of the Muslim faith increased by 141.8% during the same period, and Buddhism recorded a growth of 30.8%, Hinduism increased by 73.7%, and Sikhism by 81.7% (Statistics Canada, 2003). Together, these migratory patterns are radically transforming Québec's population (Thériault, 2006).

These migratory movements have the potential to expose immigrants and members of host communities to new realities, values, and customs. They are presenting individuals with new cultures and opportunities, and possibly, enriching their sense of self (Aron, Aron, Tudor, & Nelson, 1991), but they are also highly demanding and stressful. Immigrants can experience discrimination and be rejected by the host community, leading to highly aversive psychological problems (e.g., Ellis, MacDonald, Lincoln, & Cabral, 2008; Stevens, Volleberg, Pels, & Crijnen, 2005). Members of the host community can also become threatened by such social changes, especially if immigrants are arriving over a short period and in large numbers (Tougas, de la Sablonnière, Lagacé, & Kocum, 2003).

We argue in this chapter that immigration has implications for both individuals migrating to a new country, who will be encouraged to incorporate a new cultural identity within their sense of self, and also for members of the host community, who need to revise their conception of their own cultural identity so as to make it more inclusive, diverse, and complex. Such a task is far from easy, and we point to possible solutions for reconciling this diversity. But first, we turn to a model explaining how different social and cultural identities become integrated over time.

A Model of Multiple and Multicultural Identity Integration

Social and cultural identities do change significantly in response to a changing social context (e.g., Ethier & Deaux, 1994; Jetten, O'Brien, & Trindall, 2002). However, much research remains to be done on the actual processes through which these changes take place. Furthermore, classic intergroup theories (i.e., self-categorization theory; Turner, Hogg, Oakes, Reicher, & Wetherell, 1987) have been particularly useful for explaining short-term variations in social identities—that is, how social identities change situationally depending on the social context in which we find ourselves. However, the deeper intra-individual changes taking place over time (Cervone, 2005), as new group members incorporate a new social identity into their sense of self, need to be accounted for.

To account for these changes in social identities over time, we have recently proposed a cognitive-developmental model of social identity change and integration. We propose that identity integration occurs when multiple social identities are organized within the self-structure such that they can be simultaneously important to the overall self-concept. When integrated, connections and links are established between these different identities so that they do not feel fragmented. As a result, the self feels coherent rather than conflicted (Amiot, de la Sablonnière, et al., 2007). Hence, identity integration should have positive consequences for psychological well-being: because the integration of one's identities enables the individual to draw similarities between the different self-defining cultural characteristics, identity integration allows for a more coherent vision of the self, where cultural differences are considered complementary rather than conflictual (Amiot, de la Sablonnière, et al., 2007; Benet-Martínez, Leu, Lee, & Morris, 2002; Downie, Koestner, ElGeledi, & Cree, 2004; Benet-Martínez & Nguyen, this volume; Roccas & Brewer, 2002; Tadmor, Hong, Chiu, & No, this volume).

The positive impact of integrating cultural identities and of endorsing multiple identities (Shih, Sanchez, & Ho, this volume) is not limited to individual psychological well-being, but it also impacts directly on intergroup relations. Integrated identities have been associated with less tension between cultural groups, less discrimination, less racism, fewer negative biases toward members of other groups, and more tolerance and more openness toward immigration and immigrants (Amiot, Terry, & Callan, 2007; Brewer & Pierce, 2005; de la Sablonnière, Amiot, & Sadykova, 2009; Lipponen, Olkkonen, & Moilanen, 2004; Phinney, Ferguson, & Tate, 1997).

When developing our model of social identity development and integration, we built on a number of important intergroup models (e.g., Hornsey & Hogg, 2000; Roccas & Brewer, 2002). For instance, in their social identity complexity model, Roccas and Brewer (2002) explain how multiple social identities are organized and represented cognitively within the self. Based on crossed-categorization principles, they propose that individuals can represent their multiple social identities using four types of cognitive representations: (1) intersection (i.e., where only the conjunction or intersection of two social identities—the overlap these identities share—constitutes the person's identity), (2) dominance (i.e., one social identity is adopted and all other identities are subordinated to this one dominant identity), (3) compartmentalization (i.e., more than one group identity is important to an individual's self-concept but these identities are highly context-dependent), and (4) merger (i.e., which involves recognizing the differences among different social identities but integrating them within a more inclusive identity).

Hence, the social identity complexity model addresses the multiplicity of social identities and how these diverse identities are represented cognitively within the self at a specific point in time. Building on different intergroup (e.g., Hornsey & Hogg, 2000; Roccas and Brewer, 2002) and developmental models (e.g., Harter, 2003), our model explains how these cognitive representations of multiple social identities change over time. In doing so, we seek to account for the developmental processes involved as a new social identity is incorporated in the self, how potential conflicts between different social identities are dealt with, and how a feeling of coherence among one's multiple social identities develops over time.

More specifically, we propose that the process of integrating multiple social identities involves a number of stages. Based on developmental principles (e.g., Harter, 1999), the first stage takes place as individuals are planning to join a new social group in the future. During this *anticipatory categorization stage*, a process of self-anchoring could be operating, where the individual about to join a new social group will project his or her own personal characteristics onto this novel social ingroup (e.g., Otten & Wentura, 2001). For example, an Asian immigrant planning to come to Québec could speculate about which of her personal characteristics also apply to Québécois. Being herself a conscientious person, she could anticipate that Québécois in general will also be conscientious (i.e., a projection process). Underlying this process of projection is a more fundamental need for continuity over time (Jetten, Iyer, Tsivrikos, & Young, 2008) and for establishing cognitive links between different identities. At this first stage, this is achieved by finding similarities between one's personal identity and the new cultural identity to be integrated.

The second stage of social identity development and integration refers to *categorization*. At this point, group members are confronted with an actual change in their lives and with the existence of a new social group. This is also when group members will realize how different and discontinuous their new (i.e., new cultural group) and old (original culture) group memberships are. Intergroup dynamics are also likely to emerge. At this point, distinct identities are recognized and differences (in terms of values and norms) among social identities become highly salient. In the acculturation literature, this phenomenon is analogous to the culture clash, where immigrants feel torn between cultures as they confront diverging sets of cultural demands (e.g., Leong & Ward, 2000). This categorization stage would involve a cognitive representation of cultural identities that is analogous to Roccas and Brewer's (2002) dominance representation (i.e., where only one social identity dominates the overall self). Because of the differentiation process activated at this stage, the individual undergoing the change cannot yet consider the possibility of being part of these different cultural groups, nor does he or she perceive any similarities and cognitive links between these groups. Going back to the Asian Québécoise, when arriving in Québec, she may realize how different her original culture is from the Québec culture. She most likely will not identify as a Québécoise at this stage, given that this new identity is not yet part of her self.

It is at the *compartmentalization stage* that the new social identity becomes increasingly part of the self. With time, exposure to, and experiences gathered in the new social group, the new group member will have come to identify with his or her new social group. At this point, the new group member will also realize that he or she is part of their new social group and that this identity is becoming more and more part of the self. However, at this point, the different identities are kept in distinct "compartments" within the self, such that they do not overlap and that the similarities and linkages between these identities are not yet firmly established. The identities are also context-dependent, meaning that they are activated depending on the social context (Nguyen & Benet-Martínez, this volume; see also Roccas and Brewer's compartmentalized representation of multiple social identities).

For example, the Asian immigrant in Québec might distinctively feel like a member of her original Asian cultural group in certain situations (e.g., when interacting with family members; when taking part in traditional heritage culture celebrations like the Chinese New Year), but Québécoise in situations that are typical and highly valued in Québec (e.g., watching a hockey game with friends; studying with a Québécoise friend and explaining specific concepts in French to each other). Her identities are therefore highly contextualized and distinct and are likely to be associated with different thoughts, attitudes, and behaviors.

The fourth stage is *integration*. This last stage is crucial because it involves the realization that conflicts between identities exist and that resources must be put forward to resolve these possible conflicts (e.g., Phinney, 2003). This would take place as the Asian immigrant in Québec realizes that the behaviors she displays with Québécois, such as at work (i.e., being ambitious and self-enhancing), are contradictory to her behaviors when she interacts with members of her original cultural group (e.g., being humble and taking care of other's needs and desires), who highly value collective goals and modesty. Such contradictions and conflicts could be reconciled by finding similarities and by establishing cognitive links between her different social identities. Concretely, this could take place as the Asian Québécoise is recognizing the fundamental values that are common to both of her cultural groups (i.e., the value of hard work; doing one's best) or values that she personally cherishes and brings with her in different cultural contexts (e.g., she is a determined person, both when helping others and when accomplishing her own goals). Doing so will not only allow her to establish links between her cultural identities, but also to feel a sense of personal coherence and consistency across situations. The end result of this integration phase involves recognizing that the different social identities that compose the self are no longer context-dependent. While being different in their own ways, they can each contribute to her overall self-concept in a positive and distinct manner (e.g., Harter, 1999; Harter & Monsour, 1992).

This feeling of coherence and consistency across situations is a defining characteristic of the integration stage. However, a note of caution should be sounded here. Although identities should be particularly context-dependent at the compartmentalization stage, this capacity to identify with the most functional and adaptive social groups given the social context (e.g., Turner et al., 1987) should also take place at the integration stage. However, the important distinction between the compartmentalized and integrated stages lies in the subjective feelings of continuity, consistency, and authenticity felt over time and across different life contexts (e.g., Kernis, 2006; van Knippenberg et al., 2002; van Leeuwen et al., 2003). These feelings of consistency and continuity should be more present at the integration stage than at the compartmentalization stage. Hence, at the integration stage, although the person can adapt to a specific context and endorse the more functional and salient social identity, he or she should also feel a subjective sense of continuity and authenticity over time with all identities. A related element that distinguishes the compartmentalization and integration stages pertains to simultaneous identification. When identities are compartmentalized, if one specific identity becomes salient, then the other identities should fade significantly in importance and not come into play. In contrast, when identities are integrated, even if one identity becomes more salient or functional in a given context, the other ones do not become completely inexistent.

Apart from finding similarities among her identities so as to derive a sense of personal coherence, a second way for the immigrant to integrate her different social identities would involve identifying with a superordinate social identity—such as being human or being a "world citizen," which would be highly inclusive and would incorporate the multitude of more specific identities she possesses. This binding, overarching identity would therefore allow her to reconcile her different specific cultural identities, given that these can be regrouped and nested under this inclusive identity. Identifying with such a binding, overarching social category is analogous to Roccas and Brewer's (2002) merger representation. In the intergroup literature, studies have shown that identifying with larger and more inclusive groups led to lower ingroup bias and more tolerance (e.g., Gaertner & Dovidio, 2000; Roccas & Brewer, 2002). However, this superordinate identity should also allow one's specific identities to be recognized and respected within this superordinate whole (e.g., Hewstone & Brown, 1986; Hornsey & Hogg, 2000). It would be hard indeed to ask that group members erase and forgo all their concrete and proximal group identities (e.g., their region, culture, or nation) and identify exclusively with a large and abstract superordinate identity (e.g., being a human; being a living organism). Such a demand would be highly threatening (Hornsey & Hogg, 2000). Other theorists have proposed in a similar manner that representing the superordinate identity as complex, that is, as represented by a diversity of characteristics (i.e., not just by characteristics that are prototypical of one higher status group), yields more positive intergroup outcomes, such as increased tolerance (Mummendey & Wenzel, 1999; Waldzus, Mummendey, & Wenzel, 2005).

Social Factors Inhibiting rather than Facilitating the Integration of New Social Identities

While our argumentation up to now has focused on an individual level of analysis, social and motivational factors also play a fundamental role in either facilitating or inhibiting the integration of new identities. Identity integration is an effortful process (Chen & Klimoski, 2003) that requires cognitive resources (e.g., Tadmor & Tetlock, 2006) and the use of active coping strategies (Amiot, Blanchard, & Gaudreau, 2008; Amiot, Terry, Wirawan, & Grice, in press). Instead of leaving the individual to him or herself in this task, the social context needs to facilitate this process (Amiot, Terry, Jimmieson, & Callan, 2006). In this section, we highlight how social factors—and more precisely, feelings of threat and social support—represent antecedents that can inhibit rather than facilitate identity integration. Doing so has direct implications for policy design and interventions, given that we can directly act on these social factors to promote identity integration.

Threat   Important social changes such as immigration have the potential to trigger negative emotions such as threat among both immigrants and members of the host community. Social changes create a rupture in the balance of society (de la Sablonnière, Taylor, Perozzo, & Sadykova, 2009; de la Sablonnière, Tougas, & Lortie-Lussier, 2009; Rocher, 1992) and force individuals to reevaluate their conception of their cultural group. Such a reevaluation process does not come without consequences, rather, it is at the origin of feelings of threat. These feelings in turn *inhibit* the integration of new identities (e.g., Amiot et al., 2007; Benet-Martínez & Haritatos, 2005; Phinney, 2003; Terry, 2003; Terry & O'Brien, 2001).

Going back to the social context of Québec, threat is of particular importance. In this context of dramatic social change, both immigrants and members of the Québécois host community feel threatened, and such mutual feelings of threat block the integration process. Based on this observation, in the following section we will propose five concrete interventions that could be implemented to reduce (and even make use of) these feelings to promote the integration of new identities.

Social support   In contrast to feelings of threat, which inhibit the identity integration process, social support (e.g., informational, emotional, companionship) *facilitates* the integration of a new social identity when one joins a new social group. Developmental scholars agree that social support from one's environment is crucial to optimal development, including identity development (e.g., Harter, 1999; Mascolo & Fischer, 1998). Research conducted during changes such as immigration and organizational mergers has revealed the importance of emotional and informational social support in predicting adjustment to these changes (Ataca & Berry, 2002; Terry, Callan, & Sartori, 1996). Applying a social identity approach to social support, Haslam, O'Brien, Jetten, Vormedal, and Penna (2005) showed that informational support had a particularly positive effect in attenuating stress when it is provided by ingroup members. When joining new groups (i.e., transition to university; joining a new virtual group), social support and the satisfaction of basic psychological needs (i.e., relatedness, competence, autonomy) in the new group context predict more active coping with this change, and lead to an increased sense of identification with the new group over time (Amiot et al., in press).

Based on these findings, the five interventions we propose below (i.e., in the section "Concrete Implications of the Theoretical Model and Empirical Findings for Policy Design and Social Interventions"), aim at concretely increasing aspects of social support that will promote the integration of social identities. This should be done in such a way that the different cultural identities are valued and recognized, and by realizing that each cultural group is interdependent and contributes in its own ways to the superordinate whole. The utility of the strategy of social creativity (Tajfel & Turner, 1979) in this context will also be discussed.

Dramatic Social Changes in Québec, Immigration, and Strong Feelings of Threat

As mentioned at the beginning of the chapter, Québec has recently witnessed deep cultural transformations. Historically, Québec has struggled to maintain its culture and French language, given its geopolitical situation in a mainly English-speaking North America (e.g., Bourhis, 2001). More recently, the province massively welcomed large numbers of increasingly diverse immigrant groups to compensate for its decreasing birthrate and aging population and to fill its social, political, and economic needs (Institut de la statistique du Québec, 2000, 2007; Ministère de l'immigration et des communautés culturelles, 2000; Statistics Canada, 2003). While avidly seeking to preserve its own cultural distinctiveness among these diverse groups, Québec also claims to value principles of multiculturalism, tolerance, and openness to the world (Ministère de l'immigration et des communautés culturelles, 2009). These contradictory goals put Québec in a peculiar situation.

On the one hand, and possibly partly due to Québec's geopolitical situation and historically threatened identity (real or perceived), immigrants and members of visible minorities experience discrimination in Québec (e.g., Bourhis, Montreuil, Helly, & Jantzen, 2007). For example, studies conducted among Québec public servants have revealed systematic discrimination against members of cultural minorities (Barrette & Bourhis, 2004). In addition, many studies and surveys have suggested that Québécois are more racist than other Canadians. According to a recent survey, 33% of Canadian respondents reported having witnessed derogatory or racist comments toward Arab or Muslim communities. This percentage rises to 42% in the province of Québec (Presse Canadienne/Léger Marketing, 2001). In another survey conducted for *Maclean's Magazine*, *Global TV*, and *The Citizen* (November 2002), 44% of Canadians said they were in favor of a reduction in the immigration of individuals from Islamic countries. The highest percentage, 48%, was observable in Québec (Helly, 2004).

On the other hand, politicians and public figures have been highly reluctant to recognize the existence of this discrimination and racism in Québec. For example, when asked to comment on the results of a survey revealing the racist attitudes of Québécois, Jean Charest, Québec's prime minister, vehemently stated: "Québécois are not racist. I see the contrary. I see a society that is proud of its diversity, proud of the fact that we have different cultural trends present in a society that is mostly Francophone." The Mayor of Montréal, Gérald Tremblay, refused to believe in the "pretended racism of Montréalers" (Beauvais, 2007). According to Fo Neimi, director of the Centre for Research-Action on Race Relations in Montréal, Québec has always been hesitant to openly disclose its problems concerning discrimination (Lightman, 2006). It is in this particular context of latent identity threat coupled with an official endorsement of multicultural ideals that we wish to propose solutions.

The Debate on Reasonable Accommodations

A recent example reveals how delicate the issues of the Québécois identity and the integration of immigrants into Québec society are. In 2006–2007, a real media frenzy and political craze centered around the issue of "reasonable accommodations." Reasonable accommodations refer to "an arrangement that falls under the legal sphere that aims at relaxing the application of a standard in favor of an individual who is threatened of being discriminated against because of personal traits that are protected by law" (Commission de consultation sur les pratiques d'accommodement reliées aux différences culturelles, 2007,

p. 41). Whereas the notion of reasonable accommodation was not debated much within the population in the past, today it is a concept that raises much interest and even heated debates among Québécois. In fact, in the last 30 years, following the increase in cultural diversity in Québec, new requests for reasonable accommodations have been put forward. While the requests were originally made by individuals on the basis of handicap, sexual orientation, or gender, current requests mostly concern cultural or religious issues. Such requests have two important consequences (de la Sablonnière et al., 2007): (1) they challenge the preexisting cultural identity of Québécois, and (2) they instill a feeling of threat among both immigrants and host-community Québécois, and particularly French-speaking Québécois.

One of the most publicized examples of reasonable accommodation occurred when a community sport center, located next to a Jewish orthodox school, was asked by members of the Montréal Jewish Hassidic community to ensure that the windows of a coed workout room be covered so that it would be impossible to see through the windows from the outside. While the community center had originally agreed to replace the clear windows with opaque windows ("to preserve good neighbor relations"), the media reported the story and people in Québec began discussing the issue. The story continued to be covered in the media for several weeks and was hotly debated by the population (e.g., in phone-ins on the radio and letters published in mainstream newspapers). Members of the community center also signed a petition expressing their public disapproval of the replacement of the clear glass with opaque, in order to meet the Hassidic community's request. Finally, the managers of the community center conducted a survey among its members and decided to resolve the issue by putting up blinds at the clear-glass windows (Shields, 2007).

In this particular example, both members of the Québécois host community and members of the minority Jewish community felt threatened. In this context, host-community Québécois wanted to express the high value they set on personal freedom (i.e., dressing as one likes) and felt threatened by being required to accommodate to a cultural minority group's request, especially if this request was guided by religious concerns. In fact, since the 1960s, French Québécois people have fought for increased laicism in the public sphere and against a highly controlling Catholic church. Members of the Jewish community, on the other hand, wanted to affirm important values of their culture and religion, such as appreciating (and exposing children to) propriety through a more conventional dress code. This mutual feeling of threat poisons

Table 3.1 Summary of the Five Interventions

Intervention	Description	Examples of actions involved
1. Acknowledging intergroup tensions	Acknowledging the existence of discrimination and racism	– Enforcing laws to reprimand discrimination – Creating honors to those who implement principles of multiculturalism
2. Acknowledging mutual feelings of threat	Understanding that the feeling of threat felt by members of diverse cultural groups is at the center of any intergroup tensions and that it is important, for all cultural groups, to make the necessary efforts to reduce it	– Perspective taking – Openly discuss the mutual feeling of threat (e.g., in round tables, in educational contexts)
3. Developing a new inclusive identity	Developing a new identity that encompasses both the identity of members of the host community and the members of diverse cultural origins, so that all members belong to the same ingroup	– Redefining identities with public discussions involving the media – Addressing identity issues in classrooms – Helping bicultural individuals to increase their identity coherence (e.g., in hospitals, in schools) – Including the immigrants and other cultural groups in the host society's teaching of history
4. Offering and receiving social support	Ensuring that immigrants receive adequate social support to facilitate their integration in the host society	– Providing social support to immigrants (e.g., more accessibility to learning the language of the host culture, in classrooms) – Pairing an immigrant family with a family from the host society upon arrival
5. Valuing the strengths of all groups	Ensuring that different cultural identities are equally valued within a multicultural society and acknowledging the strengths and specificity of each cultural group within the society as a whole	– With the media, highlighting the economic and cultural contributions of the immigrants and diverse cultural groups in the host culture's society – Recognizing immigrants' working qualifications and diplomas

intergroup relations and inhibits the complete integration of Québécois from diverse cultural origins into Québec society.

Concrete Implications of the Theoretical Model and Empirical Findings for Policy Design and Social Interventions

Extending on the work of de la Sablonnière and her colleagues (2007), we propose five interventions for facilitating immigrants' integration of a new cultural identity and use the Québec context as an example (see Table 3.1). The ultimate goal of these interventions is to promote well-being and tolerance among both immigrants and members of the Québécois host community.

Intervention 1

The first step toward a better integration of new immigrants with the Québécois identity is to *acknowledge the existence of discrimination and racism in Québec*. As mentioned above, Québécois people do display discrimination toward immigrants and members of cultural minorities. To fully integrate diverse cultural groups in Québec society, it is imperative that the entire population first recognizes the existence of the important tensions existing between different cultural groups in Québec (see Cameron & Turner, this volume). Such a recognition will then make it possible to engage in concrete behaviors to reduce racism and discrimination. Acknowledging the presence of racist and discriminatory behaviors in a multiethnic society is essential to ensure its functioning (Ford, Grossman, & Jordan, 1997). This collective awareness is a necessary step toward the development of harmonious relations between different cultural groups (Ramsey & Latting, 2005). Of course, doing so is threatening, but admitting to this reality will bring transparence to the integration process. It will also liberate immigrants somewhat from the pressure and the entire responsibility of integrating within an officially multicultural Québec society that is allegedly "free of racism."

Laws already exist in Canada to reprimand discrimination (e.g., at work, in the housing sector). To ensure that this first intervention reaches its goals, such laws should be firmly enforced by the Canadian government, and ways be devised to ensure the effective and contingent punishment of individuals who violate these laws. Apart from such a punitive measure, honors could also be created and promoted across the country to acknowledge individuals whose work directly implemented the principles of multiculturalism.

Intervention 2

The second intervention aims to develop an *understanding that the feeling of threat felt by members of diverse cultural groups is at the center of the intergroup tensions and that it is important, for all cultural groups, to make the necessary efforts to reduce it.* Toward this aim, both immigrants and members of the Québécois host community should realize that this feeling is not exclusive to members of their ingroup, but extends also to members of diverse cultural groups (Galinsky & Moskowitz, 2000). For example, a French-speaking Québécois can feel threatened if he learns that Muslim immigrants are asking to eat a different type of meat (other than pork) while eating at a sugar shack (i.e., a traditional type of restaurant usually located in the countryside in Québec, which serves dishes made up of pork, potatoes, beans, and maple syrup). However, French-speaking Québécois should also consider that Muslims can feel threatened by a culture whose traditional food includes pork, given that this contradicts their cultural and religious views.

Therefore, instead of assuming that an immigrant is aiming to destroy Québec's cultural heritage and values when he is asking to eat something other than pork at the sugar shack, the French-speaking Québécois could consider that this immigrant is actively participating in Québec culture and that in this context, he also wants to affirm some aspects of his culture that are important to him. Likewise, instead of concluding that Québécois have immoral dietary traditions, this immigrant could try to understand the Québécois traditional diet through the historical context of the province (e.g., pigs were a useful source of food and highly resilient animals in the harsh Québec winter!). In this process, members of all groups should refrain from being guided exclusively by strong and spontaneous emotional reactions. Rather, we believe that feelings of threat can be used nonjudgmentally as guides that inform us about what is most personally and culturally relevant to our ingroup. A certain level of empathy and perspective-taking from members of all groups will also be required. This perspective-taking process could lead to an awareness of experiencing common human feelings and even to the realization that we are all part of the same super-ordinate human ingroup. To implement this intervention, this mutual feeling of threat should be openly discussed. The context of education appears particularly well suited to this. In this context teachers could take a very active role in leading these discussions, encouraging perspective-taking, and devising activities (e.g., based on history; geography; by informing students how widespread issues of diversity are throughout the world) and classroom debates aimed at eliciting these mutual feelings.

Intervention 3

A third intervention aiming to facilitate immigrants' integration of the Québécois identity involves *developing a new Québécois identity that encompasses both the identity of members of the Québécois host community and Québécois of diverse cultural origins, so that the term "Québécois" can be applicable to a diversity of cultural groups.* To do this, both host-community Québécois and Québécois of diverse cultural origins should incorporate the different cultural identities within their conception of what being Québécois involves. This integration implies reconceptualizing the Québécois identity according to the current social context, so that the term "Québécois" includes members of a diversity of cultural groups (e.g., Gaertner & Dovidio, 2000).

Such a cognitive reconceptualizing of the Québécois identity will have very concrete implications in terms of intergroup relations. It will imply that a young woman originating from Iraq who wears a hijab in the streets of Trois-Rivières (i.e., a relatively large city in Québec where 90% of residents are of French Canadian origin) will be considered by host-community Québécois to be as much Québécoise as they themselves are. We realize this is a major challenge, especially in light of research showing that the label "Québécois" typically defines individuals living in Québec who speak French, who have a Franco-Canadian heritage, and who support the sovereignty of Québec (e.g., Taylor & Sigal, 1982).

This intervention is in line with theoretical models such as the ingroup projection model (Mummendey & Wenzel, 1999; Waldzus et al., 2005), Hornsey and Hogg's (2000) integrative model of subgroup relations, and some research originating from the common ingroup identification model (Dovidio, Gaertner, & Validzic, 1998). According to these models, for positive intergroup relations to emerge, different subgroups within a superordinate category need to be represented and respected, and to contribute distinctly to defining this large and abstract category. This intervention is also consonant with the Canadian literature on bilingualism which shows that it is possible for bilingual individuals to identify with their different (and some-times conflictual) linguistic groups (e.g., Clément, Noels, & Deneault, 2001). Nevertheless, for this to happen, these different identities have to all be valued socially, and acquiring one should not be made at the expense of the other (Clément et al., 2001). The social context is thus crucial in promoting and valuing all cultural identities and making sure these are contributing to defining the superordinate and inclusive Québécois identity.

Implementing Intervention 3 will require a good deal of effort and creativity. We foresee a number of problems that might arise in the pro-cess. First, it is essential that immigrants from diverse cultural origins invest their efforts into integrating the Québécois identity in their over-all sense of self, but not by rejecting or relinquishing their own original cultural identity (i.e., without *assimilating* into the Québec context; Berry, 1997). This integration implies that Québécois of diverse cul-tural origins feel *both*, for example, Asian and Québécoise. To this aim, some interventions have already been devised to help bicultural indi-viduals redefine their different cultural identities and increase identity coherence which could be offered to targeted individuals (Schwartz, Montgomery, & Briones, 2006). Such interventions could be adapted to the specific Canadian context and offered through hospitals and CLSCs (community health centers) in Québec.

Second, some members of the Québécois host community might be highly reluctant to develop a broader and more inclusive conception of the Québécois identity, such as individuals who identify highly as Québécois (Crisp, Stone, & Hall, 2006), or for whom the Québécois identity is already predominant in their overall sense of self. Given French-speaking Québécois' historical struggle to preserve their lan-guage and culture and their latent feelings of threat, it should be made clear that promoting a complex and multicultural superordi-nate Québécois identity does not mean that this will be done at the expense of specific groups within Québec (i.e., Francophones), nor to the detriment of the highly effective linguistic laws preserving the French language (e.g., Bill 101; Bourhis, Montaruli, & Amiot, 2007). Furthermore, promoting the cultural development of Québécois from diverse cultural origins does not signify that all of their demands for reasonable accommodations be met.

Finally, when developing a broad and inclusive conception of the Québécois identity, it will be necessary to stress that for members of the host community, endorsing such an inclusive superordinate identity does not mean that they will have to directly and *personally* identify as a member of, say, the Latino cultural group or Haitian culture (e.g., by learning their languages). Rather, it is through identification with the inclusive and complex Québécois superordinate identity that members of the Québécois host community will come to feel that they belong to the same ingroup as Québécois who originate from the Latino or the Haitian culture.

In sum, we consider that it is crucial that host-community members make a collective effort to include diverse cultural groups in their conceptualizing of the Québécois identity. From the point of view of immigrants, doing so should greatly facilitate the integration of the new Québécois identity: for them, such an inclusive superordinate identity will be easier to relate to and will also allow to cognitively "bind" their original and new cultural identities. Essentially, the goal is to eliminate the exclusive connotation of the term "Québécois." Despite being a challenging intervention to implement, we are hopeful that it is achievable.

This feeling of hope is based on two concrete observations: first, in Québec, there have been signs of improvement over time in the relations between the Francophone and the Anglophone communities—two historically conflictual groups (the "two solitudes"). This could be partly attributable to increased dialogue between these two communities and an openness to acknowledge mutual feelings of threat (de la Sablonnière, 2008; de la Sablonnière & Taylor, 2006). Second, in recent political speeches and publications, a new meaning has been given to the term "Québécois." For example, when he was prime minister of Québec, Lucien Bouchard delivered a speech in front of the Anglophone community on March 11, 1996 in which he encouraged the Francophone community of Québec to adopt a more progressive and open vision of Québécois (Chambers, 2003). This openness to reconceptualizing and broadening the Québécois identity was also manifested by the historian Jocelyn Létourneau (2004). According to him, the term "Québécois" refers to all individuals who have invested their labor to build Québec society. Hence, despite the challenges involved in developing a broader and more inclusive superordinate Québécois identity, these recent examples are encouraging.

Intervention 4

This intervention aims at *ensuring that immigrants receive adequate social support to facilitate their integration into Québec society. Immigrants should also be active in this process and should seek out such support at different levels (e.g., cultural, social, interpersonal, job-related, health, etc.) and from different sources (i.e., from their original cultural group; from the Québécois host community).* The beneficial role of social support in intergroup relations has been found to be particularly beneficial when it is provided by ingroup members (e.g., Haslam et al., 2005).

In the context of immigration, we propose that it is crucial that immigrants receive support from a variety of sources and groups. For instance, if immigrants receive support exclusively from members of their original cultural group but not from members of the host community more generally, this could very well foster exclusive identification with their original cultural group and block the development of the new cultural identity (e.g., segregation strategy; Berry, 1997; see also Amiot & de la Sablonnière, 2008). Furthermore, during an important life change such as immigrating to a new country, it might be particularly useful to receive social support from broader sources and from diverse groups, given the stressful nature of this life change and the many needs that will have to be fulfilled (e.g., emotional, informational, job-related, linguistic). In such a situation, the individual may benefit from these diverse sources of social support, each one allowing specific needs to be satisfied (Amiot et al., in press). Identifying with a broad and inclusive superordinate identity (i.e., a multicultural Québécois identity; see Intervention 3) may hence become particularly beneficial in the context of immigration so that immigrants can gain support from diverse ingroup sources and fully benefit from each.

Intervention 5

This intervention aims at *ensuring that different cultural identities are equally valued within a multicultural Québec society and acknowledging the strengths and specificity of each cultural group within global society.* Through this intervention, we wish to stress one general principle: all social groups are interdependent and we should become aware of this interdependence and even harness its potential. We said earlier that it is possible for an individual to identify with his or her different social and cultural groups and that identifying with one group does not necessarily involve the diminution or the relinquishment of the other (e.g., Clément et al., 2001). However, for this to be possible, social groups have to be equally valued. If one cultural group is more valued than the other, then the most socially valued identity may also become predominant in the individual's overall self (Amiot, de la Sablonnière, et al., 2007).

Therefore, the fifth intervention aims at valuing the specificity of each cultural group within Québec society as a whole and ensuring that each contributes distinctively to the superordinate society. Doing so will allow immigrants to fully realize how their specific cultural background can contribute to Québec society and that each is valuable (see also Verkuyten, this volume). This should then facilitate their integration of the Québécois identity. Immigrants in Québec clearly have a lot of skills and motivation to offer to the global society. In fact, they participate in the economy, help absorb the costs associated with the aging population, increase the birthrate, and enrich artistic and scientific milieux. Attesting to the strong motivation of immigrants to integrate into Québec society, children of immigrant parents generally succeed better in school in comparison to children from nonimmigrant parents: they have better grades and a higher percentage graduate from high school (Ballivy, 2008).

However, statistics from the 2001 Canadian census reveal that immigrants in Québec have higher unemployment rates (12%) than the nonimmigrant Québécois population (8%). Also, a report from the Ministry of Relations with Citizens and Immigration (Ministère des relations avec les citoyens et de l'immigration, 2003) noted that the exclusion of immigrants from the workforce was partly due to the nonrecognition of their qualifications and training outside of Québec. Without implying that equivalences should be automatically granted between all qualifications, an effort should definitely be made to make maximum use of immigrants' knowledge, skills, and high motivation. The goal of this intervention involves ensuring that immigrants contribute to Québec society to their full potential. In line with these propositions, the Québec and Canadian governments are currently in the process of devising new ways to recognize immigrants' working qualifications and diplomas obtained in other countries. This is definitely a foot in the right direction and efforts should ensure that such an intervention is fully implemented.

How can we make sure that different cultural identities will be equally valued? Toward this aim, both immigrants and members of the host community could use the strategy of social creativity. Not only should each social group realize its particularities, strengths, competencies, and how these can complement one another when undertaking common projects within a society, but we should also directly question the superiority and value of some cultural groups over others. To do so, we need to put things in perspective. Some values clearly predominate in our capitalist societies, such as money, productivity, and dominance. Social groups that have more social prestige currently in the world distinguish themselves positively from other groups on these (currently) valued dimensions of comparison. However, other dimensions are highly important as well, and might even become strikingly necessary to value as we face new challenges (e.g., global warming; health problems in Africa), such as respect of life and its conservation, as well as health and well-being. Some groups (e.g., Aboriginals) clearly outperformed others (i.e., their colonizers) on these alternative dimensions of comparison. Perhaps it is time to put things into perspective and start being creative as to what the contribution and the "real" value of each social group is to the superordinate whole.

Conclusion

The literature in social psychology suggests that integrated cultural identities predict higher psychological well-being and more positive intergroup relations. To illustrate how we can facilitate the integration of diverse cultural identities, the particular case of Québec was used as an example for intervention. Five interventions were proposed: acknowledging the problem and the mutual feelings of threat experienced by members of diverse cultural groups, redefining the Québécois superordinate identity as inclusive and complex, providing broad social support to immigrants, and valuing each cultural identity and its contribution to the superordinate society. Although the implementation of these interventions will require effort, creativity, and sensitivity to the groups' particular context, we are hopeful that these interventions will lead to constructive social changes.

Acknowledgments

The writing of this chapter was facilitated thanks to grants from the Fonds québécois pour la recherche sur la sociét ét la culture (FQRSC) to Catherine Amiot and Roxane de la Sablonnière and to a grant from Social Sciences and Humanities Research Council of Canada (SSHRC) to Catherine Amiot. We thank the members of the *Social Change and Identity Laboratory* for their thoughts on some of the ideas presented in this chapter and Maya Yampolsky for her very useful comments.

Note

1   The term host community is employed in this chapter very inclusively and includes different groups within Québec society (i.e., Anglophones,

Francophones, members of diverse cultural groups who have already settled in the province of Québec). Ultimately, with time, immigrants will also become part of the Québécois host community.

References

Allocution du premier ministre du Québec, M. Lucien Bouchard, devant la communauté anglophone du Québec. Montréal, le lundi 11 mars 1996, au théâtre Centaur. Retrieved October 20, 2007, from www.premier-ministre .gouv.qc.ca/salle-de-presse/discours/1996/mars/1996-03-11.shtm.

Amiot, C. E., Blanchard, C. M., & Gaudreau, P. (2008). The self in change: A longitudinal investigation of coping and self-determination processes. *Self and Identity, 7*, 204–224.

Amiot, C. E., & de la Sablonnière, R. (2008). Immigrants in Québec: Toward an explanation of how multiple and potentially conflictual linguistic identities become integrated. *Diversité Urbaine, 4*, 145–161.

Amiot, C. E., de la Sablonnière, R., Terry, D. J., & Smith, J. R. (2007). Development and integration of social identities in the self: Toward a cognitive-developmental model. *Personality and Social Psychology Review, 11*, 364–388.

Amiot, C. E., Terry, D. J., & Callan, V. J. (2007). Status, equity, and social identification during an intergroup merger: A longitudinal study. *British Journal of Social Psychology, 46*, 557–577.

Amiot, C. E., Terry, D. J., Jimmieson, N. L., & Callan, V. J. (2006). A longitudinal investigation of stress and coping processes during an organizational merger: Implications for job satisfaction and organizational identification. *Journal of Management, 32*, 552–574.

Amiot, C. E., Terry, D. J., Wirawan, D., & Grice, T. (in press). Changes in social identities over time: The role of coping and adaptation processes. *British Journal of Social Psychology*.

Aron, A., Aron, E. N., Tudor, M., & Nelson, G. (1991). Close relationships as including other in the self. *Journal of Personality and Social Psychology, 60*, 241–253.

Ataca, B., & Berry, J. W. (2002). Psychological, sociocultural, and marital adaptation of Turkish immigrant couples in Canada. *International Journal of Psychology, 37*, 13–26.

Ballivy, V. (2008, January 9). Les enfants d'immigrés au tableau d'honneur [Children of immigrants on the honors list]. *La Presse*. Retrieved July 21, 2009, from http://www.immigrer.com/faq/sujet/Les-enfants-dimmigres-reussissent-mieux.html.

Barrette, G., & Bourhis, R. Y. (2004). La gestion de la diversité culturelle en emploi: Les outils de la recherche actuelle [Managing cultural diversity in the work setting: Tools from current research]. In R. Y. Bourhis (Ed.), *La diversité culturelle dans les institutions publiques québécoises: Où en sommes-*

nous à l'UQAM? Cahier des conférences et séminaires scientifiques (Vol. 9, pp. 77–99). Montréal, Canada: Chaire Concordia-UQAM en études ethniques.

Beauvais, A. (2007, January 16). Gérald Tremblay: Montréal est plutôt une ville exemple [Gérald Tremblay: Montreal is an city of example]. *Le Journal de Montréal*, 8.

Benet-Martínez, V., & Haritatos, J. (2005). Bicultural Identity Integration (BII): Components and psychosocial antecedents. *Journal of Personality, 73*, 1015–1050.

Benet-Martínez, V., Leu, J., Lee, F., & Morris, M. W. (2002). Negotiating biculturalism: Cultural frame switching in biculturals with oppositional versus compatible cultural identities. *Journal of Cross-Cultural Psychology, 33*, 492–516.

Berry, J. W. (1997). Immigration, acculturation and adaptation. *Applied Psychology: An International Review, 46*, 5–68.

Bourhis, R. Y. (2001). Reversing language shift in Quebec. In J. A. Fishman (Ed.), *Reversing language shift: Can threatened languages be saved?* (pp. 101–141). Clevedon, UK: Multilingual Matters.

Bourhis, R. Y., Montaruli, E., & Amiot, C. E. (2007). Language planning and French–English bilingual communication: Montreal field studies from 1977 to 1997. *International Journal of the Sociology of Language, 185*, 187–224.

Bourhis, R. Y., Montreuil, A., Helly, D., & Jantzen, L. (2007). Discrimination et linguicisme au Québec: Enquête sur la diversité ethnique au Canada [Discrimination and linguicism in Quebec: Survey of ethnic diversity in Canada]. *Études ethniques au Canada/Canadian Ethnic Studies, 39*, 31–50.

Brewer, M. B., & Pierce, K. P. (2005). Social identity complexity and outgroup tolerance. *Personality and Social Psychology Bulletin, 31*, 428–437.

Cervone, D. (2005). Personality architecture: Within person structures and processes. *Annual Review of Psychology, 56*, 423–452.

Chambers, G. (2003). Les relations entre anglophones et les franchophones [The relations between Anglophones and Francophones]. In M. Plourde (Ed.), *Le français au Québec: 400 ans d'histoire et de vie* (pp. 319–325). Sainte-Foy, Québec, Canada: Fides/Les Publications du Québec.

Chen, G., & Klimoski, R. J. (2003). The impact of expectations on newcomer performance in teams as mediated by work characteristics, social exchanges, and empowerment. *Academy of Management Journal, 46*, 591–607.

Clément, R., Noels, K. A., & Deneault, B. (2001). Interethnic contact, identity, and psychological adjustment: The mediating and moderating role of communication. *Journal of Social Issues, 57*, 559–577.

Commission de consultation sur les pratiques d'accommodement reliées aux différences culturelles (2007). *Vers un terrain d'entente: la parole aux citoyens* [Toward a middle ground: Citizens speak out]. Retrieved July 22, 2009, from http://www.accommodements.qc.ca/documentation/document-consultation.pdf.

Crisp, R. J., Stone, C. H., & Hall, N. R. (2006). Recategorization and subgroup identification: Predicting and preventing threats from common ingroups. *Personality and Social Psychology Bulletin, 32*, 230–243.

de la Sablonnière, R. (2008). Le bien-être psychologique des francophones et des anglophones: le rôle des points tournants de l'histoire du Québec. [Psychological well-being of Francophones and Anglophones: The role of turning points in Québec's history]. *Diversité Urbaine*, 131–144.

de la Sablonnière, R., Amiot, C. E., & Sadykova, N. (2009). *Integration of cultural identities: Processes and consequences. Journal of Cross-Cultural Psychology.* Manuscript submitted for publication.

de la Sablonnière, R., Pinard Saint-Pierre, F., Perozzo, C., Debrosse, R., Coulombe, F. S., Auger, É., et al. (2007). *Vers une intégration réciproque des identités culturelles: un sens à la crise symptomatique des accommodements raisonnables* [Toward a reciprocal integration of cultural identities: Making sense of the reasonable accommodation crisis]. Memoir presented to the Commission on practices of accommodation concerning cultural differences.

de la Sablonnière, R., & Taylor, D. M. (2006). Changements sociaux et linguistiques: une menace seulement pour les anglophones? [Social and linguistic change: A threat only for the Anglophones?]. In P. Georgeault & M. Pagé (Eds.), *Le français, langue de la diversité québécoise* (pp. 235–256). Montréal, Canada: Québec Amérique.

de la Sablonnière, R., Taylor, D. M., Perozzo, C., & Sadykova, N. (2009). Reconceptualizing relative deprivation in the context of dramatic social change: The challenge confronting the people of Kyrgyzstan. *European Journal of Social Psychology, 39*, 325–345.

de la Sablonnière, R., Tougas, F., & Lortie-Lussier, M. (2009). Dramatic social change in Russia and Mongolia: Connecting relative deprivation to social identity. *Journal of Cross-Cultural Psychology, 40*, 327–348.

Dovidio, J. F., Gaertner, S. L., & Validzic, A. (1998). Intergroup bias: Status, differentiation, and a common ingroup identity. *Journal of Personality and Social Psychology, 75*, 109–120.

Downie, M., Koestner, R., ElGeledi, S., & Cree, K. (2004). The impact of cultural internalization and integration on well-being among tricultural individuals. *Personality and Social Psychology Bulletin, 30*, 305–314.

Eccles, J. S., & Midgley, C. (1990). Changes in academic motivation and self-perception during early adolescence. In R. Montemayor, G.R. Adams, & T. P. Gullotta (Eds.), *From childhood to adolescence: A transitional period* (pp. 134–156). Newbury Park, CA: Sage.

Ellis, B. H., MacDonald, H. Z., Lincoln, A. K., & Cabral, H. J. (2008). Mental health of Somali adolescent refugees: The role of trauma, stress, and perceived discrimination. *Journal of Consulting and Clinical Psychology, 76*, 184–193.

Ethier, K. A., & Deaux, K. (1994). Negotiating social identity when contexts change: Maintaining identification and responding to threat. *Journal of Personality and Social Psychology, 67*, 243–251.

Fisher, C. D. (1986). Organizational socialization: An integrative review. *Research in Personnel and Human Resource Management, 4*, 101–145.

Ford, T. E., Grossman, R. W., & Jordan, E. A. (1997). Teaching about unintentional racism in introductory psychology. *Teaching of Psychology, 24,* 186–188.

Gaertner, S. L., & Dovidio, J. F. (2000). *Reducing intergroup bias: The common ingroup identification model.* Philadelphia, PA: Psychology Press/Taylor & Francis.

Galinsky, A. D., & Moskowitz, G. B. (2000). Perspective-taking: Decreasing stereotype expression, stereotype accessibility, and in-group favoritism. *Journal of Personality and Social Psychology, 78,* 708–724.

Harter, S. (1999). *The construction of the self: A developmental perspective.* New York: Guilford Press.

Harter, S. (2003). The development of self-representations during childhood and adolescence. In R. R. Leary & J. P. Tangney (Eds.), *Handbook of Self and Identity* (pp. 610–642). New York: Guilford Press.

Harter, S., & Monsour, A. (1992). Developmental analysis of conflict caused by opposing attributes in the adolescent self-portrait. *Developmental Psychology, 28,* 251–260.

Haslam, S. A., O'Brien, A., Jetten, J., Vormedal, K., & Penna, S. (2005). Social identity, social support, and the experience of stress. *British Journal of Social Psychology, 44,* 355–370.

Helly, D. (2004). Le traitement de l'islam au Canada [The treatment of Islam in Canada]. *Revue Européenne des Migrations Internationales, 20,* 47–71.

Hewstone, M., & Brown, R. J. (1986). Contact is not enough: An intergroup perspective. In M. Hewstone & R.J. Brown (Eds.), *Contact and conflict in intergroup encounters* (pp. 1–44). Oxford, UK: Blackwell.

Hornsey, M. J., & Hogg, M. A. (2000). Assimilation and diversity: An integrative model of subgroup relations. *Personality and Social Psychology Review, 4,* 143–156.

Institut de la statistique du Québec (2000). *Perspectives démographiques du Québec,* 1996–2041. Régions administratives, régions métropolitaines et municipalités régionales de comté. Québec, Canada.

Institut de la statistique du Québec (2007). *Naissances et taux de natalité, Québec, 1900–2006* [Births and birthrates, Quebec, 1900–2006]. Retrieved October 27, 2007, from http://www.stat.gouv.qc.ca/donstat/societe/demographie/naisn_deces/naissance/401.htm.

Jetten, J., Iyer, A., Tsivrikos, D., & Young, B. M. (2008). When is individual mobility costly? The role of economic and social identity factors. *European Journal of Social Psychology, 38,* 866–879.

Jetten, J., O'Brien, A., & Trindall, N. (2002). Changing identity: Predicting adjustment to organizational restructure as a function of subgroup and superordinate identification. *British Journal of Social Psychology, 41,* 281–297.

Kernis, M. H. (Ed.) (2006). *Self-esteem issues and answers: A sourcebook of current perspectives.* New York: Psychology Press.

Leong, C. H., & Ward, C. (2000). Identity conflict in sojourners. *International Journal of Intercultural Relations, 24,* 763–776.

Létourneau, J. (2004). *Le Québec, les Québécois: un parcours historique.* Saint-Laurent, Québec, Canada: Fides.

Lightman, N. (2006, April 10). Quebec report highlights systemic discrimination against black communities. *McGill Daily.* Retrieved October 1, 2007, from http://www.mcgilldaily.com/view.php?aid=5104.

Lipponen, J., Olkkonen, M.-E., & Moilanen, M. (2004). Perceived procedural justice and employee responses to an organizational merger. *European Journal of Work and Organizational Psychology, 13,* 391–413.

Mascolo, M. F., & Fischer, K. W. (1998). The development of self through the coordination of component systems. In M. D. Ferrari & R.J. Sternberg (Eds.), *Self-awareness: Its nature and development* (pp. 332–384). New York: Guilford Press.

Ministère de l'immigration et des communautés culturelles. (2000). *Tableaux sur l'immigration au Québec, 1995–1999* [Tables on immigration in Quebec, 1995–1999]. Retrieved July 22, 2009, from http://www.micc.gouv.qc.ca/publications/fr/recherches-statistiques/Immigration-QC-1995-1999.pdf.

Ministère de l'immigration et des communautés culturelles (2009). *Tableaux sur l'immigration permanente au Québec, 2004–2008* [Tables on permanent immigration in Quebec, 2004–2008]. Retrieved July 22, 2009, from http://www.micc.gouv.qc.ca/publications/fr/recherches-statistiques/Immigration-Quebec-2004-2008.pdf.

Ministère des relations avec les citoyens et de l'immigration (2003). *Rapport annuel de gestion 2002–2003* [Annual report 2002–2003]. Retrieved July 22, 2009, from http://www.micc.gouv.qc.ca/publications/fr/ministere/rapport-annuel/Rapport-annuel-2002-2003.pdf.

Moreland, R. L., & Levine, J. M. (2001). Socialization in organizations and work groups. In M. E. Turner (Ed.), *Groups at work: Theory and research* (pp. 69–112). Mahwah, NJ: Erlbaum.

Mummendey, A., & Wenzel, M. (1999). Social discrimination and tolerance in intergroup relations: Reactions to intergroup difference. *Personality and Social Psychology Review, 3,* 158–174.

Otten, S., & Wentura, D. (2001). Self-anchoring and ingroup favoritism: An individual-profiles analysis. *Journal of Experimental Social Psychology, 37,* 525–532.

Perry, M. J., & Mackun, P. J. (2001, April). *Population change and distribution, 1990 to 2000.* Retrieved October 13, 2008, from http://www.census.gov/prod/2001pubs/c2kbr01-2.pdf.

Phinney, J. S. (2003). Ethnic identity and acculturation. In K. M. Chun, P. Balls Organista, & G. Marín Gerardo (Eds.), *Acculturation: Advances in theory, measurement, and applied research* (pp. 63–81). Washington, DC: American Psychological Association.

Phinney, J. S., Ferguson, D., & Tate, J. (1997). Intergroup attitudes among ethnic minority adolescents: A causal model. *Child Development, 68*, 955–969.

Presse Canadienne/Léger Marketing (2001). *Immigration et racisme après le 11 septembre* [Immigration and racism after September 11]. Retrieved October 1, 2007, from http://www.legermarketing.com/documents/spclm/011105FR.pdf.

Ramsey, J., & Latting, J. K. (2005). A typology of intergroup competencies. *Journal of Applied Behavioral Science, 41*, 265–284.

Roccas, S., & Brewer, M. B. (2002). Social identity complexity. *Personality and Social Psychology Review, 6*, 88–106.

Rocher, G. (1992). *Introduction à la sociologie générale*. Ville LaSalle: Éditions Hurtubise HMH.

Schwartz, S. J., Montgomery, M. J., & Briones, E. (2006). The role of identity in acculturation among immigrant people: Theoretical propositions, empirical questions, and applied recommendations. *Human Development, 49*, 1–30.

Shields, A. (2007, March 20). Accommodements raisonnables—des fenêtres claires munies de stores pour le YMCA du Parc [Reasonable accommodations—Clear windows with blinds for the YMCA du Parc]. *Le Devoir*. Retrieved July 21, 2009, from http://www.ledevoir.com/2007/03/20/135813.html.

Statistics Canada (2003). *Major religious denominations, Quebec, 1991 and 2001*. Retrieved October 27, 2007, from http://www12.statcan.ca/english/census01/Products/Analytic/companion/rel/tables/provs/qcmajor.cfm.

Statistics Canada (2005). Ethnocultural diversity in Canada: Prospects for 2017. Retrieved July 30, 2009 from http://www.statcan.gc.ca/pub/11-008-x/2005003/article/8968-eng.pdf.

Statistics Canada (2007). *Population by immigrant status and period of immigration, 2006 counts, for Canada, provinces and territories*. Retrieved July 30, 2009 from http://www12.statcan.ca/census-recensement/2006/dp-pd/hlt/97–557/T403–eng.cfm?Lang=E&T=403&GH=4&SC=1&S=99&0=A< http://www12.statcan.ca/census-recensement/2006/dp-pd/hlt/97–557/T403–ng.cfm?Lang=E&T=403&GH=4&SC=1&S=99&0=A>.

Stevens, G. W. J. M., Volleberg, W. A. M., Pels, T. V. M., & Crijnen, A. A. M. (2005). Predicting internalizing problems in Moroccan immigrant adolescents in the Netherlands. *Social Psychiatry and Psychiatric Epidemiology, 40*, 1003–1011.

Tadmor, C. T., & Tetlock, P. E. (2006). Biculturalism: A model of the effects of second-culture exposure on acculturation and integrative complexity. *Journal of Cross-Cultural Psychology, 37*, 173–190.

Tajfel, H., & Turner, J. C. (1979). An integrative theory of intergroup conflict. In W. G. Austin & S. Worschel (Eds.), *The psychology of intergroup relations* (pp. 33–46). Hillsdale, NJ: Erlbaum.

Taylor, D. M., & Sigal, R. J. (1982). Defining "Québécois". The role of ethnic heritage, language, and political orientation. *Études ethniques au Canada/Canadian Ethnic Studies, 82,* 59–70.

Terry, D. J. (2003). A social identity perspective on organizational mergers: The role of group status, permeability, and similarity. In S. A. Haslam, D. van Knippenberg, M. J. Platow, & N. Ellemers (Eds.), *Social identity at work: Developing theory for organizational practice* (pp. 223–240). New York: Psychology Press.

Terry, D. J., Callan, V. J., & Sartori, G. (1996). A test of a stress-coping model of adjustment to a large-scale organizational change. *Stress Medicine, 12,* 105–122.

Terry, D. J., & O'Brien, A. T. (2001). Status, legitimacy, and ingroup bias in the context of an organizational merger. *Group Processes and Intergroup Relations, 4,* 271–289.

Thériault, L. (2006). Notes for the allocution of the Minister of Immigration and Cultural Communities of Quebec. Presentation at the Chambre de commerce du Montréal Métropolitain.

Tougas, F., de la Sablonnière, R., Lagacé, M., & Kocum, L. (2003). Intrusiveness of minorities: Growing pains for the majority group? *Journal of Applied Social Psychology, 33,* 283–298.

Turner, J. C., Hogg, M. A., Oakes, P. J., Reicher, S. D., & Wetherell, M. (1987). *Rediscovering the social group: A self-categorization theory.* Oxford, UK: Blackwell.

United Nations (2002). *Number of world's migrants reaches 175 million mark: Migrant population has doubled in twenty-five years.* Retrieved July 22, 2009, from http://www.un.org/esa/population/publications/ittmig 2002/press-release-eng.htm.

van Knippenberg, D., van Knippenberg, B., Monden, L., & Lima, F. (2002). Organizational identification after a merger: A social identity perspective. *British Journal of Social Psychology, 41,* 233–252.

van Leeuwen, E., van Knippenberg, D., & Ellemers, N. (2003). Continuing and changing group identities: The effects of merging on social identification and ingroup bias. *Personality and Social Psychology Bulletin, 29* (6), 679–690.

Waldzus, S., Mummendey, A., & Wenzel, M. (2005). When "different" means "worse": In-group prototypicality in changing intergroup contexts. *Journal of Experimental Social Psychology, 41,* 76–83.

4

Costs and Benefits of Switching among Multiple Social Identities

Margaret Shih, Diana T. Sanchez, and Geoffrey C. Ho

It used to be a big thing for me—finding where I belonged. Do I belong with black people? Do I belong with white people? Do I belong with biracial people? And now it's like I belong wherever I am. Whatever group I'm in, I can belong there if I want.

Chela Delgado (Gaskins, 1999, p. 16)

I went into a store in Tallahassee to buy a computer and even the black salesman ignored me and went to help the white young females from Florida State who were probably buying a video camera half the price of a computer. I was in there to spend money, but it took forty-five minutes to get help.

Ernest White (Gaskins, 1999, p. 135)

The first quote was made by a young woman of African American and European descent describing the challenges she faces in finding a sense of belonging in relation to the communities associated with her different racial identities. The second quote was from a young man of black and French Canadian descent. He describes the challenges he faces in getting help in a store because of his racial identity. These quotes provide vivid examples of how social identities shape people's experiences as they navigate their social world.

A great deal of research has documented the harmful impact of people's devalued social identities, stereotypes, or stigmas. For instance, stigmatized individuals tend to receive less help (Crosby, Bromley, & Saxe, 1980) and face "glass ceilings" in terms of career advancement

(Morrison & Von Glinow, 1990). Stigmatized individuals also receive fewer positive nonverbal cues (Word, Zanna, & Cooper, 1974), are exposed more frequently to awkward social interactions (Hebl, Tickle, & Heatherton, 2000), and are at greater risk of negative health outcomes associated with discrimination (Gee, Spencer, Chen, & Takeuchi, 2007).

Having stigmatized identities may not inevitably lead to negative outcomes and experiences. This chapter examines one process through which possessing multiple identities might buffer individuals from poor outcomes. Individuals possess multiple social identities that may be more or less prominent in different social contexts. For instance, consider a young Japanese male student in three different social situations: when with his Japanese friends, he might identify as Japanese; when at a family gathering, he might identify as young person; or, when in physical education class, he might identify with his gender. Moreover, he could be identified with any combination of these identities. Individuals possess multiple social identities and can identify in many different ways in different social situations. In any given situation, individuals with devalued identities may also switch to identify with other identities that may be valued. Because individuals possess multiple social identities, individuals belonging to devalued social groups may not be destined to poor adjustment outcomes. In this chapter, we discuss the benefits and costs of identity switching, factors that may moderate the effectiveness of identity switching, and the implications for social policy makers.

There is a great deal of evidence documenting that possessing multiple identities protects psychological well-being (see Linville, 1987; Roccas & Brewer, 2002). In this chapter, we consider people with multiple identities as those having numerous roles (e.g., mother, wife, teacher), or those having multiple stigmatized or nonstigmatized social identities (e.g., female, ethnic minority, American). Role Accumulation and Self-Complexity Theory propose that individuals who have multiple identities have a more complex self that buffers against stress-related illness and depression (Linville, 1987). Possessing a larger number of identities has also been shown to lead to better psychological health outcomes such as increased self-efficacy (Adelmann, 1994a), higher self-esteem and life and job satisfaction (Miller, Moen, & Dempster-McClain, 1991; Pietromonaco, Manis, & Frohardt-Lane, 1986), and multiple opportunities to gain social support (Hong & Seltzer, 1995). Furthermore, having a greater number of identities has been demonstrated to lower psychological distress and anxiety (Thoits, 1983, 1986), decrease health interference (Coleman, Antonucci, & Adelmann, 1987), lower rates of depression (Adelmann, 1994b; Gore &

Mangione, 1983; Kandel, Davies & Raveis, 1985; Thoits, 1983) reduce marital-induced stress (Kandel et al., 1985), and diminish rates of psychological disorders (Sachs-Ericsson & Ciarlo, 2000).

Importantly, the benefits of multiple identities are not limited to individuals with only valued social identities. Research has shown that socially devalued groups, such as women and Mexicans, reap the same psychological benefits from multiple identities as those with valued social identities (Adelmann, 1993, 1994a, 1994b; Burton, Rushing, Ritter, & Rakocy, 1993; Haavio-Mannila, 1986; Helson, Elliot, & Leigh, 1990; Jackson, 1997; Pietromonaco et al., 1986; Rushing, Ritter, & Burton, 1992; Sachs-Ericsson & Ciarlo, 2000; Waldron & Jacobs, 1989; Wilsnack & Cheloha, 1987). For example, Jackson (1997) found that both non-Hispanic whites and Mexican Americans benefit from multiple identities because of the increased opportunities to maintain self-esteem and healthy adjustment outcomes through memberships in cultural and religious institutions. Thus, having devalued or stigmatized identities does not overshadow the benefits that multiple identities can contribute to well-being.

This chapter examines one process through which possessing multiple identities might buffer individuals from poor outcomes. Specifically, we examine how individuals with multiple identities have the capacity to take advantage of adaptive identities through the process of identity switching. We review some of the benefits and costs associated with identity switching and discuss factors that may moderate the relationship between identity switching and outcomes. Finally, we discuss several implications from this chapter for social policy makers to consider.

Identity Adaptiveness

Certain social identities may be stigmatized in one social context but respected in another because stereotypes and stigmas are social constructions (Crocker & Quinn, 2000). As a result, social identities will have varying levels of *identity adaptiveness* in different social domains. Pittinsky, Shih, and Ambady (1999) define identity adaptiveness as the degree to which an identity is associated with a positive stereotype in a given context. They also suggest that identities can be adaptive in one social domain, but maladaptive in another.

For example, consider an African American individual in an academic or athletic test situation. In the athletic test situation, the African American identity would be relatively adaptive because African Americans are stereotyped to be talented at athletics (e.g., Biernat and Manis, 1994).

However, the African American identity would not be adaptive in an academic test situation, because African Americans are not stereotyped to be academically talented (e.g., Sailes, 1996). Thus, there are contexts in which the value of membership in a certain social group, such as African American, is high, and contexts in which the value of membership in the same group is low. In other words, the adaptiveness of an identity varies as a function of the social context (Amiot & de la Sablonnière, this volume; Pittinsky, Shih, & Ambady, 1999).

Identity Switching: Emphasizing the Optimally Adaptive Identity

One strategy individuals use to protect themselves from the negative consequences of negative social identities is to emphasize the identities that are optimally adaptive (Hogg & Abrams, 1988; Pittinsky et al., 1999). This idea is supported by much research recognizing that individuals may fluctuate between their social identities for a series of cognitive and motivational reasons (See Banaji & Prentice, 1994 for a review; Brewer, 1991; Sanchez, Shih, & Garcia, 2009; Steele, 1988). For instance, work on optimal distinctiveness theory finds that individuals will selectively associate and distance themselves from their different identities to establish an optimum level of tension between their desires for differentiation and assimilation (Brewer, 1991). Similarly, research into self-categorization theory suggests that individuals seek to maintain a positive identity through highlighting and selecting self-relevant categories that maximize the positivity of their self-concept (Turner, 1987). That is, individuals who find themselves in contexts in which one identity is maladaptive can increase the salience of other more facilitative identities (Hogg & Abrams, 1988; Pittinsky et al., 1999). Work on self-affirmation shows that a person who finds herself in situations in which her sense of self-worth is threatened repairs the damage by affirming another part of themselves (Steele, 1988). For instance, a woman taking a math test situation, a situation in which her female identity may threaten her confidence, may self-affirm by reminding herself that she is a good mother, which could protect her from the threat of negative stereotypes about women and math.

We propose that individuals switch among their different identities in a process that may be analogous to *frame switching*. The term frame switching, as coined by LaFromboise, Coleman, and Gerton (1993), refers to the shifting of cultural frameworks to adapt to cues in the social environment and occurs in bicultural individuals. This process assists biculturals in accessing the sets of thoughts, actions, and behaviors associated with the cultural identity that is most appropriate to the situation.

Identity switching can be differentiated from cultural frame switching in some important ways. Specifically, most of the work used to advocate the benefits of frame switching has focused on cultural competence and awareness, such as bilingualism, bicultural involvement, and bicultural awareness (LaFromboise et al., 1993). Identity switching, on the other hand, focuses on individuals' changes in the framing of their self-definitions in different contexts. Hence, identity switching centers on the perceptual as opposed to the behavioral.

Benefits and Goals Achieved through Identity Switching

Several goals can be achieved through the process of identity switching. First of all, identity switching enables individuals to access adaptive identities in a situation. This allows the individuals themselves, as well as others, to see them in the most advantageous light. There is evidence that individuals spontaneously switch their identity orientations across situations in reaction to varying levels of adaptiveness for an identity (Sanchez et al., 2009). For example, Pittinsky et al. (1999) found that individuals orient themselves more positively toward identities that are adaptive in a given situation. Specifically, in a math test situation, Asian American women recalled more positive ethnicity-related memories, because Asians are stereotyped to be talented at math. However, in a verbal test situation, Asian American women recalled more positive gender-related memories, because women are stereotyped to be talented verbally.

Research on multiracial identity also finds that multiracial individuals engage in strategic identity switching to access identities that are more adaptive to the situation. For instance, *passing* is an example of a strategy that involves identity switching which multiracial individuals can use to achieve their interpersonal goals in certain contexts. Passing involves bringing the more adaptive component racial identity to the forefront and burying the less adaptive component identities (Daniel, 1992).

A second goal that individuals can achieve through identity switching is the maintenance of self-esteem. Individuals strive to maintain a positive sense of self-worth (Baumeister, 1995). Since self-esteem is intricately tied to group membership (Luhtanen & Crocker, 1992; Tajfel & Turner, 1986), situations that threaten a social identity can be harmful to individual self-esteem. One way to maintain a positive sense of self-worth is through the management of group memberships. Therefore, it is likely that in such a situation, when a social identity is not adaptive, individuals will want to change it or seek to exit the maladaptive social identity through social mobility strategies (Tajfel & Turner, 1986).

Thirdly, there is evidence demonstrating that individuals can avoid the negative consequences associated with one identity by focusing on an alternate identity. Work on stereotype threat finds the negative stereotypes about a group can hurt the performance of individuals in that group (Steele, 1997). For example, African American students performed worse on an academic test when the negative stereotype about African American students and academic ability was salient (Steele & Aronson, 1995). Similar results were found for women on a math test (Spencer, Steele, & Quinn, 1999) and for the elderly on a memory test (Levy, 1996) when the categorically self-relevant negative stereotypes were activated. However, work on stereotype susceptibility finds that members of the negatively stereotyped group can avoid the decline in performance by focusing on an alternate identity (Shih et al., 1999). Specifically, women, stereotyped to be poor at math, could avoid performing worse on a math test, as predicted by stereotype threat theory, by focusing on alternate identities. Also, Asian American women performed worse on a math test when their female identity was made salient, but better on the same test when their Asian identity, an identity associated with math talent, was made salient (Shih et al., 1999; see Figure 4.1).

More recently, Crisp, Bache, & Maitner (2009) found that female *psychology* majors experienced a stereotype threat effect while female *engineering* majors experienced a stereotype boost effect on a math test following a negative gender comparison (i.e., "men are better than women at math"). This evidence suggests that individuals may actively choose to construe themselves in terms of their most adaptive identity, even in the face of a situational prime that could activate a maladaptive identity. Hence, identity switching may be an active process which individuals can use to avoid stereotype threat, as opposed to a passive process whereby individuals would be largely influenced by situational primes.

Costs Associated with Identity Switching

While there is a great deal of work suggesting that multiple identities can be adaptive or utilized in ways to avoid negative stereotypes and

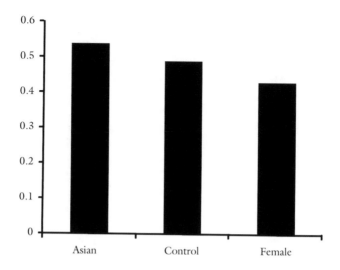

Figure 4.1   Math test performance across identity salience conditions (Shih et al., 1999).

take advantage of positive identities (e.g. Cross, Smith, & Payne, 2002; Shih et al., 1999), there is also evidence showing that switching among multiple identities carries some potential risks or costs.

Constant identity switching can potentially lead to self-concept instability or a fragmented sense of self. For instance, Donahue, Robins, Roberts, and John (1993) argue that highlighting multiple self-aspects creates a complex structure of self-knowledge which may lead to a more fragmented sense of self. In other words, while identity switching may help individuals take advantage of identity adaptiveness, constantly switching among multiple identities also carries the risk of highlighting the instability and inconsistency across identities.

In addition, self-concept stability models propose that chronically unstable self-concepts lead to poor psychological health (e.g., Rosenberg, 1979; Savin-Williams & Demo, 1983; Verkuyten, 1995). For example, the failure to foster unified racial identities has been found to have devastating psychological consequences, including anxiety, depression, academic underachievement, delinquency, substance abuse, and suicidal behavior (Gordon, 1964; Hauser, 1972; McCroy & Freeman, 1986; Park, 1928, 1931; Piskacek & Golub, 1973; Stonequist, 1937).

There is also some evidence to suggest that individuals who incessantly switch identities may suffer some negative consequences. Work

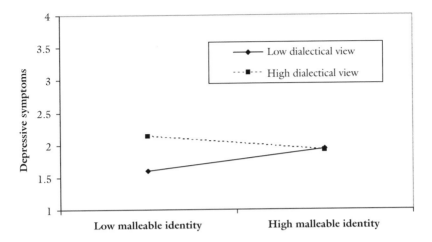

Figure 4.2 Relationship between identity malleability and depressive symptoms as a function of dialectical view (Sanchez et al., 2009).

on multiracial individuals finds that those individuals who have a more malleable racial identity and switch among racial identification across different situations tend to exhibit poorer psychological health (Sanchez et al., 2009). Moreover, this relationship is stronger among those who have low dialectical self-views and have little tolerance for change, inconsistency, and contradiction within the self (Sanchez et al., 2009; see Figure 4.2).

Moderating Factors

The preceding discussion summarizes the potential positive and negative consequences of identity switching. In the following section, we discuss some factors that may determine whether a net benefit or net cost results from an individual engaging in identity switching.

Inter-domain and Intra-domain Identity Switching

Individuals possess multiple identities across different domains (i.e., inter-domain identities). For example, a person can be a Native American within the domain of ethnicity and female within the domain of gender. Individuals can also possess multiple identities within a single domain (i.e., intra-domain identities). For example, a person can be Chinese and American within the domain of culture. Similarly, a person could be Black and White within the domain of race.

Because an individual may have multiple inter-domain and intra-domain identities, he or she may therefore switch identities between separate domains (i.e., *inter-domain identity switching*) or identities within a single domain (i.e., *intra-domain identity switching*). We propose that inter-domain identity switching is more susceptible to the positive effects of identity switching while intra-domain identity switching is more susceptible to the negative effects of identity switching. To elaborate, people generally have the capacity to view themselves through the lens of different identities which correspond to various social contexts (i.e., inter-domain identity switching). That is, a man may view himself as a father when he is with his son, a marketing manager at work, a pitcher on the baseball team, or an African American when with his friends. This type of inter-domain identity switching is quite common for most individuals in their daily lives, and because of its normality, should be understood and supported by social and societal groups. Hence, the capacity to switch identities between domains is generally adaptive, as it allows for an individual to select the optimal identity for any given context (as discussed in preceding sections).

Intra-domain identity switching occurs when individuals view themselves differentially within a single domain of their lives. However, individuals who engage in intra-domain identity switching receive less guidance from society about what it means to switch among these different identities or how to define their social identities, because society often has not yet established an understanding of what it means to possess multiple social identities within a single domain. In other words, since social identities are often socially constructed, society often doesn't have established categories for those who may possess multiple social identities within a domain. Consider the case of Castor Semenya, a South African runner who won a gold medal in the 800-meter race in the 2009 World Championships, but was found, after testing, to have both male and female sexual organs. In this case, Castor Semenya possessed characteristics society associated with the male category (a socially established identity), and also characteristics associated with the female category (also a socially established identity). However, society has not yet established a strong understanding for what it means for somebody who might belong to both the male and female category. This led to a great deal of discussion about the criteria used for establishing gender categories, and ultimately, whether Castor Semenya would be eligible to keep her medal in the women's race. As an interesting side note, the attention drawn to this issue may lead society to develop a stronger understanding of what it means to be able to fit into multiple gender categories, potentially establishing it as a more common identity in the future. In sum, multiple intra-domain social identities are often less established (e.g., White and Asian in ethnicity) relative to multiple inter-domain identities (e.g., White in ethnicity, male in gender, and lawyer in vocation).

Because possessing multiple identity within a domain is less common, individuals with multiple intra-domain identities receive less social guidance regarding how to define their social identities and what it means to switch among intra-domain identities. For example, multiracial people, those who have multiple racial identities, have few role models on how to best navigate their multiple racial identity options (Shih & Sanchez, 2005), and may be negatively viewed by others if they were to change their racial identification often. Individuals with multiple intra-domain identities may also receive less institutional support for their identities (Amiot & de la Sablonnière, this volume). For example, multiracial people were not given the option to identify with their multiple racial identities on the U.S. Census until recently. Similarly, Castor Semenya is finding resistance in participating in female track and field competitions, but has not been given an alternative venue in which she can compete. Thus, individuals with multiple intra-domain identities may be more vulnerable to negative psychological outcomes because they may feel abnormal, stigmatized, or confused when attempting to intra-domain identity switch.

Number of Identities

Individuals with a large number of identities may have greater capacity to leverage adaptive identities because they have a larger number of identities from which they can choose. Social identity theory predicts that when an individual's positive social identity is threatened, the individual may respond through several strategies, two examples of which are "social mobility," which involves exiting from the devalued social identity, and "social creativity," which involves changing the basis of comparison between the devalued social identity and the comparison identity (Tajfel & Turner, 1979). Individuals with many identities have an increased capability for social mobility because they have multiple groups to which they migrate. They also have increased capability for social creativity because they can draw on many different identities as their basis for social comparison.

Tolerance for Ambiguity

Work on cultural orientations suggests that some individuals have greater tolerance for ambiguity, change, and contradiction in the self (dubbed *dialectical self-views*; Spencer-Rodgers, Peng, Wang, & Hou, 2004). For instance, work finds that people from Eastern cultures and traditions may be more likely to have dialectical self-views than those from Western cultures because of deep-rooted Eastern religious and philosophical traditions that promote acceptance of contradiction and change (Spencer et al., 2004). In addition, Easterners report greater variability in self-aspects across contexts (English & Chen, 2007). Thus, individuals with a greater tolerance of ambiguity and change may be more resistant to the potential negative effects of identity switching.

There is some empirical evidence to support the buffering effects of dialectical self-views on negative consequences. Research on identity switching among multiracial individuals finds that individuals having high dialectical self-views buffered multiracial people from the negative psychological health outcomes associated with malleable racial identifications (Sanchez et al., 2009).

Multiple Identity Integration

The degree to which an individual views his or her multiple identities as compatible may also impact the likelihood of beneficial outcomes resulting from identity switching. Research on bicultural identity integration (see Amiot & de la Sablonnière, this volume; Nguyen & Benet-Martínez, this volume; Tadmor, Hong, Chiu, & No, this volume) finds that bicultural individuals who view their cultural identities as highly compatible are more likely to cultural frame-switch in the direction of the corresponding cultural stimuli (Benet-Martínez, Leu, & Lee, 2002), exhibit lower stress, cultural isolation, and discrimination (Benet-Martínez & Haritatos, 2005), and experience greater psychological adjustment and psychological outcomes (Chen, Benet-Martínez, & Bond, 2008).

On the other hand, incompatible identities may lead to "friction" and psychological discomfort when the individual attempts to identity switch. This may occur because individuals with low identity integration see their identities as conflicting, which may increase the difficulty of switching between identities. Hence, psychological discomfort will arise for these individuals as a function of their basic desire for consistency (Cialdini & Trost, 1998), which if unmet, may result in cognitive dissonance (Festinger, 1957) and harm the individual's positive self-concept (Cialdini & Goldstein, 2004).

Policy Implications

The preceding discussion presents several implications for social policies. Policymakers can enact policies to facilitate identity adaptiveness in three ways: (1) by increasing the total number of identity options, (2) by increasing the positivity of neutral and negative social identities, and (3) by increasing the neutrality with which social policy makers frame their tasks and programs.

Increasing the Number of Identity Options: Recognizing Identities

Social policies that increase the total number of identity options available for individuals can produce beneficial outcomes. Specifically, this can be accomplished through the recognition of a greater number of identities, which would allow individuals to have a wider range of options from which to choose when identity switching. As discussed in the preceding section regarding number of identities, individuals with a wider range of identities to choose from when identity switching may have a greater probability of locating the optimal adaptive identity for the situation.

Consider the case of the multiracial movement that pushes for the recognition of multiracial identity groups. On official forms, multiracial individuals have generally had to identify themselves with one or more of their monoracial component identities, but not as a separate multiracial group. For instance, the 2000 U.S. Census allowed individuals of multiracial descent to check off more than one race, but did not offer a multiracial category option. In this situation, multiracial individuals have the option of identifying with one or all of his or her component monoracial identities, but not as multiracial. This omission in the 2000 Census may cause multiracial individuals to be less aware of their mixed heritage and be less able or willing to switch to the multiracial identity when it is adaptive. For instance, during a discussion on race relations, an individual of mixed race descent may have the opportunity to highlight his or her mixed background to offer a perspective that individuals from monoracial backgrounds may not have. However, the multiracial individual may be unable (due to lack of social identity salience) or unwilling (due to lack of social identity recognition) to switch to the multiracial identity and be unable to provide his or her unique perspective.

In addition, recognizing a greater number of social identities and groups enhances identity adaptiveness because there will be more social programs targeted toward a wider range of identities. For instance, since the census is used for planning and allocating resources, omitting a multiracial category may lead policymakers to overlook the needs of multiracial individuals. Thus, multiracial individuals may find that they need to identify with one of their monoracial component identities, rather than their mixed identity, to access government sponsored social programs or communities to join. While the resources and services offered to monoracial minority groups may address some of the needs of multiracial individuals, there may be other needs specific to multiracial groups that may not be met. Thus, recognizing more identities, such as a multiracial group, may allow social programs targeted at addressing needs of different communities to offer services that are more targeted and effective.

Addressing Stereotypes: Destigmatizing Identities

Social policies can destigmatize negative identities by altering the expectations associated with these identities. This will, in effect, increase the adaptiveness of the stigmatized identity and lower the need to identity switch, thereby lessening the risks or costs associated with identity switching. Specifically, in cases where there is scientific evidence disconfirming negative stereotypes for a group in a particular domain, the evidence can be presented and promoted to increase the adaptiveness of the identity in that domain. This stereotype disconfirming information could mitigate the threat experienced by the individual encountering a self-relevant negative stereotype when identity switching is restricted (due to low capacity, situational priming, etc.) or the associated costs of switching outweigh the benefits. In fact, there is evidence that educating individuals about the invalidity of performance stereotypes can reduce the stereotype threat effect (see Aronson, Fried, & Good, 2002; Good, Aronson, & Inzlicht, 2003; Johns, Schmader, & Martens, 2005).

To illustrate, Hyde, Lindberg, Linn, Ellis, and Williams (2008) recently examined government-mandated standardized math tests for 7.2 million students from 2nd through to 11th grade and found that gender differences in math performance were negligible. If stereotype-disconfirming scientific information of this type were to be more widely disseminated, the negative stereotype of female math performance inferiority could be attenuated or abolished and the female identity would possess increased adaptiveness in the math performance domain. Hence, females who are unable to identity switch or do not wish to identity switch can still avoid stereotype threat in the math domain because the stereotype's credibility has been undermined by the information illustrating the adaptiveness of the female identity in the math domain.

In addition to presenting scientific information to destigmatize devalued identities, successful role models can be promoted or used as case studies to illustrate the adaptiveness of the devalued identity. Recent studies have suggested that the presence of in-group role models exhibiting counter-stereotypic behavior alleviates the effects of stereotype threat among individuals belonging to negatively stereotyped groups (e.g., Marx & Goff, 2005; Marx & Roman, 2002; McGlone, Aronson, & Kobrynowicz, 2006). These role models may act as powerful stereotype disconfirmations that increase the adaptiveness of the stigmatized identity which, in turn, increase performance in the specific domain. For instance, Barack Obama has been proclaimed a role model among African Americans (e.g., Gomstyn, 2008; Pitts, 2008; Reyes, 2008). One study found that Obama's ascendancy as a role model for African Americans has been purported to create an "Obama Effect" whereby African American students were inferior in performance on standardized verbal tests relative to White Americans prior to Obama's presidential election victory, but were on par with White Americans after the victory (Marx, Ko, & Friedman, in press). Hence, the presence of competent in-group role models may decrease identity switching and its costs because of increased identity adaptiveness.

If competent in-group role models are in short supply, social policies to increase training of the targeted group in the specific domain could be the first step in increasing the adaptiveness of an identity within a social context in the future. For instance, social programs aimed at addressing the underrepresentation of women in the science, technology, engineering, and math (STEM) fields, would do well to focus on the experiences and training of women in the STEM fields, rather than simply focusing on the number of women in the field. Focusing on the training women receive in the STEM fields would ensure that there will be highly qualified women in these fields who can serve as role models. These successful women role models will provide a credible source to debunk negative stereotypes and replace them with positive stereotypes. Thus, women, when provided with successful role models, may find that their female identity has increased adaptiveness in STEM fields. This resultant increase in female identity adaptiveness may obviate the need for identity switching and eliminate the associated costs of identity switching.

At the same time, it is important to keep in mind that policies highlighting role models cannot be haphazardly adopted. Work on reactance effects finds that highlighting exemplars that are seen as outliers (e.g., Einstein for intelligence) elicit social comparison processes leading to worse performance (Dijksterhuis et al., 1998). More recently, a second study on minority students in a summer program failed to find the "Obama effect" (Aronson, Jannone, McGlone, & Johnson-Campbell, 2009), suggesting that the "Obama effect" observed in the previous studies may be limited to a self-selected group of individuals. Thus, policymakers looking to highlight role models to improve academic performance for disadvantaged groups should carefully consider the characteristics of the students whose performance they want to improve, and also the method through which they highlight the role model, being careful not to activate social comparison processes.

Neutrality in Framing of Tasks and Social Situation

Studies have found that framing a task in different ways elicits different reactions and outcomes from people. In one study, Shih & Chui (2009) found that when a box construction task was called a "building task," a task that males are stereotyped to be good at, male participants among male–female pairs were more likely to take on the leadership role (i.e., being the first to contradict their partner and being the first to make a suggestion). However, when the task was called an "arts and crafts" task, a task that females are stereotyped to be good at, the female participant in the male–female pair more often took the leadership role. Similarly, studies have found that framing situation in different ways also influences performance. For instance, Wraga, Duncan, Helt, Jacobs, & Sullivan (2006) asked female participants to complete an imagined self-rotation task and found that females who were told that the task was a "perspective-taking task," a task in which women were expected to excel, performed significantly better on the task than participants who were told that the task was a "spatial task," a task in which women were not expected to excel. The results of these studies demonstrate the differential effects of framing on people's behaviors and performance.

Based on this evidence, we propose that it may be beneficial for social policy makers to consider increasing the neutrality in the framing of their programs, tasks, and social situations (in situations where the policy affects multiple social groups). This neutrality in framing will allow individuals to interpret situations in ways that are more adaptive to their identities, which may in turn produce more positive outcomes. Consider the case of a professor instituting a course teaching graduate students how to perform data analysis on experiments through linear models (e.g., ANOVA, GLM, Regression). The professor could label the program as a statistics class called "Linear Statistical Models." However, this *statistical* framing of the class might threaten females and other groups stereotyped to be poor math performers. However, the professor can also frame the class with a more *general* name such as "Analysis of Designed Experiments in Social Science Research." This might allow females and other groups to interpret the class in a way that is more adaptive to their identities. For instance, a female's graduate student identity (instead of her female identity) may be activated in this relatively neutral name framing because she saw the term "social science research." This would decrease the chances of her female identity threatening her class performance and increase the chances of her graduate student identity increasing her class performance because of associated stereotypes.

Conclusion

In this chapter, we explored the relationship between identity switching and adjustment outcomes. Research has found a relationship between possessing multiple identities and positive outcomes, such as higher life satisfaction and higher self-esteem. One potential process through which multiple identities can produce these positive outcomes is through individuals taking advantage of identity adaptiveness by identity switching. That is, individuals can switch among their identities in different situations to identities that are adaptive to the situations, and deemphasize identities that are maladaptive. At the same time, while identity switching can produce positive results, identity switching can also carry risks, such as identity fragmentation. Several factors influencing the likelihood of identity switching eliciting positive or negative outcomes include the individual's type of identity switching, number of identities, tolerance for ambiguity, and level of identity integration. Social policies can help to facilitate identity adaptiveness by increasing the number of identities individuals have, by destigmatizing devalued identities and by framing situations in neutral non-stereotyped ways.

References

Adelmann, P. (1993). Psychological well-being and homemaker vs. retiree identity among older women. *Sex Roles, 29*, 195–212.

Adelmann, P. (1994a). Multiple roles and physical health: Gender and ethnic comparisons. *Research on Aging, 16*, 142–165.

Adelmann, P. (1994b). Multiple roles and psychological well-being in a national sample of older adults. *Journal of Gerontology, 49*, s277–s285.

Aronson, J., Fried, C. B., & Good, C. (2002). Reducing the effects of stereotype threat on African American college students by shaping theories of intelligence. *Journal of Experimental Social Psychology, 38*, 113–125.

Aronson, J., Jannone, S., McGlone, M., & Johnson-Campbell, T. (2009). The Obama effect: An experimental test. *Journal of Experimental Social Psychology, 45*, 957–960.

Banaji, M. R., & Prentice, D. A. (1994). The self in social context. *Annual Review of Psychology, 45*, 297–332.

Baumeister, R. F. (1995). Self and identity: An introduction. In A. Tesser (Ed.), *Advanced social psychology*. New York: McGraw-Hill.

Benet-Martínez, V., & Haritatos, J. (2005). Bicultural Identity Integration (BII): Components and socio-personality antecedents. *Journal of Personality, 73*, 1015–1050.

Benet-Martínez, V., Leu, J., & Lee, F. (2002). Negotiating biculturalism: Cultural frame switching in biculturals with oppositional versus compatible cultural identities. *Journal of Cross-Cultural Psychology, 33*, 492–516.

Biernat, M., & Manis, M. (1994). Shifting standards and stereotype-based judgments. *Journal of Personality and Social Psychology, 66*, 5–20.

Brewer, M. B. (1991). The social self: On being the same and different at the same time. *Personality and Social Psychology Bulletin, 17*, 475–482.

Burton, R. P., Rushing, B., Ritter, C., & Rakocy, A. (1993). Roles, race and subjective well-being: A longitudinal analysis of elderly men. *Social Indicators Research, 28*, 137–156.

Chen, S. X., Benet-Martínez, V., & Bond, M. H. (2008). Bicultural identity, bilingualism, and psychological adjustment in multicultural societies: Immigration-based and globalization-based acculturation. *Journal of Personality, 76*(4), 803–838.

Cialdini, R. B., & Goldstein, N. J. (2004). Social influence: Compliance and conformity. *Annual Review of Psychology, 55*, 591–621.

Cialdini, R. B., & Trost, M. R. (1998). Social influence: social norms, conformity, and compliance. In D. T. Gilbert, S.T. Fiske, & G. Lindzey (Eds.), *The handbook of social psychology* (4th ed., Vol. 2, pp. 151–92). Boston: McGraw-Hill.

Coleman, L. M., Antonucci, T. C., & Adelmann, P. K. (1987). Role involvement, gender, and well-being. In F. J. Crosby (Ed.), *Spouse, parent, worker: On gender and multiple roles* (pp. 138–153). New Haven, CT: Yale University Press.

Crisp, R. J., Bache, L. M., & Maitner, A. T. (2009). Dynamics of social comparison in counter-stereotypic domains: Stereotype boost, not stereotype threat, for women engineering major. *Social Influence, 4,* 171–184.

Crocker, J., & Quinn, D. M. (2000). Social stigma and the self meaning, situations and self-esteem. In T. F. Heatherton, R.E. Klede, R. M. Hebl, & J.G. Hull (Eds.), *The social psychology of stigma.* New York: Guilford Press.

Crosby, F., Bromley, S., & Saxe, L. (1980). Recent unobtrusive studies of black and white discrimination and prejudice: A literature review. *Psychological Bulletin, 87,* 546–563.

Cross, W., Smith, L., & Payne, Y. (2002). *Black identity: A repertoire of daily enactments.* In P. Pedersen, J. Draguns, W. Lonner, & J. Trimble (Eds.), *Counseling across cultures* (5th ed., pp. 93–108). Thousand Oaks, CA: Sage.

Daniel, G. R. (1992). Beyond Black and White: The new multiracial consciousness. In M. P. Root (Ed.), *Racially mixed people in America* (pp. 333–341). Newbury Park, CA: Sage.

Dijksterhuis, A., Spears, R., Postmes, T., Stapel, D. A., Koomen, W., van Knippenberg, A., & Scheepers, D. (1998). Seeing one thing and doing another: Contrast effects in automatic behavior. *Journal of Personality and Social Psychology, 75,* 862–871.

Donahue, E. M., Robins, R. W., Roberts, B. W., & John, O. P. (1993). The divided self: Concurrent and longitudinal effects of psychological adjustment and social roles on self-concept differentiation. *Journal of Personality and Social Psychology, 64,* 834–846.

English, T., & Chen, S. (2007). Culture and self-concept stability: Consistency across and within contexts among Asian Americans and European Americans. *Journal of Personality and Social Psychology, 93,* 478–490.

Festinger, L. (1957). *A theory of cognitive dissonance.* Stanford, CA: Stanford University Press.

Gaskins, P. (1999). *What are you? Voices of mixed-race young people.* New York: Holt.

Gee, G. C., Spencer, M., Chen, J., & Takeuchi, D. T. (2007). A nationwide study of discrimination and chronic health conditions among Asian Americans. *American Journal of Public Health, 97*(7), 1275–1282.

Gomstyn, A. (2008, November 5). ABC news online, Obama as a role model: Students, educators share excitement. http://abcnews.go.com/US/story?id=6184328&page=1

Good, C., Aronson, J., & Inzlicht, M. (2003). Improving adolescents' standardized test performance: An intervention to reduce the effects of stereotype threat. *Journal of Applied Developmental Psychology, 24,* 645–662.

Gordon, A. (1964). *Intermarriage: Interethnic, interracial, interfaith.* Boston: Beacon Press.

Gore, S., & Mangione, T. W. (1983). Social roles, sex roles and psychological distress: Additive and interactive models of sex differences. *Journal of Health & Social Behavior, 24,* 300–312.

Haavio-Mannila, E. (1986). Inequalities in health and gender. *Social Science and Medicine, 22,* 141–149.

Hauser, S. (1972). Black and White identity development: *Aspects and Perspectives. Journal of Youth and Adolescence, 1,* 113–130.

Hebl, M. R., Tickle, J., & Heatheron, T. F. (2000). Awkward moments in interactions between nonstigmatized and stigmatized individuals. In T. F. Heatherton, R.E. Kleck, M. R. Hebl, & J.G. Hull (Eds.), *The social psychology of stigma* (pp. 275–306). New York: Guilford Press.

Helson, R., Elliot, T., & Leigh, J. (1990). Number and quality of roles. *Psychology of Women Quarterly, 14,* 83–101.

Hogg, M. A., & Abrams, D. (1988). *Social identification: A social psychology of intergroup relations and group processes.* London: Routledge.

Hong, J., & Seltzer, M. M. (1995). The psychological consequences of multiple roles: The nonnormative case. *Journal of Health & Social Behavior, 36,* 386–398.

Hyde, J. S., Lindberg, S. M., Linn, M. C., Ellis, A. B., & Williams, C. C. (2008). Diversity–gender similarities characterize math performance. *Science, 321*(5888), 494–495.

Jackson, P. B. (1997). Role occupancy and minority mental health. *Journal of Health and Social Behavior, 38,* 237–255.

Johns, M., Schmader, T., & Martens, A. (2005). Knowing is half the battle – teaching stereotype threat as a means of improving women's math performance. *Psychological Science, 16,* 175–179.

Kandel, D. B., Davies, M., & Raveis, V. H. (1985). The stressfulness of daily social roles for women: Marital, occupational and household roles. *Journal of Health & Social Behavior, 26,* 64–78.

LaFromboise, T., Coleman, H. L. K., & Gerton, J. (1993). Psychological impact of biculturalism: Evidence and theory. *Psychological Bulletin, 114*(3), 395–412.

Levy, B. (1996). Improving memory in old age through implicit self-stereotyping. *Journal of Personality and Social Psychology, 71,* 1092–1107.

Linville, P. W. (1987). Self-complexity as a cognitive buffer against stress-related illness and depression. *Journal of Personality and Social Psychology, 52,* 663–676.

Luhtanen, R., & Crocker, J. (1992). A collective self-esteem scale: Self-evaluation of one's social identity. *Personality & Social Psychology Bulletin, 18,* 302–318.

Marx, D. M., & Goff, P. A. (2005). Clearing the air: The effect of experimenter race on targets' test performance and subjective experience. *British Journal of Social Psychology, 44,* 645–657.

Marx, D. M., Ko, S. J., & Friedman, R. A.(in press). The "Obama Effect": How a salient role model reduces race-based performance differences. *Journal of Experimental Social Psychology.*

Marx, D. M., & Roman, J. S. (2002). Female role models: Protecting women's math test performance. *Personality and Social Psychology Bulletin, 28,* 1183–1193.

McCroy, R. G., & Freeman, E. (1986). Racial identity issues among mixed-race children. *Social Work in Education, 8,* 150–153.

McGlone, M., Aronson, J., & Kobrynowicz (2006). Stereotype threat and the gender gap in political knowledge. *Psychology of Women Quarterly, 30,* 392–398.

Miller, M. L., Moen, P., & Dempster-McClain, D. (1991). Motherhood, multiple roles, and maternal well-being: Women of the 1950s. *Gender & Society, 5,* 565–582.

Morrison, A. M., & Von Glinow, M. (1990). Women and minorities in management. *American Psychologist, 45,* 200–208.

Park, R. E. (1928). Human migration and the marginal man. *American Journal of Sociology, 33,* 881–893.

Park, R. E. (1931). Mentality of racial hybrids. *American Journal of Sociology, 36,* 534–551.

Pietromonaco, P. R., Manis, J., & Frohardt-Lane, K. (1986). Psychological consequences of multiple social roles. *Psychology of Women Quarterly, 10,* 373–381.

Piskacek, V., & Golub, M. (1973). *Children of interracial marriages.* In I. R. Stuart & L.E. Abt (Eds.), *Interracial marriage: Expectations and realities* (pp. 53–61). New York: Grossman.

Pittinsky, T. L., Shih, M., & Ambady, N. (1999). Identity adaptiveness: Affect across multiple identities. *Journal of Social Issues: Special Issue: Prejudice and intergroup relations: Papers in honor of Gordon W. Allport's centennial, 55,* 503–518.

Pitts, B. (2008, August 26). CBS News online, Obama Effect touching a new generation. http://www.cbsnews.com/stories/2008/08/26/eveningnews/main4386451.shtml

Reyes, R. P. (2008). Barack Obama: The new role model for Black children. The Student Operated Press. http://thesop.org/index.php?article=14029.

Roccas, S., & Brewer, M. B. (2002). Social identity complexity. *Personality and Social Psychology Review, 6,* 88–106.

Rosenberg, M. (1979). *Conceiving the self.* New York: Basic Books.

Rushing, B., Ritter, C., & Burton, R. P. (1992). Race differences in the effects of multiple roles on health: Longitudinal evidence from a national sample of older men. *Journal of Health & Social Behavior, 33,* 126–139.

Sachs-Ericsson, N., & Ciarlo, J. A. (2000). Gender, social roles, and mental health: An epidemiological perspective. *Sex Roles: Special Issue, 43,* 605–628.

Sailes, G. A. (1996). An investigation of campus stereotypes: The myth of Black athletic superiority and the dumb jock stereotype. In R. E. Lapchick

(Ed.), *Sport in society: Equal opportunity or business as usual?* (pp. 193–202). Thousand Oaks, CA: Sage.

Sanchez, D. T., Shih, M., & Garcia, J. A. (2009). Juggling multiple racial identities: Malleable racial identification and psychological well-being. *Cultural Diversity and Ethnic Minority Psychology, 15*, 243–254.

Savin-Williams, R. C., & Demo, D. H. (1983). Situational and transituational determinants of adolescent self-feelings. *Journal of Personality and Social Psychology, 44*, 824–833.

Shih, M., Pittinsky, T. L., & Ambady, N. (1999). Stereotype susceptibility: Identity salience and shifts in quantitative performance. *Psychological Science, 10*, 80–83.

Shih, M. J., & Chui, W. (2009). Building and Arts: Leadership in cross gender dyads. Manuscript in preparation.

Shih, M. J., & Sanchez, D. T. (2005). Perspectives and research on the positive and negative implications of having multiple racial identities. *Psychological Bulletin, 131*, 569–591.

Spencer, S. J., Steele, C. M., & Quinn, D. M. (1999). Stereotype threat and women's math performance. *Journal of Experimental Social Psychology, 35*, 4–28.

Spencer-Rodgers, J., Peng, K., Wang, L., & Hou, Y. (2004). Dialectical self and psychological well-being. *Personality and Social Psychology Bulletin, 30*, 1416–1432.

Steele, C. M. (1988). *The psychology of self-affirmation: Sustaining the integrity of the self.* In L. Berkowitz (Ed.), *Advances in experimental social psychology* (Vol. 21, pp. 261–302). New York: Academic Press.

Steele, C. M. (1997). A threat in the air: How stereotypes shape intellectual identity and performance. *American Psychologist, 52*, 613–629.

Steele, C. M., & Aronson, J. (1995). Stereotype threat and the intellectual test performance of African-Americans. *Journal of Personality and Social Psychology, 69*, 797–811.

Stonequist, E. V. (1937). *The marginal man: A study in personality and culture conflict.* New York: Russell & Russell.

Tajfel, H., & Turner, J. C. (1979). An integrative theory of intergroup conflict. In W. G. Austin & S. Worchel (Eds.), *The social psychology of intergroup relations* (pp. 7–24). Monterey, CA: Brooks/Cole.

Tajfel, H., & Turner, J. C. (1986). *The social identity theory of intergroup behavior.* In S. Worchel & W. Austin (Eds.), *Psychology of intergroup relations* (pp. 7–24). Chicago: Nelson-Hall.

Thoits, P. A. (1983). Multiple identities and psychological well-being: A reformulation of the social isolation hypothesis. *American Sociological Review, 48*, 174–187.

Thoits, P. A. (1986). Multiple identities: Examining gender and marital status differences in distress. *American Sociological Review, 48*, 174–187.

Turner, J. C. (1987). *Rediscovering the social group: A self categorization theory.* Oxford, UK: Basil Blackwell.

Verkuyten, M. (1995). Self-esteem, self-concept stability, and aspects of ethnic identity among minority and majority youth in the Netherlands. *Journal of Youth and Adolescence, 24*(2), 155–175.

Waldron, I., & Jacobs, J. A. (1989). Effects of multiple roles on women's health: Evidence from a national longitudinal study. *Women & Health, 15,* 3–19.

Wilsnack, R. W., & Cheloha, R. (1987). Women's roles and problem drinking across the lifespan. *Social Problems, 34,* 231–248.

Word, C. D., Zanna, M. P., & Cooper, J. (1974). The nonverbal mediation of self-fulfilling prophecy effects of interracial interactions. *Journal of Experimental Social Psychology, 10,* 109–120.

Wraga, M., Duncan, L., Helt, M., Jacobs, E. C., & Sullivan, K. (2006). Neural basis of stereotype-induced shifts in women's mental rotation performance. *Social Cognitive and Affective Neuroscience, 2,* 12–19.

Part II

Culture

5

Multicultural Identity
What It Is and Why It Matters

Angela-MinhTu D. Nguyen and Verónica Benet-Martínez

Multicultural Identity: What It Is and Why It Matters

> I think of myself not as a unified cultural being but as a communion of different cultural beings. Due to the fact that I have spent time in different cultural environments, I have developed several cultural identities that diverge and converge according to the need of the moment.
>
> (*Sparrow, 2000, p. 190*)

The global increase in intercultural contact owing to factors such as immigration, speed of travel and communication, and international corporate presence is difficult to ignore. Undoubtedly, multiculturalism and globalization influence how people see themselves and others, and how they organize the world around them. The year 2009 marks the beginning of Barack Hussein Obama's U.S. presidential administration. Not only does Obama exemplify the word "multiculturalism"—as a biracial individual from a multicultural family who has lived in various countries—several of his key advisors have also lived outside the United States (Bartholet & Stone, 2009), and almost half of his cabinet are from racial or ethnic minorities (Wolf, 2009). In fact, in his inaugural speech, Obama stated that multiculturalism is a national strength (Obama, 2009), and since then, he has deliberately set out to select a diverse cabinet, based on the premise that multicultural individuals have insights, skills, and unique psychological experiences that contribute to society.

The prevalence and importance of multiculturalism has long been acknowledged in psychology (e.g., Hermans & Kempen, 1998; LaFromboise, Coleman, & Gerton, 1993), yet the phenomenon has been investigated empirically only since the late 1990s. However, the study of multicultural identities has exciting implications for the field of psychology, and for social and personality psychology in particular, as the issue of how individuals develop a sense of community, national, cultural, ethnic, and racial group membership becomes particularly meaningful in situations of cultural clashing, mixing, and integration (Baumeister, 1986; Phinney, 1999). Furthermore, the social and individual factors that influence multicultural identity provide psychologists with another window through which to study individual variations in self-concept dynamics. In fact, as Phinney eloquently said (1999): "increasing numbers of people find that the conflicts are not between different groups but between different cultural values, attitudes, and expectations *within themselves* [italics added]" (p. 27). Lastly, the study of multicultural identity affords unique methodological tools. By virtue of having two or more cultures that can be independently manipulated, multicultural individuals give researchers a quasi-experimental design ideal for the study of how culture affects behavior (Hong, Morris, Chiu, & Benet-Martínez, 2000). In addition, previously identified cross-cultural differences can be replicated in experiments with multicultural individuals (Sanchez-Burks, Lee, Choi, Nisbett, Zhao, & Koo, 2003). Furthermore, these cross-cultural differences can be examined while controlling for variables that confound national comparisons (e.g., gross national product) by using multicultural individuals in a within-subjects design.

Despite the world's long history of intercultural contact and mixing, empirical research on multicultural identity has begun only since the late 1990s, with the increase of cultural diversity in academia, politics, and the media. In this chapter, we define and discuss the constructs of multiculturalism and multicultural identity from both an individual and societal perspective, and also quickly summarize the relevant issues in acculturation theory, from which current cultural identity research took its roots. Second, we identify some concerns in multicultural identity research, such as how to best measure and conceptualize this type of identity, and the issue of individual and group differences. With regard to the latter, we pay special attention to the construct of Bicultural Identity Integration (BII) and its correlates. The implications of multiculturalism research, particularly benefits for the individual as well as society at large, are also reviewed. Finally, we discuss the relevance of multicultural identity theory and research to other types of multiple identities (e.g., bisexual identity).

Multiculturalism: Individual and Societal Level

Who is multicultural? There are many definitions of multiculturalism, ranging from general (i.e., based on demographic characteristics) to psychologically specific conceptualizations (e.g., cultural identifications or orientations). Broadly speaking, those who are mixed-race and mixed-ethnic, those who have lived in more than one country (such as expatriates, international students, immigrants, refugees, and sojourners), those reared with at least one other culture in addition to the dominant mainstream culture (such as children of immigrants or colonized people), and those in intercultural relationships may all be considered multicultural (Berry, 2003; Padilla, 2006).[1] In the United States alone, multicultural individuals may include the 13% who are foreign-born, the 34% who are non-White, and the 20% who speak a language other than English at home (U.S. Census Bureau, 2006). High numbers of multicultural individuals can also be found in other nations where migration is strong (e.g., Canada, Australia, Western Europe, Singapore) or where there is a history of colonization (e.g., Hong Kong).

Psychologically, there is no commonly agreed definition of multiculturalism. Loosely speaking, multicultural individuals are those whose self-label (e.g., "I am multicultural") or group self-categorization (e.g., "I am American" and "I am Chinese"; "I am Chinese-American") reflects their cultural pluralism. More specifically, multiculturalism can be defined as the experience of having been exposed to and having internalized two or more cultures (Hong et al., 2000; Nguyen & Benet-Martínez, 2007). Relatedly, multicultural identity is the condition of having strong attachments with and loyalties toward these different cultures (Benet-Martínez & Haritatos, 2005). Notice then that multicultural identity is only one component (although perhaps the most important one) of the more complex and multidimensional notion of multiculturalism. That is, an individual who has been exposed to and has learned more than one culture is a multicultural person, but only when this individual expresses an attachment with and loyalty to these cultures can we say that the individual has a multicultural identity.

Multiculturalism is a broader term referring to more than one culture (i.e., two cultures, three cultures, four cultures, and so on), whereas biculturalism is a more specific term referring to exactly two cultures. Although the terms "multicultural" and "bicultural" are typically used to describe individuals, they can also be used to describe nations (e.g., bicultural Canada, where Anglophone and Francophone cultures coexist), and institutions and policies (e.g., multicultural education). Although the term is recent, the concept of biculturalism dates back to the origins of modern Canada (1774, when British authorities allowed French Canadians full use of their language, system of civil law, and freedom to practice their Roman Catholicism). Biculturalism should not be confused with bilingualism (having fluency in two languages), although these terms are conceptually related, since often (but not always), bicultural individuals and institutions are also bilingual.

Multicultural ideology and policies advocate that society and organizations should include and equally value distinct cultural groups (Fowers & Richardson, 1996). Although the term multiculturalism is typically used to acknowledge the presence of the distinct cultures of immigrant groups, sometimes it can also be applied to acknowledge the presence of indigenous peoples in colonized nations. One assumption behind the multicultural ideology is that public acceptance and recognition of one's culture and opportunities for multicultural interactions are crucial for self-worth and well-being (Burnet, 1995). Support for this argument is found in counseling (Sue & Sue, 2003), education (Banks & Banks, 1995), corporate (Plaut, Thomas, & Goren, in press), and developmental contexts (Berry, Phinney, Sam, & Vedder, 2006; Yip, Seaton, & Sellers, 2006). Work closely examining multicultural attitudes and their effects from both the minority and majority perspectives (e.g., Verkuyten, this volume; Verkuyten, 2009; Verkuyten & Martinovic, 2006) reveals some interesting moderating factors. First, cultural and ethnic minorities (e.g., Turkish, Moroccan) are more likely to endorse multiculturalism than members of an ethnic majority group (e.g., Dutch). Second, multiculturalism is positively associated with self-esteem among ethnic-minority individuals who identify strongly with their ethnic group, while this interactive effect does not exist for majority individuals. Further, strength of ethnic identification is positively related to endorsement of multiculturalism for minority individuals, while the link between ethnic identification and multiculturalism is negative among majority individuals.

Multiculturalism has been formally adopted as an official policy in nations such as Canada, Australia, and the Netherlands, for reasons that vary from country to country. Multicultural policies influence the structures and decisions of governments to ensure that political and economic resources are allocated equitably to all represented cultural groups. Examples of government-endorsed multicultural policies are dual citizenship, government support for media outlets (e.g., newspapers, television, radio) in minority languages, support for cultural minority holidays, celebrations, and community centers, and acceptance of traditional and religious codes of dress and behavior in the public sphere (e.g., work, school).

Acculturation and Multiculturalism

Multicultural identity and acculturation are tightly intertwined, with multi/biculturalism being one of four ways to acculturate; therefore, we review the development of acculturation theory and the definition of biculturalism from an acculturation standpoint before delving further into our discussion of multicultural identity.

Traditional views of acculturation (the process of learning or adapting to a new culture) asserted that to acculturate means to assimilate—rejecting one's ethnic or original culture and adopting the new or dominant culture (Berry, 2003). In other words, acculturation originally was conceptualized as a unidimensional, one-directional, and irreversible process of moving toward the new mainstream culture and away from the original ethnic culture (Trimble, 2003). However, a wealth of acculturation studies conducted since the mid-1980s (see Sam & Berry, 2006 for a review) support acculturation as a bidimensional, two-directional, multi-domain complex process, in which assimilation into the mainstream culture is not the only way to acculturate. In other words, equating acculturation with assimilation is simply inaccurate.

The bidimensional model of acculturation is based on the premise that acculturating individuals have to deal with two central issues, which comprise the two cultural orientations of acculturation (Berry, 2003): (1) the extent to which they are motivated or allowed to retain identification and involvement with the culture of origin, now the non-majority, ethnic culture; and (2) the extent to which they are motivated or allowed to identify with and participate in the mainstream, dominant culture. The negotiation of these two central issues results in four distinct acculturation positions: assimilation (involvement and identification with the dominant culture only), integration/biculturalism (involvement and identification with both cultures), separation (involvement and identification with the ethnic culture only), or marginalization (lack of involvement and identification with either culture; see Rudmin, 2003 for a thorough discussion of this strategy). Empirical work on these four acculturation attitudes or strategies reveals that, at least at the individual level, the most common strategy used by immigrant and cultural minorities is integration/biculturalism, followed by separation, assimilation, and marginalization (Berry et al., 2006; Sam & Berry, 2006). Further, there is now robust evidence supporting the psychometric validity of the multidimensional model of acculturation and its advantages over unidimensional models in predicting a wide array of outcomes (Flannery, Reise, & Yu, 2001; Ryder, Allen, & Paulhus, 2000).[2]

Additional support for the idea that individuals can simultaneously hold two or more cultural orientations is provided by recent socio-cognitive experimental work showing that bicultural individuals shift between their two cultural orientations in response to cultural cues, a process called "cultural frame-switching" (CFS; Hong et al., 2000; Verkuyten & Pouliasi, 2006). Bicultural individuals' ability to engage in CFS has been documented in multiple behavioral domains such as attribution (Benet-Martínez, Leu, Lee, & Morris, 2002; Cheng, Lee, & Benet-Martínez, 2006; Hong et al., 2000; Verkuyten & Pouliasi, 2002), personality self-views (Ramirez-Esparza, Gosling, Benet-Martínez, Potter, & Pennebaker, 2006; Ross, Xun, & Wilson, 2002), identity (Verkuyten & Pouliasi, 2002), self-construals (Gardner, Gabriel, & Lee, 1999), and cooperation (Wong & Hong, 2005), among others. Note that CFS is not merely a knee-jerk response to cultural cues; rather, it occurs when a particular cultural schema influences behavior to the extent that it is cognitively accessible (it has been recently activated by explicit or implicit cues) and applicable (it is relevant to the situation; Hong, Benet-Martínez, Chiu, & Morris, 2003; Tadmor, No, Hong, & Chiu, this volume).

Lastly, it is important to point out that the acculturation perspective does not presuppose that multicultural individuals internalize and use their different cultures globally and uniformly. Acculturation changes can take place in many different domains of life: language use or preference, social affiliation, communication style, cultural identity and pride, and cultural knowledge, beliefs, and values (Zane & Mak, 2003); and acculturation changes in some of these domains may occur independently of changes in other components. For instance, a Japanese American bicultural individual may endorse Anglo-American culture behaviorally and linguistically and yet be very Japanese (ethnic culture) in terms of her/his values and attitudes. Similarly, a Mexican American bicultural individual can behave in ways that are predominantly Mexican (e.g., speak mostly Spanish, live in a largely Mexican neighborhood) and yet display great pride and attitudinal attachment with American culture. In fact, some recent acculturation work suggests that, independently of how much the mainstream culture is internalized and practiced, immigrants and their descendents often adhere to the ethnic cultural values even more strongly than members of their home country, probably because they can become gradually "encapsulated" within the norms and values of an earlier era in their homeland (Kim-Jo, Benet-Martínez, & Ozer, in press).

Thus far, the discussion of acculturation and multiculturalism has been at the individual level, but acculturation is also tied to multiculturalism at the societal level. At the national level, there are strategies corresponding to the individual acculturation strategies above (Berry, 2003; see Figure 5.1). Countries with public policies that promote the assimilation of acculturating individuals are described as melting pots. Those that encourage separation are referred to as segregationist, and those that promote marginalization are labeled exclusionary. Most importantly, national policies supporting the integration/biculturalism strategy are considered multicultural. For example, Canada's multicultural policies encourage ethnic and cultural groups to maintain, develop, and share their cultures with others as well as to accept and interact with other groups (Berry, 1984). Although acculturating individuals by and large prefer the bicultural or integration strategy, in reality, most host countries are melting pots, encouraging the assimilation of acculturating individuals into the dominant culture (Van Oudenhoven, Ward, & Masgoret, 2006; Verkuyten,

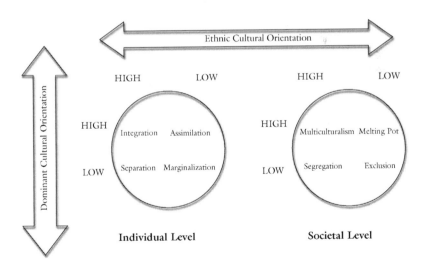

Figure 5.1   Acculturation and multiculturalism at the individual versus societal levels. Adapted from Berry, 2003.

this volume). Consequently, when national policies and dominant groups' acculturation attitudes do not match with acculturating individuals' strategies, conflicts and problems in intergroup relations may arise (Bourhis, Moïse, Perreault, & Senécal, 1997; Jasinskaja-Lahti, Liebkind, Horenczyk, & Schmitz, 2003). Thus, public policies regarding acculturation and biculturalism undoubtedly can affect intercultural relations within a country, especially as changing global migration patterns diversify many nations around the world.

Multiculturalism: Operationalization and Measurement

Acculturation, and the narrower constructs of multiculturalism or biculturalism, have been operationalized and measured in a variety of ways, including unidimensional scales, bidimensional scales (e.g., median-split, addition, multiplication, and subtraction methods), direct measures of acculturation strategies, cultural identification question(s), or simple demographic questions. An exhaustive review of the available instruments and theoretical and psychometric issues involved in measuring biculturalism (and acculturation) is beyond the scope of this chapter (see Arends-Tóth & van de Vijver, 2006; Zane & Mak, 2003 for excellent reviews). Accordingly, we provide instead a practical and brief summary of the available approaches and their pros and cons.

Early attempts at measuring biculturalism relied on bipolar, single-dimension scales that explicitly or implicitly reflected a unidirectional view of acculturation. In this framework, low scores or the starting point of the scale typically reflected separation, and high scores or the other end of the scale reflected assimilation, with biculturalism being tapped by middle scores or the midpoint of the scale (e.g., Cuéllar, Harris, & Jasso, 1980; Rotheram-Borus, 1990; Suinn, Rickard-Figueroa, Lew, & Vigil, 1987). These unidimensional scales should be avoided because they equate involvement and identification with one culture to a lack of involvement and identification with the other culture. In addition, these scales confound biculturalism and marginalization. For example, a scale item may be "Who do you associate with?" and the response choices may be labeled with 1 = *mostly individuals from the ethnic culture*, 2 = *individuals from both the ethnic and dominant cultures equally*, 3 = *mostly individuals from the dominant culture*. A bicultural individual would select "2" because he/she has many friends from both cultures, but a marginalized individual may also select "2" because his/her lack of socialization with members from each culture is similar.

With the increased adoption of the bidimensional model of acculturation came an increase in the number of bidimensional scales, where involvement with ethnic and dominant cultures is measured in two separate multi-item scales. With this method, biculturalism can be operationalized in different ways. Typically, bicultural individuals are those who have scores above the median (e.g., Ryder et al., 2000; Tsai, Ying, & Lee, 2000) or midpoint (e.g., Donà & Berry, 1994) on both cultural orientations. More recently, cluster analyses (e.g., Lee, Sobal, & Frongillo, 2003) and latent class analyses (e.g., Stevens, Pels, Vollebergh, & Crijnen, 2007) have also been used to create categories of acculturation strategies, including the integration or bicultural strategy. This typological approach allows researchers to differentiate bicultural individuals from other acculturating types (assimilated, separated, or marginalized) but does not provide a biculturalism score. Other, non-typological ways of operationalizing biculturalism when using bidimensional scales are to add the two cultural orientation subscale scores (e.g., Cuéllar, Arnold, & Maldonado, 1995) or combine them into an interaction term (Birman, 1998) so that low and high scores represent low and high levels of biculturalism, respectively. One caveat of these last two methods is the difficulty in differentiating between individuals who have medium scores on both cultural scales and those who score very high on one scale and low on the other. Lastly, some researchers have used a method where scores on the two cultural orientation scales are subtracted from another, so that scores close to zero denote biculturalism (Szapocznik, Kurtines, & Fernandez, 1980). This approach is not recommended because, like unidimensional measurement, it makes bicultural and marginalized individuals indistinguishable from each other. Obviously, two key advantages of these multidimensional approaches are that the cultures of interest (e.g., ethnic, mainstream, and religious cultures), regardless of their number, can be independently assessed, and that their measurement can be tailored to particular acculturating groups (e.g., mixed-race individuals, sojourners, etc.).

Some researchers prefer to measure the acculturation strategies directly (e.g., Berry, Kim, Power, Young, & Bujaki, 1989). These instruments typically include four scales with statements capturing favorable attitudes toward the integration (biculturalism), assimilation, separation, and marginalization strategies. Because each individual receives a score on each of these acculturation strategies, a bicultural individual would be someone whose highest score is on the integration subscale. This widely used approach has some advantages over traditional acculturation scales (e.g., it allows us to measure the construct of biculturalism *attitudes* directly) but it suffers from some nontrivial conceptual and psychometric limitations (e.g., low score reliabilities, lack of scale independence; see Kang, 2006; Rudmin, 2003; Zane & Mak, 2003 for reviews).

When time or reading levels are compromised, researchers may choose to measure biculturalism with one or two questions. For instance, bicultural individuals can be those who self-identify with a hyphenated label (e.g., Persian-American) rather than an ethnic (e.g., Persian) or a national (e.g., American) label, those who endorse the label "bicultural" (vs. "monocultural"), or those who score above the midpoint on two single items stating "I feel/am U.S. American" and "I feel/am Chinese" (e.g., Benet-Martínez & Haritatos, 2005). Lastly, we should warn against the common practice of using demographic variables such as generational status, legal residence, or linguistic ability and preference as a proxy for psychological acculturation (e.g., Buriel, Calzada, & Vasquez, 1982). As mentioned earlier, bicultural involvement and identification can occur at different rates for different life domains, for different individuals, and for different cultural groups, and demographic variables seem to be poor to modest predictors of these changes (Phinney, 2003; Schwartz, Pantin, Sullivan, Prado, & Szapocznik, 2006).

Individual and Group Differences in Multicultural Identity

"I had been rowing back and forth, in a relentless manner, between two banks of a wide river. Increasingly, what I wanted was to be a burning boat in the middle of the water, visible to both shores yet indecipherable in my fury."

(*lê thi diem thúy, 2003*)

The process of negotiating multiple cultural identities is complex and multifaceted. A careful review of the early (and mostly qualitative) work on this topic in the acculturation (e.g., Padilla, 1994; Phinney & Devich-Navarro, 1997) and popular (e.g., Chavez, 1994; O'Hearn, 1998) literatures reveals that multicultural individuals often talk about their multiple cultural attachments in complicated ways, including both positive and negative terms. Multiculturalism can be associated with feelings of pride, uniqueness, and a rich sense of community and history, while also bringing to mind identity confusion, dual expectations, and value clashes. Further, multicultural individuals deal differently with the implications of different cultural and racial stereotypes and the pressures coming from their different communities for loyalties and behaviors (LaFromboise et al., 1993). An important issue, then, is how particular personality dispositions, contextual pressures, and acculturation and demographic variables impact the process of multicultural identity formation and the meanings associated with this experience.

Although most acculturating individuals use the integration/biculturalism strategy (Berry et al., 2006), research on acculturation has almost exclusively focused on individual differences *across* acculturation strategies rather than *within* acculturation strategies. Yet, not all bicultural individuals are alike. Early theoretical work on this issue is worth reviewing, even if briefly. In a seminal review of the biculturalism phenomenon, LaFromboise et al. (1993) described two biculturalism modes: *alternation* and *fusion*. Alternating bicultural individuals switch their behaviors in response to situational cultural demands, whereas fused bicultural individuals are oriented to a third emerging culture that is distinct from each of their two cultures (e.g., Chicano culture). Birman (1994) expanded on LaFromboise et al.'s (1993) framework to describe four types of bicultural individuals: *blended* (i.e., fused), *instrumental* (individuals behaviorally oriented to both cultures but identified with neither), *integrated* (individuals behaviorally oriented to both cultures but identified with only their ethnic culture), and *explorers* (behaviorally oriented to the dominant culture but identified with only their ethnic culture). Phinney and Devich-Navarro's (1997) qualitative and quantitative study sought to empirically integrate Berry's (1990), LaFromboise et al.'s (1993), and Birman's (1994) conceptual models of biculturalism. This study identified two bicultural types which were given labels similar to those in LaFromboise et al.'s study: *blended biculturals*—who felt positively about both cultures and did not feel conflicted, and *alternating biculturals*—who also identified with both cultures but saw conflict between them.

These researchers are credited with calling attention to bicultural individuals and for advancing this area of research; however, a conceptual limitation of the above typologies is their confounding of identity and behavioral markers. Specifically, whereas the labels "blended" and "fused" refer to identity-related aspects of the bicultural experience (e.g., seeing oneself as Asian American or Chicano), the label "alternating" refers to the behavioral domain, that is, the ability to engage in cultural frame-switching (Benet-Martínez et al., 2002). Naturally, individuals' subjective experience of their identity and their behavior/competencies do not have to map onto each other (Roccas &

Brewer, 2002). For instance, a bicultural individual may have a blended or fused identity (e.g., someone who is proud of being both Jewish and American) and also alternate between speaking mainstream English and Yiddish, depending on the context. Thus the labels "blended" and "alternating" do not seem to tap different types of bicultural individuals but rather different components of the bicultural experience (i.e., identity vs. behaviors).

Bicultural Identity Integration (BII)

After an extensive review and synthesis of the empirical and qualitative acculturation and multiculturalism literature, Benet-Martínez et al. (2002) proposed the theoretical construct of Bicultural Identity Integration (BII) as a framework for investigating individual differences in bicultural identity organization. BII captures the degree to which "biculturals perceive their mainstream and ethnic cultural identities as compatible and integrated vs. oppositional and difficult to integrate" (Benet-Martínez et al., 2002, p. 9). As an individual difference variable, BII thus focuses on bicultural individuals' subjective perceptions of managing dual cultural identities (i.e., how much their dual cultural identities intersect or overlap). The emphasis here is on subjective (i.e., the perception of) cultural overlap and compatibility because, as was found in a study of over 7,000 acculturating adolescents in 13 countries, objective cultural differences do not seem to relate to adjustment (Berry et al., 2006).

Bicultural individuals with high BII tend to see themselves as part of a hyphenated culture (or even part of a combined, emerging "third" culture), and find the two cultures largely compatible and easy to integrate. Bicultural individuals with low BII, on the other hand, tend to see themselves as living "in-between cultures" and report seeing the two cultures as largely conflictual and disparate. In summary, bicultural individuals high and low on BII identify with both mainstream (e.g., American) and ethnic (e.g., Chinese) cultures but differ in their ability to create a synergistic, integrated cultural identity. Theoretically, BII may relate to other identity constructs, such as nonoppositional vs. oppositional identity (Ogbu, 1993) and identity synthesis vs. confusion (Schwartz, 2006), but these relationships still need to be explored empirically.

Recent studies on BII are beginning to elucidate the relationships between BII and relevant behavioral, cognitive, and social variables. For example, BII has been found to moderate the process of cultural frame-switching (Benet-Martínez et al., 2002; Cheng et al., 2006; Zou, Morris, & Benet-Martínez, 2008). Specifically, bicultural individuals with high BII respond to the activation of the corresponding (e.g., Chinese or American) cultural meaning system by providing responses that are culturally congruent (e.g., stronger external attributions after seeing Chinese primes, and stronger internal attributions after seeing American primes). Bicultural individuals with low BII, however, display the reverse effect. That is, they provide culturally incongruent responses to cultural primes (e.g., stronger external attributions to American primes and stronger internal attributions to Chinese primes). These contrastive responses suggest an automatic or unconscious reactance against the cultural expectations of a given situation, a phenomenon often reported in academic and popular depictions of identity conflict (e.g., Ogbu, 2008; Roth, 1969). BII has also been linked to having (1) richer social networks (Mok, Morris, Benet-Martínez, & Karakitapoglu-Aygun, 2007); (2) moderately complex cultural schemas (Benet-Martínez, Lee, & Leu, 2006); (3) higher creative performance (Cheng, Sanchez-Burks, & Lee, 2008); (4) higher psychological adjustment, even after controlling for neuroticism (Chen, Benet-Martínez, & Bond, 2008); (5) more overlapping perceptions of one's own cultural ingroups (Miramontez, Benet-Martínez, & Nguyen, 2008); and (6) stronger preference for culturally blended persuasive appeals (Lau-Gesk, 2003).

Recent work shows that BII is not a unitary construct, as initially suggested in earlier work (Benet-Martínez et al., 2002). Instead, BII seems to involve two independent psychological constructs, cultural conflict and cultural distance, each representing unique and separate aspects of the dynamic intersection between mainstream and ethnic cultural identities in bicultural individuals (Benet-Martínez & Haritatos, 2005). Cultural distance captures the degree of dissociation or compartmentalization vs. overlap perceived between the two cultural orientations (e.g., "I see myself as a Chinese in the U.S." vs. "I am a Chinese-American"). Cultural conflict, on the other hand, captures the degree of tension or clash vs. harmony perceived between the two cultures (e.g., "I feel trapped between the two cultures" vs. "I do not see conflict between the Chinese and American ways of doing things"). (See Table 5.1 for scale items and Benet-Martínez and Haritatos (2005, Table 2) for the factor structure of the scale.) The psychometric independence of cultural conflict and distance suggests that these constructs are formative (i.e., causal) rather than reflective (i.e., effect) indicators of BII (Bollen & Lennox, 1991). That is, rather than a latent construct with two resulting dimensions (cultural distance and conflict), BII should perhaps be

Table 5.1 Bicultural Identity Integration Scale (BIIS-1)

Cultural distance
  1. I am simply a Chinese who lives in North America.
  2. I keep Chinese and American cultures separate.
  3. I feel Chinese American (R).
  4. I feel part of a combined culture (R).

Cultural conflict
  5. I am conflicted between the American and Chinese ways of doing things.
  6. I feel like someone moving between two cultures.
  7. I feel caught between the Chinese and American cultures.
  8. I don't feel trapped between the Chinese and American cultures (R).

Note. The BIIS-1 can be used with any ethnic minority culture and any host culture. To adapt this scale, substitute the ethnic minority culture for "Chinese," the host culture for "American," and the host country or continent for "North America." Adapted from Benet-Martínez and Haritatos (2005).

understood as emerging or resulting from (rather than leading to) variations in cultural distance and conflict. Thus, behaviors, attitudes, and feelings described by cultural researchers under the rubric of low BII (e.g., the feelings reported by the bicultural individual quoted earlier) may in fact be largely capturing the phenomenology of the more basic experience of cultural conflict and/or cultural distance.

Cultural distance and conflict are each associated with different sets of personality, performance-related, and contextual antecedents (Benet-Martínez & Haritatos, 2005), which explains the very different phenomenological experiences of biculturalism in the existing literature. Specifically, as indicated by path analyses, cultural distance is predicted by having a close-minded disposition, lower levels of cultural competence (particularly with regard to the mainstream culture), experiencing strains in the linguistic domain (e.g., being self-conscious about one's accent), and living in a community that is not culturally diverse. Cultural conflict, on the other hand, is largely predicted by having a neurotic disposition, experiencing discrimination, and having strained intercultural relations (e.g., being told that one's behavior is "too American" or "ethnic"). In summary, cultural distance is particularly linked to performance-related personal and contextual challenges (e.g., cognitive rigidity, low linguistic fluency, culturally limited surroundings), while cultural conflict stems from strains that are largely intra- and interpersonal in nature (e.g., nervousness, social prejudice, and rejection).

Group Differences in Multiculturalism

Multicultural individuals may belong to one of the following five groups based on the voluntariness, mobility, and permanence of contact with the dominant group: immigrants, refugees, sojourners, ethnic minorities, and indigenous people (Berry, Kim, Minde, & Mok, 1987). Immigrants arrive in the host country voluntarily and usually with the intention to stay, whereas refugees arrive in the host country by force or due to lack of other alternatives. Like immigrants, sojourners, such as expatriates and international students, also arrive in the host country voluntarily, but their stay is usually temporary. Ethnic minorities and indigenous people are those born in the host country, but indigenous people differ from ethnic minorities in that the host country was involuntarily imposed upon them (e.g., via colonization). The ethnic minority group may be divided into second-generation individuals (whose parents are immigrants or refugees) and third- or later-generation individuals (whose parents were born in the host country; Padilla, 2006). Many mixed-race or mixed-ethnic individuals are also multicultural, regardless of their acculturating group status (Padilla, 2006).

There may be group-level differences among the groups mentioned above with regard to their levels of BII due to their group's history in the host country, their relations with members of the dominant group, the current political and socioeconomic situation, and other structural variables. For instance, immigrants and sojourners chose to migrate to the host country for economic or educational opportunities, and many have the option of returning to their native countries; thus, relative to the other groups, this type of multicultural individual may be more focused on opportunities and less focused on cultural issues. Consequently, cultural differences may not necessarily be internalized or translated into the experience of cultural identity conflict. Conversely, refugees and indigenous people are often forced into contact with the dominant culture, and the involuntary nature of this contact (e.g., refugees may want to return to their native countries, but this is not possible due to conflicts between the host and native countries or within their native countries) magnifies cultural differences and identity conflict. Relatedly, African Americans, with their history of involuntary slavery and expatriation, may also experience more cultural conflict than other groups. Lastly, there are reasons to think that feelings of cultural conflict may also be common among mixed-heritage individuals and second-generation individuals (at least relative to immigrants and sojourners). Mixed-race and mixed-ethnic individuals are often given (implicit or explicit) messages suggesting that they are not "enough" of one culture or the other (Root, 1998). Likewise, second-generation ethnic minorities are considered not "ethnic" enough by both their parents and dominant-culture peers with regard to certain cultural "markers" (e.g., ethnic language fluency), while also not being considered part of the mainstream culture (Padilla, 2006).

In addition to the voluntariness of contact and group expectations, variables such as generational status and cultural socialization may also play a role in BII, particularly the experience of cultural distance. Immigrants first learn their ethnic culture in their native country and later learn the dominant culture in the host country, thus their competencies and associations with each culture may be more compartmentalized and situation-specific (i.e., high cultural distance) compared to other groups. This dissociation may also occur among second-generation ethnic minorities for whom dominant and ethnic cultures are largely relegated to the public (e.g., work) and private (e.g., home) spheres, respectively. However, other second- and later-generation ethnic minorities (e.g., Chicano individuals) may be reared with a blend of both cultures, and thus the structure and experience of their identities may be more blended (i.e., low cultural distance). All in all, notice that the above propositions focus on the *relative* level of perceived cultural distance or conflict across groups—that is, we do not assert that some groups perceive cultural distance or conflict while others do not.

Psychological Consequences of Multiculturalism

What impact, if any, does multiculturalism have on individuals and the larger society? The issue of whether multiculturalism is beneficial is often theoretically and empirically debated. Some researchers contend that the integration/biculturalism strategy, as compared to the other three acculturation strategies (separation, assimilation, marginalization), is the most ideal, leading to greater benefits in all areas of life (e.g., Berry, 1997; Phinney, Horenczyk, Liebkind, & Vedder, 2001). However, others have argued that this is not always the case, because the process of dealing with two cultures places a burden on the individual and can lead to stress, isolation, and identity confusion (e.g., Gordon, 1964; Rudmin, 2003; Vivero & Jenkins, 1999). While some researchers have found positive links between biculturalism and adjustment (e.g., Szapocznik & Kurtines, 1980; Ward & Kennedy, 1994), others have found no link or a negative one (e.g., Burnam, Hough, Karno, Escobar, & Telles, 1987; Rotheram-Borus, 1990). In other words, findings have been mixed with regard to the direction and magnitude of these associations (Myers & Rodriguez, 2003; Rogler, Cortes, & Malgady, 1991).

A recent meta-analysis suggests that these seemingly contradictory findings may be attributable to the ways in which biculturalism has been measured (Nguyen & Benet-Martínez, 2009; see also our review of measurement issues in this chapter). Across the 83 studies and 23,197 participants examined in this meta-analysis, biculturalism was found to have a significant and positive relationship with psychological and sociocultural adjustment. However, the magnitude of this association was moderated by the type of acculturation scales used (see Figure 5.2). When only studies using direct measures of acculturation strategies were included, the relationship was weak to moderate ($r = .21$). However, when only studies using unidimensional scales were included, the relationship was strong ($r = .54$). Finally, when only studies using bidimensional scales were used (i.e., biculturalism measured via scores above the median or midpoint on both cultural orientations, the addition method, the multiplication method, or cluster or latent class analysis), the relationship between biculturalism and adjustment was even stronger ($r = .70$). In other words, biculturalism is related to better adjustment, but this relationship is best detected when biculturalism is measured bidimensionally. Perhaps involvement with two or more cultures (vs. the cultural relinquishing that characterizes assimilation or

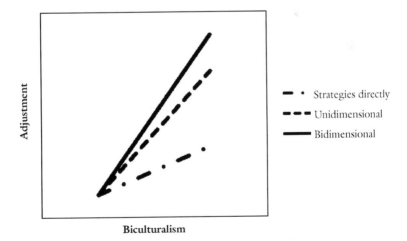

Figure 5.2   Effect size of the biculturalism–adjustment relationship by type of acculturation scale.

separation) facilitates the acquisition of cognitive and social skills as well as wider behavioral repertoires and competencies which, in turn, buffer multicultural individuals against the psychological maladjustment (e.g., anxiety, loneliness) or sociocultural challenges (e.g., interpersonal conflicts, intercultural miscommunication) that can often characterize the acculturation experience (Padilla, 2006).

It is important to note that multiculturalism is not necessarily an individual choice; groups and intergroup relations also play a role. For example, one may want to use the integration/biculturalism strategy, but if one is never accepted into mainstream society, then the integration/biculturalism strategy may not be possible. Similarly, if one lives in a community without same-ethnic individuals, then it may not be possible to blend one's cultures, or if one consistently encounters discrimination, then it may not be possible to perceive one's cultures as harmonious. In fact, research has found that perceived discrimination, along with poor intergroup relations and perception that the dominant group is impermeable, predicted greater cultural identity conflict (Benet-Martínez & Haritatos, 2005; Lin, 2008). Although more research is needed to determine causality among intergroup relations, multiculturalism, and adjustment, public policies, such as multicultural policies regarding greater diversity, the integration of dominant and ethnic cultures, or the prohibition of disparate treatment for different groups, may influence one's multiculturalism, which in turn, may affect one's well-being.

Multiculturalism may also have significant implications for greater national success and improved national functioning (Berry, 1998; Schwartz, Montgomery, & Briones, 2006). In children and adolescents, multiculturalism is positively related to greater academic achievement (Farver, Bhadha, & Narang, 2002; Régner & Loose, 2006). These educationally successful students may be able to contribute a great deal to society when they become adults. In the workplace, multicultural individuals may also contribute to organizational success, especially when it comes to expatriate assignments, because their multicultural competence may generalize to intercultural competence, which is necessary for expatriate success (Bell & Harrison, 1996). In addition, they have skills (e.g., multilingualism, cultural frame-switching, intercultural sensitivity) that are crucial in our increasingly globalized world; thus, these individuals are ideal cultural mediators for intercultural conflicts and miscommunications within communities, nations, and internationally (see our introductory point about President Obama). More generally, it has been found that individuals with more extensive multicultural experiences, such as multicultural individuals, have greater cognitive complexity (Benet-Martínez et al., 2006), integrative complexity (Tadmor & Tetlock, 2006; Tadmor, Tetlock, & Peng, 2009), and creativity (Leung, Maddux, Galinsky, & Chiu, 2008; Maddux & Galinsky, 2009), which are necessary for innovation and progress. In sum, policies promoting biculturalism and multiculturalism may benefit bicultural individuals *and* society at large. Unfortunately, in reality, most host countries continue to encourage the assimilation strategy despite the fact that acculturating individuals by and large prefer the integration/biculturalism strategy (Van Oudenhoven et al., 2006; Verkuyten, this volume).

The Intersection of Other Types of Cultures

The terms "multicultural" or "bicultural" are typically used to refer to national or ethnic cultures; however, these terms can also be used to describe the intersection of other cultures (e.g., professional cultures, geographic cultures, generational cultures). For example, an individual from the southern region of the United States living in the northern region of the United States may be bicultural. A culture of honor, which justifies violence in defense of one's reputation, is relatively prevalent in the south but not the north; therefore, southern White males living in the north may have to adapt to the norms in the north and negotiate those two cultures (Cohen, Nisbett, Bowdle, & Schwarz, 1996). Sexual minorities, such as lesbian women, may also be bicultural, considering that they negotiate lesbian culture and mainstream heterosexual culture (Fingerhut, Peplau, & Ghavami, 2005). Furthermore, the pair of cultures to which "biculturalism" refers need not be within the same category. For example, engineering is a male-dominated occupation; therefore, women engineers may also be considered bicultural because they must negotiate their identities as women and as engineers (Cheng et al., 2008). In addition, individuals such as Turkish Dutch Muslims may be multicultural because they negotiate their ethnic culture (Turkish), the dominant culture (Dutch), and their religious culture (Muslim; Verkuyten & Yildiz, 2007). The theory and research on multiculturalism discussed in the previous research may thus also apply to these other intersections of cultures, but further research is desperately needed.

Concluding Comments

Researchers and practitioners have acknowledged the importance of multiculturalism, and noted its links to mental health, intergroup relations, and academic and occupational success (e.g., Hermans & Kempen, 1998; LaFromboise et al., 1993). Recently, multiculturalism has also taken center stage in popular culture. Earlier, it was mentioned that Obama is undoubtedly multicultural and that biculturalism may refer to cultures other than ethnic cultures. At the 2009 Radio and Television Correspondents' Dinner, John Hodgman, a humorist and actor famous for his role in Apple's Mac vs. PC commercials, delivered a speech on biculturalism and hybridity, and identified Obama as being of two worlds: the world of "nerds" and the world of "jocks" (C-SPAN, 2009). Like a nerd, Obama values science, objectivity, and the questioning of the status quo, and like a jock, Obama is likeable, confident, and fun to be around. As mentioned earlier, some bicultural individuals may experience the pressure of not being "enough" of one culture or another. In line with this, Hodgman questioned Obama's authenticity as a nerd and tested him on his nerdiness. Although delivered as a humorous speech, it accurately highlights the bicultural experience, particularly the expectations and possible strains related to that experience.[3]

Multiculturalism is indisputably a fact of life. Through exposure to and internalization of different cultures, individuals can experience different ways of learning, viewing, and reacting to the world. This experience makes these individuals' cultural identities more complex and layered and enriches their cognitive and behavioral repertoires. Recent research shows that these psychological processes lead to higher cognitive complexity and more creative and tolerant thinking. These attributes are an indispensable skill in our global world.

Notes

1   For the sake of simplicity and consistency, in this chapter we favor the broader term "multicultural" or "multiculturalism" over the term "bicultural." Regardless of the term used, we always refer to individuals and societies who position themselves between two (or more) cultures and incorporate this experience (i.e., values, knowledge, and feelings associated to each of these identities and their intersection) into their sense of self.

2   The possibility of being oriented to an emergent third culture has important implications for research on multiculturalism. The currently accepted bidimensional model of acculturation with ethnic and dominant cultural orientations might be replaced by a tridimensional model, where the third cultural orientation is the emergent third culture (Flannery et al., 2001). Moreover, this tridimensional model might be more applicable to later-generation individuals than either the unidimensional or bidimensional model of acculturation. As yet, no study has examined a third cultural orientation or compared a tridimensional model to the other models.

3   Biculturalism also appears in more mainstream outlets, such as the Hollywood blockbuster movie, *Star Trek* (Abrams, 2009). One of the central themes in this movie is Spock's mixed heritage, with a Vulcan father and human mother. The movie follows Spock from his childhood, where he struggled with being bicultural and was bullied for not being Vulcan enough, to his adulthood, where he seemed to reconcile the perceived cultural conflicts associated with his biculturalism and to embrace both identities.

References

Abrams, J. J. (Director & Producer). (2009). *Star Trek*. Paramount Pictures.

Arends-Tóth, J. V., & van de Vijver, F. J. R. (2006). Assessment of psychological acculturation. In D. L. Sam & J.W. Berry (Eds.), *Cambridge Handbook of Acculturation Psychology* (pp. 142–60). Cambridge, UK: Cambridge University Press.

Banks, J. A., & Banks, C. M. (1995). *Handbook of research on multicultural education*. New York: Macmillan.

Bartholet, J., & Stone, D. (2009, January 17). A team of expatriates. *Newsweek*. Retrieved from: http://www.newsweek.com/id/180207.

Baumeister, R. (1986). *Identity: Cultural change and the struggle for self*. New York: Oxford University Press.

Bell, M. P., & Harrison, D. A. (1996). Using intra-national diversity for international assignments: A model of bicultural competence and expatriate adjustment. *Human Resource Management Review, 6*, 47–74.

Benet-Martínez, V., & Haritatos, J. (2005). Bicultural identity integration (BII): Components and psychosocial antecedents. *Journal of Personality, 73*, 1015–1050.

Benet-Martínez, V., Lee, F., & Leu, J. (2006). Biculturalism and cognitive complexity: Expertise in cultural representations. *Journal of Cross-Cultural Psychology, 37*, 386–407.

Benet-Martínez, V., Leu, J., Lee, F., & Morris, M. (2002). Negotiating biculturalism: Cultural frame switching in biculturals with oppositional versus compatible cultural identities. *Journal of Cross-Cultural Psychology, 33*, 492–516.

Berry, J. W. (1984). Multicultural policy in Canada: A social psychological analysis. *Canadian Journal of Behavioural Science, 16*, 353–370.

Berry, J. W. (1990). Psychology of acculturation. In J. Berman (Ed.), *Cross-Cultural Perspectives: Nebraska Symposium on Motivation* (pp. 201–234). Lincoln: University of Nebraska.

Berry, J. W. (1997). Immigration, acculturation, and adaptation. *Applied Psychology: An International Review, 46*, 5–34.

Berry, J. W. (1998). Social psychological costs and benefits of multiculturalism: A view from Canada. *Trames, 2*, 209–233.

Berry, J. W. (2003). Conceptual approaches to acculturation. In K. M. Chun, P.B. Organista, & G. Marín (Eds.), *Acculturation: Advances in theory, measurement, and applied research* (pp. 17–37). Washington, DC: American Psychological Association.

Berry, J. W., Kim, U., Minde, T., & Mok, D. (1987). Comparative studies of acculturative stress. *International Migration Review, 21*, 491–511.

Berry, J. W., Kim, U., Power, S., Young, M., & Bujaki, M. (1989). Acculturation attitudes in plural societies. *Applied Psychology: An International Review, 38*, 185–206.

Berry, J. W., Phinney, J. S., Sam, D. L., & Vedder, P. (2006). Immigrant youth: Acculturation, identity, and adaptation. *Applied Psychology: An International Review, 55*, 303–332.

Birman, D. (1994). Acculturation and human diversity in a multicultural society. In E. J. Trickett, R.J. Watts, & D. Birman (Eds.), *Human diversity: Perspective on people in context* (pp. 261–284). San Francisco: Jossey-Bass.

Birman, D. (1998). Biculturalism and perceived competence of Latino immigrant adolescents. *American Journal of Community Psychology, 26*, 335–354.

Bollen, K., & Lennox, R. (1991). Conventional wisdom on measurement: A structural equation perspective. *Psychological Bulletin, 110*, 305–314.

Bourhis, R. Y., Moïse, L. C., Perreault, S., & Senécal, S. (1997). Towards an interactive acculturation model: A social psychological approach. *International Journal of Psychology, 32*, 369–386.

Buriel, R., Calzada, S., & Vasquez, R. (1982). The relationship of traditional Mexican American culture to adjustment and delinquency among three generations of Mexican American male adolescents. *Hispanic Journal of Behavioral Sciences, 4*, 41–55.

Burnam, M. A., Hough, R. L., Karno, M., Escobar, J. I., & Telles, C. A. (1987). Acculturation and lifetime prevalence of psychiatric disorders among Mexican Americans in Los Angeles. *Journal of Health and Social Behavior, 28*, 89–102.

Burnet, J. (1995). Multiculturalism and racism in Canada. In J. Hjarno (Ed.), *Multiculturalism in the Nordic societies* (pp. 43–50). Copenhagen, Denmark: TemaNord.

Chavez, D. (1994). *Face of an angel.* New York: Farrar, Straus, and Giroux.

Chen, S. X., Benet-Martínez, V., & Bond, M. H. (2008). Bicultural identity, bilingualism, and psychological adjustment in multicultural societies:

Immigration-based and globalization-based acculturation. *Journal of Personality*, *76*, 803–838.

Cheng, C., Lee, F., & Benet-Martínez, V. (2006). Assimilation and contrast effects in cultural frame-switching: Bicultural Identity Integration (BII) and valence of cultural cues. *Journal of Cross-Cultural Psychology*, *37*, 742–760.

Cheng, C.-Y., Sanchez-Burks, J., & Lee, F. (2008). Connecting the dots within: Creative performance and identity integration. *Psychological Science*, *19*, 1178–1184.

Cohen, D., Nisbett, R. E., Bowdle, B. R., & Schwarz, N. (1996). Insult, aggression, and the southern culture of honor: An "experimental ethnography." *Journal of Personality and Social Psychology*, *70*, 945–960.

C-SPAN (2009). 2009 Radio and Television Correspondents' Dinner. Retrieved June 28, 2009, from: http://www.c-spanarchives.org/library/index.php?main_page=product_video_info&products_id=287153–1.

Cuéllar, I., Arnold, B., & Maldonado, R. (1995). Acculturation Rating Scale for Mexican Americans—II: A revision of the original ARSMA scale. *Hispanic Journal of Behavioral Sciences*, *17*, 275–304.

Cuéllar, I., Harris, L. C., & Jasso, R. (1980). An acculturation scale for Mexican American normal and clinical populations. *Hispanic Journal of Behavioral Sciences*, *2*, 199–217.

Donà, G., & Berry, J. W. (1994). Acculturation attitudes and acculturative stress of Central American refugees. *International Journal of Psychology*, *29*, 57–70.

Farver, J. A. M., Bhadha, B. R., & Narang, S. K. (2002). Acculturation and psychological functioning in Asian Indian adolescents. *Social Development*, *11*, 11–29.

Fingerhut, A. W., Peplau, L. A., & Ghavami, N. (2005). A dual-identity framework for understanding lesbian experience. *Psychology of Women Quarterly*, *29*, 129–139.

Flannery, W. P., Reise, S. P., & Yu, J. (2001). An empirical comparison of acculturation models. *Personality and Social Psychology Bulletin*, *27*, 1035–1045.

Fowers, B. J., & Richardson, F. C. (1996). Why is multiculturalism good? *American Psychologist*, *51*, 609–621.

Gardner, W. L., Gabriel, S., & Lee, A. Y. (1999). "I" value freedom, but "we" value relationships: Self-construal priming mirrors cultural differences in judgment. *Psychological Science*, *10*, 321–326.

Gordon, M. M. (1964). *Assimilation in American life*. New York: Oxford University Press.

Hermans, H. J. M., & Kempen, H. J. G. (1998). Moving cultures: The perilous problem of cultural dichotomies in a globalizing society. *American Psychologist*, *53*, 1111–1120.

Hong, Y. Y., Benet-Martínez, V., Chiu, C. Y., & Morris, M. W. (2003). Boundaries of cultural influence: Construct activation as a mechanism for cultural differences in social perception. *Journal of Cross-Cultural Psychology*, *34*, 453–464.

Hong, Y. Y., Morris, M. W., Chiu, C. Y., & Benet-Martínez, V. (2000). Multicultural minds: A dynamic constructivist approach to culture and cognition. *American Psychologist, 55,* 709–720.

Jasinskaja-Lahti, I., Liebkind, K., Horenczyk, G., & Schmitz, P. (2003). The interactive nature of acculturation: Perceived discrimination, acculturation attitudes and stress among young ethnic repatriates in Finland, Israel and Germany. *International Journal of Intercultural Relations, 27,* 79–97.

Kang, S.-M. (2006). Measurement of acculturation, scale formats, and language competence: Their implications for adjustment. *Journal of Cross-Cultural Psychology, 37,* 669–693.

Kim-Jo, T., Benet-Martínez, V., & Ozer, D. (in press). Culture and conflict resolution styles: The role of acculturation. *Journal of Cross-Cultural Psychology.*

LaFromboise, T., Coleman, H. L., & Gerton, J. (1993). Psychological impact of biculturalism: Evidence and theory. *Psychological Bulletin, 114,* 395–412.

Lau-Gesk, L. G. (2003). Activating culture through persuasion appeals: An examination of the bicultural consumer. *Journal of Consumer Psychology, 13,* 301–315.

lê, d. t. t. (2003). *The gangster we are all looking for.* New York: Random House.

Lee, S.-K., Sobal, J., & Frongillo, E. A. (2003). Comparison of models of acculturation: The case of Korean Americans. *Journal of Cross-Cultural Psychology, 34,* 282–296.

Leung, A. K.-y., Maddux, W. W., Galinsky, A. D., & Chiu, C.-y. (2008). Multicultural experience enhances creativity: The when and how. *American Psychologist, 63,* 169–181.

Lin, E.-Y. (2008). Family and social influences on identity conflict in overseas Chinese. *International Journal of Intercultural Relations, 32,* 130–141.

Maddux, W. W., & Galinsky, A. D. (2009). Cultural borders and mental barriers: The relationship between living abroad and creativity. *Journal of Personality and Social Psychology, 96,* 1047–1061.

Miramontez, D. R., Benet-Martínez, V., & Nguyen, A.-M. D. (2008). Bicultural identity and self/group personality perceptions. *Self and Identity, 7,* 430–445.

Mok, A., Morris, M., Benet-Martínez, V., & Karakitapoglu-Aygun, Z. (2007). Embracing American culture: Structures of social identity and social networks among first-generation biculturals. *Journal of Cross-Cultural Psychology, 38,* 629–635.

Myers, H. F., & Rodriguez, N. (2003). Acculturation and physical health in racial and ethnic minorities. In K. M. Chun, P.B. Organista, & G. Marin (Eds.), *Acculturation: Advances in theory, measurement, and applied research* (pp. 163–185). Washington, DC: American Psychological Association.

Nguyen, A.-M. D., & Benet-Martínez, V. (2007). Biculturalism unpacked: Components, individual differences, measurement, and outcomes. *Social and Personality Psychology Compass, 1,* 101–114.

Nguyen, A.-M. D., & Benet-Martínez, V. (2009). *Biculturalism is linked to adjustment: A meta-analysis.* Manuscript submitted for publication.

Obama, B. H. (2009, January 21). Inaugural address. Retrieved July 8, 2009, from: http://www.whitehouse.gov/blog/inaugural-address/.

Ogbu, J. U. (1993). Differences in cultural frame of reference. *International Journal of Behavioral Development, 16,* 483–506.

Ogbu, J. U. (2008). Minority status, oppositional culture, and schooling. New York: Routledge.

O'Hearn, C. C. (1998). *Half and half: Writers on growing up biracial and bicultural.* New York: Pantheon Books.

Padilla, A. M. (1994). Bicultural development: A theoretical and empirical examination. In R. G. Malgady & O. Rodriguez (Eds.), *Theoretical and conceptual issues in Hispanic mental health* (pp. 20–51). Melbourne, FL: Krieger.

Padilla, A. M. (2006). Bicultural social development. *Hispanic Journal of Behavioral Sciences, 28,* 467–497.

Phinney, J. S. (1999). An intercultural approach in psychology: Cultural contact and identity. *Cross-Cultural Psychology Bulletin, 33,* 24–31.

Phinney, J. S. (2003). Ethnic identity and acculturation. In K. M. Chun, P.B. Organista, & G. Marin (Eds.), *Acculturation: Advances in theory, measurement, and applied research* (pp. 63–81). Washington, DC: American Psychological Association.

Phinney, J. S., & Devich-Navarro, M. (1997). Variations in bicultural identification among African American and Mexican American adolescents. *Journal of Research on Adolescence, 7,* 3–32.

Phinney, J. S., Horenczyk, G., Liebkind, K., & Vedder, P. (2001). Ethnic identity, immigration, and well-being: An interactional perspective. *Journal of Social Issues, 57,* 493–510.

Plaut, V. C., Thomas, K. M., & Goren, M. J. (in press). Is multiculturalism or colorblindness better for minorities? *Psychological Science,.*

Ramirez-Esparza, N., Gosling, S., Benet-Martínez, V., Potter, J., & Pennebaker, J. (2006). Do bilinguals have two personalities? A special case of cultural frame-switching. *Journal of Research in Personality, 40,* 99–120.

Régner, I., & Loose, F. (2006). Relationship of sociocultural factors and academic self-esteem to school grades and school disengagement in North African French adolescents. *British Journal of Social Psychology, 45,* 777–797.

Roccas, S., & Brewer, M. B. (2002). Social identity complexity. *Personality and Social Psychology Review, 6,* 88–107.

Rogler, L. H., Cortes, D. E., & Malgady, R. G. (1991). Acculturation and mental health status among Hispanics: Convergence and new directions for research. *American Psychologist, 46,* 585–597.

Root, M. P. P. (1998). Experiences and processes affecting racial identity development: Preliminary results from the biracial sibling project. *Cultural Diversity and Mental Health, 4,* 237–247.

Ross, M., Xun, W. Q. E., & Wilson, A. E. (2002). Language and the bicultural self. *Personality and Social Psychology Bulletin, 28,* 1040–1050.

Roth, P. (1969). *Portnoy's complaint.* New York: Random House.

Rotheram-Borus, M. J. (1990). Adolescents' reference-group choices, self-esteem, and adjustment. *Journal of Personality and Social Psychology, 59,* 1075–1081.

Rudmin, F. W. (2003). Critical history of the acculturation psychology of assimilation, separation, integration, and marginalization. *Review of General Psychology, 7,* 3–37.

Ryder, A. G., Alden, L. E., & Paulhus, D. L. (2000). Is acculturation unidimensional or bidimensional? A head-to-head comparison in the prediction of personality, self-identity, and adjustment. *Journal of Personality and Social Psychology, 79,* 49–65.

Sam, D. L., & Berry, J. W. (2006). *Cambridge Handbook of Acculturation Psychology,* Cambridge, UK: Cambridge University Press.

Sanchez-Burks, J., Lee, F., Choi, I., Nisbett, R., Zhao, S., & Koo, J. (2003). Conversing across cultures: East-West communication styles in work and nonwork contexts. *Journal of Personality and Social Psychology, 85,* 363–372.

Schwartz, S. J. (2006). Predicting identity consolation from self-construction, eudaimonistic self-discovery, and agentic personality. *Journal of Adolescence, 29,* 777–793.

Schwartz, S. J., Montgomery, M. J., & Briones, E. (2006). The role of identity in acculturation among immigrant people: Theoretical propositions, empirical questions, and applied recommendations. *Human Development, 49,* 1–30.

Schwartz, S. J., Pantin, H., Sullivan, S., Prado, G., & Szapocznik, J. (2006). Nativity and years in the receiving culture as markers of acculturation in ethnic enclaves. *Journal of Cross-Cultural Psychology, 37,* 345–353.

Sparrow, L. M. (2000). Beyond multicultural man: Complexities of identity. *International Journal of Intercultural Relations, 24,* 173–201.

Stevens, G. W. J. M., Pels, T. V. M., Vollebergh, W. A. M., & Crijnen, A. A. M. (2007). Problem behavior and acculturation in Moroccan immigrant adolescents in the Netherlands: Effects of gender and parent-child conflict. *Journal of Cross-Cultural Psychology, 38,* 310–317.

Sue, D. W., & Sue, F. (2003). *Counseling the culturally diverse: Theory and practice* (4th ed.). New York: Wiley.

Suinn, R. M., Rickard-Figueroa, K., Lew, S., & Vigil, P. (1987). The Suinn-Lew Asian Self-Identity Acculturation Scale (SL-ASIA). *Educational and Psychological Measurement, 47,* 401–407.

Szapocznik, J., & Kurtines, W. M. (1980). Acculturation, biculturalism and adjustment among Cuban Americans. In A. M. Padilla (Ed.), *Psychological dimensions on the acculturation process: Theory, models, and some new findings* (pp. 139–159). Boulder, CO: Westview Press.

Szapocznik, J., Kurtines, W. M., & Fernandez, T. (1980). Bicultural adjustment and involvement in Hispanic-American youths. *International Journal of Cross-Cultural Relations, 4,* 353–365.

Tadmor, C. T., & Tetlock, P. E. (2006). Biculturalism: A model of the effects of second-culture exposure on acculturation and integrative complexity. *Journal of Cross-Cultural Psychology, 37,* 173–190.

Tadmor, C. T., Tetlock, P. E., & Peng, K. (2009). Acculturation strategies and integrative complexity: The cognitive implications of biculturalism. *Journal of Cross-Cultural Psychology, 40,* 105–139.

Trimble, J. E. (2003). Introduction: Social change and acculturation. In K. M. Chun, P.B. Organista, & G. Marín (Eds.), *Acculturation: Advances in theory, measurement, and applied research* (pp. 3–13). Washington, DC: American Psychological Association.

Tsai, J. L., Ying, Y.-W., & Lee, P. A. (2000). The meaning of "being Chinese" and "being American": Variation among Chinese American young adults. *Journal of Cross-Cultural Psychology, 31,* 302–332.

U.S. Census Bureau. (2006). Retrieved March 18, 2008, from: http://www.census.gov.

Van Oudenhoven, J. P., Ward, C., & Masgoret, A. M. (2006). Patterns of relations between immigrants and host societies. *International Journal of Intercultural Relations, 30,* 637–651.

Verkuyten, M. (2009). Self-esteem and multiculturalism: An examination among ethnic minority and majority groups in the Netherlands. *Journal of Research in Personality, 43,* 419–427.

Verkuyten, M., & Martinovic, B. (2006). Understanding multicultural attitudes: The role of group status, identification, friendships, and justifying ideologies. *International Journal of Intercultural Relations, 30,* 1–18.

Verkuyten, M., & Pouliasi, K. (2002). Biculturalism among older children: Cultural frame switching, attributions, self-identification and attitudes. *Journal of Cross-Cultural Psychology, 33,* 596–609.

Verkuyten, M., & Pouliasi, K. (2006). Biculturalism and group identification: The mediating role of identification in cultural frame-switching. *Journal of Cross-Cultural Psychology, 37,* 312–326.

Verkuyten, M., & Yildiz, A. A. (2007). National (dis)identification and ethnic and religious identity: A study among Turkish-Dutch Muslims. *Personality and Social Psychology Bulletin, 33,* 1448–1462.

Vivero, V. N., & Jenkins, S. R. (1999). Existential hazards of the multicultural individual: Defining and understanding "cultural homelessness". *Cultural Diversity and Ethnic Minority Psychology, 5,* 6–26.

Ward, C., & Kennedy, A. (1994). Acculturation strategies, psychological adjustment, and sociocultural competence during cross-cultural transitions. *International Journal of Intercultural Relations, 18,* 329–343.

Wolf, R. (2009, April 20). Most diverse Cabinet in history still incomplete. *USA Today.* Retrieved from: http://www.usatoday.com/news/washington/2009-04-19-cabinet_N.htm.

Wong, R. Y.-m., & Hong, Y.-y. (2005). Dynamic influences of culture on cooperation in the Prisoner's Dilemma. *Psychological Science, 16,* 429–434.

Yip, T., Seaton, E. K., & Sellers, R. M. (2006). African American racial identity across the lifespan: Identity status, identity content and depressive symptoms. *Child Development, 77,* 1504–1517.

Zane, N., & Mak, W. (2003). Major approaches to the measurement of acculturation among ethnic minority populations: A content analysis and an alternative empirical strategy. In K. M. Chun, P.B. Organista, & G. Marín (Eds.), *Acculturation: Advances in theory, measurement, and applied research* (pp. 39–60). Washington, DC: American Psychological Association.

Zou, X., Morris, M. W., & Benet-Martínez, V. (2008). Identity motives and cultural priming: Cultural (dis)identification in assimilative and contrastive responses. *Journal of Experimental Social Psychology, 44,* 1151–1159.

6

What I Know in My Mind and Where My Heart Belongs

Multicultural Identity Negotiation and its Cognitive Consequences

Carmit T. Tadmor, Ying-yi Hong, Chi-Yue Chiu, and Sun No

With the increasing globalization of the early twenty-first century more and more individuals are exposed to cultures strikingly different from their own. Early studies of the experience of living at the junction of two or more cultures stressed the negative psychological consequences of conflict, ambivalence, and a disjointed sense of self (Park, 1928; Stonequist, 1935). However, researchers now agree that immersion in different cultures can also have positive effects on psychological functioning (e.g., LaFromboise, Coleman, & Gerton, 1993). Indeed, some researchers have begun to focus on the benefits of multicultural exposure at all levels of analysis, arguing that diversity of cultural perspectives can increase tolerance and reduce prejudice (e.g., Crisp & Hewstone, 2007; Gaertner, Dovidio, Nier, Ward, & Banker, 1999; Roccas & Brewer, 2002) as well as foster flexibility, creativity, and decision quality (e.g., Cheng, Sanchez-Burks, & Lee, 2008; Chiu & Hong, 2005; Hong, Chiu, & Kung, 1997; Hong, Morris, Chiu, & Benet-Martínez, 2000; Leung & Chiu, in press; Leung, Maddux, Galinsky, & Chiu, 2008; Maddux & Galinsky, 2009; McLeod, Lobel, & Cox, 1996; Tadmor, Galinsky, & Maddux, 2009; Tadmor, Hernandez, Jang, & Polzer, 2009). Research has also begun to investigate the impact of negotiating multicultural identity on cognitive functioning, and consequently, has begun to elucidate the underlying link between multiculturalism and its associated benefits (Benet-Martínez, Lee, & Leu, 2006; Roccas & Brewer, 2002; Leung & Chiu, in press; Nguyen & Benet-Martínez, this volume; Tadmor & Tetlock, 2006; Tadmor, Tetlock, & Peng, 2009).

And yet, despite the optimistic view of the expected benefits associated with multicultural experience, incidents of racial tension, prejudice, and intergroup violence abound in multicultural societies. Culturally diverse groups often experience conflict, communication breakdown, and lack of trust leading to worse, not better performance relative to culturally homogeneous groups (e.g., Earley & Gibson, 2002). Intercultural negotiations often yield outcomes that are lower in joint gains than those that result from intracultural negotiations (Brett & Okumura, 1998). Immigrants traveling to other countries in pursuit of job opportunities with the hopes of personal and professional development often fail (Wederspahn, 1992). Research has yet to uncover the reasons for these mixed findings. Our primary goal in this chapter is to draw attention to these issues and to propose an integrative model to account for the development and cognitive consequences of multicultural identity.

Specifically, we propose there are two potential reasons for mixed findings regarding the potential advantages associated with multiculturalism. First, researchers have tended to treat multicultural experience as if it were a rather unitary concept; however, it can actually refer to different things, ranging from passive, brief, incidental exposure to a foreign culture to actively sought-after, extensive exposure to two or more cultures. Moreover, an individual can be exposed to cultures that are only minimally different from each other (e.g., an American in Canada) or to cultures that are radically different (e.g., an American in Japan). Finally, multicultural experiences can be imposed on individuals, such as in the case of many refugees, or they can be actively sought out, such as when an individual initiates a relocation assignment to a foreign land. Each of these factors—*quantity, quality, and voluntariness*— is likely to differentially affect how much multicultural knowledge is actually internalized during multicultural exposure. We argue that independent of the nature of multicultural experiences, the greater the amount of multicultural knowledge internalized, the greater the potential for the expected benefits associated with multicultural experience to come to fruition.

A second potential explanation for the mixed results may be due to failure to differentiate between *multicultural mind* and *multicultural self*, where the former refers to the acquisition of a cultural knowledge tradition and the latter refers to cultural identification with the acquired cultural knowledge tradition (e.g., Hong, Wan, No, & Chiu, 2007).

Given that knowledge tradition is the object of cultural identification, it is implausible that a person would identify with a culture without having at least some vague ideas about what constitutes the culture's knowledge tradition; however, a person may acquire and apply a cultural tradition without identifying with it (No et al., 2008; Wan, Chiu, Peng, & Tam, 2007a; Wan et al., 2007b; Zou et al., in press). We contend that although multicultural experiences can lead to the acquisition of diverse cultural knowledge traditions that in turn can lead to a variety of benefits, people's cultural identification patterns will determine the ease of accessibility to this information. Specifically, we propose that identification levels will determine the degree to which this diverse knowledge will be applied and, consequently, whether its benefits will be actualized.

Taken together, in our integrated model we propose that individuals negotiating multicultural identity will (a) integrate (or compartmentalize) ideas and practices from different cultures to different extents, and (b) decide to affiliate with or distance themselves from the stakeholding cultures, depending on the accountability pressures they face. The first factor will influence the depth of multicultural knowledge and consequently the level of cognitive flexibility, creativity, and intercultural competence obtained, whereas the second factor will influence the long-term likelihood of accessing multicultural knowledge as well as chronic changes in levels of integrative complexity.

To flesh out these ideas, we have organized the chapter into four major sections. First, we briefly review the cognitive principles that underlie application and utility of multicultural knowledge. Next, we review the psychological processes involved in the development and management of multicultural identities as well as delineate the effects of cultural identification patterns on adaptive and creative utilization of multicultural knowledge. Next, we discuss the individual and sociopolitical factors that affect the process of multicultural identity negotiation and affiliation decisions. Finally, we discuss the model's implications for immigration policies and suggest social interventions geared toward multicultural competence development.

Multicultural Mind: Application and Benefits of Multicultural Knowledge

Application of Multicultural Knowledge

Past research (see Au, Wan, & Chiu, in press; Chiu & Hong, 2005, 2006, 2007; Hong et al., 2000) has revealed the psychological principles that underlie how multicultural individuals appropriate knowledge to guide their behaviors. Very briefly, multicultural experiences expand the individual's cognitive toolkit and enable the individual to appropriate culturally applicable cognitive tools to solve problems in concrete cultural settings. That is, individuals with extensive exposure to multiple cultures have acquired and hence have at their disposal knowledge (implicit beliefs, values, norms, and practices) from the respective cultural tradition to guide their behaviors in the respective cultural communities.

Multicultural experiences also foster contextualization of cultural knowledge. Individuals with extensive multicultural experiences are aware of the culture-specificity of the knowledge items in their cognitive toolkit; they are aware of the differential connectedness of different knowledge items to different cultural traditions (e.g., for an American-Indian bicultural, the notion of human rights is more strongly connected to the American tradition and the notion of dharma is more strongly connected to the Indian tradition). Equipped with such contextualized knowledge, multicultural individuals often exhibit a high level of behavioral responsiveness to situational cues that signal the relevance of different cultural scripts. Experimental evidence supporting this idea abounds (Hong et al., 1997, 2000; Hong, Benet-Martínez, Chiu, & Morris, 2003). For example, in one experiment, Chinese American biculturals (Hong Kong Chinese, Chinese Americans) were exposed to either Chinese cultural icons (e.g., the Chinese dragon) or American cultural icons (e.g., Mickey Mouse). Incidental exposure to Chinese (vs. American) cultural icons increased these biculturals' tendency to focus on factors external to the actor to interpret an ambiguous event; they made more external (vs. internal) attributions (Hong et al., 1997, see Figure 6.1). Subsequent studies have replicated this effect, referred to as culture-priming effect or cultural frame-switching (Hong et al., 2000), on spontaneous self-construal (Ross, Xun, & Wilson, 2002), self-referential memory (Sui, Zhu, & Chiu, 2007) and cooperative behaviors (Wong & Hong, 2005), in a variety of bicultural samples (Chinese Canadians, Dutch–Greek bicultural children) using different kinds of cultural primes (e.g., language, experimenter's cultural identity; Ross et al., 2002; Verkuyten & Pouliasi, 2002; see also Verkuyten, this volume). In addition, researchers have also found neurological evidence for the culture-priming effect of self-representations (Chiao et al., in press), and have begun to investigate the effects of simultaneously activating competing cultural networks (Chiu & Cheng, 2007; Chiu, Mallorie, Keh, & Law, 2009; Tadmor et al., 2009).

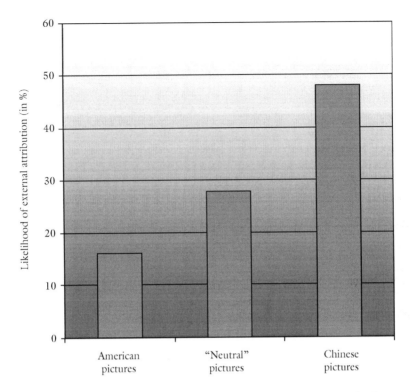

Figure 6.1 Chinese American bicultural participants' likelihood of external (vs. internal) attributions as a function of American, neutral, and Chinese cultural priming (data from Hong et al., 1997).

However, bicultural individuals do not passively respond to situational cueing of cultural knowledge. Instead, after a situational cue has called out a certain cultural knowledge item, bicultural individuals will spontaneously assess the item's applicability to solving the presenting problem in the immediate situation, and apply the item only when the item's situational appropriateness is evident. In the same vein, switching cultural frame is not a knee-jerk response to cultural cues in the environment. The evoked cultural frame will be appraised for its applicability to the judgment context before it is applied; an accessible cultural idea will not impact judgments or behaviors unless it is applicable to the task at hand. As noted, Chinese American biculturals would more likely focus on factors external to the individual actor, applying a group (vs. individual) agency perspective to interpret a stimulus event when they are primed with Chinese cultural cues than when they are primed with American cultural cues. However, this occurs only when the group (vs. individual) agency perspective is applicable in the judgment context, as when the tension between group agency and individual agency is highlighted (Hong et al., 2003).

Similarly, in Chinese cultural contexts, a cooperative (vs. competitive) script is applicable only in interaction with friends, but not in interactions with strangers. Thus, subsequent to being primed with Chinese (vs. American or culture-neutral) cultural cues, Chinese American biculturals are more cooperative when they play the Prisoner's Dilemma game with their friends. However, culture priming does not impact these biculturals' cooperative or competitive choices when they play the game with strangers (Wong & Hong, 2005). Nonetheless, when individuals encounter an ill-defined situation with unclear cultural expectations, they may perform a memory search of all pertinent past experiences to identify and select the most context-appropriate response based on the individuals' subjective reading of the situation.

In summary, culture, like other knowledge, impacts judgments and behaviors when it is activated. A cultural knowledge item will be activated when it is available, chronically or temporarily accessible, *and* applicable. Thus, retrieval of a specific cultural knowledge item is a probabilistic (as opposed to deterministic) process contingent upon the individual's chronic cultural experiences, the unfolding cultural milieu, and the situation-appropriateness of cultural knowledge. That is, culture does not rigidly determine human behaviors. Instead, like other knowledge, culture is a cognitive resource for grasping experiences and pursuing life goals.

Benefits of Multicultural Knowledge

The foregoing analysis suggests that bicultural individuals, by virtue of their multicultural experience, have at their disposal a broader set of contextualized cultural knowledge that enables them to respond flexibly and discriminatively to shifting cultural demands in the situation. Indeed, some theoreticians hold that individuals who have acquired multiple cultural knowledge traditions have more than one set of cultural tools to interpret the world (DiMaggio, 1997; Shore, 1996). Moreover, their greater awareness of a wider array of ideas, concepts, artifacts, practices, norms, habits, and values may foster competent behaviors in at least three ways: increased *integrative complexity*, greater *creative expansion*, and greater *intercultural competence*.

Integrative complexity   As a dimension of information processing, integrative complexity refers to the capacity and willingness to acknowledge the legitimacy of competing perspectives on the same issue (differentiation) and to forge conceptual links among these perspectives (integration) (Suedfeld, Tetlock, & Streufert, 1992). Within a cross-cultural context, integrative complexity reflects the degree to which people accept the reasonableness of clashing cultural perspectives on how to live and, consequently, the degree to which they are motivated to develop cognitive schemas that integrate these competing world-views (Tadmor & Tetlock, 2006). Recent research suggests that as individuals who have had extensive multicultural experiences repeatedly shift cultural frames in response to changing situational cues, they are likely to develop more complex modes of thinking than individuals who lack such experiences. Cognitively complex multicultural individuals are likely to engage in effortful processing of cues and recognize the self-relevance of cultural information (Benet-Martínez et al., 2006; Nguyen & Benet-Martínez, this volume).

Research on bilingualism has provided some indirect support for this suggestion. For example, compared to monolingual children, bilinguals have been found to be more successful in solving a card-sorting task that required an understanding of conflicting rules (Bialystok, 2001). Bilinguals' more advanced use of higher-order rules allows them to see things from different perspectives and understand that different judgments are appropriate for different situations. More direct evidence comes from a recent study (Benet-Martínez et al., 2006) showing that Chinese American biculturals' free descriptions of both American and Chinese cultures are more complex than those of Anglo-American monoculturals.

Multiculturals' greater levels of integrative complexity, in turn, are likely to foster both enhanced creative abilities as well as more competent intercultural interactions.

Creativity   Creativity is typically defined as the process of bringing into being something that is both novel and useful (Amabile, 1996). The creative cognition approach, a major psychological approach to understanding creativity, suggests that accessibility of different knowledge traditions is critical to the generation of creative ideas. According to this approach (Smith, Ward, & Finke, 1995), creative conceptual expansion—a cognitive process that takes place when attributes of seemingly irrelevant concepts are added to an existing concept to extend its conceptual boundary—can lead to creative performance (Hampton, 1997; Wan & Chiu, 2002; Ward, Smith, & Vaid, 1997). The underlying logic is that exposure to and acquisition of different sets of knowledge equips the individual with a broader set of concepts that can then be utilized for creative expansion.

Within the cultural context, if individuals are frequently exposed to only a single cultural lens, it becomes a learned routine that automatically filters how individuals view their world (Briley & Wyer, 2002; Chiu & Hong, 2005; Ng & Bradac, 1993; Tadmor & Tetlock, 2006). Although culture provides conventional tools for sense making and problem solving, it can also impede creativity through reliance on highly accessible exemplars and a relatively constrained conceptual network (Ward, 1994). In contrast, the acquisition of multicultural knowledge traditions and the resulting integrative complexity should foster creativity directly by providing access to a wider base of ideas and concepts that can be retrieved and integrated into novel combinations. The process of acquiring new cultural knowledge can also increase the psychological readiness to recruit and seek out ideas from unfamiliar sources to use as inputs in the creative process, thereby allowing continued exposure to a wide range of new ideas, norms, and practices (Chiu & Hong, 2005; Leung & Chiu, in press; Leung et al., 2008; Maddux & Galinsky, 2009).

Some early findings have provided indirect evidence for the potential of multicultural experience to facilitate creativity. For example, at the individual level, research has documented that a high proportion of prominent creators and leaders are first- or second-generation immigrants (Goertzel, Goertzel, & Goertzel, 1978). Bilingualism research has further shown that compared to monolinguals, bilinguals are more creative and are more successful in a variety of cognitive tasks (Bialystok, 2001). At the group level, culturally heterogeneous groups have sometimes been found to be more creative and more flexible and tolerant of ambiguous information than culturally homogeneous groups. Culturally heterogeneous groups also tend to reach higher-quality decisions (e.g., Elron, 1997; McLeod, Lobel, & Cox, 1996; Watson, Kumar, & Michaelsen, 1993; also see Nemeth & Kwan, 1987). Finally, at the societal level, research has shown that civilizations are more likely to prosper after they open themselves to the foreign influences which ensue from immigration (Simonton, 1997).

More recent research has provided direct support for the hypothe-sized relationship. For example, at the individual level, there is evidence that time spent living abroad is positively correlated with creativity and that temporarily priming foreign living experiences can further enhance creative tendencies for individuals who have previously lived abroad. These relationships are mediated by the degree to which individuals have adapted to different cultures (Maddux & Galinsky, 2009), pro-viding support for the suggestion that it is the acquisition of cultural knowledge that lies at the heart of the creative benefits associated with multicultural exposure. Similarly, among European American univer-sity students, those who have had more experiences with other cultures have a greater tendency to sample ideas from other cultures and inte-grate them in a creative conceptual expansion task (Leung & Chiu, in press). Furthermore, direct evidence has also been found for the causal effect of multicultural exposure on creativity. In one study (Leung & Chiu, in press), relative to European Americans who were exposed to a monocultural slideshow of American or Chinese culture, those who were exposed to a multicultural slideshow of American and Chinese cul-tures showed increased creative performance on tasks completed both immediately after exposure and almost a week later (see Figure 6.2). Most recent research has further demonstrated the creative utility of multicultural experiences at both the dyadic and group levels of analy-ses (Tadmor et al., 2009; Cheng, Mor, & Morris, 2009). Importantly, all the studies reviewed in this section relied on creativity tasks that do not require culturally specific knowledge, thereby indicating that the creative benefits related to multicultural experiences are not limited to the cultural domain.

Notably, it appears that in order for the creative benefits of mul-ticultural experiences to materialize it is necessary that the difference between cultural knowledge networks be salient. Indeed, as illustrated in Leung and Chiu's research (in press), exposing European Americans to only Chinese culture did not result in increased creativity. Only simultaneous exposure to both Chinese and American culture yielded creative benefits. As shown in Figure 6.2, it is when cultural networks are mentally placed side by side that individuals are able to perceive the conceptual contrast between the ideas in each network and are able to utilize their increased complexity to integrate or synthesize the seemingly incompatible ideas from different cultural sources. Thus, it seems that it is not enough to have access to competing cultural infor-mation; rather it is how the information is processed in the mind of individuals that is crucial for the actualization of the creative benefits

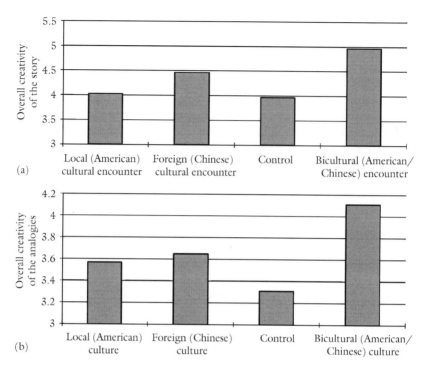

Figure 6.2 Creative performance following exposure to American culture only, Chinese culture only, and Chinese and American cultures simultaneously. The participants were European Americans, and the creativity task was (a) rewriting the Cinderella story for children in Turkey immediately following the exposure and (b) constructing creative analogies of time 4–7 days after the exposure. Data from Leung & Chiu (in press).

of multicultural experiences (Leung & Chiu, in press; Tadmor et al., 2009).

Intercultural Competence In multicultural communications, multicultural knowledge allows individuals to discover, adjust, and integrate new attitudes and values from foreign cultures (Casmir, 1992). As such, knowledge of other cultures may help to establish common ground in intercultural interactions, such as during international business negotiations or management of culturally heterogeneous work teams (e.g., Earley & Ang, 2003; Earley & Gibson, 2002; Tadmor, 2006). Specifically, given that each culture may prescribe different kinds of behaviors and norms that are deemed acceptable, multiculturals' ability to modify their thoughts and behaviors to suit the cultural context should allow them to facilitate smoother interactions with members of each culture (Triandis, 1975).

In contrast, individuals who lack multicultural knowledge, given that they can only rely on a single cultural lens to construe reality, are likely to run into difficulties when interacting with members of new cultures. Consistent with this idea, Chinese Americans, who are familiar with both Chinese and American culture, are likely to know that Americans are more motivated by gains than are Chinese. Therefore, when Chinese Americans tried to persuade a Chinese or an American to purchase an insurance policy, they were found to use more gain-focused arguments for an American than for a Chinese target. American participants' choice of persuasive messages, however, was not affected by the target's ethnic identity (see Chiu & Hong, 2005).

In addition, accurate knowledge of another culture is linked to better intercultural interaction quality. For example, Mainland Chinese university students in Hong Kong who have more accurate knowledge of the values of their host culture have more satisfactory interactions with the local students and the university staff than students who have less accurate knowledge (Li & Hong, 2001). In contrast, lack of multicultural knowledge may lead to misperception, misinterpretation, and even fear of interacting with members of foreign cultures (Cushner & Brislin, 1996).

Importantly, as we suggested in the case of creativity, multiculturals' cultural sensitivity may also be the result of their greater levels of integrative complexity, which provide them not only with a more nuanced understanding of intercultural variation but also with an awareness that there are many viable and legitimate constructions of reality (Tadmor & Tetlock, 2006; also see Bennett, 2004).

In summary, there is considerable evidence that as high-quality and voluntary multicultural experiences accumulate, individuals broaden their multicultural knowledge, which in turn facilitates integrative complexity, creative expansion, and intercultural competence. Nevertheless, multicultural individuals may choose not to recruit multicultural knowledge as behavioral guides. We propose that one determinant of multicultural knowledge application is how equally identified individuals are with their multiple cultural networks. In the next section, we review evidence that suggests that the more an individual identifies with more than one culture, the more likely the individual will access and apply these cultural networks, and the more likely the potential benefits of multiculturalism should come to fruition.

Multicultural Self: Patterns of Cultural Identification

When individuals are exposed to and acquire a second cultural tradition (or more), they do not just retrieve their knowledge of the pertinent cultures. Rather issues of cultural identification (i.e., defining the self with reference to these cultural traditions) come to the fore (Hong, Roisman, & Chen, 2006; Sussman, 2000). As individuals turn their knowledge traditions into objects of reflection, these knowledge networks are cognitively juxtaposed and their significance with reference to prior cultural experiences and current intercultural relations is evaluated.

Although early research on acculturation was based on the assumption that changes in cultural identity take place along a single continuum that moves from one cultural identity (i.e., culture of origin) to the other (i.e., the host culture's identity), more recent research has emphasized the multidimensionality of cultural selves and has conceptualized home and host cultural identities as orthogonal domains. Consequently, individuals are seen as capable of having more than one cultural identity, each of which can independently vary in strength (Berry, 1997; LaFromboise et al., 1993; Ryder, Alden, & Paulhus, 2000; also see Crisp & Hewstone, 2007; Hong et al., 2006; Roccas & Brewer, 2002).

Until recently, the factors that affect intrapsychic attitudes toward acculturation as well as the role played by second-culture exposure in shaping cognitive, affective, and motivational processes has received little attention (Benet-Martínez, Leu, Lee, & Morris, 2002). In their Acculturation Complexity Model, Tadmor & Tetlock (2006) have attempted to address these gaps by modeling the impact of second-culture exposure on acculturation choice and on individual cognition and coping skills. Specifically, the model delineates: (a) the factors that affect individuals' adoption and achievement of specific acculturation strategies, and (b) the differential effects that second-culture exposure can have on the integrative complexity of social cognitive functioning.

Development of Multicultural Identities

According to the Acculturation Complexity Model (Tadmor & Tetlock, 2006), as individuals who are exposed to a second culture become aware of the different and potentially conflicting cultural traditions which exist in each cultural milieu, internal and external *accountability* pressures will affect whether individuals will affiliate or distance themselves from the stakeholding cultures, where accountability refers to the need to justify one's thoughts and actions to significant others in accord with shared norms. This pressure to account for behavior is rooted in people's fundamental need for social approval, whether as an end in itself, as a way to bolster their self-worth, or as a way to procure power over scarce resources (Tetlock, 2002). How people respond to accountability demands will depend, however, on the types of accountability pressure they experience.

Accountability pressures can come from inside or outside the individual. External accountability refers to the matrix of all interpersonal relationships in which an individual is engaged and to which s/he feels s/he must answer for particular attitudes and behaviors. However, the existence of an external audience is not necessary for the creation of accountability pressures. People often internalize the voices of those with whom they feel strong affinity (Ashforth, Kreiner, & Fugate, 2000). This type of audience internalization makes it difficult to escape evaluative scrutiny (Tetlock, 2002). In addition, the audience to whom the individual is accountable need not be uniform. It can represent a single unified set of values or a complex, even flatly contradictory set of values (Tetlock, 2002). Within the cultural context, a single audience refers to one composed of perspectives with a unified cultural orientation (e.g., an exclusively Chinese audience valuing harmony), whereas a mixed audience refers to one composed of at least two distinct cultural perspectives (e.g., a combination of Chinese and Americans, with the former valuing harmony and the latter debate).

Ultimately, if the individual becomes accountable to a single audience, motivated by the desire to align multicultural identities with prior experiences and current goals and affordances, s/he will foster allegiance primarily with a single identity. In contrast, if a person becomes accountable to a mixed audience composed of both his/her old and new cultural groups, a dual-identity pattern will be sought.

The model further stipulates that people who seek dual identification will experience more severe cultural dissonance during acculturation than those who seek single identification. This happens because the mixed accountability pressures facing such individuals require them to justify their conduct to representative members of both cultural groups simultaneously. By contrast, individuals who seek single identification and who are held accountable to a single cultural constituency experience less conflict (Tadmor, 2006; Tetlock, 1992; also see Baumeister, 1986). Drawing on cognitive consistency theories (Roccas & Brewer, 2002; Tetlock, 1986), the model suggests that the more severe the cultural conflict, the greater the need to resort to more effortful, integratively complex solutions. Repeated exposure to cultural conflicts will lead to the development of increasingly automatic coping responses, either simple (for single identifiers) or complex (for dual identifiers). Finally, it is suggested that it is through the resolution of multiple instances of dissonance that acculturation takes place and sustained identity shifts ensue. Based on how multicultural identities are structurally represented—dual or single identification—different likelihoods of accessing each cultural knowledge network will result.

Likelihood of Accessing Multicultural Knowledge

As previously suggested, multicultural individuals' responses to cultural cues involve more than automatic cognitive processes. Such individuals do not automatically shift cultural frames in response to situational cues, but rather fashion their reactions based on their motives to embrace or disavow particular cultural identities (Zou, Morris, & Benet-Martínez, 2008). Indeed, there is evidence that the effects of cultural frame-switching are partially mediated by the activation of cultural identities—a cultural icon activates its attendant cultural identity, which in turn leads to culturally congruent responses (Verkuyten & Pouliasi, 2006; also see Briley & Wyer, 2002). Research further shows that when identification with a culture is strong, perceptions of the social world are filtered through the lens of that culture and individuals shift their responses to match cultural prototypes (assimilative responses; No et al., 2008; Zou et al., 2008). In contrast, when individuals disidentify with a culture, they demonstrate a contrast effect, shifting their responses away from the cued culture and responding in accordance to the norms of their preferred cultural identity (Zou et al., 2008).

Based on this conceptualization, we contend that a person's identification pattern may regulate accessibility to cultural knowledge. The more strongly an individual identifies with a *single* culture, the more likely this individual would be motivated to habitually access and rigidly apply only its attendant knowledge network (Tadmor, 2006; cf., Abelson, 1959). In support of this suggestion, it has been shown that among people who have been exposed to two cultures, those who identify strongly with Culture A (rather than with Culture B) tend to more strongly endorse values that are prototypical features of Culture A (Wan et al., 2007a). Studies have also shown that when individuals view their culture as conflicting rather than compatible, they exhibit a contrast effect (Benet-Martínez et al., 2002). In contrast, when individuals are equally identified with both cultures, both cultural knowledge networks are likely to become more salient and chronically accessible than when identification patterns are unequal. Not only are dual identifiers likely to view multicultural knowledge as relevant self-concepts and therefore more likely to access it (Markus, 1977), but with their greater levels of integrative complexity, they can readily appreciate cultural differences and simultaneously access both cultural knowledge networks, despite their apparent dissimilarities and contradictions (Tadmor and Tetlock, 2006).

Implications for Cultural Competence

Given dual identifiers' more chronic access to multicultural knowledge, they are likely to exhibit greater cultural competence across domains than single identifiers. Empirical research has provided support for this suggestion. For example, Tadmor, Tetlock et al. (2009) find in samples of both Israelis living in the United States and Asian Americans that dual identifiers expressed more integratively complex thoughts about both culture- and work-related topics than did single identifiers. Providing support for the causal effect of dual identification, Tadmor, Tetlock et al. (2009) further find that Asian Americans primed with dual identification show a preference for a more complex thinking style than do those primed with a single identification. In addition, Tadmor, Tetlock et al. (2009) find that dual identifiers are more creative than single identifiers. Similarly, Cheng et al. (2009) find that greater levels of perceived compatibility between two identities (i.e., Asian and American; female and engineer) predict higher levels of creative performance. Finally, a plethora of research has demonstrated the positive effects of dual identification for intercultural competence and greater tolerance toward outgroup members (e.g., Brewer & Pierce, 2005; Crisp & Hewstone, 2007; Dovidio, Gartner, & Validzic, 1998; Hornsey & Hogg, 2000; Roccas & Brewer, 2002).

These findings suggest that mere exposure to foreign cultures is insufficient to actualize the potential cognitive benefits of multiculturalism. Rather what is crucial is how individuals internally represent the different cultures. Indeed, past research has found large variations in how people manage and experience dual cultural identities (e.g., Benet-Martínez et al., 2002, LaFromboise et al., 1993; Phinney & Devich-Navarro, 1997; Tsai, Ying, & Lee, 2000). One variation—the extent of lopsided identification with one culture versus balanced identification with both cultures—appears to be directly related to degree of cultural competence achieved.

In this section we propose that although cultural knowledge gained from multicultural experiences may provide individuals with a wider array of intellectual resources to choose from, a person's accountability matrix and the resulting cultural identification pattern will determine whether multiple cultural networks are likely to be simultaneously accessible. In the remaining sections, we explore the factors that affect people's perceived accountability pressures and what type of interventions can be used to increase the probability of dual identification.

Factors Affecting the Management of Multicultural Identities

Researchers have paid considerable attention to the relation between demographics, personality, and situational characteristics and the preferences for the different patterns of multicultural identities (Berry, 1997; Bourhis, Moïse, Perreault, & Senécal, 1997; Padilla & Perez, 2003; Roccas & Brewer, 2002). From our perspective, what these characteristics have in common is that they all affect the type of accountability pressure a person will feel. Indeed, according to social cognition researchers (e.g., Fiske, 1993), people's cognitive processes stem from their pragmatic goals, which themselves derive from multiple sources, including internal person-related variables and external situational constraints. Hence we contend that the cognitive organization of cultures and affiliation decisions will depend in part on multicultural individuals' *internal* motivational concerns and in part on the *external* sociopolitical determinants of these individuals' accountability to the stakeholding cultures.

Internal Factors

When the dominant motivational concerns call for adherence to conventional norms in one's own culture, individuals, independent of their amount of multicultural experiences, tend to resist ideas from foreign cultures. Three motivational factors that have been shown to promote cultural conformity are *need for cognitive closure*, *existential terror*, and *essentialization of race*.

The need for cognitive closure (NFCC), or the need for firm answers, may limit people's willingness to affiliate with multiple cultures. Indeed, research has shown that because cultural conventions provide definite answers with high consensual validity and individuals with high NFCC prefer firm answers and dislike ambiguity, these individuals are particularly motivated to follow cultural conventions (Chao, Zhang, & Chiu, in press; Chiu, Morris, Hong, & Menon, 2000; Fu et al., 2007). By contrast, low-NFCC individuals do not reliably prefer one set of cultural norms to the other. If anything, they display a slight tendency to endorse counter-normative responses (Fu et al., 2007). Research further shows that high- (vs. low-) NFCC immigrants adhere more strongly to a single cultural identification. Because the specific reference group at entry offers clear direction on how to behave, think and feel, it provides high-NFCC individuals with the certainty they desire. Which culture high-NFCC individuals choose to identify with and stay accountable to would depend on whether the social support they experience during the initial stay in a new culture comes mainly from their culture of origin or from their new culture (Kosic, Kruglanski, Pierro, & Mannetti, 2004). Finally, high- (vs. low-) NFCC American Chinese bicultural individuals are less susceptible to situational cueing of culture-characteristic judgments; instead, contrast effects have been observed (Fu et al., 2007).

These findings resonate with the dispositional version of the Acculturation Complexity Model (Tadmor & Tetlock, 2006; Tadmor, Tetlock et al., 2009), which hypothesizes that those disposed to have more complex thinking styles are more likely to develop a dual-identification pattern, because these individuals' chronic tolerance for dissonance (Crockett, 1965) allows them to internalize contradictory aspects of both cultures. Taken together, these results suggest that if high-NFCC individuals who adhere strongly to a single cultural tradition and habitually access knowledge from this tradition only, they (compared to low-NFCC individuals) should exhibit lower levels of cultural competence. In support of this hypothesis, Leung and Chiu (in press) show that the association between multicultural experiences and willingness to recruit ideas from unfamiliar cultures is significantly attenuated when individuals are placed under conditions that elicit high NFCC (see Figure 6.2).

A second motivational factor is mortality salience. According to the Terror Management Theory (TMT; Greenberg, Solomon, & Pzszczynski, 1997), when individuals are reminded of their eventual finitude, they will experience existential terror. To cope with it, they will increase their adherence to cultural conventions and, through this strategy, obtain a sense of symbolic immortality—the body may perish after death, but the culture one belongs to will continue to propagate (Solomon, Greenberg, Schimel, Arndt, & Pzszczynski, 2004). Moreover, when such a cultural defense mindset is activated, it will motivate a search for positive distinctiveness of the threatened culture and a desire to defend the viability of the culture against erosive effects of the foreign culture (Chiu, 2007). Research has provided ample evidence for this suggestion, showing that increasing mortality salience in the situation results in stronger identification with the threatened culture (Kashima, Halloran, Yuki, & Kashima, 2004), more favorable responses to people who support their cultural worldview and less favorable responses to people who threaten it (Greenberg et al., 1990), and that ingroup threat leads to lower social identity complexity (Roccas & Brewer, 2002; see also Brewer, this volume).

Once again, given that multicultural individuals who are confronted with mortality threat are more likely to identify with and adhere to a single cultural tradition, we would expect them to also show limited cultural competence relative to individuals who do not receive such threats. Indeed, research has shown that mortality salience increases affective aversion toward creative activities (Arndt, Greenberg, Solomon, & Pzszczynski, 1999), and that existential terror moderated the positive association between multicultural experiences and receptiveness to ideas from foreign cultures (Leung & Chiu, in press).

Finally, Hong and her colleagues (Chao, Chen, Roisman, & Hong, 2007; Hong, Chao, & No, in press; No et al., 2008) proposed that biculturals' beliefs about race—whether race is an essentialist entity (reflecting biological essence, is unalterable, and indicative of abilities and traits) or a socially constructed, dynamic construct—predict the extent to which they can successfully achieve psychological adaptation to both cultures. The researchers contend that an essentialist race belief would lower the perceived permeability between racial group boundaries. Therefore, ethnic minorities holding an essentialist race theory would have a harder time integrating experiences with both their ethnic and host cultures.

Consistent with this idea, Chao et al. (2007) find that Chinese Americans with stronger endorsement of an essentialist race theory exhibited higher skin conductance reactivity when talking about their own bicultural experiences, suggesting that an essentialist race theory is associated with more effortful defense. No et al. (2008) further find that when presented with Korean culture primes, Korean American participants responded by assimilating their responses toward the primes, irrespective of their lay race beliefs. However, when presented with American culture primes, theory of race moderated participants' responses: those who endorsed the social constructionist race theory assimilated toward the primes, whereas those who strongly endorsed essentialist beliefs did not show such assimilation. Thus it appears that an essentialist race belief also leads to greater reliance on a single cultural network.

External Factors

Importantly, even when individuals are internally motivated to integrate multiple identities, external factors may limit the identification options available to them. Two obvious factors that may affect the propensity to develop dual identification are *friendship ties* and *acculturation orientations* of the host community.

First, accountability pressures are likely to depend to a large extent on the nature of people's friendship and acquaintance patterns and on the psychological functions that these relationships serve (Bochner, 1982; Tadmor & Tetlock, 2006). For example, Novakovic (1977) showed that the ethnicity of one's closest friends predicts acculturation patterns of Yugoslavian children living in Australia. Over time, participants with friends from both cultures develop greater dual identification than children with friends from only one cultural group. Similarly, Feldman and Rosenthal (1990) found that Chinese high-schoolers living in Australia tend to become more unitarily identified with the local Australian culture than Chinese high-schoolers living in the United States. They explain that because in Australia the Chinese population is small, Chinese children have no choice but to create new friendships with Australians, and, consequently, develop greater levels of identification with Australian culture. In contrast, the Chinese population in the United States is relatively vast, and therefore the children are not pressured to give up their culture of origin. Hence, they could maintain friendships with both cultural groups and identify with both.

Second, immigrants' adoption of a particular multicultural identity negotiation strategy is further influenced by the acculturation preferences of the host community (e.g., Berry, 1997; Bourhis et al., 1997; Montreuil & Bourhis, 2001). For example, if mainstream cultural members endorse an integration orientation, accepting the rights of immigrants to adopt mainstream culture while simultaneously retaining their heritage cultural identity, immigrants are more likely to develop a dual identification pattern than if mainstream cultural members endorse an assimilation, segregation, or exclusionist orientation.

In summary, it appears that successful management of multicultural identities depends on both internal and external factors. Given that there are important benefits linked to accessing and applying multicultural knowledge, the next section details specific policy initiatives that will facilitate the development of equal identification and the integration of multicultural knowledge.

Social Intervention and Policy Implications

We have presented evidence for the potential benefits of multicultural knowledge and multicultural identification. The conclusions we reach in the present review have implications on policies and programming of public attitudes directed toward promoting multicultural integration in the society (Berry, 1999). We argue that future policy decisions should facilitate people's chances of gaining extended multicultural experiences while discouraging factionalism and separatism within societies. These policies should be most effective if they are carried out in social milieux that encourage tolerance, social-political and economic equality, and intermingling among individuals of diverse cultural backgrounds—qualities that many multicultural societies struggle to possess still today (Esses, Wagner, Wolf, Preiser, & Wilbur, 2006; Zick, Pettigrew, & Wagner, 2008). In the remainder of this section we review existing ideologies regarding multiculturalism and discuss their implications on promoting multicultural identification and maximizing access to multicultural knowledge.

Multiculturalism and immigration are inextricably linked; social policies intended to promote multicultural knowledge and experiences are tied to immigration policy (Deaux, 2008). Social policies fostering multicultural integration may target individuals, members of the dominant group, and the society at large. Policies targeting individuals may have greater chances of success if they encourage the development of accountability to multiple cultural audiences. Examples of such policies include mixed schooling for fostering cross-cultural friendship networks (Mendoza-Denton & Page-Gould, 2008; Turner & Brown, 2008).

Three multiculturalism ideologies have shaped the debates surrounding immigration-related social policies: assimilation, colorblind, and multiculturalism ideologies. The assimilation ideology mandates that immigrants abandon their previous language and cultural distinctiveness for the host-country language and culture (Bourhis et al., 1997). Extreme forms of assimilation ideology argue that national identification with the host country is incompatible with multicultural identification (Verkuyten, 2009), and immigrants are expected to relinquish their heritage identity and knowledge entirely. The colorblind ideology advocates the irrelevance of race (or country of origin) to individual outcomes or treatment by others in the host country (Knowles, Lowery, Hogan, & Chow, 2009). Lastly, the multiculturalism (pluralism) ideology supports tolerance for diverse cultures and accepts equal participation from all groups (Liu, 2007).

While assimilation and colorblind policies may sometimes help reduce conflict and increase tolerance, they may run the risk of wiping out the advantages that multiculturalism can confer. This is because the goal of assimilation policies is to eliminate all other cultural influences other than the national culture of the host country, and the goal of colorblind policies is to downplay both negative and positive influences of race and culture on individual performance and outcomes (Verkuyten, 2006; Verkuyten, this volume). In contrast, multicultural policies that promote genuine acceptance of members of immigrant backgrounds are more likely to foster balanced identifications with multicultural cultures and the achievement of a cohesive liberal democracy.

Yet, existing evidence indicates that in many societies, promoting multiculturalism is an uphill battle. For multiculturalism policies to succeed, immigrant/minority members and dominant/host members of the society must be equally invested in these policies (Berry, 2006). Nonetheless, rallying society-wide support for these policies could be challenging. Findings in the United States show that Americans, whether Black, Asian, or White, predominantly equate Americanness with being White (Devos & Banaji, 2005).

Nonetheless, there are reasons to remain hopeful. Despite the tension between New Zealand Maori (indigenous people of New Zealand) and Pakeha (people of European descent in New Zealand) over the distribution of economic resources (Sibley, Liu, Duckitt, & Khan, 2008), the two groups have had a long-standing legal and social agreement that both groups contribute equally to the national culture and identity (Sibley & Liu, 2004). When Maori and Pakeha were tested for implicit preferences for their own group, no strong biases emerged (Sibley & Liu, 2007), suggesting that both groups support a bicultural national partnership for New Zealand, at least at an implicit level.

In summary, future policies need to address not only the means to increase multicultural civic engagement and participation from all groups, but also address the deeper roots of cultural insecurity among the host majority, which could lead to divisiveness, prejudice, and discrimination against immigrants. Efforts to implement such changes can be constructively directed to offering effective training programs and social interventions that (a) facilitate multicultural learning, (b) reduce cultural and racial essentialism, and create open, safe environments where identity threats are minimized. Such interventions would hopefully promote a society where all individuals, majority and minority alike, would benefit from the meeting of multiple cultures.

Conclusion

In an increasingly interdependent world, understanding the interplay of multiculturalism and social cognitive functioning has become critical. In this chapter, we have proposed two factors that influence multicultural identity negotiation. The first factor focuses on the multicultural mind that grows out of multicultural experiences. The second factor deals with the multicultural self and the inclinations to affiliate with or distance oneself from the stakeholding cultures. We have suggested that although greater levels of multicultural knowledge can potentially yield important psychological benefits, including enhanced integrative complexity, creativity, and intercultural competence, the actualization of these potentials depends in part on how individuals resolve their identity concerns. Specifically, we propose that multicultural individuals who balance their identifications with multiple cultures are inclined to habitually access the cultures' attendant knowledge networks, and are therefore likely to benefit from multicultural experiences. On the contrary, having preclosed identification with a single culture because of internal motivational factors or external sociopolitical pressures will thwart these advantages, and even lead to attitudinal rigidity, extremism, and intolerance. Although minority groups are particularly likely to encounter these potential problems, mainstream cultural members will also be affected, particularly when they feel that the "purity" of their cultural group is contaminated by other cultures (Chiu, 2007). We close by inviting researchers and practitioners to work together to promote a constructive multicultural social agenda to empower the individual and to benefit the society at large.

References

Abelson, R. P. (1959). Modes of resolution of belief dilemmas. *Journal of Conflict Resolution, 3*(4): 343–352.

Amabile, T. M. (1996). *Creativity in context.* Boulder, CO: Westview Press.

Arndt, J., Greenberg, J., Solomon, S., Pzszczynski, T., & Schimel, J. (1999). Creativity and terror management: Evidence that creative activity increases guilt and social projection following mortality salience. *Journal of Personality and Social Psychology, 77,* 19–32.

Ashforth, B. E., Kreiner, G. E., & Fugate, M. (2000). All in a day's work: Boundaries and micro role transitions. *Academy of Management Review, 25,* 472–491.

Au, E., Wan, W., & Chiu, C.-y. (in press). The social and cultural context of cognition: A knowledge perspective. In S. Kreitler & K. A. Renninger (Eds.), *Cognition and motivation: Forging an interdisciplinary perspective.* Cambridge, UK: Cambridge University Press.

Baumeister, R. F. (1986). *Identity: Cultural change and the struggle for self.* Oxford, UK: Oxford University Press.

Benet-Martínez, V., Lee, F., & Leu, J. (2006). Biculturalism and cognitive complexity: Expertise in cultural representations. *Journal of Cross-Cultural Psychology, 37,* 386–407.

Benet-Martínez, V., Leu, J., Lee, F., & Morris, M. W. (2002). Negotiating biculturalism—cultural frame switching in biculturals with oppositional versus compatible cultural identities. *Journal of Cross-Cultural Psychology, 33,* 492–516.

Bennett, M. J. (2004). Becoming interculturally competent. In J. Wurjzel (Ed.), *Toward multiculturalism: A reader in multicultural education* (pp. 62–77). Newton, MA: Intercultural Resource Corporation.

Berry, J. W. (1997). Immigration, acculturation, and adaptation. *Applied Psychology: An International Review, 46,* 5–68.

Berry, J. W. (1999). Intercultural relations in plural societies. *Canadian Psychology/Psychologie canadienne, 40,* 12–21.

Berry, J. W. (2006). Mutual attitudes among immigrants and ethnocultural groups in Canada. *International Journal of Intercultural Relations, 30,* 719–734.

Bialystok, E. (2001). *Bilingualism in development: Language, literacy, and cognition.* New York: Cambridge University Press.

Bochner, S. (1982). The social psychology of cross-cultural relations. In S. Bochner (Ed.), *Cultures in contact: Studies in cross-cultural interaction* (pp. 5–44). Oxford, UK: Pergamon Press.

Bourhis, R. Y., Moïse, L. C., Perreault, S., & Senécal, S. (1997). Towards an interactive acculturation model: A social psychological approach. *International Journal of Psychology, 32,* 369–386.

Brett, J. M., & Okumura, T. (1998). Inter- and intracultural negotiations: U.S. and Japanese negotiators. *Academy of Management Journal, 41,* 495–510.

Brewer, M. B., & Pierce, K. P. (2005). Social identity complexity and outgroup tolerance. *Personality and Social Psychology Bulletin, 31,* 428–437.

Briley, D. A., & Wyer, R. S. (2002). The effect of group membership salience on the avoidance of negative outcomes: Implications for social and consumer decisions. *Journal of Consumer Research, 29,* 400–415.

Casmir, F. L. (1992). Third-culture building: A paradigm shift for international and intercultural communication. *Communication Yearbook, 16,* 407–428.

Chao, M., Chen, J., Roisman, G., & Hong, Y. (2007). Essentializing race: Implications for bicultural individuals' cognition and physiological reactivity. *Psychological Science, 18,* 341–348.

Chao, M. M., Zhang, Z.-X., & Chiu, C.-y. (in press). Adherence to perceived norms across cultural boundaries: The role of need for cognitive closure and ingroup identification. *Group Processes and Intergroup Relations*,.

Cheng, C.-y., Mor, S., & Morris, M. W. (2009). *Culture in mind(s) of creative teams: Multicultural exposure and cultural habits as catalysts for team creativity*. Manuscript in preparation.

Cheng, C.-y., Sanchez-Burks, J., & Lee, F. (2008). Connecting the dots within: Creative performance and identity integration. *Psychological Science*, *1*, 1178–1184.

Chiao, J. Y., Harada, T., Komeda, H., Li, Z., Mano, Y., Saito, D., Parrish, T. B., Sadato, N., & Iidaka, T.(in press). Dynamic cultural influences on neural representations of the self. *Journal of Cognitive Neuroscience*.

Chiu, C.-y. (2007). Managing cultures in a multicultural world: A social cognitive perspective. *Journal of Psychology in Chinese Societies*, *8*, 101–120.

Chiu, C.-y., & Cheng, S. Y. Y. (2007). Toward a social psychology of culture and globalization: Some social cognitive consequences of activating two cultures simultaneously. *Social and Personality Psychology Compass*, *1*, 84–100.

Chiu, C.-y., & Hong, Y.-y (2005). Cultural competence: Dynamic processes. In A. Elliot & C. S. Dweck (Eds.), *Handbook of motivation and competence* (pp. 489–505). New York: Guilford Press.

Chiu, C.-y., & Hong, Y. (2006). *Social psychology of culture*. New York: Psychology Press.

Chiu, C.-y., & Hong, Y.-y (2007). Cultural processes: Basic principles. In E. T. Higgins & A. E. Kruglanski (Eds.), *Social psychology: Handbook of basic principles* (pp. 785–809). New York: Guilford Press.

Chiu, C.-y., Mallorie, L., Keh, H.-T., & Law, W. (2009). Perceptions of culture in multicultural space: Joint presentation of images from two cultures increases ingroup attribution of culture-typical characteristics. *Journal of Cross-Cultural Psychology*, *40*, 282–300.

Chiu, C.-y., Morris, M. W., Hong, Y. Y., & Menon, T. (2000). Motivated cultural cognition: The impact of implicit cultural theories on dispositional attribution varies as a function of need for closure. *Journal of Personality and Social Psychology*, *78*, 247–259.

Crisp, R. J., & Hewstone, M. (2007). Multiple social categorization. In M. P. Zanna (Ed.), *Advances in Experimental Social Psychology* (vol. 39, pp. 163–254). San Diego, CA: Academic Press.

Crockett, W. H. (1965). Cognitive complexity and impression formation. In B. A. Maher (Ed.), *Progress in experimental personality research* (pp. 47–90). New York: Academic Press.

Cushner, K., & Brislin, R. W. (1996). *Intercultural interactions: A practical guide*. (2nd ed.). Thousand Oaks, CA: Sage.

Deaux, K. (2008). To be an American: Immigration, hyphenation, and incorporation. *Journal of Social Issues*, *64*, 925–943.

Devos, T., & Banaji, M. R. (2005). American = White? *Journal of Personality and Social Psychology, 88,* 447–466.

DiMaggio, D. (1997). Culture cognition. *Annual Review of Sociology, 23,* 263–287.

Dovidio, J. F., Gartner, S. L., & Validzic, A. (1998). Intergroup bias: Status, differentiation, and a common ingroup identity. *Journal of Personality and Social Psychology, 75,* 109–120.

Earley, P. C., & Ang, S. (2003). *Cultural intelligence: Individual interactions across cultures.* Stanford, CA: Stanford University Press.

Earley, P. C., & Gibson, C. B. (2002). *Multinational work teams: A new perspective.* Mahwah, NJ: Erlbaum.

Elron, E. (1997). Top management teams within multinational corporations: effects of cultural heterogeneity. *Leadership Quarterly, 8,* 393–412.

Esses, V., Wagner, U., Wolf, C., Preiser, M., & Wilbur, C. J. (2006). Perceptions of national identity and attitudes toward immigrants and immigration in Canada and Germany. *International Journal of Intercultural Relations, 30,* 653–669.

Feldman, S. S., & Rosenthal, D. A. (1990). The acculturation of autonomy expectations in Chinese high schoolers residing in two western nations. *International Journal of Psychology, 25,* 259–281.

Fiske, S. T. (1993). Social cognition and social perception. In M. R. Rosenzweig & L. W. Porter (Eds.), *Annual review of psychology* (pp. 155–194). Palo Alto, CA: Annual Reviews.

Fu, J. H. Y., Morris, M. W., Lee, S. L., Chao, M., Chiu, C-y., & Hong, Y. (2007). Epistemic motives and cultural conformity: Need for closure, culture, and context as determinants of conflict judgments. *Journal of Personality and Social Psychology, 92*(2): 191–207.

Gaertner, S., Dovidio, J., Nier, J., Ward, C., & Banker, B. (1999). Across cultural divides: The value of a superordinate identity. In D. Prentice & D. Miller (Eds.), *Cultural divides: Understanding and overcoming group conflict.* New York: Russell Sage Foundation.

Goertzel, M. G., Goertzel, V., & Goertzel, T. G. (1978). *300 eminent personalities: A psychosocial analysis of the famous.* San Francisco: Jossey-Bass.

Greenberg, J., Pzszczynski, T., Solomon, S., Resenblatt, A., Veeded, M., & Kirkland, S. (1990). Evidence of terror management theory II: The effects of mortality salience on reactions to those who threaten or bolster the cultural worldview. *Journal of Personality and Social Psychology, 58,* 308–318.

Greenberg, J., Solomon, S., & Pzszczynski, T. (1997). Terror management theory of self-esteem and cultural worldviews: Empirical assessments and conceptual refinements. In M. P. Zanna (Ed.), *Advances in experimental social psychology* (vol. 29, pp. 61–139). New York: Academic Press.

Hampton, J. A. (1997). Emergent attributes in combined concepts. In T. B. Ward, S. M. Smith, & J. Vaid (Eds.), *Creative thought: An investigation of conceptual structures and processes* (pp. 83–110). Washington, DC: American Psychological Association.

Hong, Y., Benet-Martínez, V., Chiu, C., & Morris, M. W. (2003). Boundaries of cultural influence: Construct activation as a mechanism for cultural differences in social perception. *Journal of Cross-Cultural Psychology, 34,* 453–464.

Hong, Y., Chao, M., & No, S.(in press). Dynamic interracial/intercultural processes: The role of lay theories of race. *Journal of Personality.*

Hong, Y., Chiu, C., & Kung, T. M. (1997). Bringing culture out in front: Effects of cultural meaning system activation on social cognition. In K. Leung, Y. Kashima, U. Kim, & S. Yamaguchi (Eds.), *Progress in Asian social psychology* (vol. 1, pp. 135–146). Singapore: Wiley.

Hong, Y., Morris, M. W., Chiu, C., & Benet-Martínez, V. (2000). Multicultural minds: A dynamic constructivist approach to culture and cognition. *American Psychologist, 55,* 709–720.

Hong, Y., Roisman, G. I., & Chen, J. (2006). A model of cultural attachment: A new approach for studying bicultural experience. In M. H. Bornstein & L. R. Cote (Eds.), *Acculturation and parent–child relationships: Measurement and development* (pp. 135–170). Mahwah, NJ: Erlbaum.

Hong, Y., Wan, C., No, S., & Chiu, C. (2007). Multicultural identities. In S. Kitayama & D. Cohen (Eds.), *Handbook of cultural psychology.* New York: Guilford Press.

Hornsey, M. J., & Hogg, M. A. (2000). Subgroup relations: A comparison of mutual intergroup differentiation and common ingroup identity models of prejudice reduction. *Personality and Social Psychology Bulletin, 26,* 242–256.

Kashima, E. S., Halloran, M., Yuki, M., & Kashima, Y. (2004). The effects of personal and collective mortality salience on individualism: Comparing Australians and Japanese with higher and lower self-esteem. *Journal of Experimental Social Psychology, 40,* 384–392.

Knowles, E. D., Lowery, B. S., Hogan, C. M., & Chow, R. M. (2009). On the malleability of ideology: Motivated construals of color blindness. *Journal of Personality and Social Psychology, 96,* 857–869.

Kosic, A., Kruglanski, A. W., Pierro, A., & Mannetti, L. (2004). The social cognitions of immigrants' acculturation: Effects of the need for closure and reference group at entry. *Journal of Personality and Social Psychology, 86,* 796–813.

LaFromboise, T., Coleman, H. L. K., & Gerton, J. (1993). Psychological impact of biculturalism: Evidence and theory. *Psychological Bulletin, 114,* 395–412.

Leung, A. K.-y., & Chiu, C.-y. (in press). Multicultural experiences, idea receptiveness, and creativity. *Journal of Cross-Cultural Psychology.*

Leung, A. K.-y., Maddux, W. W., Galinsky, A. D., & Chiu, C.-y. (2008). Multicultural experience enhances creativity—The when and how. *American Psychologist, 63,* 169–181.

Li, Q., & Hong, Y.-y. (2001). Intergroup perceptual accuracy predicts real-life intergroup interactions. *Group Processes and Intergroup Relations, 4,* 341–354.

Liu, S. (2007). Living with others: Mapping the routes to acculturation in a multicultural society. *International Journal of Intercultural Relations, 31,* 761–778.

Maddux, W. W., & Galinsky, A. D. (2009). Cultural borders and mental barriers: The relationship between living abroad and creativity. *Journal of Personality and Social Psychology, 96,* 1047–1061.

Markus, H. (1977). Self-schemata and processing information about the self. *Journal of Personality and Social Psychology, 35,* 63–78.

McLeod, P. L., Lobel, S. A., & Cox, T. H., Jr. (1996). Ethnic diversity and creativity in small groups. *Small Group Research, 27,* 248–264.

Mendoza-Denton, R., & Page-Gould, E. (2008). Can cross-group friendships influence minority students' well-being at historically White universities? *Psychological Science, 19,* 933–939.

Montreuil, A., & Bourhis, R. Y. (2001). Majority acculturation orientations towards "valued" and "devalued" immigrants. *Journal of Cross-Cultural Psychology, 32,* 698–719.

Nemeth, C. J., & Kwan, J. L. (1987). Minority influence, divergent thinking, and detection of correct solutions. *Journal of Applied Social Psychology, 17,* 786–797.

Ng, S. H., & Bradac, J. (1993). *Power in language: Verbal communication and social influence.* Newbury Park, CA: Sage.

No, S., Hong, Y., Liao, H., Lee, K., Wood, D., & Chao, M. M. (2008). Lay theory of race affects and moderates Asian Americans' responses toward American culture. *Journal of Personality and Social Psychology, 95,* 991–1004.

Novakovic, J. (1977). *The assimilation myth revisited: Rejection of home culture by second generation Yugoslav immigrant children as a function of age, friendship group, and sex.* Unpublished honors thesis, School of Psychology, University of New South Wales.

Padilla, A. M., & Perez, W. (2003). Acculturation, social identity, and social cognition: A new perspective. *Hispanic Journal of Behavioral Sciences, 25,* 35–55.

Park, R. E. (1928). Human migration and the marginal man. *American Journal of Sociology, 5,* 881–893.

Phinney, J. S., & Devich-Navarro, M. (1997). Variations in bicultural identification among African American and Mexican American adolescents. *Journal of Research on Adolescence, 7,* 3–32.

Roccas, S., & Brewer, M. B. (2002). Social identity complexity. *Personality and Social Psychology Review, 6,* 88–106.

Ross, M., Xun, W. Q. E., & Wilson, A. E. (2002). Language and the bicultural self. *Personality and Social Psychology Bulletin, 28,* 1040–1050.

Ryder, A. G., Alden, L. E., & Paulhus, D. L. (2000). Is acculturation unidimensional or bidimensional? A head-to-head comparison in the prediction of personality, self-identity, and adjustment. *Journal of Personality and Social Psychology, 79,* 49–65.

Shore, B. (1996). *Culture in mind: Cognition, culture, and the problem of meaning.* New York: Oxford University Press.

Sibley, C. G., & Liu, J. H. (2004). Social dominance and Pakeha attitudes towards the general principles and resource-specific aspects of bicultural policy. *New Zealand Journal of Psychology, 33,* 88–99.

Sibley, C. G., & Liu, J. H. (2007). New Zealand = bicultural? Implicit and explicit associations between ethnicity and nationhood in the New Zealand context. *European Journal of Social Psychology, 37,* 1222–1243.

Sibley, C. G., Liu, J. H., Duckitt, J., & Khan, S. S. (2008). Social representations of history and the legitimation of social inequality: The form and function of historical negation. *European Journal of Social Psychology, 38,* 542–565.

Simonton, D. K. (1997). Foreign influence and national achievement: The impact of open milieus on Japanese civilizations. *Journal of Personality and Social Psychology, 72,* 86–94.

Smith, S. M., Ward, T. B., & Finke, R. A. (1995). *The creative cognition approach.* Cambridge, MA: MIT Press.

Solomon, S., Greenberg, J., Schimel, J., Arndt, J., & Pszczynski, T. (2004). Human awareness of morality and evolution of culture. In M. Schaller & C. S. Crandall (Eds.), *The psychological foundations of culture* (pp. 15–40). Mahwah, NJ: Erlbaum.

Stonequist, E. V. (1935). The problem of marginal man. *American Journal of Sociology, 7,* 1–12.

Suedfeld, P., Tetlock, P. E., & Streufert, S. (1992). Conceptual/integrative complexity. In C. P. Smith (Ed.), *Motivation and personality: Handbook of thematic content analysis* (pp. 393–400). Cambridge, UK: Cambridge University Press.

Sui, J., Zhu, Y., & Chiu C.-y., (2007). Bicultural mind, self-construal, and recognition memory: Cultural priming effects on self- and mother-reference effect. *Journal of Experimental Social Psychology, 43,* 818–824.

Sussman, N. M. (2000). The dynamic nature of cultural identity throughout cultural transitions: Why home is not so sweet. *Personality and Social Psychology Review, 4,* 355–373.

Tadmor, C. T. (2006). *Biculturalism: The plus side of leaving home? The effects of second-culture exposure on integrative complexity and its consequences for overseas performance.* Unpublished doctoral dissertation, University of California, Berkeley.

Tadmor, C. T., Galinsky, A. D., & Maddux, W. W. (2009). *Biculturalism: Dual identification with home and host cultures predicts creative and professional performance.* Manuscript to be submitted for publication.

Tadmor, C. T., Hernandez, P., Jang, S., & Polzer, J. T. (2009). *The influence of multiculturalism and self-verification on creativity in culturally diverse dyads.* Manuscript to be submitted for publication.

Tadmor, C. T., & Tetlock, P. E. (2006). Biculturalism: A model of the effects of second-culture exposure on acculturation and integrative complexity. *Journal of Cross-Cultural Psychology, 37,* 173–190.

Tadmor, C. T., Tetlock, P. E., & Peng, K. (2009). Biculturalism and integrative complexity: Testing the Acculturation Complexity Model. *Journal of Cross-Cultural Psychology, 40,* 105–139.

Tetlock, P. E. (1986). A value pluralism model of ideological reasoning. *Journal of Personality and Social Psychology, 50,* 819–827.

Tetlock, P. E. (1992). The impact of accountability on judgment and choice: Toward a social contingency model. *Advances in Experimental Social Psychology, 25,* 331–376.

Tetlock, P. E. (2002). Social functionalist frameworks for judgment and choice: Intuitive politicians, theologians, and prosecutors. *Psychological Review, 109,* 451–471.

Triandis, H. C. (1975). Culture training, cognitive complexity, and interpersonal attitudes. In R. W. Brislin, S. Bochner, & W. J. Lonner (Eds.), *Cross-cultural perspectives on learning* (pp. 39–77). Beverly Hills, CA: Sage.

Tsai, J. L., Ying, Y., & Lee, P. A. (2000). The meaning of "being Chinese" and "being American": Variation among Chinese American young adults. *Journal of Cross-Cultural Psychology, 31,* 302–332.

Turner, R. N., & Brown, R. (2008). Improving children's attitudes toward refugees: An evaluation of a school-based multicultural curriculum and an anti-racist intervention. *Journal of Applied Social Psychology, 38,* 1295–1328.

Verkuyten, M. (2006). Multicultural recognition and ethnic minority rights: A social identity perspective. *European Review of Social Psychology, 17,* 148–184.

Verkuyten, M. (2009). Support for multiculturalism and minority rights: The role of national identification and out-group threat. *Social Justice Research, 22,* 31–52.

Verkuyten, M., & Pouliasi, K. (2002). Biculturalism among older children: Cultural frame switching, attributions, self-identification, and attitudes. *Journal of Cross-Cultural Psychology, 33,* 596–609.

Wan, C., Chiu, C. -y., Peng, S., & Tam, K.-p. (2007a). Measuring cultures through intersubjective norms: Implications for predicting relative identification with two or more cultures. *Journal of Cross-Cultural Psychology, 38,* 213–226.

Wan, C., Chiu, C.-y., Tam, K.-p., Lee, S.-l., Lau, I. Y.-m., & Peng, S.-q. (2007b). Perceived cultural importance and actual self-importance of values in cultural identification. *Journal of Personality and Social Psychology, 92,* 337–354.

Wan, W. W.-n. & Chiu, C.-y. (2002). Effects of novel conceptual combination on creativity. *Journal of Creative Behavior, 36,* 227–240.

Ward, T. B. (1994). Structured imagination: The role of conceptual structure in exemplar generation. *Cognitive Psychology, 27,* 1–40.

Ward, T. B., Smith, S. M., & Vaid, J. (1997). Conceptual structures and processes in creative thought. In T. B. Ward, S. M. Smith, & J. Vaid (Eds.), *Creative thought: an investigation of conceptual structures and processes.* Washington, DC: American Psychological Association.

Watson, W. E., Kumar, K., & Michaelsen, L. K. (1993). Cultural diversity's impact on interaction process and performance: Comparing homogenous and diverse task groups. *Academy of Management Journal, 36,* 590–602.

Wederspahn, G. M. (1992). Costing failures in expatriate human resource management. *Human Resource Planning, 15,* 27–35.

Wong, R. Y., & Hong, Y. (2005). Dynamic influences of culture on cooperation in the prisoner's dilemma. *Psychological Science, 16,* 429–434.

Zick, A., Pettigrew, T. F., & Wagner, U. (2008). Ethnic prejudice and discrimination in Europe. *Journal of Social Issues, 64,* 233–251.

Zou, X., Morris, M. W., & Benet-Martínez, V. (2008). Identity motives and cultural priming: Cultural (dis)identification in assimilative and contrastive responses. *Journal of Experimental Social Psychology, 44,* 1151–1159.

Zou, X., Tam, K.-p., Morris, M. W., Lee, S.-l., Lau, Y.-m., & Chiu, C.-y. (in press). Culture as *common* sense: Perceived consensus vs. personal beliefs as mechanisms of cultural influence. *Journal of Personality and Social Psychology.*

Part III

Intergroup Attitudes

7

Multiculturalism and Tolerance
An Intergroup Perspective

Maykel Verkuyten

> These movements form part of the wider struggle for recognition of identity and difference or, more accurately, of identity-related differences. Their demand for recognition goes far beyond the familiar plea for toleration, for the latter implies conceding the validity of society's disapproval and relying on its self-restraint.
>
> *(Parekh, 2000, p. 1)*

How to deal with cultural and religious differences? That is a question that is hotly debated in many societies and in all kinds of settings, such as cities, neighborhoods, organizations, and schools. Cultural and religious plurality raises difficult questions, particularly when group positions are at stake and incompatible demands are involved. Various approaches for dealing with diversity have been proposed. The description of multicultural realities has led to prescriptions for dealing with diversity. In general, and as illustrated in the quote above, a distinction can be made between *multicultural* approaches that focus on the recognition and active support of group differences (Modood, 2007) and classical liberal approaches that emphasize the depoliticization of these differences and argue for the *toleration* of diversity (Barry, 2001).

The latter approaches claim that tolerance is sufficient for dealing adequately with diversity because it gives individual citizens the freedoms and rights to define and develop their own identities. It is argued that precisely because of the importance of culture and religion in people's lives these should be neutralized as a political force in which group-specific claims are made (Sniderman & Hagendoorn, 2007). Historically, the concept of tolerance evolved from efforts to deal with the harmful and violent effects of religious conflicts (Walzer, 1997). The presence of a great number of Muslims in western European countries has given a renewed urgency to the idea of tolerance as a mechanism for dealing with diversity. Islam has emerged as the focus of immigration and diversity debates in Europe (Zolberg & Long, 1999) and is at the heart of what is perceived as a "crisis of multiculturalism" (Modood, 2007).

Proponents of multiculturalism argue, however, that "mere" tolerance is not enough, and that multiculturalism should involve active support for cultural difference. Multiculturalism implies that differences are not ignored or eliminated but to some extent publicly affirmed, recognized, and valued. The withholding of recognition or misrecognition is seen as a form of oppression (Taylor, 1992). Toleration would be an act of generosity from the powerful, who grudgingly agree to put up with minorities. In doing so the larger society's disapproval of minority identities and practices is implicitly affirmed. For many minority members, the end result of toleration would be a poor substitute for the recognition and affirmation that they would deserve and need.

This chapter examines some key social psychological aspects of tolerance and multiculturalism. The emphasis is on intergroup factors such as perceived threats, ingroup identification and group evaluations. In addition, the focus is on majority-group members. Toleration presupposes that one has a disproportionate amount of power in society to suppress the behavior in question, and the majority-group members' responses to multiculturalism are likely to have clear repercussions for group relations.

I will first discuss tolerance and several intergroup factors underlying toleration. Subsequently, I will address the complexity of toleration by looking at people's reasoning about various forms and domains of tolerance. Next, I will address the question of majority-group members' support for multicultural recognition. Then, I will consider multiculturalism in relation to ingroup reappraisal and to outgroup evaluation. Finally, I will discuss the relationship between the endorsement of the ideology of multiculturalism and tolerance of specific minority practices. Most of the research examples that will be given are concerned with the Dutch context. One reason is that our research is predominantly conducted in the Netherlands. Another reason is that the most overt and ambitious European experiment in multiculturalism was developed in the Netherlands, but the recent retreat of multiculturalism is also most evident there (Joppke, 2004).

Tolerance

Tolerance can be conceptualized in various ways, such as the valuing and celebrating of difference, a generalized positive attitude toward outgroups, the absence of prejudice, and the putting up with something that one disapproves of or is prejudiced against. I am concerned here with this last meaning of tolerance, which is a key condition for citizenship and democracy (Sullivan & Transue, 1999). Tolerance for dissenting practices is not the absence of prejudice, but rather a separate construct that emphasizes forbearance and not begrudging other people their own ways. Tolerance is an option when one dislikes something or someone and is the opposite of discrimination; when one endures or refrains from action although other's beliefs and practices are disapproved of or rejected.

Tolerance is critical for cultural diverse societies because the hotly debated questions and issues are about concrete practices and actions. Should Sikhs be allowed to wear a turban rather than a helmet on construction sites or a crash helmet when riding a motorcycle? Should the practice of forced marriages among some immigrant groups be accepted? Should a light form of female circumcision (*sunna*) be allowed? Should all images of pigs be banned from pictures in public offices because these might offend Muslims' feelings? It is around these concrete questions that cultural and religious diversity are put to the test and ways of life can collide.

Theoretically, the focus on tolerance allows for an examination of its difference with prejudice. According to Gibson (2006, p. 26) this is "one of the most important tasks of future research." Most often, the expectation is that both are closely connected because they are grounded, for example, in personal attributes such as authoritarianism (Altemeyer, 1988) and social dominance (Sidanius & Pratto, 1999). However, the conceptual distinction implies that it should be possible that prejudiced attitudes go together with tolerance. Furthermore, intolerance can have other bases than outgroup dislike. A generalized positive attitude toward an outgroup does not have to imply the acceptance of specific rights or practices of outgroup members. For example, positive affect toward Muslims does not have to mean that one accepts actions that go against operative public norms that govern the civic relations between people (Parekh, 2000), like Muslim teachers who refuse to shake hands with children's parents of the opposite sex, and civil servants wearing a burqa or a niqab. Principled conservatism rather than prejudice can underlie the opposition to specific rights for minority groups (Sniderman & Piazza, 1993).

In a survey study among ethnic Dutch adolescents tolerance was examined in terms of the willingness to accept a Muslim teacher and to accept a Muslim giving a public speech at one's school (Van der Noll, Poppe, & Verkuyten, in press). It turned out that almost a third of the participants had a prejudicial attitude toward Muslims but also accepted the Muslim teacher and the public speech. Furthermore, there were participants (12.5%) with a positive attitude toward Muslims and who gave intolerant answers to the two cases (see also Sniderman & Hagendoorn, 2007). These results indicate that prejudice toward Muslims and intolerance of public activities by members of this group are relatively distinct. Generalized negative affect toward Muslims does not necessarily imply the rejection of specific rights and actions, and a neutral or generalized positive affect does not have to imply an unconditional acceptance of practices. The empirical distinction between prejudice and political tolerance has also been found in other studies (e.g., Gibson & Gouws, 2003). It indicates that research on cultural diversity should not only focus on negative evaluations and feelings but should also consider when and why people tolerate specific practices.

Research on political tolerance has focused on the role of personality characteristics such as dogmatism, insecurity, and adherence to tradition (see Vogt, 1997). Additionally, there is work on the role of political expertise, political participation, and commitment to democratic values as determinants of tolerance (Sullivan & Transue, 1999). However, relatively little attention is given to intergroup factors such as perceived threats and ingroup identification. Tolerance presupposes group differences and implies that one group has the power to suppress the disliked or threatening behavior of the other. In his review, Gibson (2006) argues that research on tolerance needs to examine different types of threat and that the antecedents of threat perception are poorly understood.

In our study among ethnic Dutch adolescents (Van der Noll et al., in press), and in agreement with studies on political tolerance, it turned out that perceived group threat is a key determinant of tolerance. Both symbolic and safety threat were independently and negatively related to tolerance of Muslims. Thus, differences in norms, beliefs, and values that threaten one's worldview (symbolic threat), as well as the belief that the presence of Muslims leads to increased violence and vandalism (safety threat), did fuel negative reactions toward practices and rights of Muslims (see also Sniderman & Hagendoorn, 2007). In addition, ingroup identification was found to be positively associated with symbolic and safety threat, but did not have a direct effect on tolerance. Participants who identified relatively strongly with the Dutch ingroup were more sensitive and concerned about things that might harm Dutch society and culture. In turn, feelings of threat were associated with less tolerance.

Social Reasoning

To tolerate is to allow, but this does not imply a refusal to judge and that nothing can be affirmed. Tolerance is not relativism or an unconditional acceptance of difference. Developmental and political science research has shown that tolerance is not a global construct. Tolerance depends on whom, what, and when people are asked to tolerate dissenting beliefs and practices. For example, Wainryb, Shaw, and Maianu (1998) found that adolescents were more tolerant of beliefs and practices based on dissenting information than dissenting moral values. The same has been found in an experimental study among ethnic Dutch adolescents' tolerant judgments of Muslims' political rights and dissenting beliefs and practices (Verkuyten & Slooter, 2007). Participants took into account various aspects of what they were asked to tolerate and the sense in which they should be tolerant. The nature and the social implication of the behavior, and the underlying belief type, all made a difference to the tolerant judgments. For example, the level of tolerance was lower when the social implications were greater, and participants were more tolerant of practices based on dissenting cultural beliefs than on dissenting moral beliefs.

Furthermore, accepting that people hold dissenting beliefs does not have to imply that one tolerates the public expression of such beliefs or the actual practices based on such beliefs (Vogt, 1997). These dimensions of tolerance can trigger different levels of acceptance. In their study, Wainryb and colleagues (1998) found, for example, that European American children and early adolescents were more tolerant of dissenting speech than practices (see also Witenberg, 2002). Similarly, Verkuyten and Slooter (2007) found that Dutch adolescents were more tolerant of Muslim parents, publicly arguing for differential gender treatment of children or for a very light form of female circumcision, than for the actual acts themselves. This higher acceptance of the public expression of the dissenting beliefs is consistent with the idea of free speech. It can be seen as stimulating debate, which is important for the democratic process and as causing less direct harm or injustice than the actual acts.

However, higher acceptance of public expressions of beliefs compared to the actual practices based upon these beliefs depends on the intergroup context. Specifically, Muslims trying to persuade co-believers to engage in a dissenting practice can be perceived as a threat to the majority ingroup. In one study (Gieling, Thijs, & Verkuyten, in press) we examined ethnic Dutch participants' perceptions of four concrete cases of specific practices that are not illegal but that are hotly debated in Dutch society: the wearing of a headscarf by Muslim women, the refusal to shake hands with males by a female Muslim teacher, the founding of separate Islamic schools, and the public expression of the view that homosexuals are inferior people by an imam. We focused not only on the participants' tolerance of these practices but also on their acceptance of people trying to mobilize other Muslims. Participants were asked whether the different Muslim actors should be allowed to campaign in order to try to convince others to do the same thing. This social mobilization of Muslims is typically seen as threatening to Dutch identity and culture (Sniderman & Hagendoorn, 2007; Velasco González, Verkuyten, Weesie, & Poppe, 2008;) and therefore the participants were expected to be less tolerant of Muslims campaigning for ingroup support for the particular practice than of the actual practice itself. The findings clearly showed this to be the case. Campaigning for support and persuading others implies mobilizing Muslims, for example, to start wearing a headscarf, to stop shaking hands with people of the opposite sex, and to found more Islamic schools. Politicians and the media tend to present these practices as "backward" and as threatening Dutch identity and culture (see Scroggins, 2005; Vasta, 2007). They would undermine the secular and Christian traditions of the Netherlands. Trying to persuade other Muslims to act similarly is seen as contributing to the "Islamization of Dutch society," and therefore leads to lower acceptance compared to the act itself.

These findings for tolerance show that it is important to examine the social reasoning behind the evaluation of cultural and religious practices. Social psychological research on cultural diversity tends to focus on stereotypes and group evaluations. What is also needed, however, is an understanding of the underlying criteria that people use to determine whether particular acts and practices are acceptable. Social cognitive domain theory (see Smetana, 2006; Turiel, 2002), for example, proposes that people use moral (e.g., fairness, justice), social-conventional (e.g., group norms, traditions), and psychological (e.g. autonomy, personal preferences) reasoning to evaluate and reason about specific behaviors and situations.

The findings in our research (Gieling et al., in press; Study 1) indicate that the four cases were indeed seen as referring to the three domains, with the wearing of a headscarf predominantly considered to involve the personal domain, the founding of Islamic schools and the refusal to shake hands as triggering more social conventional concerns, and the imam's speech raising moral issues. This distinction between the three domains was found independently of age, educational level, and gender. Furthermore, in agreement with the domain theory, it turned out (Study 2) that tolerance was highest in the personal domain and lowest in the moral domain, with the social conventional domain in between. Thus, the participants were found to be most tolerant of Muslim students wearing a headscarf and least tolerant of the imam's speech. The cases of the Islamic school and the refusal to shake hands, both mainly matters of social convention, fell in between. This difference was found for both types of tolerance: for the actual practices and for Muslims trying to persuade others to engage in the same practices.

Tolerance is the most basic level of positive relations between groups. Nevertheless, it is crucial because it is the first and necessary step toward civility, and foundational for a just society (Vogt, 1997). A diverse, equal, and peaceful society does not require that we all like each other, but it does necessarily mean that people tolerate one another. Multicultural proponents argue, however, that "mere" tolerance is not enough. It would be a poor substitute for the affirmation and recognition of cultural diversity that minority members deserve and need. Multiculturalism goes beyond toleration, for it involves active support for group differences and the remaking of the public sphere in order to fully include minority identities.

Multicultural Recognition

The Endorsement of Multiculturalism

Empirical studies on multiculturalism attitudes indicate that the general support for multiculturalism is not very strong among majority groups in many Western countries. Apart from Canada, where majority members have been found to favor multiculturalism (e.g., Berry & Kalin, 1995), studies in other countries have found moderate support, such as in Australia, (e.g. Ho, 1990) and the United States (e.g., Citrin, Sears, Muste, & Wong, 2001; Wolsko, Park, & Judd, 2006), or low support, such as in Germany, Switzerland, Slovakia, and the Netherlands (e.g.,

Arends-Tóth & Van de Vijver, 2003; Piontkowski, Florack, Hoelker, & Obdrzálek, 2000; Zick, Wagner, van Dick, & Petzel, 2001).

In many (European) countries multiculturalism is typically seen as identity-threatening for the majority group and identity-supporting for minority groups (e.g., McLaren, 2003; Van Oudenhoven, Prins, & Buunk, 1998). Majority group members tend to see ethnic minorities and their desire to maintain their own culture as a threat to their cultural dominance and group identity. Following social psychological theories that emphasize the role of group status and interests in the dynamics of intergroup relations (e.g., Sherif, 1966; Sidanius & Pratto, 1999; Tajfel & Turner, 1979) it can be expected that groups are less in favor of multiculturalism when it goes against their material and symbolic interests. Hence, it is likely that multiculturalism appeals more to ethnic minority groups than to majority group members, who in turn endorse assimilation more strongly. Several studies in different countries have confirmed this expectation (Verkuyten, 2005; Wolsko et al., 2006), including a study examining multicultural attitudes among majority and immigrant groups in 21 European countries (Schalk-Soekar, 2007).

Encouraging people to recognize and appreciate cultural differences may create a backlash among majority group members because it is seen as jeopardizing the ingroup's position and identity (Correll, Park, & Smith, 2008; Sniderman & Hagendoorn, 2007). The support for multiculturalism is particularly low when it is perceived as causing harm to the ingroup. In several experiments, Lowery, Unzueta, Knowles, and Goff (2006) showed that majority-group members supported policies that benefited minorities only when these did not harm the ingroup. Furthermore, when a policy's outcome was framed in terms of ingroup loss, majority-group identity was negatively related to support for the policy. However, there was no association between group identity and policy support when the outcome was framed in terms of minority gain or when there was no change in the majority-group position.

Ingroup Identification

National identity and national identification are central to debates on immigration and cultural diversity. This is the case in settler countries such as Australia and the United States (e.g., Huntington, 2004), and also in non-settler European societies that have a historically established majority group, like the Netherlands and Germany (Joppke, 2004).

Ingroup identification is important for understanding how the majority group responds to cultural and religious diversity (see Verkuyten,

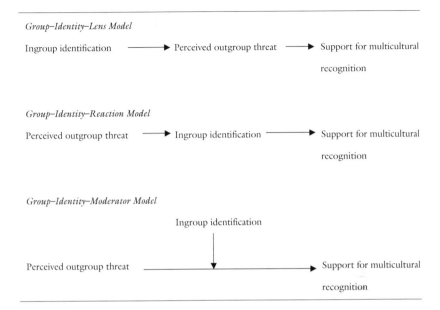

Group–Identity–Lens Model

Ingroup identification   ⟶   Perceived outgroup threat   ⟶   Support for multicultural recognition

Group–Identity–Reaction Model

Perceived outgroup threat   ⟶   Ingroup identification   ⟶   Support for multicultural recognition

Group–Identity–Moderator Model

Ingroup identification

Perceived outgroup threat   ⟶   Support for multicultural recognition

Figure 7.1 Three models for the role of ingroup identification in the relationship between outgroup threat and the support for multicultural recognition.

2007). In general, the more majority-group members identify with their own group the more they can be expected to try to protect their group's interests and status position, for example by emphasizing assimilation. Theoretically, the question is how exactly ingroup identification is involved in these reactions. For example, ingroup identification of the majority group can be an antecedent of perceived outgroup threat, a consequence of perceived threat, and can also moderate the relationship between outgroup threat and the support for multicultural recognition and minority rights (see Figure 7.1).

The "group-identity-lens" model (Eccleston & Major, 2006) hypothesizes that ingroup identification is an antecedent of perceived outgroup threat and will affect the support for multicultural recognition indirectly, via its association with threat. This model is in line with self-categorization theory (Turner & Reynolds, 2001) that posits that when a particular social identity is salient it provides a "lens" through which the perceiver sees the world and makes sense of it. Group identity functions as a group lens that makes people sensitive to anything that concerns or could harm their group. Thus, higher group identification will lead to greater threat perceptions, and these perceptions result in a particular response (see Riek, Mania, & Gaertner, 2006).

The second "group-identity-reaction" model is based on the idea that perceiving group threat leads individuals to identify more strongly with their ingroup and that stronger identification leads to more negative outgroup attitudes. People can cope with outgroup threats by adopting group-based strategies that increase ingroup identification (e.g., Jetten, Branscombe, Schmitt, & Spears, 2001). Research among racial and ethnic minority groups shows that increased perceptions of discrimination predicts increased ingroup identification (Schmitt & Branscombe, 2002; Verkuyten & Yildiz, 2007). The position of majority groups is different, however. In most west European countries, indigenous majority groups have a relatively secure position and ethnic group boundaries are rather impermeable. These conditions imply that threats posed by immigrants and ethnic minorities are unlikely to lead to stronger national identification (Verkuyten & Reijerse, 2008).

The "group-identity-moderator" model predicts that ingroup identification interacts with outgroup threat to predict the support for multiculturalism and minority rights. This model is in line with social identity theory (Tajfel & Turner, 1979). The idea is that perceived threat has different effects, depending on national identification, because the motivational meanings of perceived threat are different. Compared to low identifiers, those with high ingroup identification are more likely to be concerned about their group, especially when the position and value of the group identity is at stake (e.g., Bizman & Yinon, 2001; Branscombe & Wann, 1994).

I examined these three models in three survey studies among ethnic Dutch participants (Verkuyten, 2009). The group-identity-lens model predicts that outgroup threat mediates the relationship between ingroup identification and the support for multiculturalism and minority rights, the group-identity-reaction model argues that ingroup identification is the mediator, and the moderator model predicts a significant effect of the interaction between ingroup identification and outgroup threat on the support for multiculturalism and minority rights (see Figure 7.1). The results of the three studies were similar and in line with self-categorization theory, which argues that group identity makes people sensitive and vigilant to anything that concerns or could harm their group. Regression analyses showed that the group-identity-lens model fitted the data, and there was no evidence for the group-identity-reaction model or the group-identity-moderator model. Ingroup national identification was positively related to perceived outgroup threat, and threat, in turn, was negatively related to the support for multiculturalism and minority rights. Thus, group identification seems to lead to greater threat perception and, once threat is perceived, it leads to less support for immigrants and ethnic minorities.

Multiculturalism and Ingroup Reappraisal

> *Interviewer*: "Is that right, you think it is enriching too, these, er, different cultures?"*Interviewee*: "Oh, absolutely. You get this wider perspective. You don't just – this conventional, narrow Holland and, er, all that, er, you get a wider perspective, you know, you, you start taking more of an interest in other cultures too."

This quote is from a study on multiculturalism in the Netherlands (Verkuyten, 2004), and illustrates Pettigrew's (1997) proposition of "deprovincialization." Through intergroup contact you can "get this wider perspective," a self-critical view that goes beyond "this conventional, narrow Holland." Pettigrew (1997, 1998) argued that intergroup contact not only affects attitudes toward outgroups but also involves a reappraisal and distancing from the ingroup. Especially for majority-group members, contact can lead to the insight that the traditions, customs, norms, and values of one's group are not the only ways to manage and look at the world. Positive contact may broaden the majority-group members' horizon by acknowledging and recognizing the value of other cultures and thereby put the taken-for-granted own cultural standards into perspective. Limited experiences make the ingroup appear the center of the world and its norms and customs provide the self-evident and invariant standards for judgment. Positive intergroup contact enriches people's views of the social world, making them less ingroup-centric and giving them more pluralistic standards of judgment. Ingroup norms and customs are put into perspective and cultural differences are recognized and appreciated (Schmid & Hewstone, this volume).

Pettigrew (1998) discusses the result of European surveys showing that outgroup friendship is related to less national pride among majority-group members. In another study, using a German national probability sample, he showed that positive contact is negatively associated with the strength of German identity (Pettigrew, 2009). These findings suggest that intergroup contact can lead to less provincialism or a distancing from the ingroup. However, in these studies the mediating role of multiculturalism was not examined.

Multicultural approaches involve learning about differences and diversity and imply that one's own cultural standards are considered more relative (e.g., Leung, Maddux, Galinsky, & Chiu, 2008). For majority-group members this learning typically implies a reshaping of their views on their ingroup (Hogan & Mallott, 2005; Nagda, Kim, & Truelove, 2004; Cameron & Turner, this volume). Multiculturalism encompasses the ideological view that nuances and puts into perspective the majority's group identity and culture. Some evidence for this comes from four studies among ethnic Dutch participants (Verkuyten, 2005). In two surveys there was a tendency for the endorsement of multiculturalism to be negatively associated with ingroup evaluation. In addition, in two experimental studies Dutch participants tended to have lower ingroup evaluation in a multicultural compared to an assimilationist situational context.

Additional evidence comes from three large-scale surveys among ethnic Dutch participants in which the relationship between quantity of outgroup contact and ingroup distance (ingroup identification and ingroup feelings) was examined (Verkuyten, Thijs, & Bekhuis, in press). Following the deprovincialization thesis, more positive contact with ethnic outgroups was expected to lead to a higher endorsement of multiculturalism, that, in turn, was expected to be related to a stronger distancing from the ingroup. The findings in all three studies supported the deprovincialization thesis. In Study 1, higher opportunity for interethnic contact was associated with a stronger endorsement of multiculturalism and, in turn, multiculturalism was related to lower ingroup identification and fewer positive global feelings toward the Dutch ingroup. Study 2 focused on self-reported quantity of contact, and the endorsement of multiculturalism was again found to mediate the relationship between contact and ingroup identification and ingroup feelings. In Study 3 the alternative explanation of feelings of outgroup threat playing a mediating role was taken into account. It turned out that threat did mediate the relationship between contact and ingroup distance but the endorsement of multiculturalism also was an independent mediator.

Thus, intergroup contact helps to make ingroup cultural standards relative rather than invariant and self-evident. Contact can stimulate reflecting on one's own group and a more critical ingroup orientation. A wider perspective that goes beyond "this conventional, narrow Holland" is the result, and gaining distance from the dominant majority group can also help to form a less provincial view on minority outgroups. Multiculturalism involves active support for cultural differences and discouragement against outgroup negativity and disapproval. It can stimulate ingroup criticism but the focus tends to be on the acceptance and evaluation of minority outgroups.

Multiculturalism and Outgroup Evaluations

Multiculturalism is a difficult and controversial issue that leads to a lot of confusion, ambivalence, and debate. Ginges and Cairns (2000) found that Australian citizens saw the multicultural policy as beneficial for the country and as increasing social equality, but people also mentioned disadvantages such as a threat to the status quo, and to the unity and stability of the country. Among Dutch majority members, Breugelmans and Van de Vijver (2004) found a positive social norm involving support for multiculturalism and a negative social norm referring to multiculturalism as a threat. Both social norms were predictors of multicultural attitudes (see also Verkuyten, 2004). Thus, encouraging people to recognize and appreciate cultural differences may create a backlash among (especially highly identified) majority-group members because it can be seen as threatening the ingroup's position and identity (Correll et al., 2008; Sniderman & Hagendoorn, 2007).

However, a central aim of multiculturalism is to provide and promote a context for outgroup acceptance and recognition. Multiculturalism is expected to contribute to favorable intergroup relations. There is supporting evidence for this in educational settings (e.g., Hogan & Mallott, 2005) and also in social psychological research. Using survey data in the United States, Wolsko and colleagues (2006), for example, found that people who endorse multiculturalism see ethnic groups as more different from each other, but at the same time, view ethnic outgroups in a more positive manner. Thus, the group thinking inherent in multiculturalism seems to promote perceived group differences as well as a reduced tendency to evaluate the ingroup more positively than the outgroup (see also Ryan, Hunt, Weible, Peterson, & Casas, 2007). Furthermore, in three studies in the Netherlands it was found that the more Dutch-majority participants endorsed multiculturalism the more likely they tended to be to evaluate the outgroup positively (Velasco González et al., 2008; Verkuyten, 2005).

These associations do not tell us anything about causal effects. Some experimental studies have directly examined the effects of multiculturalism on intergroup relations. Wolsko, Park, Judd, and Wittenbrink (2000), for example, examined the impact of exposure to multicultural and colorblind ideologies on intergroup judgments among white participants in the United States. They found stronger stereotyping and

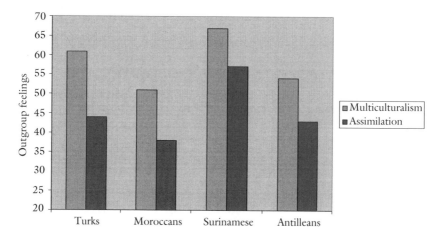

Figure 7.2 Mean scores for outgroup feelings toward four ethnic outgroups by experimental condition.

greater use of category information in their multicultural condition compared to colorblindness. In addition, compared to the control participants, there was less pro-white attitudinal bias in both ideological conditions. Richeson and Nussbaum (2004) also studied white participants, examining them for automatic and explicit forms of racial attitudes. Participants exposed to a message endorsing colorblindness showed greater racial bias on both forms of racial attitudes than those exposed to a message endorsing a multicultural perspective. In two experimental studies in the Netherlands, multicultural and assimilation ideology were made salient in separate conditions. There were two different versions of a questionnaire that were divided randomly among the participants. One version focused on multiculturalism and another on assimilationism (see Verkuyten, 2005). Figure 7.2 shows the combined results for the ethnic group feelings in the two studies and toward four ethnic minority groups (see Coenders, Lubbers, Scheepers, & Verkuyten, 2008). The finding is clear: Dutch participants had more positive outgroup evaluations toward the four groups in the multicultural condition compared to the assimilation condition.

However, these positive effects of multiculturalism might be restricted to low ethnic-conflict situations. In two experiments, Correll and colleagues (2008) showed that when conflict is low, white participants who were induced to accept the multicultural ideology exhibited less prejudice than controls, whereas they expressed greater bias in high-conflict or zero-sum situations in which the outcomes for the ingroup were harmed. Thus, people tend to be more negative toward minorities when they experience a multicultural ideological setting as challenging or undermining the interests and resources of their ingroup (Lowery et al., 2006). When the setting is not experienced as causing ingroup harm, support for and acceptance of minority groups is more likely.

It also should be noted that social psychological research tends to focus on multiculturalism as an abstract ideological notion and examines the effects on general group evaluations. However, as is well known from attitude research, abstract or principle considerations differ from (the lack of) support for practical implications and situations. This raises the question whether the endorsement of multiculturalism implies the acceptance of controversial and concrete practices and actions.

Multiculturalism and Tolerance

Studies on political thinking and behavior show that people tend to support democratic rights in the abstract but often do not endorse the same rights in concrete circumstances (see Vogt, 1997). It is one thing to endorse the freedom of speech and demonstration in general, and another thing to apply these freedoms to, for example, radical Muslim groups living in a secular or Christian country, or a politician arguing that Islam is an inferior religion and that the Koran should be forbidden.

However, higher endorsement of multicultural ideology has been found to be related to more tolerant judgments of concrete practices. In one of our studies it turned out that multiculturalism was directly associated with tolerance of Muslims, and this association was partially mediated by symbolic threat and safety threat (Van der Noll et al., in press). Individuals who endorsed multicultural recognition more strongly perceived less symbolic as well as less safety threat. These findings are in line with previous research (Velasco González et al., 2008; Ward & Masgoret, 2006) and with Berry's (2006) argument that multicultural recognition can provide confidence, trust, and security among everyone living in pluralistic societies. A view that cultural diversity is good for society implies an acceptance and positive evaluation of practices and behaviors of outgroup members. In addition to these indirect effects, the endorsement of multicultural recognition was also directly related to tolerance of Muslims. Hence, multiculturalism seems to provide a general ideological view about the importance of cultural diversity that not only reduces a sense of group threat but also emphasizes that people should be recognized and valued in their group identity, and that there should be social equality and equal rights and opportunities. This result is in agreement with research that has shown that beliefs about democratic processes and the protection of minority rights is a primary source of political tolerance (McClosky & Brill, 1983; Sullivan, Piereson, & Marcus, 1982). Thus, the ideology of multiculturalism was strongly, and directly and indirectly, related to the acceptance of actual practices by Muslims.

In another study we also found that participants who more strongly endorsed multicultural recognition were more tolerant of practices of Muslims (Gieling et al., in press). However, the role of multiculturalism was moderated by domain. Individuals who endorsed multicultural recognition tended to tolerate practices that were considered to belong to the personal and the conventional domain but were less accepting in the moral domain. The endorsement of the value of cultural diversity appears not to be unlimited. There are different kinds of diversity, and some are more problematic than others. Moral diversity, for example, is problematic when one wants to build cohesive communities, and this kind of diversity also tends to be incoherent. Take the example of the acceptance of homosexuality. The acceptance of homosexuality is a matter of personal opinion when one accepts it oneself but does not expect others to do so. It becomes conventionally regulated when one argues that everyone in one's own group or society should accept it but people in other groups or societies need not. But if one sees the acceptance of homosexuality as a moral issue one thinks that everyone else in all communities should support it, for example, as a basic human right. In that case it becomes difficult to tolerate that others think differently and act against it.

Multiculturalism does not imply moral relativism in which all practices and ideas are judged equally right and acceptable (Lukes, 2008). Respecting other cultural communities and their practices is difficult when concerns and considerations of others' welfare and fairness are involved. Already 5-year-old children have been shown to think that some beliefs are relative and others not and that their judgments of relativism differ from their tolerant judgments of divergent beliefs (Wainryb, Shaw, Langley, Cottam, & Lewis, 2004). Thus, in our study participants were found to make a distinction between practices that they evaluated negatively but considered a personal matter, practices that violate conventional norms, and practices that go against moral beliefs. The level of tolerance did not only differ between these domains, but intergroup factors (ingroup identification and the endorsement of multicultural recognition) appeared to be less important for the acceptance of outgroup practices that evoke moral concerns. Low and high identifiers and low and high endorsers of multiculturalism were equally negative in the moral domain but not toward practices that were seen as personal or matters of social convention. For these, high identifiers and low multiculturalists were more intolerant. Theoretically, this means that a combination of social psychological intergroup theories and social domain theory (see Killen, Margie & Sinno, 2006) can improve our understanding of the many and hotly debated controversies in diverse cultural and religious societies.

Discussion

Accommodating diverse cultures and religions is an inescapable feature of societies all around the world. Questions of cultural diversity give rise to lively and important debates in many spheres of life. Some argue that tolerance is sufficient for dealing adequately with diversity. An emphasis on cultural differences and group rights would be unnecessary and would fuel essentialist group thinking, separatism, and conflict. Proponents of multiculturalism, however, reason that "mere" tolerance is not enough and that multiculturalism should involve active support for cultural difference.

This chapter has discussed some of our social psychological research on tolerance and multiculturalism. The understanding of people's acceptance of dissenting practices is important for developing adequate interventions to improve tolerance, which is foundational for equality and the development of harmonious intergroup relations. Most lines of thinking argue that the reduction of stereotypes and prejudice is necessary for these kinds of relationships to develop. However, our knowledge and ability to reduce stereotypes and prejudice remains limited. Generalized perceptions and negative beliefs and feelings do not appear to be easy to change or to reject. The importance of tolerance is that it keeps the negative beliefs and feelings from becoming negative actions, thereby forming the first crucial step toward civility or the last barrier to conflict (Vogt, 1997). People may disagree with one another and may have stereotypes and prejudiced attitudes, but should at least agree about how to disagree. Tolerance does not imply indifference, and relativism that is found in some forms of multiculturalism celebrates diversity and argues that one should refrain from value judgments about other groups (Lukes, 2008). Tolerance always has limits and does not involve a full acceptance and valuing of all social practices of other groups, such as potentially harmful activities, illiberal internal rules, and ingroup oppression of, for example, some Muslim women and children.

Research shows that people evaluate different practices differently and that tolerance is not a single construct. A decision of whether a particular practice should be tolerated always involves a variety of personal, social conventional, and moral considerations. People can be both tolerant and intolerant of diversity because they take into account various aspects of what they are asked to tolerate, the sense in which they should be tolerant, and who they are expected to tolerate. This means, for example, that we should develop a better understanding of people's reasoning about the acceptance of dissenting beliefs and practices. It also means that effective civics education has to focus on the related questions of what should and what should not be tolerated and why.

Furthermore, it is important to think about ways to manage and change threat perceptions, because outgroup threat is a strong predictor of intolerance. A focus on multiculturalism is one possibility, since perceived threats tend to be lower among those individuals who endorse multicultural recognition. In addition, people who endorse the value of cultural diversity more strongly appear to be more tolerant and to have a more positive attitude toward minority outgroups. They also tend to have a less "provincial" or wider perspective with a more critical and nuanced stance toward their ingroup. Thus, in addition to tolerance, an emphasis on cultural diversity and multicultural recognition can be a promising avenue for improving intergroup relations. However, it is important to stimulate multicultural recognition without ignoring majority-group members' concerns for their ingroup's outcomes. Multiculturalism requires the majority group to relinquish some of its power and status and often raises concerns for the ingroup. Thus, multicultural ideologies can create a backlash among majority-group members in the form of increased hostility and decreased support for social equality (Sniderman & Hagendoorn, 2007).

It is centrally important to examine how multiculturalism is presented and defined, and the ways it is actually implemented and practiced. Multicultural recognition is often seen as undermining the majority group's identity or harming their interests. But it can also be construed as being a fundamental part of, for example, the national self-image or the organizational or institutional identity, and as beneficial for society as a whole or for one's organization or institution. Obviously, this is easier in some contexts than in others. Multicultural education in schools is often less difficult to implement than changing traditional corporate cultures, or national self-understandings. Furthermore, there are important differences between schools, and between organizations or countries. For example, in contrast to settler countries like Australia, Canada, and the United States, where almost all citizens have an immigrant background, European countries have a long history of established majority groups and issues of immigration and cultural diversity are relatively novel. European multiculturalism is not as clearly entangled with issues of national self-understanding and ethnic minority-group members are more strongly expected to adopt the dominant group's way of life. In European countries, multiculturalism is clearly on the retreat, and not only because of national self-understandings and the lack of public support for official multicultural policies and initiatives (Joppke, 2004). There are also serious problems of cultural and economic integration, social cohesion, self-segregation of minorities and their children, and a one-sided emphasis on group differences.

The importance and benefits of tolerance should not be underestimated. Its emphasis on civic identity and the individual's freedom to define and develop their own identities and ways of life offers crucial spaces for cultural diversity. However, minority-group members do not only want to be accepted and tolerated as individual citizens with equal opportunities and rights, but many of them also want to be recognized and respected as members of their cultural or religious group.

References

Altemeyer, B. (1988). *Enemies of freedom: Understanding right-wing authoritarianism*. San Francisco: Jossey-Bass.

Arends-Tóth, J., & Van De Vijver, F. J. R. (2003). Multiculturalism and acculturation: Views of Dutch and Turkish–Dutch. *European Journal of Social Psychology, 33,* 249–266.

Barry, B. (2001). *Culture and equality*. Cambridge, UK: Polity Press.

Berry, J. W. (2006). Mutual attitudes among immigrants and ethnocultural groups in Canada. *International Journal of Intercultural Relations, 30,* 719–734.

Berry, J. W., & Kalin, R. (1995). Multicultural and ethnic attitudes in Canada. An overview of the 1991 national survey. *Canadian Journal of Behavioural Sciences, 27,* 301–320.

Bizman, A., & Yinon, Y. (2001). Intergroup and interpersonal threats as determinants of prejudice: The moderating role of in-group identification. *Basic and Applied Social Psychology, 23,* 191–196.

Branscombe, N. R., & Wann, D. L. (1994). Collective self-esteem conse-quences of outgroup derogation when a valued social identity is on trial. *European Journal of Social Psychology, 24,* 641–657.

Breugelmans, S. M., & Van de Vijver, F. J. R. (2004). Antecedents and com-ponents of majority attitudes toward multiculturalism in the Netherlands. *Applied Psychology: An International Review, 53,* 400–422.

Citrin, J., Sears, D. O., Muste, C., & Wong, C. (2001). Multiculturalism in American public opinion. *British Journal of Political Science, 31,* 247–275.

Coenders, M., Lubbers, M., Scheepers, P., & Verkuyten, M. (2008). More than two decades of changing ethnic attitudes in the Netherlands. *Journal of Social Issues, 64,* 269–286.

Correll, J., Park, B., & Smith, J. A. (2008). Colorblind and multicultural prej-udice reduction strategies in high-conflict situations. *Group Processes and Intergroup Relations, 11,* 471–491.

Eccleston, C. P., & Major, B. N. (2006). Attributions to discrimination and self-esteem: The role of group identification and appraisal. *Group Processes and Intergroup Relations, 9,* 147–162.

Gibson, J. L. (2006). Enigmas of intolerance: Fifty years after Stouffer's com-munism, conformity, and civil liberties. *Perspectives on Politics, 4,* 21–34.

Gibson, J. L., & Gouws, A. (2003). *Overcoming intolerance in South Africa: Experiments in democratic persuasion.* New York: Cambridge University Press.

Gieling, M., Thijs, J., & Verkuyten, M.(in press). Tolerance of practices by Muslim actors: An integrative social-developmental perspective. *Child Devel-opment.*

Ginges, J., & Cairns, D. (2000). Social representations of multiculturalism: A faceted analysis. *Journal of Applied Social Psychology, 30,* 1345–1370.

Ho, R. (1990). Multiculturalism in Australia: A survey of attitudes. *Human Relations, 43,* 259–272.

Hogan, D. E., & Mallott, M. (2005). Changing racial prejudice through diversity education. *Journal of College Student Development, 46,* 115–125.

Huntington, S. (2004). *Who we are: The challenges to American national iden-tity.* New York: Simon & Schuster.

Jetten, J., Branscombe, N. R., Schmitt, M. T., & Spears, R. (2001). Rebel with a cause: Group identification as a response to perceived discrimination from the mainstream. *Personality and Social Psychology Bulletin, 27,* 1204–1213.

Joppke, C. (2004). The retreat of multiculturalism in the liberal state: theory and policy. *British Journal of Sociology, 55,* 237–257.

Killen, M., Margie, N. G., & Sinno, S. (2006). Morality in the context of intergroup relations. In M. Killen & J. Smetana (Eds.), *Handbook of moral development* (pp. 155–183). Mahwah, NJ: Erlbaum.

Leung, A. K.-y., Maddux W. W., Galinsky, A. D., & Chiu, C.-y. (2008). Mul-ticultural experience enhances creativity: The when and how. *American Psychologist, 63,* 169–181.

Lowery, B. S., Unzueta, M. M., Knowles, E. D., & Goff, P. A. (2006). Concern for the in-group and opposition to affirmative action. *Journal of Personality and Social Psychology, 90,* 961–974.

Lukes, S. (2008). *Moral relativism: Big ideas/small books.* New York: St Martin's Press.

McClosky, H., & Brill, A. (1983). *Dimensions of tolerance: What Americans believe about civil liberties.* New York: Basic Books.

McLaren, L. M. (2003). Anti-immigrant prejudice in Europe: Contact, threat perception, and preferences for the exclusion of migrants. *Social Forces, 81,* 908–36.

Modood, T. (2007). *Multiculturalism.* Cambridge, UK: Polity Press.

Nagda, B. A., Kim, C., & Truelove, Y. (2004). Learning about difference, learning with others, learning to transgress. *Journal of Social Issues, 60,* 195–214.

Parekh, B. (2000). *Rethinking multiculturalism: Cultural diversity and political theory.* London: Macmillan.

Pettigrew, T. F. (1997). Generalized intergroup contact effects on prejudice. *Personality and Social Psychology Bulletin, 23,* 173–185.

Pettigrew, T. F. (1998). Intergroup contact theory. *Annual Review Psychology, 49,* 65–85.

Pettigrew, T. F. (2009). Secondary transfer effect of contact: Do intergroup contact effects spread to noncontacted outgroups? *Social Psychology, 40,* 55–65.

Piontkowski, U., Florack, A., Hoelker, P., & Obdrzálek (2000). Predicting acculturation attitudes of dominant and non-dominant groups. *International Journal of Intercultural Relations, 24,* 1–26.

Richeson, J. A., & Nussbaum, R. J. (2004). The impact of multiculturalism versus color-blindness on racial bias. *Journal of Experimental Social Psychology, 40,* 417–423.

Riek, B. M., Mania, E. W., & Gaertner, S. L. (2006). Intergroup threat and outgroup attitudes: A meta-analytic review. *Personality and Social Psychology Review, 10,* 336–353.

Ryan, C. S., Hunt, J. S., Weible, J. A., Peterson, C. R., & Casas, J. F. (2007). Multicultural and colorblind ideology, stereotypes, and ethnocentrism among Black and White Americans. *Group Processes and Intergroup Relations, 10,* 617–637.

Schalk-Soekar, S. (2007). *Multiculturalism: A stable concept with many ideological and political aspects.* Tilburg, The Netherlands: Tilburg University.

Schmitt, M. T., & Branscombe, N. R. (2002). Meaning and consequences of perceived discrimination in advantaged and privileged social groups. In W. Stroebe & M. Hewstone (Eds.), *European Review of Social Psychology* (vol. 12, pp. 167–199). London: Wiley.

Scroggins, D. (2005, June 27). The Dutch–Muslim cultural war. *The Nation,* 21–25.

Sherif, M. (1966). *In common predicament. Social psychology of intergroup conflict and cooperation.* Boston: Houghton Mifflin.

Sidanius, J., & Pratto, F. (1999). *Social dominance: An intergroup theory of social hierarchy and oppression.* Cambridge, UK: Cambridge University Press.

Smetana, J. G. (2006). Social-cognitive domain theory: Consistencies and variations in children's moral and social judgments. In M. Killen & J. Smetana (Eds.), *Handbook of moral development* (pp. 117–153). Mahwah, NJ: Erlbaum.

Sniderman, P. M., & Hagendoorn, L. (2007). *When ways of life collide: Multiculturalism and its discontents in the Netherlands.* Princeton, NJ: Princeton University Press.

Sniderman, P. M., & Piazza, T. (1993). *The scar of race.* Cambridge, MA: Harvard University Press.

Sullivan, J. L., Piereson, J., & Marcus, G. E. (1982). *Political tolerance and American democracy.* Chicago: University of Chicago Press.

Sullivan, J. L., & Transue, J. E. (1999). The psychological underpinnings of democracy: A selective review of research on political tolerance, interpersonal trust, and social capital. *Annual Review of Psychology, 50,* 625–650.

Tajfel, H., & Turner, J. (1979). An integrative theory of intergroup conflict. In W. G. Austin & S. Worchel (Eds.), *The social psychology of intergroup relations* (pp. 33–47). Monterey, CA: Brooks/Cole.

Taylor, C. (1992). The politics of recognition. In A. Gutmann (Ed.), *Multiculturalism: Examining the politics of recognition* (pp. 25–73). Princeton, NJ: Princeton University Press.

Turiel, E. (2002). *The culture of morality.* Cambridge, UK: Cambridge University Press.

Turner, J. C., & Reynolds, K. J. (2001). The social identity perspective in intergroup relations: Theories, themes, and controversies. In R. Brown & S. Gaertner (Eds.), *Blackwell handbook in social psychology. Vol. 4: Intergroup processes* (pp. 133–152). Oxford, UK: Blackwell.

Van der Noll, J., Poppe, E., & Verkuyten, M.(in press). Political tolerance and prejudice: Differential reactions towards Muslims in the Netherlands. *Basic and Applied Social Psychology.*

Van Oudenhoven, J. P., Prins, K. S., & Buunk, B. P. (1998). Attitudes of minority and majority members towards adaptation of immigrants. *European Journal of Social Psychology, 28,* 995–1013.

Vasta, E. (2007). From ethnic minorities to ethnic majority policy: Multiculturalism and the shift to assimilation in the Netherlands. *Ethnic and Racial Studies, 30,* 713–740.

Velasco González, K., Verkuyten, M., Weesie, J., & Poppe, E. (2008). Prejudice towards Muslims in the Netherlands: Testing the integrated threat theory. *British Journal of Social Psychology, 47,* 667–685.

Verkuyten, M. (2004). Everyday ways of thinking about multiculturalism. *Ethnicities, 4,* 53–74.

Verkuyten, M. (2005). Ethnic group identification and group evaluation among minority and majority groups: Testing the multicultural hypotheses. *Journal of Personality and Social Psychology, 88*, 121–138.

Verkuyten, M. (2007). Multicultural recognition and ethnic minority rights: A social identity perspective. In W. Stroebe & M. Hewstone (Eds.), *European Review of Social Psychology* (vol. 17, pp. 148–184). London: Wiley.

Verkuyten, M. (2009). Support for multiculturalism and minority rights: The role of national identification and out-group threat. *Social Justice Research, 22*, 31–52.

Verkuyten, M., & Reijerse, A. (2008). Intergroup structure and identity management among ethnic minority and majority groups: The interactive effects of perceived stability, legitimacy and permeability. *European Journal of Social Psychology, 31*, 106–121.

Verkuyten, M., & Slooter, L. (2007). Tolerance of Muslim beliefs and practices: Age related differences and context effects. *International Journal of Behavioral Development, 31*, 467–477.

Verkuyten, M., Thijs, J., & Bekhuis, H.(in press). Intergroup contact and ingroup reappraisal: Testing the deprovincialization thesis. Manuscript under review.

Verkuyten, M., & Yildiz, A. A. (2007). National (dis)identification and ethnic and religious identity: A study among Turkish-Dutch Muslims. *Personality and Social Psychology Bulletin, 33*, 1448–1462.

Vogt, W. P. (1997). *Tolerance and education: Learning to live with diversity and difference.* London: Sage.

Wainryb, C., Shaw, L. A., Langley, M., Cottam, K., & Lewis, R. (2004). Children's thinking about diversity of belief in the early school years: Judgments of relativism, tolerance, and disagreeing persons. *Child Development, 75*, 687–703.

Wainryb, C., Shaw, L. A., & Maianu, C. (1998). Tolerance and intolerance: Children's and adolescents' judgements of dissenting beliefs, speech, persons, and conduct. *Child Development, 69*, 1541–1555.

Walzer, M. (1997). *On toleration.* New Haven, CT: Yale University Press.

Ward, C., & Masgoret, A. (2006). An integrative model of attitudes toward immigrants. *International Journal of Intercultural Relations, 30*, 671–682.

Witenberg, R. T. (2002). Reflective racial tolerance and its development in children, adolescents and young adults: Age related difference and context effects. *Journal of Research in Education, 12*, 1–8.

Wolsko, C., Park, B., & Judd, C. (2006). Considering the tower of Babel: Correlates of assimilation and multiculturalism among ethnic minority and majority groups in the United States. *Social Justice Research, 19*, 277–306.

Wolsko, C., Park, B., Judd, C. M., & Wittenbrink, B. (2000). Framing interethnic ideology: Effects of multicultural and color-blind perspectives on judgements of groups and individuals. *Journal of Personality and Social Psychology, 78*, 635–654.

Zick, A., Wagner, U., van Dick, R., & Petzel, T. (2001). Acculturation and prejudice in Germany: Majority and minority perspectives. *Journal of Social Issues, 57,* 541–557.

Zolberg, A. R., & Long, L. W. (1999). Why Islam is like Spanish: Cultural incorporation in Europe and the United States. *Politics and Society, 27,* 5–38.

8

Diversity Experiences and Intergroup Attitudes

Christopher L. Aberson

Diversity Experiences and Intergroup Attitudes

This chapter focuses on the impact of diversity experiences on intergroup attitudes. The first section develops a definition of diversity experiences. Specifically, I distinguish between diversity experiences and intergroup contact. The second section examines the impact of diverse educational (e.g., ethnic study courses, cultural celebrations) and work experiences (e.g., diversity training) on intergroup attitudes (e.g., attitudes toward other ethnic groups, ability to take the perspective of members of other groups). As many diversity experiences are voluntary, the third section discusses predictors of participation in diversity experiences. This section focuses on who chooses to participate in diversity experiences and the impacts of voluntary participation on conclusions about the diversity experience–intergroup attitude relationship. To develop further an understanding of the causal mechanisms underlying how diversity experiences improve attitudes, the fourth section examines research and theory relevant to factors that mediate this relationship. Specifically, I explore variables such as intergroup anxiety and perspective taking that potentially explain why diversity experiences improve intergroup attitudes. The fifth section focuses on the implications of the research for social and educational policies, with concrete suggestions for pre-college education and programs seeking to enhance support for affirmative action. Finally, I identify gaps in present knowledge and suggest avenues for future investigation.

Defining Diversity Experiences

For the purpose of this chapter, I define diversity experiences as experiences that provide opportunities for individuals to learn about people from different backgrounds without necessarily engaging in contact with people from those backgrounds. These experiences might include completing coursework focused on diversity issues (e.g., a Gender Roles or Race and Inequality course), attending events devoted to diversity (e.g., Indigenous People's Week or National Coming Out Day), or participating in diversity training (e.g., a workshop addressing equal opportunity practices).

How diversity experiences differ from intergroup contact is particularly important. Intergroup contact broadly refers to experiences of personal interaction with members of other groups (outgroups). For example, a White person engaged in a friendship with a Hispanic person is experiencing intergroup contact, as is a heterosexual man who works with a gay man (see Allport, 1954; Pettigrew, 1998 for overviews). The present definition of a diversity experience does not require contact with outgroup members. This does not mean that diversity experiences may not include components of outgroup contact, only that contact on its own does not fit the definition. Whereas outgroup contact certainly involves experience with diversity, there is already compelling research supporting the positive impacts of contact on intergroup attitudes (e.g., Pettigrew & Tropp, 2006). Instead, my focus on diversity experiences involves issues such as diversity education and organizational diversity training. To give some examples of the distinction, I define experiences such as a course in the psychology of prejudice or attending a workshop on Islamic cultures as representing a diversity experience. Similarly, attending an organizational workshop on improving communication in diverse teams is also a diversity experience. On the other hand, I define sharing a dormitory room with a student from a different ethnic background, having a close outgroup friend, or working collaboratively with outgroup members at work as contact experiences, but not diversity experiences. I address empirical evidence of the distinctiveness of these topics at the end of the following section.

Educational and Work Experiences

This section addresses the impacts of educational and workplace diversity experiences on intergroup attitudes. In general, the most extensive

Table 8.1 Summary of Findings and Limitations for Educational Settings

	Large-scale studies	*Small-scale studies*
Types of diversity experiences	Classroom experiences (e.g., ethnic studies courses), activities outside the classroom (e.g., diversity workshops), intergroup dialogues	Intergroup dialogues, classroom experiences, activities outside the classroom, diversity educational programs
Positive impact of experiences	More positive intergroup attitudes, greater citizenship engagement, increased support for equality, better perspective taking, more positive interactions with ethnic outgroup members	Increased understanding of privilege, greater endorsement of the importance of diversity, better perspective taking, more democratic sentiments, increased political engagement
Strength of evidence	Strong and consistent results from several large-scale longitudinal research studies	Mixed results from quasi-experimental and correlational studies
Limitations and under-investigated questions	Most data reflect voluntary experiences, mediated effects under-researched, few controlled experiments	Small sample sizes may account for failure to find effects, few controlled experiments or mediation analyses

evidence in this area comes from longitudinal studies in higher education settings, with fewer studies employing experimental designs and examining workplace or pre-college programs. Longitudinal studies are particularly important as these studies track changes in student attitudes over long periods of time. Table 8.1 summarizes results for educational studies.

Large-scale Studies in Higher Educational Settings

A number of large-scale educational studies demonstrate considerable relationships between curricular (e.g., courses) and co-curricular (e.g., cultural celebration, workshops) diversity experiences and intergroup attitudes. Broadly, experiences with diversity relate to more positive attitudes toward outgroups, increased support for equality, and greater endorsement of policies designed to promote equality, such as affirmative action.

One prominent data source from the University of Michigan's Michigan Student Study (MSS) highlights numerous benefits of diversity experiences. The project involved longitudinal data collection from 1990 to 1994, measuring incoming students yearly through their fourth year at the institution. Most analyses defined diversity experiences as reflecting some or all of the following components: The extent of exposure to information or activities devoted to understanding other groups and interracial or interethnic relationships in courses, readings, lectures, and discussions; whether students perceived that a specific course or program had an important impact on their diversity views; and participation in activities at the university such as Hispanic Heritage Celebration, Native American Month or Annual Pow Wow, Martin Luther King Symposium, Asian American Awareness Week, Black History Month, or Intergroup Dialogues (see Gurin, 1992).

There is a great deal of work based on the MSS, with the findings compelling, especially for the positive impacts of diversity experiences on White students. For example, Whites with more diversity experiences demonstrated greater political engagement, appreciation for other perspectives, and better learning outcomes than did students with fewer experiences (Gurin, 1999; Gurin, Nagda, & Lopez, 2004, Study 2). Similarly, others found that diversity experiences predicted increased support for educational equity and awareness of inequality for White students (Lopez, 1993, 2004; Lopez, Holliman, & Peng, 1995). Still another study examining changes in White, Asian American, and African American students' attitudes toward affirmative action over four years found greater diversity experience related to increases in support for affirmative action, even after controlling for a host of additional predictors of affirmative action attitudes (Aberson, 2007a).

The Cooperative Institutional Research Program (CIRP) also provides extensive longitudinal data addressing diversity experiences (see Astin, 1993). This work examined students from nearly 200 institutions across the United States in their fourth year of college (1989) and then again five years later (1994). Enrollment in college diversity courses promoted greater citizenship engagement (e.g., community action) and greater racial/cultural engagements (e.g., acceptance of persons of other races) five years after college for most groups, with the most consistent benefits observed for White students, even after controlling for informal interactions (e.g., socializing with students of different backgrounds; Gurin, Dey, Hurtado, & Gurin, 2002).

Another large-scale study of diversity experiences comes from the Preparing Students for a Diverse Democracy project. This work followed students from 10 campuses across the United States from admission to their second year in college. Most analyses of these data collapsed across ethnicity; however, the sample was predominantly White. Consistent with the Michigan and CIRP findings, participation in diversity courses related to greater support for diversity and equity and more support for race-based initiatives (Hurtado, 2003). Students with more curricular diversity participation (e.g., courses that included readings or materials on race, ethnicity, gender, and oppression) showed more positive attitudes toward gay men and lesbians (Engberg, Hurtado, & Smith, 2007). In addition, for students in most majors, diversity courses and co-curricular activities related positively to their self-reported strengths in areas such as being able to work cooperatively with diverse people, tolerance of others with different beliefs, perspective taking, and motivation to learn about outgroups (Engberg, 2007). For White, African American, Asian American, and Latino students, co-curricular activities or opportunities to participate in intensive discussions with students of different backgrounds related to perceptions of more positive interactions with ethnic outgroup members (Saenz, Ngai, & Hurtado, 2007). Also, a subsample of the data found that students enrolled in a course on social diversity reported more positive interactions with other ethnic groups compared to students enrolled in a traditional course (Laird, Engberg, & Hurtado, 2005).

Still another large-scale longitudinal study (1996–2001) examined attitudes of students at the University of California, Los Angeles (Sidanius, Levin, van Laar, & Sears, 2008). This work found that for White students, greater ethnic study course content associated with more outgroup friends in the final year of measurement, even after controlling for factors such as pre-college attitudes and experiences. Additionally, for Asian American students (a majority group on campus), more ethnic studies content related to reduced modern racism (van Laar, Sidanius, & Levin, 2008).

Small-scale Educational Studies

A number of smaller studies also addressed the impact of diversity experiences. Several demonstrated results broadly consistent with the larger studies, but others failed to show effects. For example, students who reported discussing diversity in their courses showed stronger understandings of privilege and prejudice (Mayhew & Fernández, 2007), students who completed a multiracial dormitory dialogue program more strongly endorsed the importance of diversity compared to students who had just started the program and those who had not participated (Muthuswamy, Levine, & Gazel, 2006), students who completed a diversity course requirement demonstrated less modern racism than students who had just begun the course (Chang, 2002), diversity course participation related to positive increases in motivation to control prejudice and desire to promote social justice and inclusion (Zúñiga, Williams, & Berger, 2005), and students enrolled in a first-year diversity education program exhibited greater perspective-taking ability, democratic sentiments, and political engagement than a matched group of students who did not enroll (Gurin et al., 2004, Study 1).

One increasingly prominent diversity experience in educational settings is the intergroup dialogue. An intergroup dialogue involves facilitated face-to-face learning experiences that engage students from different groups in discussions of differences and commonalities, social inequalities, and approaches to working together to achieve equality (Zúñiga, Nagda, Chesler, & Cytron-Walker, 2007). A number of studies demonstrated that completion of courses involving intergroup dialogues related to positive outcomes, including increased understanding of outgroup perspectives (Hurtado, 2003) and desires to bridge intergroup differences (Nagda, 2006; Nagda, Kim, & Truelove, 2004).

Despite the positive impacts reported above, a number of studies found no benefits for diversity experiences. For example, students who completed a civic learning program with a strong multicultural focus showed similar diversity orientations as students who did not participate (Longerbeam & Sedlacek, 2006). Another study found that a series of diversity workshops failed to impact diversity awareness (Brown, 2004). Similarly, a course designed to improve diversity competence found that, for White men, the course not only failed to improve attitudes toward gay men and lesbians, but also related to less positive attitudes toward women (Hood, Muller, & Seitz, 2001). Additionally, a review that focused on pre-post and comparison group studies found mixed evidence for positive effects of diversity education with regard to attitudes toward specific groups or skill acquisition (Kulik & Roberson, 2008). I suggest several explanations for these mixed results in the section on gaps in present knowledge and future research directions.

Organizational Diversity Training

Many organizations seek to improve relationships among workers through diversity training. Surveys of U.S. organizations indicate that roughly two-thirds use some form of diversity training (Esen, 2005), with estimates indicating that diversity training is a U.S.$8 billion industry (Hansen, 2003). Although many organizations use some form of diversity training, the effectiveness of such programs for improving intergroup attitudes is questionable.

With regard to whether diversity training affects intergroup attitudes, it appears that the best answer is "we're not sure" (Paluck, 2006, p. 579). Addressing impacts of training on improving organizational diversity, diversity training impacts opportunities for women and minorities considerably less than more directed programs such as creating bodies within the organization responsible for promoting diversity (e.g., a diversity taskforce) and implementing mentoring programs (Kalev, Dobbin, & Kelly, 2006).

The mixed effectiveness of diversity training highlights several shortcomings in program design. First, training is difficult to evaluate, as most organizations introduce programs organization-wide, making comparison-group studies difficult (Agars & Kottke, 2004). Supporting this proposition, an extensive review indicated that most research in the area involves field studies using only post-intervention measures without control groups (Paluck & Green, 2009). Others note failures of popular programs (e.g., Blue-eyes Brown-eyes) to consider theory in program design (Pendry, Driscoll, & Field, 2007; see also van Knippenberg & van Ginkel, this volume). Theory-driven experimental investigations of the effectiveness of organizational training are lacking.

Although there are clearly shortcomings in both theoretical grounding and evidence for the effectiveness of diversity training, it is important to recognize that many discussions of program effectiveness in the psychological literature focus primarily on whether diversity training improves intergroup attitudes (also see Cameron & Turner, this volume and Verkuyten, this volume for a more extensive discussion of these issues). Many organizations, however, use diversity training as a single piece of a broader diversity enhancement program that might include an affirmative action plan, diversity committees, mentoring, and staff devoted to equal opportunity issues. It may be that evaluations of diversity training ignore critical components of organization diversity plans that contribute to improved intergroup attitudes.

Evidence for the Distinctiveness of Diversity Experiences and Contact

Although I make the distinction between diversity experiences and contact experiences, it is important to note that the two variables are related. For example, in the UCLA study, diversity experiences such as enrollment in ethnic studies courses related to more outgroup friendships for White students (van Laar et al., 2008). In studies employing majority White samples, participation in diversity courses did not impact quantity of interactions with diverse peers but it did relate to more positive contact experiences with diverse peers (Laird, 2005). Also, curricular experiences such as attending racial/cultural awareness programs and discussion of racial issues related to greater frequency of cross-ethnic contact (Gottfredson et al., 2008). In each of the studies cited, the observed effects appear relatively small (e.g., correlation of $<.40$). Diversity experiences and intergroup contact are related, but not so strongly as to dispute their status as distinct constructs.

Predicting Engagement in Diversity Experiences

This section addresses predispositions to participate in diversity experiences. Many of the studies in the previous section examined voluntary diversity experiences, so it is important to address whether certain characteristics (e.g., greater willingness to engage in cross-ethnic contact) relate to greater participation in these experiences. Several studies examining engagement in university-level diversity experiences suggest considerable differences between students who participated in diversity experiences and those who did not. For example, White students enrolled in a program involving courses and workshops focused on diversity issues tended to be those with more pre-college openness to diversity (Nagda, Gurin, & Johnson, 2005). Similarly, students who arrived at college with stronger pluralistic orientations signed up for more diversity courses and workshops (Engberg, 2007), those with more diverse pre-college friends indicted stronger intentions to enroll in diversity courses (Milem & Umbach, 2003), and students with a greater awareness of inequality or support for educational equity were more likely to participate in curricular diversity (Lopez, 2004). More generally, Whites who valued diversity reported a stronger interest in contact with outgroup members (Tropp & Bianchi, 2007). These studies suggest that students who arrive at college open to diversity and with more diverse contact experiences tend to be the ones who are most likely to take advantage of voluntary diversity experiences.

Similar findings exist in the organizational realm. For example, employees' interest in attending voluntary diversity training related to their knowledge of equal opportunity procedures and their competency in dealing with diversity (Kulik, Pepper, Roberson, & Parker, 2007). Taken together with the university studies, these data call into question whether predispositions explain the links between diversity experiences and improved intergroup attitudes.

Some work mitigates concerns about the role of pre-college attitudes on diversity participation. For example, diversity experiences predicted improvements in attitudes toward affirmative action, even after controlling for pre-college openness to diversity (Aberson, 2007a). In addition, after controlling for a wide range of pre-college openness and attitude variables, greater diversity participation still related to more positive cross-ethnic interactions for most students (Saenz et al., 2007).

There also remains the possibility that interactions between experiences and openness drive findings. It could be that those who are more initially open to diversity show greater attitude change following diversity experiences than those who are less open. Consistent with this proposition, a course providing structured interracial dialogues increased confidence in perspective-taking ability, but only for individuals who valued the dialogic process (Nagda & Zúñiga, 2003). Students who come to experiences more open to diversity may be more strongly influenced by the experience, may enjoy the events more, and may become more committed to attending future events. The issue of motivation to participate in diversity experiences presents a serious challenge to data supporting the effectiveness of voluntary programs promoting diversity experiences.

Mediators of the Diversity Experience–Intergroup Attitude Relationship

This section focuses on empirical studies addressing mediators of the diversity experience–attitude relationship and examines theory relevant to mediation. A mediating variable is one that accounts for how and why one variable influences another. In the context of the relationship between diversity experiences and improved intergroup attitudes, mediating variables address what it is about diversity experiences that potentially lead to attitude improvement. That is, mediators suggest why diversity experiences relate to improved attitudes.

Empirical Studies Examining Mediators

Despite considerable support for the relationship between diversity experiences and intergroup attitudes, relatively little work addresses mediators of the relationship. That is, there is presently not a clear picture of how diversity experiences improve attitudes. Below I review the limited evidence for mediated effects.

In a study of dialogue processes, factors related to openness to diversity and willingness to consider outgroup perspectives mediated relationships between diversity participation and the desire to bridge differences between groups (Nagda, 2006). Similarly, desire to learn about racial differences mediated the relationship between dialogue participation and confidence in abilities to take action to reduce prejudice and promote diversity (Nagda et al., 2004). In another study, motivation to learn about the outgroup mediated the relationship between participation in co-curricular activities and pluralistic orientations (Engberg, 2007). Willingness to consider other perspectives and the desire to learn about other groups appear conceptually similar to social psychological constructs such as perspective taking and empathy (e.g., Davis, 1994). At a general level, taking outgroup perspectives (e.g., Vescio, Sechrist, & Paolucci, 2003) and empathy for outgroup members (e.g., Stephan & Finlay, 1999) consistently relate to improved attitudes toward outgroups.

Other results however, failed to show mediated relationships. For example, intergroup anxiety, a well-established mediator of contact–intergroup attitude relationship (e.g., Stephan et al., 2002), failed to mediate relationships between curricular experiences and attitudes toward ethnic outgroups and lesbians, gays, and bisexuals (Engberg, 2007; Engberg et al., 2007).

Theory and Empirical Results Suggesting Additional Mediating Variables

One theoretical model that proposes several mediators potentially relevant to the impact of diversity experiences is Integrated Threat Theory (ITT). ITT posits that threats to the ingroup promote negative attitudes toward outgroups (Stephan & Stephan, 2000). Threats include intergroup anxiety, realistic threat (e.g., perceived barriers to the ingroup's welfare), symbolic threat (e.g., threats to the ingroup's values), and negative stereotyping. Antecedents to threat include contact, ingroup identification, status, and perceived intergroup conflict. ITT proposes that antecedents influence attitudes through their effects on threat (i.e., that threats mediate the relationship between antecedents and attitudes). Of the antecedent variables addressed in ITT, contact appears conceptually closest to diversity experiences. As discussed earlier in the chapter, contact and diversity experiences are distinct constructs. However, it may be the case that both types of experiences work through similar routes to improve attitudes. For example, a Christian's contact experience, such as a friendship with a Muslim, might improve attitudes toward Muslims by enhancing understanding of Muslim perspectives. This might also be accomplished through diversity experiences such as a course focused on religious diversity. Given these issues, a good starting point for examining mediators of the diversity experience–intergroup attitude relationship is consideration of mediators of the contact–intergroup attitude relationship (see also Schmid & Hewstone, this volume).

Several studies present extensive data on mediators of the contact–intergroup attitude relationship, finding that contact predicted threats in the expected directions (i.e., better quality of contact related to feeling less threatened), and that threats mediated contact impacts on attitudes (e.g., Aberson & Gaffney, 2009; Aberson & Haag, 2007; Stephan et al., 2002). Additionally, meta-analytic evidence found factors not addressed in ITT such as knowledge, empathy, and perspective taking, mediated the contact–attitude relationship (Pettigrew & Tropp, 2008).

As discussed earlier, there is some evidence that perspective taking and empathy mediate the diversity experience–attitude relationship. Additionally, there is considerable data demonstrating that intergroup dialogues and other diversity experiences relate to perspective taking and empathy. For example, diversity courses and intergroup dialogues associated with better perspective-taking ability (Hurtado, 2003). Analyses of the MSS data found a relationship between diversity experiences and greater perspective taking among White students (Gurin et al., 2004). Similarly, students with more diversity-course enrollment showed more empathy regarding prejudice (Spanierman, Todd, & Anderson, 2009) and greater enthusiasm for learning about new perspectives (Gottfredson et al., 2008). Taken together with the mediation studies involving willingness to consider other perspectives and related variables, these data suggest a promising role for perspective taking and empathy in mediating the diversity experience–intergroup attitude relationship. That is, it appears that enhanced perspective taking and empathy are important components of successful diversity experiences.

Relevant to intergroup anxiety, intergroup dialogues increased willingness to engage in interactions with outgroup members and increased appreciation of differences (Nagda, 2006). More classroom diversity experiences related to positive changes in Universal Diversity Orientation, a construct that involves issues such as ease with outgroup members and desire to learn more about outgroups (Spanierman, Neville, Liao, Hammer, & Wang, 2008). Additionally, for White and Latino students, enrollment in ethnic studies courses related to more outgroup friendships (van Laar, Sidanius, & Levin, 2008), suggesting that these courses weakened barriers to contact such as intergroup anxiety. Others, however, found no relationship between diversity experiences, intergroup dialogues, and reduced intergroup anxiety (Engberg, 2007; Engberg et al., 2007; Hurtado, 2003).

Extensive evidence for the role of mediated effects is not presently available and existing results provide mixed effects. Taken as a whole, the results described in this section suggest an important role for increasing perspective taking and empathy in mediating the impacts of diversity experiences on intergroup attitudes. Although mixed results exist for intergroup anxiety, it may be the case that experiences designed specifically to reduce anxiety would produce greater improvements in intergroup attitudes. It appears that no studies examined the mediating role of knowledge, realistic threat, symbolic threat, or negative stereotypes. These variables are established mediators of the contact–intergroup attitude relationship, so investigating their impact on the diversity experience–intergroup attitude relationship seems a logical step. Mediation addresses the causal mechanisms promoting attitude improvements. A better understanding of these mechanisms would suggest improvements to programs promoting diversity experiences. For example, if intergroup anxiety mediates the diversity experience–intergroup attitude relationship, this suggests that programs that explicitly focus on reducing intergroup anxiety will impact attitudes more strongly than those that do not.

Social Policy Implications

There are several policy implications inherent in the results of studies reviewed in the previous sections. First, it appears that, despite limitations in knowledge of mediating mechanisms, college diversity experiences do relate to improved intergroup attitudes. This suggests that colleges and universities should make diversity courses and related workshops part of their standard curriculum.

Data on predispositions find that pre-college characteristics such as openness to diversity, appreciation of diversity, and diverse friendships relate to greater participation in diversity experiences at the college level and promote effective diversity training experiences in organizations. This suggests that efforts directed at younger people (i.e., before college and before entering the workforce) that foster openness to diversity facilitate effective diversity experiences later in life. Several existing programs show promising results at this level. For example, a program designed around common identity approaches increased cross-ethnic friendships among first- and second-grade students (Houlette et al., 2004), and elementary and secondary-school programs employing intergroup dialogue approaches appear to improve intergroup attitudes (Fernandez, 2001; Tiven, 2001). The influence of pre-college and pre-workforce attitudes suggests considerable benefits for increased implementation of programs for children and adolescents.

Also relevant is the relationship between diversity beliefs and support for affirmative action. Research regarding the relationship between belief in the value of diversity and support for affirmative action demonstrated positive relationships with support for affirmative action in general (Aberson & Haag, 2003) and support for specific affirmative-action policies such as those employing banding or tiebreak procedures (Aberson, 2007b). In each of these studies, diversity beliefs predicted attitudes even when controlling for other relevant beliefs such as belief in meritocracy, fairness of affirmative action, and prevalence of discrimination. Openness to diversity may be a key component to promoting support for social policies such as affirmative action. This suggests that programs that promote openness to diversity facilitate enhanced support for affirmative action.

Gaps in Our Knowledge and Suggestions for Future Research

This section identifies gaps in our present knowledge and suggests avenues for future investigation. Although several large-scale studies found positive relationships between diversity experiences and intergroup attitudes, it is important to recognize that each study, despite use of statistical controls and longitudinal approaches, was correlational.

Selection issues limit the strength of the conclusions of these studies (e.g., people open to diversity seek out diversity experiences). There are few controlled experiments addressing the impact of diversity experiences on attitudes (Paluck & Green, 2009). Definitive conclusions about the causal role of diversity experiences in changing attitudes requires further investigation employing stronger research designs.

Statistical power appears limited for many small-scale investigations. Two extensive reviews of diversity education in academic and organizational settings found that roughly half of the studies reviewed employed samples of fewer than 100 participants (Kulik & Roberson, 2008; Paluck & Green, 2009). In general, a larger proportion of the small sample studies failed to detect effects, suggesting that the mixed effects found in the literature may be a function of inadequate statistical power.

Another issue is whether diversity experiences should be voluntary or mandated. When freely choosing experiences, participants who are initially more open to diversity are the most likely to seek out diversity experiences. Data on pre-college attitudes support the proposition that those students who begin college more open to diversity tend to engage in more diversity experiences (e.g., Nagda et al., 2005). Voluntary experiences appear to "preach to the choir." However, it is not clear whether or not mandating experiences is effective.

Turning the focus to organizational diversity training, theory-driven designs and evaluation are lacking. Studies of common diversity training suggest several areas where social psychological theories and research might considerably improve approaches (Pendry et al., 2007). There remain numerous unanswered questions regarding issues such as the value of focusing on differences and what difference to address, the role of emotions, whether minority presence is necessary, whether or not to address stereotypes, and whether training should be voluntary (Paluck, 2006). In short, it appears that diversity trainers and academics have largely failed to work together to design appropriate evaluations and optimal programs that employ theory-driven interventions and adequate field experiments to test effectiveness (Paluck & Green, 2009).

There are few studies clearly addressing mediation of the diversity experience–intergroup attitude relationship. Not surprisingly, it remains unclear which types of interventions actually work (Hurtado, Griffin, Arellano, & Cuellar, 2008; Stephan, Renfro, & Stephan, 2004). An increased focus on mediation will clarify how diversity experiences improve intergroup attitudes and guide program design to effect optimal attitude change.

Finally, although prominent large-scale studies contribute a great deal to the literature, most include definitions of diversity experiences that focus primarily on quantity of attendance at workshops or related events. Future work will benefit from addressing issues of the quality of such experiences as well as students' levels of engagement.

Conclusions

Knowledge regarding the positive impacts of diversity experiences on intergroup attitudes should be expanded. However, despite a number of methodological limitations, the role of diversity experiences in promoting positive intergroup attitudes appears promising. The clearest conclusion drawn from this review is that students who participated in more diversity experiences demonstrate more positive attitudes toward outgroup members and a host of other positive outcomes. The next step for researchers in this area is to firmly establish the causal effects of such programs and to develop stronger evidence regarding which programs work and why.

References

Aberson, C. L. (2007a). Diversity experiences predict changes in attitudes toward affirmative action. *Cultural Diversity and Ethnic Minority Psychology, 13,* 285–294.

Aberson, C. L. (2007b). Diversity, merit, fairness, and discrimination beliefs as predictors of support for affirmative action policy actions. *Journal of Applied Social Psychology, 37,* 2451–2474.

Aberson, C. L., & Gaffney, A. M. (2009). An integrated threat model of implicit and explicit attitudes. *European Journal of Social Psychology, 39,* 808–830.

Aberson, C. L., & Haag, S. C. (2003). Beliefs about affirmative action and diversity and their relationship to support for hiring policies. *Analyses of Social Issues and Public Policy, 3,* 121–138.

Aberson, C. L., & Haag, S. C. (2007). Contact, anxiety, perspective taking, and stereotype endorsement as predictors of implicit and explicit biases. *Group Processes and Intergroup Relations, 10,* 179–201.

Agars, M. D., & Kottke, J. L. (2004). Models and practice of diversity management: A historical review and presentation of a new integration theory. In M. S. Stockdale & F.J. Crosby (Eds.), *The psychology and management of workplace diversity* (pp. 55–77). Malden, MA: Blackwell.

Allport, G. W. (1954). *The nature of prejudice.* Reading, MA: Addison-Wesley.

Astin, A. W. (1993). *What matters in college?* San Francisco: Jossey-Bass.

Brown, E. L. (2004). What precipitates change in cultural diversity awareness during a multicultural course: The message or the method? *Journal of Teacher Education, 55,* 325–340.

Chang, M. J. (2002). The impact of undergraduate diversity course requirement on students' racial views and attitudes. *Journal of General Education, 51,* 21–42.

Davis, M. H. (1994). *Empathy: A social psychological approach.* Madison, WI: Brown & Benchmark.

Engberg, M. E. (2007). Educating the workforce for the 21st century: A cross-disciplinary analysis of the impact of the undergraduate experience on students' development of a pluralistic orientation. *Research in Higher Education, 48,* 283–317.

Engberg, M. E., Hurtado, S., & Smith, G. C. (2007). Developing attitudes of acceptance toward lesbian, gay, and bisexual peers: Enlightenment, contact, and the college experience. *Journal of Gay & Lesbian Issues in Education, 4,* 49–77.

Esen, E. (2005). *Workplace diversity practices survey report.* Alexandria, VA: Society for Human Resource Management.

Fernandez, T. (2001). Building "bridges" of understanding through dialogue. In D. Schoem & S. Hurtado (Eds.), *Intergroup dialogue: Deliberative democracy in school, college, community, and workplace* (pp. 45–58). Ann Arbor, MI: University of Michigan Press.

Gottfredson, N. C., Panter, A. T., Daye, C. E., Allen, W. A., Wightman, L. F., & Deo, M. E. (2008). Does diversity at undergraduate institutions influence student outcomes? *Journal of Diversity in Higher Education, 1,* 80–94.

Gurin, G. (1992). *The Michigan Study: Expectations and experiences of first-year students with diversity.* Ann Arbor: University of Michigan, Office of Academic Multicultural Initiatives.

Gurin, P. (1999). *Expert report of Patricia Gurin.* Retrieved from http://www.umich.edu/~urel/admissions/legal/expert/summ.html.

Gurin, P., Dey, E. L., Hurtado, S., & Gurin, G. (2002). Diversity and higher education: Theory and impact on educational outcomes. *Harvard Educational Review, 72,* 330–366.

Gurin, P., Nagda, B. A., & Lopez, G. E. (2004). The benefits of diversity in education for democratic citizenship. *Journal of Social Issues, 60,* 17–34.

Hansen, F. (2003). *Workforce, 82,* 28–32.

Hood, J. N., Muller, H. J., & Seitz, P. (2001). Attitudes of Hispanics and Anglos surrounding a workforce diversity intervention. *Hispanic Journal of Behavioral Sciences, 23,* 444–458.

Houlette, M. A., Gaertner, S. L., Johnson, K. M., Riek, B. M., Dovidio, J. F., & Banker, B. S. (2004). Developing a more inclusive social identity: An elementary school intervention. *Journal of Social Issues, 60,* 35–55.

Hurtado, S. (2003). Preparing college students for a diverse democracy: Final report to the U.S. Department of Education, OERI, Field Initiated Studies Program. Ann Arbor, MI: Center for the Study of Higher and Postsecondary Education.

Hurtado, S., Griffin, K. A., Arellano, L., & Cuellar, M. (2008). Assessing the value of climate assessments: Progress and future directions. *Journal of Diversity in Higher Education, 1*, 204–221.

Kalev, A., Dobbin, F., & Kelly, E. (2006). Best practices or best guesses? Assessing the efficacy of corporate affirmative action and diversity policies. *American Sociological Review, 71*, 589–617.

Kulik, C. T., Pepper, M. B., Roberson, L., & Parker, S. K. (2007). The rich get richer: Predicting participation in voluntary diversity training. *Journal of Organizational Behavior, 28*, 753–769.

Kulik, C. T., & Roberson, L. (2008). Common goals and golden opportunities: Evaluations of diversity education in academic and organizational settings. *Academy of Management Learning & Education, 7*, 309–331.

Laird, F. N. (2005). College students' experiences with diversity and their effects on academic self-confidence, social agency, and disposition toward critical thinking. *Research in Higher Education, 46*, 365–387.

Laird, F. N., Engberg, M. E., & Hurtado, S. (2005). Modeling accentuation effects: Enrolling in a diversity course and the importance of social action engagement. *Journal of Higher Education, 76*, 448–476.

Longerbeam, S. D., & Sedlacek, W. E. (2006). Attitudes toward diversity and living-learning outcomes among first- and second-year college students. *NASPA Journal, 43*, 40–55.

Lopez, G. E. (1993). The effects of group contact and curriculum on White, Asian American, and African American students' attitudes. *Dissertation Abstracts International, 54*(07): 3900B (UMI No. 9332125).

Lopez, G. E. (2004). Interethnic contact, curriculum and attitudes in the first year of college. *Journal of Social Issues, 60*, 75–94.

Lopez, G. E., Holliman, D., & Peng, T. (1995). Beyond zero-sum diversity: Student support for educational equity. *Educational Record, 76*, 55–62.

Mayhew, M. J., & Fernández, S. D. (2007). Pedagogical practices that contribute to social justice outcomes. *Review of Higher Education, 31*, 55–80.

Milem, J. F., & Umbach, P. D. (2003). The influence of pre-college factors on students' predispositions regarding diversity activities in college. *Journal of College Student Development, 44*, 611–624.

Muthuswamy, N., Levine, T. R., & Gazel, J. (2006). Interaction-based diversity initiative outcomes: An evaluation of an initiative aimed at bridging the racial divide on a college campus. *Communication Education, 55*, 105–121.

Nagda, B. A. (2006). Breaking barriers, crossing boundaries, building bridges: Communication processes in intergroup dialogues. *Journal of Social Issues, 62*, 553–576.

Nagda, B. A., Gurin, P., & Johnson, S. M. (2005). Living, doing and thinking diversity: How does pre-college diversity experience affect first-year students' engagement with college diversity? In R. Feldman (Ed.), *Improving the first year of college: Research and practice* (pp. 73–108). Mahwah, NJ: Erlbaum.

Nagda, B. A., Kim, C. W., & Truelove, Y. (2004). Learning about difference, learning with others, learning to transgress. *Journal of Social Issues, 60*, 195–214.

Nagda, B. A., & Zúñiga, X. (2003). Fostering meaningful racial engagement through intergroup dialogues. *Group Processes and Intergroup Relations, 6*, 111–128.

Paluck, E. L. (2006). Diversity training and intergroup contact: A call to action research. *Journal of Social Issues, 62*, 577–595.

Paluck, E. L., & Green, D. P. (2009). Prejudice reduction: What works? A review and assessment of research and practice. *Annual Review of Psychology, 60*, 339–367.

Pendry, L. F., Driscoll, D. M., & Field, S. C. T. (2007). Diversity training: Putting theory into practice. *Journal of Occupational and Organizational Psychology, 80*, 27–50.

Pettigrew, T. F. (1998). Intergroup contact theory. *Annual Review of Psychology, 49*, 65–85.

Pettigrew, T. F., & Tropp, L. R. (2006). A meta-analytic test of intergroup contact theory. *Journal of Personality and Social Psychology, 90*, 751–783.

Pettigrew, T. F., & Tropp, L. R. (2008). How does intergroup contact reduce prejudice? meta-analytic tests of three mediators. *European Journal of Social Psychology, 38*, 922–934.

Saenz, V. B., Ngai, H. N., & Hurtado, S. (2007). Factors influencing positive interactions across race for African American, Asian American, Latino, and White college students. *Research in Higher Education, 48*, 1–38.

Sidanius, J., Levin, S., van Laar, C., & Sears, D. O. (2008). *The diversity challenge: Social identity and intergroup relations on the college campus.* New York: Russell Sage Foundation.

Spanierman, L. B., Neville, H. A., Liao, H., Hammer, J. H., & Wang, Y. (2008). Participation in formal and informal campus diversity experiences: Effects on students' racial democratic beliefs. *Journal of Diversity in Higher Education, 1*, 108–125.

Spanierman, L. B., Todd, N. R., & Anderson, C. J. (2009). Psychosocial costs of racism to whites: Understanding patterns among university students. *Journal of Counseling Psychology, 56*, 239–252.

Stephan, C. W., Renfro, L., & Stephan, W. G. (2004). The evaluation of multicultural education programs: techniques and a meta-analysis. In W. G. Stephan & W. P. Vogt (Eds.), *Education programs for improving intergroup relations: Theory, research and practice* (pp. 227–242). New York: Teachers College Press.

Stephan, W. G., Boniecki, K. A., Ybarra, O., Bettencourt, A., Ervin, K. S., Jackson, L. A., McNatt, P. S., & Renfro, C. L. (2002). The role of threats in racial attitudes of Blacks and Whites. *Personality and Social Psychology Bulletin, 28*, 1242–1254.

Stephan, W. G., & Finlay, K. (1999). The role of empathy in improving inter-group relations. *Journal of Social Issues, 55,* 729–743.

Stephan, W. G., & Stephan, C. W. (2000). An integrated threat theory of prejudice. In S. Oskamp (Ed.), *Reducing prejudice and discrimination* (pp. 23–46). Hillsdale, NJ: Erlbaum.

Tiven, L. (2001). Student voices: The ADL's World of Difference institute peer training program. In D. Schoem & S. Hurtado (Eds.), *Intergroup dialogue: Deliberative democracy in school, college, community, and workplace* (pp. 59–73). Ann Arbor: University of Michigan Press.

Tropp, L. R., & Bianchi, R. A. (2007). Interpreting references to group membership in context: Feelings about intergroup contact depending on who says what to whom. *European Journal of Social Psychology, 37,* 153–170.

van Laar, C., Sidanius, J., & Levin, S. (2008). Ethnic-related curricula and intergroup attitudes in college: Movement toward and away from the in-group. *Journal of Applied Social Psychology, 38,* 1601–1638.

Vescio, T. K., Sechrist, G. B., & Paolucci, M. P. (2003). Perspective taking and prejudice reduction: The mediational role of empathy arousal and situational attributions. *European Journal of Social Psychology, 33,* 455–472.

Zúñiga, X., Nagda, B. A., Chesler, M., & Cytron-Walker, A. (2007). Inter-group dialogues in higher education: Meaningful learning about social justice. *ASHE-ERIC Higher Education Report Series, 32*(4): 1–128.

Zúñiga, X., Williams, E. A., & Berger, J. B. (2005). Action-oriented democratic outcomes: The impact of student involvement with campus diversity. *Journal of College Student Development, 46,* 660–678.

Part IV

Intergroup Relations

9

The Effects of Crossed Categorizations in Intergroup Interaction

Norman Miller, Marija Spanovic, and Douglas Stenstrom

Human history chronicles examples of dissatisfied groups of people who yearn for, seek out, and ultimately find their "promised land." One such example is that of Europeans fleeing to America in search of religious freedoms. On their quest, these groups encounter other groups with whom they either coexist peacefully, assimilate, or fight. Even in the most peaceful of circumstances, the creation of new societies is a challenge that creates further subdivisions and separates groups whose visions differ from those of others. Human movements and the processes that occur in emergent and changing societies create diverse social settings wherein most people can distinctively be categorized on the basis of their race, ethnicity, citizenship, political affiliation, social status, religion, gender, sexual orientation, occupation, etc. This chapter examines how crossing two or more dimensions of categorization influences bias. It also examines the factors that moderate the effects of crossed categorization on bias.

Diversity and Social Categorization

Diversity is often challenging as each group strives for power, self-government, or civil rights, and societies differ in the ways in which they deal with it. For example, at some point in their history many societies attempt to minimize intergroup differentiation. In the United

Table 9.1 Crossed Categorization Studies that Have Demonstrated Differential Bias as a Function of Moderating Conditions

Study	Moderator	Findings
Crisp & Hewstone (2000a)	Positive incidental affect	ii = io = oi = oo (equivalence)
Ensari & Miller (2001)	Personalization	ii = io = oi = oo (equivalence)
Urada & Miller (2000)	Positive incidental affect and dominance	Ii = Io
Crisp & Beck (2001)	High id. and greater differentiation	Decreased bias
Stone & Crisp (2007)	Subgroup id. = superordinate id.	Decreased bias
Crisp et al. (2005)	Subgroup id. = crossed or superord. id.	Decreased bias
Urada et al. ((2007); Exp. 1)	Multiple group membership	I = Io = Ioo = Iooo > O
Urada et al. ((2007); Exp. 1)	Multiple group membership	O = Oi < Oii = Oiii = I
Ensari et al. (in press)	Positive integral affect and relevance	Ii = Oi = Oi > Oo (social inclusion)
Vanbeselaere (2000)	Category importance	i = Io = Oi > Oo (social inclusion)
Crisp et al. (2006)	Common ingroup identity	ii = io = oi > oo (social inclusion)
Crisp & Hewstone (2001b)	Ingroup primes	ii = io = oi > oo (social inclusion)
Ensari & Miller (1998)	Positive integral affect	ii = Oi > io > oo (hierarchical rejection)
Ensari & Miller (2001)	Category salience	Ii > Oi = Oo (dominance)
van Knippenberg et al. (1994)	Relevance	Ii > Oi = Oo (dominance)
Kenworthy et al. (2003)	Neutral affect	ii > io = oi > oo (additivity)
Ensari & Miller (1998)	Neutral affect	ii > io = oi > oo (additivity)
Ensari & Miller (1998)	Negative integral affect	ii > io > Oi = oo (hierarchical acceptance)
Ensari et al. (in press)	Negative integral affect and relevance	Ii > Io > Oi = Oo (hierarchical acceptance)
Urada et al. ((2007); Exp.2)	Multiple group membership	I > Io = Ioo = Iooo = O
Urada et al. ((2007); Exp.2)	Multiple group membership	O = Oi = Oii = Oiii < I
Kenworthy et al. (2003)	Negative incidental affect	ii > io = oi = oo (social exclusion)
Crisp & Beck (2001)	High id. and decreased differentiation	Increased bias
Stone & Crisp (2007)	Subgroup id. > superordinate id.	Increased bias

Note. Studies are ordered (top to bottom) in terms of increasing overall bias against outgroups.

States, a common belief is that ethnic and racial differences should be eliminated via assimilation (Schlesinger, 1992). Communist countries similarly attempted to eliminate status differentiation by creating nations wherein all people belonged to the same social class. Given these and other instances throughout history, it is interesting to note that no country, nation, or state in human history has eliminated intergroup differentiation. Moreover, in many cases elimination of differences is frowned upon and as a result, societies are left to deal with differences, biases, and conflicts that stem from intergroup differences.

Some patterns of diversity, however, may not be as problematic as others. For example, anthropological evidence suggests that societies wherein distinct groups are nested within a superordinate category exhibit more conflict than those in which groups combine in such a way that members are simultaneously categorized along several different dimensions (LeVine & Campbell, 1972). In the former case, simple categorization occurs within the superordinate category. Any given person is either a member of their own group (ingroup member) or a member of a different group (outgroup member). In the latter case, multiple categorization occurs because others are either ingroups or outgroups on numerous dimensions of categorization, making their ingroup or outgroup status ambiguous.

The crossed categorization (CC) research paradigm, which simultaneously examines two dimensions of categorization, is a simplified representation of this latter case. In it, some persons are ingroup members on both dimensions of categorization, others are ingroup members on one dimension of categorization and outgroup members on another, and yet others are outgroup members on both dimensions of categorization. For example, crossing gender and race can result in four new categories: Asian females, Asian males, White females, and White males. From a standpoint of an Asian female, other Asian females are double ingroup members (ii), Asian males and White females belong to crossed or mixed groups (io or oi), whereas White males are double outgroup members (oo). Aside from being a simplified depiction of existing diversity patterns, the CC paradigm implicitly suggests an intervention for the reduction of intergroup bias.

Categorization of people into ingroups and outgroups leads to category differentiation such that differences within groups are weakened and differences between them are accentuated (Doise, 1978). At the same time ingroups are typically evaluated more favorably than outgroups (Brewer, 1979; Mullen, Brown, & Smith, 1992; Oakes, Haslam, & Turner, 1994; Tajfel, 1959). However, when one dimension of categorization is crossed with another dimension, the process of weakening differences within groups and accentuating differences between them (Campbell, 1956) can be counteracted by the simultaneous operation of these same processes on the other dimension. Specifically, relative to simple categorization, category differentiation is greater when participants evaluate double outgroups and it is weaker when they evaluate crossed groups (Arcuri, 1982; Deschamps & Doise, 1978; Rehm, Lilli, & Van Eimeren, 1988; Vescio, Judd, & Kwan, 2004). Thus, as a result of decreased category differentiation, bias is often reduced in the CC paradigm compared to simple categorization. Indeed, several studies show that, compared to simple categorization, CC reduces bias (Deschamps & Doise, 1978; Vanbeselaere, 1987, 1991). Other studies, however, show no reduction in bias (Brown & Turner, 1979; Singh, Yeoh, Lim, & Lim, 1997; Vescio et al., 2004) (see Table 9.1).

How can we account for the inconsistent findings? Mullen, Migdal, and Hewstone (2001) meta-analytically compared the magnitude of intergroup bias in a CC paradigm with that in a simple categorization paradigm. They found that the resulting bias reduction depended on the definition of bias. In a simple categorization paradigm, bias is defined as a difference between ingroup and outgroup evaluations. However, in the CC paradigm there are four groups and consequently, there are several different ways in which bias can be conceptualized. The category differentiation (reduction) model defines bias as the difference between the evaluations of double ingroups and double outgroups (Doise, 1978). According to the category conjunction (dissimilarity) model, bias is defined as a difference between the evaluations of double ingroups and all other groups combined (Rogers, Miller, & Hennigan, 1981). Finally, in the composite bias model, the evaluation of double ingroup is compared to the evaluation of all other groups and the difference is then averaged. Mullen et al. (2001) found that in both category differentiation (reduction) and in category conjunction (dissimilarity) models, bias was increased in the CC paradigm, by comparison to simple categorization. When the composite bias definition was utilized, however, the CC paradigm reduced bias compared to simple categorization. Mullen et al. (2001) also examined each portion of the composite bias separately and showed that, relative to simple categorization, crossed categorization reduces bias toward crossed or mixed groups, but it increases it toward double outgroups. However, these comparisons were not made separately for the designs that employed within- vs. between-group comparisons. Most studies rely on within-group designs, which, by making comparison salient, are likely to produce a contrast effect when comparing double outgroups with crossed groups. That is, in within-group designs, double outgroups may be judged more harshly than in between-group designs. In turn, this may explain the finding that CC increases bias toward double outgroups, arguing that, instead, this negative effect for double outgroups may be artifactual because the relative frequency of within- vs. between-group designs is confounded with outcome. Furthermore, irrespective of which of the three definitions of bias is used, CC increased bias in artificial groups by comparison with simple categorization, but decreased it in real groups. Thus, this further testifies that CC may be a viable option for interventions that are aimed at reducing bias. Mullen et al. (2001) also found that as the size of double ingroup decreased, bias increased. Perhaps the inverse relation between numerosity and distinctiveness accounts for this effect by augmenting the double ingroup's differentiation. In other words, small double ingroups may be more distinctive and hence, better differentiated from their outgroups. In turn, this may lead to greater bias.

Moreover, given that people belong to many different overlapping categorizations, comparing simple to crossed categorizations may be of limited utility in that the CC paradigm better maps onto most societies than does simple categorization. Consequently, it is perhaps not surprising that most CC research has ignored this comparison and instead merely examined different patterns of evaluations within the CC paradigm. Several different patterns have been found, but amongst them, the most common one is the additivity pattern (Crisp & Hewstone, 1999). An additivity pattern describes an outcome wherein double ingroups are evaluated most positively, double outgroups are evaluated most negatively, and mixed groups are somewhere in between the two extremes (ii > io = oi > oo; Hagendoorn & Henke, 1991; Hewstone, Islam, & Judd, 1993; Vanbeselaere, 1991). With respect to the goal of reducing societal conflict, however, the most desirable pattern is the equivalence pattern wherein all four target groups are evaluated equally (ii = io = oi = oo; Brown & Turner, 1979; Deschamps & Doise, 1978; Vanbeselaere, 1987). In the social inclusion or conjunction similarity pattern, any target person with an ingroup membership on either or both dimensions is evaluated more positively than the double outgroup (ii = io = oi > oo; Brown & Turner, 1979, Vanbeselaere, 1991). Conversely, in the social exclusion or conjunction dissimilarity pattern, the double ingroup is evaluated more positively than any target with outgroup membership on both or either dimension (ii > io = oi = oo; Eurich-Fulcher & Schofield, 1995; Vanbeselaere, 1987). Category dominance occurs when only the membership on the dominant (i.e., the most salient or the most important) dimension garners attention, whereas membership on the non-dominant dimension is ignored ($Ii = Io > Oi = Oo$; Arcuri, 1982; Hagendoorn & Henke, 1991; Hewstone et al., 1993; Stangor, Lynch, Duan, & Glass, 1992). An additional pattern is the hierarchical ordering or hierarchical acceptance pattern (Brewer, Ho, Lee, & Miller, 1987; Hewstone et al., 1993; Triandis & Triandis, 1960). In this pattern—a combination of the category dominance and social exclusion patterns—categorization on the second dimension depends on categorization on the first. As in category dominance, one dimension is more dominant than the other dimension of categorization. Membership on the non-dominant dimension, however, is ignored only when targets belong to the outgroup on the dominant dimension. When, instead, they belong to the ingroup on the dominant dimension ($Ii > Io > Oi = Oo$), perceivers do attend to it. Its variant is a hierarchical derogation (or hierarchical rejection) pattern wherein outgroup membership on the first dimension determines differentiation ($Ii = Io > Oi > Oo$).

The sections that follow will examine the circumstances under which each of the patterns emerge and the moderators that are implicated in their occurrence. Urban and Miller's (1998) meta-analysis identified four factors that moderate CC effects: affective valence, cognitive load, category dominance, and personalized interaction. Additional factors that have been investigated are categorization when more than two groups are involved (Urada, Stenstrom, & Miller, 2007), strength of identification with one's ingroup (Crisp, Walsh, & Hewstone, 2006; Experiment 3), and the induction of a shared superordinate identity (Crisp, Walsh, & Hewstone, 2006; Experiments 1 and 2). Given the breadth of research showing that affective valence influences crossed categorization, we begin by first discussing affective variables, and then proceed to other factors—factors that can more readily be conceptualized as cognitive and motivational variables. We then discuss the recent extension of the CC paradigm into the workplace. Intergroup interaction frequently occurs in diverse work settings. In these settings, aside from bias, team performance is of interest. Thus, researchers recently have extended the CC paradigm into the workplace to examine team performance as a consequence of different patterns of diversity (Homan, van Knippenberg, Van Kleef, & De Dreu, 2007; Sawyer, Houlette, & Yeagley, 2006; van Knippenberg & van Ginkel, this volume). These factors will be further examined in the following sections, and where applicable, integrated with other factors relevant to diversity, such as a positive attitude toward multicultural ideology.

Affective Valence

Affect frequently colors our judgment about the world. For example, if someone makes us angry or afraid, we might be inclined to avoid, dislike, and distrust that person. Bower's (1981) associative network theory proposes that feelings are nodes in an associative network. Our moods elicit mood-congruent memories. A bad mood caused by someone's insensitive remark may trigger memories of other people who have hurt us in the past. This type of affect is known as *integral* affect and, as suggested in the previous example, it is induced by the targets of evaluation. By cueing other related memories, affect serves to protect us from making mistakes or from being hurt in the future. Moreover, affect has a similar function even when it is *incidental*, which refers to affect that is independent of the intergroup context or any particular target of evaluation. In other words, if we happen to be in a bad mood when we meet somebody, we may mistakenly judge that person as unlikable. Schwartz and Clore (1983) argue that this occurs because feelings function as information. When in a bad mood, we misattribute the cause of our mood to people or circumstances that surround us. Positive affect acts similarly in that we tend to like those that make us laugh and feel at ease, or those who make us feel good. Moreover, negative affect induces a more vigilant processing style, whereas positive affect induces heuristic processing (Forgas, 2000). These models of mood and social judgment regard positive affect as deleterious because it does not elicit the careful and perhaps more cautious processing that occurs under negative mood. Isen, Niedenthal, & Cantor (1992), however, view the effects of positive affect positively in that it induces broader and more inclusive categorization and augments creativity.

Studying affect in the context of intergroup interaction is important because the presence of both positive and negative affect often marks such interactions. When interacting with outgroup members in a benign setting, one may experience positive affect as a result of learning about a novel and interesting social category. Interactions with conflict-arousing outgroups, however, typically induce intergroup anxiety (Stephan & Stephan, 1985) or other negative emotions. Since Urban and Miller (1998) found that affect moderates CC effects, researchers have experimentally manipulated both incidental and integral negative and positive affect within the CC paradigm. Models of mood and social judgment suggest that positive and negative mood will differentially impact evaluations of mixed targets in the CC paradigm. Thus, for instance, a positive mood may increase the salience of the ingroup membership of a mixed (i.e., neutral) target, whereas a negative mood may increase the salience of the mixed target's outgroup membership.

Crisp and Hewstone (2000a) studied the effects of *positive incidental affect* in the CC paradigm by giving experimental participants false performance feedback. As expected from the mood and social judgment models, evaluations of the mixed targets were raised to the level of double ingroup target. Unexpectedly, however, the double outgroup target was raised to that same level, resulting in an equivalence pattern. The equivalence pattern likely occurred because positive affect induced more inclusive categorizations and thereby caused all four CC targets to have been seen as belonging to the same superordinate category (Dovidio, Gaertner, Isen, & Lowrance, 1995; Isen & Daubman, 1984). Alternatively, this pattern may have occurred because this experiment involved crossing of two minimal or relatively unimportant groups. Thus, when positive affect was combined with low-category importance, it led to maximal inclusion. Either way, given that the equivalence pattern is the most optimal outcome in that all outgroup members are evaluated as favorably as ingroup members, the work by Crisp and Hewstone (2000a) points to useful avenues of effective interventions for easing conflicting intergroup interactions. Directly inducing positive incidental affect within the context or establishing inclusive categorizations may lead to more positive crossed categorized interactions.

In a related investigation of positive incidental affect, Urada and Miller (2000) used autobiographical recollections to manipulate positive incidental affect. They argued that mixed targets possess both positive and negative characteristics. Since they lack either strong positive or strong negative cues, they should not be impacted by positive and negative affect unless one of the dimensions of categorization is more important. Indeed, when one dimension of categorization dominated the other, positive incidental affect caused the evaluation of the Io target to be raised to the level of Ii target. These results are consistent with Bower's (1981) and Isen et al.'s (1992) models. These results likely occurred because positive affect induced participants to focus on a dominant ingroup membership, while disregarding the less dominant outgroup membership. The implication of the research is that incidental affect, although unrelated to any particular target, plays a crucial role in directing the focus of attention amongst the various group memberships that may exist. Bicultural individuals, for example, are routinely faced with having to choose between the sometimes conflicting information about their multiple cultural identities. At any given moment, their focus or perception of themselves and others may be dictated by the combination of incidental affect and the dominant group memberships.

In a related fashion, *negative incidental affect* creates a focus on the outgroup memberships rather than the ingroup membership. Models of mood and social judgments predict that when in a negative mood, the outgroup membership of a mixed target may become more salient and mood-congruent judgments may ensue. Targets who possess an outgroup membership on either dimension will be evaluated more negatively than those who are clearly ingroup members, thereby pro-ducing a social exclusion pattern. Kenworthy, Canales, Weaver, and Miller (2003) induced negative incidental mood by rudely interrupt-ing participants during a difficult anagram task. As expected, a social exclusion pattern occurred in the negative affect condition, whereas an additivity pattern emerged in the neutral affect condition. An induction of sadness produced this same exclusion pattern. When anger and sad-ness were integrated meta-analytically across their four studies, anger was shown to produce a stronger effect than sadness. Furthermore, anger and sadness did not differ on the avoidance measure of affiliation, whereas they differed on the approach measure of aggression. Unlike the anger condition, which produced higher levels of aggression, the sadness condition did not differ from neutral affect condition. Thus, consistent with other research, these negative affects differed in the degree to which they elicit approach versus avoidance (Frijda, Kuipers, & ter Schure, 1989).

Ensari and Miller (1998) examined the effects of *positive and negative integral affect* in a CC paradigm. Participants read a bogus news-paper article wherein outgroup members (all belonging to a single outgroup category) praised their ingroup. This elicited both positive affect and an increase in the salience of the outgroup category that had provided praise. Participants then stated their preference for four novel CC targets (ii, Oi, io, oo), one of whom (Oi) contained an out-group membership on the same categorization dimension as the group that had provided praise. Thus, only the preferences for the Oi target should be affected by the positive affect and the category dominance simultaneously induced by it, whereas evaluations of the other targets should conform to the typical additivity pattern. As expected, posi-tive affect produced a hierarchical rejection pattern (ii = Oi > io > oo), wherein the induction of positive affect led participants to prefer a mixed target who shared the outgroup membership with the persons who had provided the praise as much as they preferred a double ingroup target. The neutral affect condition, wherein the descriptive remarks participants read about Disneyland were designed to make none of the four crossed categorization targets any more salient than another, produced the typical additivity pattern ($ii > oi = io > oo$).

Ensari, Stenstrom, Pedersen, and Miller (in press), in addition to manipulating positive affect, also manipulated the relevance of the four CC targets. In the relevant condition, each of them possessed a membership on the category dimension containing the outgroup that had provided compliments (Ii, Io, Oi, and Oo). In the irrelevant condition, only the Oi target shared such membership (ii, Oi, io, and oo). In addition, importance-type relevance was co-varied with the previously described manipulation of fit-type relevance by coordinating an alleged future discussion topic with the category membership of the dominant (complimenting) category dimension (I or O in the relevant condition, but not for the O category of the Oi target in the irrelevant condition). Thus, in the condition containing both fit and importance relevance, when liberal participants received compliments from conservatives, the future discussion topic was made to concern comparative college funding of the relevant campus political organization (the *College Democrat Organization* and *College Republican Organization*) "on the basis of membership rolls, as opposed to equal funding," the latter having been alleged to be the current policy. By contrast, in the irrelevant condition, although there was fit relevance for the Oi target, the future discussion topic—a change in on-campus parking regulations—had no connection to the category memberships of any of the four CC targets. Thus, when preceded by compliments from conservatives, the discussion topic in the relevant condition had bearing for evaluations of all four targets (the Ii, Io, Oi, and OO targets), whereas in the irrelevant condition, it had no bearing for any of them. These two conditions allowed comparison between the Oi target that contained both importance- and fit-type relevance (in the relevant condition) with the Oi target that only had fit-type relevance (in the irrelevant condition). Interestingly, the target evaluations in the two compliment conditions conformed to the social inclusion pattern ($Ii = Io = Oi > Oo$), whereas in the control condition they again exhibited an additivity pattern (see Figure 9.1).

Although this effect was expected in the relevant condition, its occurrence in the irrelevant condition was anomalous, failing to match the hierarchical pattern found in this same condition by Ensari and Miller (1998). The only difference between the two studies was that in Ensari et al. (in press) all targets shared a superordinate identity with the participant, being students from the same university, whereas in Ensari and Miller (1998) the targets' ingroup/outgroup distinctions involved

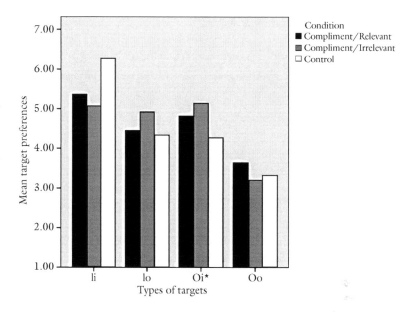

Figure 9.1   Means of target preferences (Ensari et al., in press).

non-students as well as students at another university. Perhaps the inadvertent priming of a superordinate identity interacted with the positive mood induction to augment its impact, thereby producing a social inclusion pattern rather than the previously obtained hierarchical pattern. Nonetheless, the results further testify to the broader categorization that can occur under positive affect.

Using a similar design, Ensari and Miller (1998) also manipulated negative integral affect. This time, however, participants read a bogus newspaper article wherein outgroup members insulted their ingroup. This elicited negative affect and increased the salience of the category that had provided the insult. Participants were then asked to evaluate novel targets who had nothing to do with the insulting person, with the exception of a shared outgroup membership for the Oi target on one dimension of categorization. Thus, participants were given an opportunity to displace onto a novel target the anger caused by a prior insult. Again, only the Oi target was expected to be influenced by the manipulations, whereas preferences for the remaining three targets were expected to conform to the additivity pattern. As expected, a hierarchical acceptance pattern emerged (ii > io > Oi = oo) in the negative affect condition, whereas an additivity pattern occurred in the neutral affect condition.

Cognitive Variables

Cognitive variables found to moderate CC effects were cognitive over-load and differential importance between the two category dimensions (Urban & Miller, 1998). When category information is readily avail-able, cognitive overload tends to increase reliance on it. When category information is not readily present, it decreases stereotyping (Gilbert & Hixon, 1991). Cognitive overload in CC studies produced a social exclusion pattern (Urban & Miller, 1998). Cognitive overload is often stressful and can contribute to the emergence of negative affect (Marco & Suls, 1993; Repetti, 1993). Thus, it is not surprising that cogni-tive overload produced the pattern that is expected to occur under negative incidental affect. Moreover, these results contrast with those of Ensari and Miller (1998) and Ensari et al. (in press) wherein inte-gral, as opposed to incidental negative affect was induced, but parallel those of Kenworthy et al. (2003), who also induced negative inciden-tal affect. Thus, they further suggest that it is the negative incidental affect induced by cognitive overload that subsequently leads to a social exclusion pattern.

When the importance of one dimension of categorization exceeds that of another, a dominance pattern emerges (Urban & Miller, 1998). These results are believed to occur because a more important dimension is more salient or more relevant to the participants (Miller, Kenworthy, Canales, & Stenstrom, 2006). Experimental evaluation of category importance has produced mixed results. Vanbeselaere (2000) crossed real with hypothetical groups and failed to find support for category dominance as a result of differential relevancy of the crossed targets. This result may have occurred because the hypothetical group inad-vertently possessed category importance. Ensari and Miller ((1998), Study 2) also failed to find support for differential relevancy of the crossed targets. Recall that in the high relevancy conditions, on one of the dimensions of categorization, each target shared a category mem-bership with the persons who provided the insult. In the irrelevant condition only the Oi target shared a category membership with the source of insult. Perhaps the failure of target evaluations of relevant groups to differ from those of irrelevant groups occurred because the manipulation of relevancy was too weak.

As previously indicated, Ensari et al. (in press) strengthened this rel-evancy manipulation by co-varying importance-type relevance with the previously discussed manipulation of fit-type relevance. In Ensari et al. (in press), each of the four CC targets shared a category dimension with the outgroup that had been insulting. Importance-type relevance refers to the importance of the category dimension to the actor. As indicated, Ensari et al. (in press) induced importance-type relevance by leading participants to believe that the topic of a future discussion between them and one of their CC partners was one intrinsically linked to the category that provided the insult. In the irrelevant condition, importance-type relevance was low and fit-type relevance only occurred for the Oi target—a target who shared a membership with the outgroup that had provided the insult, whereas the remaining three targets remained fit-irrelevant (ii, io, and oo). These two conditions allowed comparison between the Oi target who possessed both importance- and fit-type relevance (the relevant condition) with the Oi target who only had fit-type relevance (the irrelevant condition). As expected, the target possessing both types of relevance was less preferred as a future partner than one possessing only fit-type relevance. The relevance manipulation also impacted the evaluation of the target whose *ingroup* status was relevant to the source of the insult (Io). The preference for the Io target in the relevant condition was marginally higher than that for the io target in the irrelevant condition. Similarly, the Oo target in the relevant condition was less preferred than the oo target in the irrelevant condition. Replicating Ensari and Miller (1998), the insult condition yielded a hierarchical acceptance pattern (Ii > Io > Oi = Oo), whereas the no affect control condition yielded an additivity pattern.

Van Knippenberg, van Twuyver, and Pepels (1994) also found the expected relevancy effects in the CC paradigm by crossing gender with the university (student/teacher) dimension in a "who said what?" paradigm. By comparison to the student/teacher dimension, gender yielded more within-group errors than between-group errors. This pattern reversed, however, when the topic of conversation was made to be related to student/teacher dimension. This procedure yielded a category dominance pattern, such that membership on the university dimension was ignored when the topic of the conversation made gender relevant. Similarly, membership on the gender dimension was ignored when the university dimension became relevant.

By assimilating the Oi target to the Oo target—in a category dominance pattern—the presence of a dominant category essentially reverses the beneficial effects of the presence of an ingroup category on a non-dominant dimension. In other words, ingroup membership of the Oi target is completely ignored. Thus, it seems important to attempt to minimize the negative effects of category dominance. One potential for accomplishing this is by adding multiple non-dominant ingroup memberships. When targets are simple, people identify stimuli

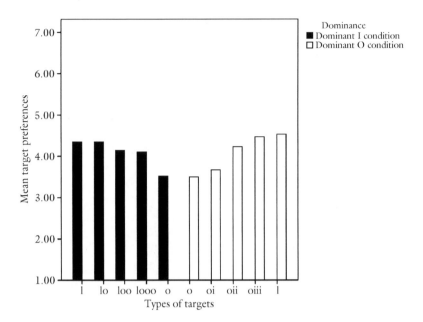

Figure 9.2   Trimmed means of target preferences (Urada et al., 2007).

in terms of all the attributes that they posses. Typically, an additive rule is used when integrating information (Anderson, 1965, 1967, 1968). However, when stimuli are more complex, people use a feature detection strategy (Prinz & Sheerer-Neumann, 1974). In CC contexts with multiple groups, this means that targets will be meta-categorized into *ingroup-like* or *outgroup-like* categories. A target possessing a dominant outgroup on one dimension and non-dominant ingroup on another dimension will be categorized as outgroup-like (Urada et al., 2007). However, a target who possesses both a dominant outgroup membership and two or more non-dominant ingroup memberships is categorized as ingroup-like (see Figure 9.2). Furthermore, a target with a dominant ingroup membership is still perceived as ingroup-like even after the addition of three non-dominant outgroup memberships.

These patterns of results only occurred when participants assessed their preferences for future interaction with the CC targets. When their task was to exclude targets, target-person differences were then attended to and an outgroup derogation pattern occurred. Specifically, a target with a dominant outgroup membership was perceived as outgroup-like regardless of how many non-dominant ingroup memberships he or she possessed. By contrast, a target with a dominant ingroup membership and with one or more non-dominant outgroup memberships was also perceived as outgroup-like. It may be worth noting that this latter set of results occurred in an online study, which may have contributed to such harsh evaluation of CC targets.

The processes underlying these effects clearly need elaboration and testing. One potentially interesting aspect is that knowledge of targets' additional category memberships may serve to further individuate them. Individuation creates recognition of a person's distinct identity, promoting an awareness of the distinctiveness of individual persons. Individuation reduces the better than average effect (Alicke, Koltz, Brietenbecher, Yurak, & Vredenburg, 1995), increases the perception of intra-category differences and intra-category variability (Brewer, Dull, & Lui, 1981), allows the outgroup to be seen less as a unit, and thus diminishes intergroup bias (Wilder, 1978). In the context of CC research such potential individuation effects makes the somewhat counterintuitive prediction that a target person identified as Ooooo will be better liked than one identified as Oo or O. Specifically, in some circumstances, an Ooooo target may be perceived as not clearly belonging to any category, but instead, as a unique individual who, as a consequence of having a multitude of group memberships and/or personal characteristics, is seen as highly individuated. Even though each group may know of many Ooooo targets, each outgroup designation may represent a different outgroup membership for each person, thereby precluding the forming of a clear and coherent Ooooo category within the culture or society.

Another factor leading to assimilation of crossed categorization targets is an induction of a superordinate or common ingroup identity. Consistent with other research, in a control condition, the crossing of two minimal group categories produced the typical additive pattern. When, in addition, both a common ingroup was made salient and the crossed groups lacked importance, it produced a social inclusion pattern (Crisp et al., 2006) whereas for important crossed groups, the additive pattern remained. Ordinarily, a salient superordinate identity reduces bias (Gaertner & Dovidio, 2000). The failure of a salient shared superordinate identity (Americans) to reduce category differentiation when the subcategories reflect important category distinctions (Blacks, Asian-Americans, Hispanics) is noteworthy in that it points to an important limitation with respect to the potential benefit of making a superordinate category membership salient. Whether such limitation extends to manipulations of the salience of shared fate remains unknown. At the same time, however, this occurrence of a social inclusion pattern within the context of a superordinate ingroup supports our interpretation of the between study difference between Ensari et al.'s (in press) replication of Ensari and Miller (1998), wherein the latter had produced a hierarchical pattern and the former yielded a social inclusion pattern. As indicated, we believe that this difference in outcomes occurred because the target in Ensari et al. shared the same superordinate identity with participants. Like Crisp et al.'s (2006) outcome with a superordinate category, Ensari et al.'s replication—which was implemented in the context of a superordinate categorization of the ingroup and outgroup categories, whereas Ensari and Miller's was not—also produced a social inclusion pattern. Interestingly, in Ensari et al. both the relevant and irrelevant conditions produced a social inclusion pattern. This is contrary to Crisp et al.'s study wherein an additive pattern occurred in the important (viz. the relevant) condition. This difference likely emerged because Ensari et al. induced positive affect in addition to inadvertently priming a superordinate categorization. Thus, their manipulation of relevance may have been weaker relative to Crisp et al.'s manipulation.

A more inclusive common ingroup identity operates in the same fashion as positive affect. It seems that both processes prime ingroup identity and make ingroup membership of the crossed targets more salient. Thus, both an induction of positive affect and that of the common ingroup identity moderate CC effects by priming ingroup identity or increasing the salience of ingroup membership. Crisp and Hewstone (2000b) primed the pronoun "we" or the letter string "xxxx" while thinking about one of the four CC targets. As expected, a social inclusion pattern was observed after an ingroup prime ("we"). This finding is consistent with the idea that this general priming mechanism underlies the effects observed with respect to the positive affect and common ingroup identity.

Motivational Variables

The evidence reviewed so far indicates that reduced category differentiation leads to decreases in bias. To some group members, however, a blurring of the intergroup boundaries may be threatening. Through socialization or due to increased threat from an outgroup, some group members may become so invested in a particular group membership that they base their self-worth and even their sense of self on it. These high identifiers, just like people in general, strive for a distinct and positive sense of self (Tajfel, 1982; Tajfel & Turner, 1979). To achieve it, high identifiers need to see their ingroups as different from and better than their relevant outgroups (Abrams & Hogg, 1998; Brown, 1984; Hogg & Mullin, 1999). In these circumstances, attempts to blur intergroup boundaries or to decrease category differentiation will be met with strong resistance. Indeed, increases in intergroup similarity or reductions in intergroup distinctiveness often lead to increases in bias (Jetten & Spears, 2003).

High identifiers were less biased after generating non-shared categories about an outgroup than after generating shared or crosscutting categories (Crisp & Beck, 2001). Quite the opposite pattern appeared for low identifiers. Low identifiers were more biased after generating non-shared categories compared to categories that crosscut original group dichotomies. Similarly, inducing group members to recategorize themselves as members of a superordinate category that subsumed both their ingroup and their former outgroup also led to increased bias toward the original outgroup. This occurred, however, in a setting wherein the strength of identification with the subgroup exceeded the strength of identification with the superordinate category. When strength of identity with the subgroup was only as high as that with the superordinate category, bias was attenuated (Stone & Crisp, 2007). These results suggest that techniques based on multiple categorization will fail as an intervention strategy in circumstances wherein group members strongly identify with their ingroup. In those, however, wherein strength of identification with the crosscutting group or superordinate group equals the strength of identification in the original group, bias is reduced (Crisp, Stone, & Hall, 2005; Experiment 4).

Another approach that might address the adverse effects of distinctiveness threat among high identifiers is to introduce them to multicultural views. Multiculturalism, an ideological contrast to assimilationism, is a belief that diversity is most optimally managed by recognizing, accepting, and even cherishing group differences. Participants who were induced to think according to multicultural ideology perceived greater category differentiation, while simultaneously expressing less bias (Aberson, this volume; Verkuyten, this volume; Wolsko, Park, Judd, & Wittenbrink, 2000). Furthermore, minorities who supported multicultural views identified more strongly with their ingroups, whereas majority-group members who supported multiculturalism identified less strongly with the ingroup. Multicultural beliefs of majority groups did not influence ingroup evaluation, but they improved outgroup evaluation (cf. Verkuyten, 2005). Conversely, among minority participants, multicultural beliefs improved ingroup evaluations, but they did not influence outgroup evaluations. Minority groups typically endorse multicultural beliefs more strongly than do majority groups (Verkuyten, 2005). Therefore, there may be some benefit in presenting multicultural beliefs in a manner that is not considered threatening to majorities, particularly to those who are strongly identified with their ingroup. One reason why the making of multicultural ideology salient may be a useful approach for reducing bias is because it not only attempts to reverse harmful effects of distinctiveness threat, while increasing perceptions of category differentiation, but also it may offer an understanding of one's own and other groups. Because cherishing intergroup differences is a part of multiculturalism, multicultural attitudes may induce one to seek out multicultural opportunities, making one more likely to interact with people of different cultural origins and attend various multicultural events, and thereby increasing both contact and knowledge about cultural groups. Meta-analytic evidence clearly shows that contact reduces prejudice (Pettigrew & Tropp, 2006), a benefit that generalizes beyond those in the immediate situation (Ensari & Miller, 2002). Moreover, complex views about cultural differences may offer protection against negative stereotypes and biases (Phinney & Alipuria, 2006). Although multicultural views have not yet been investigated within the CC paradigm, it seems that such pairing may prove beneficial for reducing bias.

If multicultural attitudes indeed lead to greater complexity in the representation of group differences, then the related concept of a complex perception of one's own social identity is likely to have similar effects (Brewer, this volume; Roccas and Brewer, 2002). People vary in the degree to which they perceive their ingroups as overlapping vs. crosscutting. Those with low complexity see their groups as convergent and overlapping. For example, an individual who is both Christian and White may perceive that all Christians are White. On the other hand, those with high complexity see their groups as crosscutting. A White Christian individual with complex identity will recognize that there are many non-White Christians. Brewer and Pierce (2005) found that higher identity complexity is related to greater inclusiveness and tolerance of outgroups. This effect may have occurred because individuals with low complexity are more likely to misperceive outgroup members as belonging to double outgroups. Using a prior example, a White Christian may automatically assume that non-White targets are also not Christian, thus treating them as double outgroups. Alternatively, individuals with low complexity may process outgroups in simple terms. Thus, a White Christian will process non-Whites as simply an outgroup, disregarding any other potential dimension of categorization. In both of these alternatives, individuals with high complexity might be more likely to notice crossed or common superordinate memberships of targets.

Personalization and Decategorization

The tendency to categorize individuals into groups reflects an attempt to simplify complex social worlds (Allport, 1954; Taylor, Fiske, Etcoff, & Ruderman, 1978). Unfortunately, however, categorization of people into groups may induce one to apply harmful stereotypes, even to those individual group members who do not conform to that stereotype. In an ideal world, harmful stereotyping and unfair treatment of outgroup members would be avoided by treating each individual on an individual basis and not responding to them as members of the category within which they seem to fit. Decategorization—whether top-down (as when one receives factual information about the variability among persons comprising a social category) or bottom-up (as when one receives individuating information about a particular outgroup member)—is a strategy that offers just that. It increases one's awareness of the distinctiveness or individuality of the members who belong to a particular social category (Brewer & Miller, 1984).

Personalization of an outgroup member is a bottom-up process that increases intra-category variability via interpersonal self-other comparisons, self-disclosure, or induced empathy. It is believed to augment the familiarity and similarity that are typically associated with interpersonal liking; it induces trust, positive affect, better processing of individuating information, and reduction of anxiety; it provides an opportunity for a disconfirmation of negative outgroup stereotypes; and it leads to a less homogenous perception of an outgroup (Cook, 1978; Derlega, Harris, & Chaikin, 1973; Lazowski & Andersen, 1990; Rothbart & John, 1985; Sears, 1983; Stephan & Stephan, 1985; Whitley, Schofield, & Snyder, 1984; Wilder, 1978, 1986; Zajonc, 1980).

In their meta-analysis, Urban and Miller (1998) examined the moderating effect of individuating information within the CC paradigm. Personalization was defined to have occurred if: the level of judgment was individual rather than group; targets had names; and visual contact and cooperative interaction were present. Although this composite was labeled personalization, Miller (2002) later argued that these features represented only one aspect of personalization—individuation or knowledge about target persons' unique characteristics. As expected, individuation reduced intergroup bias and produced an equivalence pattern.

In an experimental evaluation of personalization within the CC paradigm (Ensari & Miller, 2001), participants, who were assigned to minimal groups and engaged in self-disclosure, were told that group assignments were either based on individual attributes or on category distinctions. Intergroup bias toward novel targets was reduced and an equivalence pattern was produced only in the personalization condition. By contrast, attention to one of the category distinctions produced a dominance pattern. Thus, self-disclosure was only beneficial when group assignments emphasized individual attributes as opposed to category distinctions.

Overview of the Moderators, Patterns, and the Implications for Interventions

As a whole, affective valence dramatically moderated the patterns of evaluation in the CC paradigm. The additivity pattern was produced when both categories were of equal importance to the perceiver and in conditions of neutral mood. When an induction of positive incidental affect primed superordinate categorization of unimportant CC categories, an equivalence pattern emerged. However, when one dimension dominated another, positive incidental affect yielded a dominance pattern. Negative incidental affect elicited a social exclusion pattern wherein targets who possessed an outgroup membership on either or both dimensions of categorization were evaluated more negatively than one who was clearly an ingroup member. Positive integral mood impacted the evaluation of a target who shared an outgroup membership with the source of the affect by raising it to the level of double ingroup target. Negative integral mood caused the evaluation of a mixed target who shared an outgroup membership with the source of the affect to match that of the double outgroup target. As a summary of the impact of affect valence on the CC paradigm, an induction of positive affect produced evaluations of one or more crossed targets to be raised to the level of the true ingroup member on both categories (ii) for all cases, both integral and incidental. Conversely, in all cases of both integral and incidental *negative* affect, the crossed targets were always perceived with more bias as compared to the pure ingroup member (ii). Taken as a whole, this work suggests that an intervention that makes crossed-category memberships salient will improve intergroup relations, particularly if the intergroup interaction can be structured in such a way that it produces positive affect. Cooperation in an intergroup setting may be one such source of positive affect (Johnson, Johnson, & Maruyama, 1983; Miller & Davidson-Podgorny, 1987). Improving evaluations of double outgroup targets, however, still remains a challenge. Useful future work could examine evaluations of double outgroup targets who are a source of the positive affect that typifies cooperative settings. Additionally, however, as suggested by the differential effects of distinct negative emotions (Kenworthy et al., 2003), an attention to the effects of discrete emotional states, as well as a differentiation between approach and avoidance behaviors, is likely to yield a better understanding than that provided by merely examining valence effects per se.

In addition to affective variables, cognitive variables also moderated CC effects. A meta-analytic examination of cognitive variables showed that cognitive overload in a CC setting may be harmful, as it produced a social exclusion pattern. This effect, however, has not been evaluated experimentally, suggesting a need for further corroboration. Meta-analytical results, nevertheless, reveal that CC interventions may benefit from attempts to eliminate cognitive overload. Category importance or dominance of one dimension over the other produced a category dominance pattern. This pattern is not the most desirable pattern when it comes to attempts to eliminate or reduce bias because dominance of outgroup membership on one dimension eliminates the beneficial effects of having an ingroup membership on another dimension. However, making two or more non-dominant group memberships salient seems to help, particularly if task instructions emphasize inclusion rather than exclusion of targets.

Our review of affective and cognitive variables makes it obvious that reducing differentiation typically has a beneficial effect on bias. However, motivational factors, such as strength of identification with an ingroup, show that decreased differentiation can be harmful. High identifiers resisted attempts to reduce category distinctiveness by increasing bias. Perhaps distinct intervention strategies for reducing intergroup bias should be applied to low vs. high identifiers. One potential avenue for reducing bias when strongly identified group members are faced with distinctiveness threat is to introduce them to positive attitudinal presentations of multicultural ideology, which typically leads to perceptions of increased category differentiation, while reducing bias.

Integrating affective, cognitive, and motivational moderators of CC effects, Crisp and Hewstone (2007) propose a differentiation–decategorization model of multiple categorization effects. The model distinguishes between two basic consequences of multiple categorization: decategorization and differentiation. These two processes differ in the degree of complexity used to classify social worlds. Decategorization entails complex representations of the social world wherein one is aware of the distinctiveness or individuality of the members who belong to a particular social category. Like personalization, it is effortful processing that discourages simple categorization and leads one to conclude that in some circumstances more individuated processing may be preferable. Decategorization, then, enables one to perceive that each individual can be categorized in multiple ways and it thereby reduces bias. As shown previously, personalization reduced intergroup bias and resulted in an equivalence pattern. Thus, it seems that interventions that aim to reduce intergroup bias would benefit from the use of personalization in CC settings. It may be harder, however, to achieve an equivalence pattern with real groups. Future research should examine the effects of personalization when real groups are used to form CC targets.

Quite contrary to decategorization, the typical consequence of differentiation is a simple representation of one's social world wherein, in its simplest form, the world is divided into an ingroup and an outgroup. In its most complex form, the world consists of several dimensions of categorization that either cross or converge. According to Crisp and Hewstone's (2007) model, and considering the evidence reviewed so far, converging social categories increase differentiation and thus augment bias, whereas crosscutting categories reduce differentiation and bias. This relationship is further moderated by positive and negative affect. As described above, induction of positive affect and elimination of negative affect lead to broader and more inclusive categorization. In fact, Crisp and Hewstone (2007) argue that positive mood increases the salience of ingroup membership in the mixed targets because both positive mood and ingroup membership are affectively positive (cf. Vanman & Miller, 1993). A more inclusive common ingroup identity operates in the same fashion and produces the same effect because it also primes ingroup identity and makes ingroup membership of the crossed targets more salient.

Unfortunately, priming ingroup identities does not always have beneficial effects. Moreover, as previously indicated, among strongly identified group members reduced differentiation leads to greater bias. Crisp and Hewstone (2007) argue that strongly identified group members resist the undermined distinctiveness that is a necessary consequence of reduced differentiation. However, an alternative explanation may be that strongly identified group members in fact resist the positivity that is applied to outgroups after attempts to recategorize them at a more inclusive common ingroup level. In other words, strongly identified group members may be uncomfortable sharing parts of their positive ingroup identity with their former outgroups.

Diversity in the Workplace

Immigration patterns, the influx of women into the workplace, attempts to end segregation, and affirmative-action policies have all contributed to increased diversity in organizations. Besides bias, a variable of interest in organizational settings is group performance (see Rink & Jehn, this volume; van Knippenberg & van Ginkel, this volume). Diversity in the workplace is sometimes regarded as harmful because it can lead to the creation of subgroups whose intergroup dynamic impedes the successful functioning of an organization. However, a type of diversity that has a potential to enhance group performance is informational diversity. It refers to differences in knowledge, values, and ideas (Jehn, Northcraft, & Neale, 1999; van Knippenberg & Haslam, 2003). Informational diversity can contribute to the exchange of ideas and knowledge and it can lead to error detection, better information processing, problem solving, and group effectiveness (Davis, 1969; Gruenfeld, Mannix, Williams, & Neale, 1996; Phillips, Mannix, Neale, & Gruenfeld, 2004; Tjosvold & Poon, 1998; van Knippenberg, De Dreu, & Homan, 2004). Integrating different perspectives regarding diversity, van Knippenberg et al. (2004) argued that, when it comes to group functioning, informational diversity interacts with the subgroup categorization processes. According to the faultline theory, group functioning is particularly hindered when multiple diversity dimensions converge within a group (Earley & Mosakowski, 2000; Lau & Murnighan, 1998). However, when informational diversity, for example, is crossed with other diversity dimensions, functioning of the group is enhanced.

Homan et al. (2007) created faultlines within their groups by correlating (i.e., converging) gender and personality type on a bogus personality test and then comparing the performance of these groups to groups that had no such faultlines. Furthermore, some of these groups were informationally homogeneous (all members had access to the total set of information), whereas others were heterogeneous (information was divided in two parts). Groups with faultlines performed better (i.e., experienced increased elaboration of information, less task and relationship conflict, better team climate, and more satisfaction) when informational diversity was crossed rather than when it converged with the existing faultline. Similarly, Sawyer et al. (2005) crossed racial categories with job function boundaries. As expected, crosscut diversity structure led to weakening of the faultlines, increased information sharing, and improved decision making. Task anxiety may moderate these effects in that the crossing of intergroup categories with task roles was only beneficial under conditions of low task anxiety (Marcus-Newhall, Miller, Holtz, & Brewer, 1993).

Furthermore, the previously discussed moderators of CC effects suggest ways for improving organizational performance. For example, creating a positive work environment may be important in organizations because it encourages more socially inclusive patterns. Similarly, organizations should strive to promote common ingroup identity in ways that do not threaten existing identities of its members. Previous research also indicates that there might be some benefit in structuring group tasks so that they reduce cognitive overload or increase personalization in organizations.

Summary

The reviewed literature suggests that interventions that make CC memberships salient will reduce intergroup bias. This is particularly likely to be useful under conditions of positive affect, when intergroup interaction is decategorized, and when a common ingroup identity is also induced. Besides reducing bias, making CCs salient can be useful in diverse organizations for improving team performance and climate, information sharing, and decision making.

References

Abrams, D., & Hogg, M. A. (1998). Prospects for research in group processes and intergroup relations. *Group Processes & Intergroup Relations, 1,* 7–20.

Alicke, M. D., Klotz, M. L., Breitenbecher, D. L., Yurak, T. J., & Vredenburg, D. S. (1995). Personal contact, individuation, and the better-than-average effect. *Journal of Personality and Social Psychology, 68,* 804–825.

Allport, G. W. (1954). *The Nature of Prejudice.* Cambridge, MA: Addison-Wesley.

Anderson, N. H. (1965). Averaging versus adding as a stimulus combination rule in impression formation. *Journal of Experimental Psychology, 70,* 394–400.

Anderson, N. H. (1967). Averaging model analysis of set-size effect in impression formation. *Journal of Experimental Psychology, 75*, 158–165.

Anderson, N. H. (1968). Application of a linear-serial model to a personality-impression task using serial presentation. *Journal of Personality and Social Psychology, 10*, 354–362.

Arcuri, L. (1982). Three patterns of social categorization in attribution memory. *European Journal of Social Psychology, 12*, 271–282.

Bower, G. (1981). Mood and memory. *American Psychologist, 36*, 129–148.

Brewer, M. B. (1979). In-group bias in the minimal intergroup situation: A cognitive-motivational analysis. *Psychological Bulletin, 86*, 307–324.

Brewer, M. B., Dull, V., & Lui, L. (1981). Perceptions of the elderly: Stereotypes as prototypes. *Journal of Personality and Social Psychology, 41*, 656–670.

Brewer, M. B., Ho, H.-K., Lee, J.-Y, & Miller N. (1987). Social identity and social distance among Hong Kong schoolchildren. *Personality and Social Psychology Bulletin, 13*, 156–165.

Brewer, M. B., & Miller, N. (1984). Beyond the contact hypothesis: Theoretical perspectives on desegregation. In N. Miller & M.B. Brewer (Eds.), *Groups in contact: The psychology of desegregation* (pp. 281–302). Orlando, FL: Academic Press.

Brewer, M. B., & Pierce, K. P. (2005). Social identity complexity and outgroup tolerance. *Personality and Social Psychology Bulletin, 31*, 428–437.

Brown, R. J. (1984). The effects of intergroup similarity and cooperative vs. competitive orientation an intergroup discrimination. *British Journal of Social Psychology, 21*, 21–33.

Brown, R. J., & Turner, J. C. (1979). The criss-cross categorization effect in intergroup discrimination. *British Journal of Social and Clinical Psychology, 18*, 371–383.

Campbell, D. T. (1956). Enhancement of contrast as a composite habit. *Journal of Abnormal and Social Psychology, 53*, 350–355.

Cook, S. W. (1978). Interpersonal and attitudinal outcomes in cooperating interracial groups. *Journal of Research & Development in Education, 12*, 97–113.

Crisp, R. J., & Beck, S. R. (2001). Reducing intergroup bias: The moderating role of ingroup identification. *Group Processes and Intergroup Relations, 8*, 173–185.

Crisp, R. J., & Hewstone, M. (1999). Differential evaluation of crossed category groups: Patterns, processes and reducing intergroup bias. *Group Processes Intergroup Relations, 2*, 307–333.

Crisp, R. J., & Hewstone, M. (2000a). Crossed categorization and intergroup bias: The moderating roles of intergroup and affective context. *Journal of Experimental Social Psychology, 36*, 357–383.

Crisp, R. J., & Hewstone, M. (2000b). Multiple categorization and social identity. In D. Cappoza & R. Brown (Eds.), *Social identity processes: Trends in theory and research* (pp. 149–166). Beverly Hills, CA: Sage.

Crisp, R. J., & Hewstone, M. (2007). Multiple social categorization. In M. P. Zanna (Ed.), *Advances in experimental social psychology* (Vol. 39, pp. 163–254). San Diego, CA: Elsevier Academic Press.

Crisp, R. J., Stone, C. H., & Hall, N. R. (2006). Recategorization and subgroup identification: Predicting and preventing threats from comman ingroups. *Personality and Social Psychology Bulletin, 32*, 230–243.

Crisp, R. J., Walsh, J., & Hewstone, M. (2006). Crossed categorization in common ingroup contexts. *Personality and Social Psychology Bulletin, 32*, 1204–1218.

Davis, J. H. (1969). *Group performance.* Reading, MA: Addison Wesley.

Derlega, V. J., Harris, M. S., & Chaikin, A. L. (1973). Self-disclosure reciprocity, liking and the deviant. *Journal of Experimental Social Psychology, 9*, 277–284.

Deschamps, J.-C., & Doise, W. (1978). Crossed category memberships in intergroup relations. In H. Tajfel (Ed.), *Differentiation between social groups* (pp. 141–158). Cambridge, UK: Cambridge University Press.

Doise, W. (1978). *Groups and individuals: Explanations in social psychology.* Cambridge, UK: Cambridge University Press.

Dovidio, J. F., Gaertner, S. L., Isen, A. M., & Lowrance, R. (1995). Group representations and intergroup bias: Positive affect, similarity, and group size. *Personality and Social Psychology Bulletin, 21*, 856–865.

Earley, C. P., & Mosakowski, E. (2000). Creating hybrid team cultures: An empirical test of transnational team functioning. *Academy of Management Journal, 43*, 26–49.

Ensari, N., & Miller, N. (1998). Effect of affective reactions by an out-group on preferences for crossed categorization discussion partners. *Journal of Personality and Social Psychology, 75*, 1503–1527.

Ensari, N., & Miller, N. (2001). Decategorization and the reduction of bias in the cross categorization paradigm. *European Journal of Social Psychology, 31*, 193–216.

Ensari, N., & Miller, N. (2002). The out-group must not be so bad after all: The effects of disclosure, typicality, and salience on intergroup bias. *Journal of Personality and Social Psychology, 83*, 313–329.

Ensari, N., Stenstrom, D. M., Pedersen, W. C., & Miller, N.(in press). The role of integral affect and category relevance on crossed categorization. *Group Dynamics: Theory, Research and Practice.*

Eurich-Fulcher, R., & Schofield, J. W. (1995). Correlated versus uncorrelated social categorizations: The effect on intergroup bias. *Personality and Social Psychology Bulletin, 21*, 149–159.

Forgas, J. (2000). Managing moods: Towards a dual-process theory of spontaneous mood regulation. *Psychological Inquiry, 11*, 172–177.

Frijda, N. H., Kuipers, P., & ter Schure, E. (1989). Relations among emotion, appraisal, and emotional action readiness. *Journal of Personality and Social Psychology, 57*, 212–228.

Gaertner, S. L., & Dovidio, J. F. (2000). *Reducing intergroup bias: The Common Ingroup Identity Model.* Philadelphia, PA: Psychology Press.

Gilbert, D. T., & Hixon, J. G. (1991). The trouble of thinking: Activation and application of stereotypic beliefs. *Journal of Personality and Social Psychology*, *60*, 509–517.

Gruenfeld, D. H., Mannix, E. A., Williams, K. Y., & Neale, M. A. (1996). Group composition and decision making: How member familiarity and information distribution affect process and performance. *Organizational Behavior and Human Decision Processes*, *67*, 1–15.

Hagendoorn, L., & Henke, R. (1991). The effect of multiple category membership on intergroup evaluations in a North Indian context: Class, caste and religion. *British Journal of Social Psychology*, *30*, 247–260.

Hewstone, M., Islam, M. R., & Judd, C. M. (1993). Models of crossed categorization and intergroup relations. *Journal of Personality and Social Psychology*, *64*, 779–793.

Hogg, M. A., & Mullin, B. (1999). Joining groups to reduce uncertainty: Subjective uncertainty reduction and group identification. In D. Abrams & M.A. Hogg (Eds.), *Social identity and social cognition* (pp. 249–279). Malden, MA: Blackwell.

Homan, A. C., van Knippenberg, D., Van Kleef, G. A., & De Dreu, C. K. W. (2007). Interacting dimensions of diversity: Cross-categorization and the functioning of diverse work groups. *Group Dynamics: Theory, Research, and Practice*, *11*, 79–94.

Isen, A. M., & Daubman, K. A. (1984). The influence of affect on categorization. *Journal of Personality and Social Psychology*, *47*, 1206–1217.

Isen, A. M., Niedenthal, P. M., & Cantor, N. (1992). An influence of positive affect on social categorization. *Motivation and Emotion*, *16*, 65–78.

Jehn, K. A., Northcraft, G. B., & Neale, M. A. (1999). Why differences make a difference: A field study of diversity, conflict, and performance in workgroups. *Administrative Science Quarterly*, *44*, 741–763.

Jetten, J., & Spears, R. (2003). The divisive potential of differences and similarities: The role of intergroup distinctiveness in intergroup differentiation. In W. Stroebe & M. Hewstone (Eds.), *European review of social psychology* (Vol. 14, pp. 203–241). Hove, UK: Psychology Press/Taylor & Francis.

Johnson, D. W., Johnson, R. T., & Maruyama, G. M. (1983). Interdependence and interpersonal attraction among heterogeneous and homogeneous individuals: A theoretical formulation and a meta-analysis of the research. *Review of Educational Research*, *53*, 5–54.

Kenworthy, J. B., Canales, C. J., Weaver, K. D., & Miller, N. (2003). Negative incidental affect and mood congruency in crossed categorization. *Journal of Experimental Social Psychology*, *39*, 195–219.

Lau, D., & Murnighan, K. (1998). Demographic diversity and faultlines: The compositional dynamics of organizational groups. *Academy of Management Review*, *23*, 325–340.

Lazowski, L. E., & Andersen, S. M. (1990). Self-disclosure and social perceptions: The impact of private, negative, and extreme communications. *Journal of Social Behavior & Personality*, *5*, 131–154.

LeVine, R. A., & Campbell, D. T. (1972). *Ethnocentrism: Theories of conflict, ethnic attitudes and group behavior.* New York: Wiley.

Marco, C. A., & Suls, J. (1993). Daily stress and the trajectory of mood: Spillover, response assimilation, contrast, and chronic negative affectivity. *Journal of Personality and Social Psychology, 64,* 1053–1063.

Marcus-Newhall, A., Miller, N., Holtz, R., & Brewer, M. B. (1993). Cross-cutting category membership with role assignment: A means of reducing intergroup bias. *British Journal of Social Psychology, 32,* 125–146.

Miller, N. (2002). Personalization and the promise of contact theory. *Journal of Social Issues, 58,* 387–410.

Miller, N., & Davidson-Podgorny, G. (1987). Theoretical models of intergroup relations and the use of cooperative teams as an intervention for desegregated settings. In C. Hendrick (Ed.), *Group processes and intergroup relations. Review of personality and social psychology* (Vol. 9, pp. 41–67). Thousand Oaks, CA: Sage.

Miller, N., Kenworthy, J., Canales, C., & Stenstrom, D. (2006). Explaining the effects of crossed categorization on ethnocentric bias. In R. J. Crisp & M. Hewstone (Eds.), *Multiple social categorization: Processes, models and applications* (pp. 160–188). Hove, UK: Psychology Press (Taylor & Francis).

Mullen, B., Brown, R., & Smith, C. (1992). Ingroup bias as a function of salience, relevance, and status: An integration. *European Journal of Social Psychology, 22,* 102–122.

Mullen, B., Migdal, M. J., & Hewstone, M. (2001). Crossed categorization versus simple categorization and intergroup evaluations: A meta-analysis. *European Journal of Social Psychology, 31,* 721–736.

Oakes, P. J., Haslam, S. A., & Turner, J. C. (1994). *Stereotyping and social reality.* Oxford, UK: Blackwell.

Pettigrew, T. F., & Tropp, L. R. (2006). A meta-analytic test of intergroup contact theory. *Journal of Personality and Social Psychology, 90,* 751–783.

Phillips, K. W., Mannix, E. A., Neale, M. A., & Gruenfeld, D. H. (2004). Diverse groups and information sharing: The effects of congruent ties. *Journal of Experimental Social Psychology, 40,* 497–510.

Phinney, J. S., & Alipuria, L. L. (2006). Multiple social categorization and identity among multiracial, multiethnic, and multicultural individuals: Processes and implications. In R. Crisp & M. Hewstone (Eds.), *Multiple social categorization: Processes, models and applications* (pp. 211–238). New York: Psychology Press.

Prinz, W., & Scheerer-Neumann, G. (1974). Component processes in multi-attribute stimulus classification. *Psychological Research, 37,* 25–50.

Rehm, J., Lilli, W., & Van Eimeren, B. (1988). Reduced intergroup differentiation as a result of self-categorization in overlapping categories. *A quasi-experiment. European Journal of Social Psychology, 18,* 375–379.

Repetti, R. L. (1993). Short-term effects of occupational stressors on daily mood and health complaints. *Health Psychology, 12,* 125–131.

Roccas, S., & Brewer, M. B. (2002). Social identity complexity. *Personality and Social Psychology Review*, 6, 88–106.

Rogers, M., Miller, N., & Hennigan, K. (1981). Cooperative games as an intervention to promote cross-racial acceptance. *American Educational Research Journal*, 18, 513–516.

Rothbart, M., & John, O. P. (1985). Social categorization and behavioral episodes: A cognitive analysis of the effects of intergroup contact. *Journal of Social Issues*, 41, 81–104.

Sawyer, J. E., Houlette, M. A., & Yeagley, E. L. (2006). Decision performance and diversity structure: Comparing faultlines in convergent, crosscut and racially homogenous groups. *Organizational Behavior and Human Decision Processes*, 99, 1–15.

Schlesinger, A. M. (1992). *The disuniting of America: Reflections on a multicultural society*. New York: W. W. Norton.

Schwartz, N., & Clore, G. L. (1983). Mood, misattribution, and judgments of well-being: Informative and directive functions of affective states. *Journal of Personality and Social Psychology*, 45, 513–523.

Sears, D. O. (1983). The person-positivity bias. *Journal of Personality and Social Psychology*, 44, 233–250.

Singh, R., Yeoh, B. S. E., Lim, D. I., & Lim, K. K. (1997). Cross categorization effects in intergroup discrimination: Adding vs. averaging. *British Journal of Social Psychology*, 36, 121–159.

Stangor, C., Lynch, L., Duan, C., & Glass, B. (1992). Categorization of individuals on the basis of multiple social features. *Journal of Personality and Social Psychology*, 62, 207–218.

Stephan, W., & Stephan, C. (1985). Intergroup anxiety. *Journal of Social Issues*, 41, 157–175.

Stone, C. H., & Crisp, R. J. (2007). Superordinate and subgroup identification as predictors of intergroup evaluation in common ingroup contexts. *Group Processes & Intergroup Relations*, 10, 493–513.

Tajfel, H. (1959). Quantitative judgment in social perception. *British Journal of Psychology*, 50, 16–29.

Tajfel, H. (1982). Social psychology of intergroup relations. *Annual Review of Psychology*, 33, 1–39.

Tajfel, H., & Turner, J. C. (1979). An integrative theory of intergroup conflict. In W. G. Austin & S. Worchel (Eds.), *The social psychology of intergroup relations* (pp. 33–47). Monterey, CA: Brooks/Cole.

Taylor, S. E., Fiske, S. T., Etcoff, N. L., & Ruderman, A. J. (1978). Categorical and contextual bases of person memory and stereotyping. *Journal of Personality and Social Psychology*, 36, 778–793.

Tjosvold, D., & Poon, M. (1998). Dealing with scarce resources: Open-minded interaction for resolving budget conflicts. *Group & Organization Management*, 23, 237–255.

Triandis, H. C., & Triandis, L. M. (1960). Race, social class, religion, and nationality as determinants of social distance. *Journal of Abnormal and Social Psychology*, 61, 110–118.

Urada, D., Stenstrom, D. M., & Miller, N. (2007). Crossed-categorization beyond the two-group model. *Journal of Personality and Social Psychology, 92*, 649–664.

Urada, D. I., & Miller, N. (2000). The impact of positive mood and category importance on crossed categorization effects. *Journal of Personality and Social Psychology, 78*(3), 417–433.

Urban, L. M., & Miller, N. (1998). A theoretical analysis of crossed categorization effects: A meta-analysis. *Journal of Personality and Social Psychology, 74*, 894–908.

Vanbeselaere, N. (1987). The effect of dichotomous and crossed social categorizations upon intergroup discrimination. *European Journal of Social Psychology, 17*, 143–156.

Vanbeselaere, N. (1991). The different effects of simple and crossed categorizations: A result of the category differentiation process or of differential category salience? In W. Stroebe & M. Hewstone (Eds.), *European review of social psychology* (Vol. 2, pp. 247–278). Chichester, UK: Wiley.

Vanbeselaere, N. (2000). The treatment of relevant and irrelevant outgroups in minimal group situations with crossed categorizations. *Journal of Social Psychology, 140*, 515–526.

van Knippenberg, A., van Twuyver, M., & Pepels, J. (1994). Factors affecting social categorization processes in memory. *British Journal of Social Psychology, 33*, 419–431.

van Knippenberg, D., De Dreu, C. K. W., & Homan, A. C. (2004). Work group diversity and group performance: An integrative model and research agenda. *Journal of Applied Psychology, 89*, 1008–1022.

van Knippenberg, D., & Haslam, A. S. (2003). Realizing the diversity dividend: Exploring the subtle interplay between identity, ideology, and reality. In A. Haslam, D. van Knippenberg, M. J. Platow, & N. Ellemers (Eds.), *Social identity at work: Developing theory for organizational practice* (pp. 61–77). New York: Psychology Press.

Vanman, E., & Miller, N. (1993). Applications of emotion theory and research to stereotyping and intergroup relations. In D. M. Mackie & D.L. Hamilton (Eds.), *Affect, cognition and stereotyping: Interactive processes in group perception* (pp. 213–238). San Diego, CA: Academic Press.

Verkuyten, M. (2005). Ethnic group identification and group evaluation among minority and majority groups: Testing the multiculturalism hypothesis. *Journal of Personality and Social Psychology, 88*, 121–138.

Vescio, T. K., Judd, C. M., & Kwan, V. S. Y. (2004). The crossed-categorization hypothesis: Evidence of reductions in the strength of categorization, but not intergroup bias. *Journal of Experimental Social Psychology, 40*, 478–496.

Whitley, B. E., Schofield, J. W., & Snyder, H. N. (1984). Peer preferences in a desegregated school: A round robin analysis. *Journal of Personality and Social Psychology, 46*, 799–810.

Wilder, D. A. (1978). Reduction of intergroup discrimination through individuation of the out-group. *Journal of Personality and Social Psychology, 36,* 1361–1374.

Wilder, D. A. (1986). Cognitive factors affecting the success of intergroup contact. In S. Worchel & W. Austin (Eds.), *Psychology of intergroup relations* (pp. 49–66). Chicago: Nelson Hall.

Wolsko, C., Park, B., Judd, C. M., & Wittenbrink, B. (2000). Framing interethnic ideology: Effects of multicultural and color-blind perspectives on judgments of groups and individuals. *Journal of Personality and Social Psychology, 78,* 635–654.

Zajonc, R. (1980). Feeling and thinking: Preferences need no inferences. *American Psychologist, 35,* 151–175.

10

Complexity of Superordinate Self-Categories and Ingroup Projection

Sven Waldzus

This chapter is about how diversity can beat provincial ethnocentric prejudice. More precisely, it is about how establishing a more complex system of standards leads people to be more tolerant in their judgment of other people, and of themselves. It focuses on one particular process, ingroup projection, that makes people intolerant toward deviant outgroups, and on how this process can be interrupted by inducing complexity.

Ingroup Projection as a Source of Intolerance

Behind the research presented in this chapter is a particular theoretical approach explaining intolerance toward deviants (Mummendey & Wenzel, 1999). The main idea is that those who are not like us are not only seen as different from us, but also as deviating from normative standards that we take for granted. Sometimes taking normative standards for granted is understandable, namely if these normative standards are derived from the goals and values of a certain group (Marques, Abrams, & Serôdio, 2001). For instance, scientists who fake their data are clearly deviating from the normative concept of a responsible scientist. However, sometimes things are more difficult, particularly if we have to deal with comparisons between groups within more inclusive, superordinate categories. Are social sciences less scientific than exact physical sciences? Are African Americans less American than European Americans (Devos & Banaji, 2005)? Should homosexual couples be considered as competent parents for adopted children? Groups often disagree about such issues. The reason is that members of social groups generalize attributes, values, norms, and goals of their ingroup onto superordinate categories that provide dimensions for comparisons with outgroups. As a result, groups often consider themselves to be more prototypic than they are seen from the outside. In one study, German primary-school teachers thought that they were more typical teachers than high-school teachers, and high-school teachers thought that they were more typical teachers than primary-school teachers; chopper bikers and sport bikers both claimed that their group was more similar to the prototype of bikers than the other group (Waldzus, Mummendey, Wenzel, & Boettcher, 2004). Both Germans and Italians, when comparing their own national groups with the other, associated more attributes of their own group with the word *Europeans* than the other group did (Bianchi, Mummendey, Steffens, & Yzerbyt, in press). Finally, ingroup characteristics are judged as more human than those of the outgroup, independently of their valence (Paladino & Vaes, 2009). Sometimes, only one of the two groups sees the ingroup to be more prototypical than the outgroup, whereas the other group claims equal prototypicality. Psychology students in a German university believed that they were more typical students than business students, whilst business students found themselves equally prototypical in comparison with psychology students (Wenzel, Mummendey, Weber, & Waldzus, 2003). In studies of implicit association, White Americans showed a stronger association between their own group and America than between African and Asian Americans and America, while African Americans associated their group equally strongly with America as White Americans (Devos & Banaji, 2005). Such asymmetries in ingroup projection are important and will be discussed in more detail later on.

Comparisons in terms of prototypicality are self-relevant, which is why people are often passionate about them. According to self-categorization theory (Turner, Hogg, Oakes, Reicher, & Wetherell, 1987) part of our self-concept consists of hierarchically structured self-categories (e.g., social psychologists, psychologists, scientists, human beings) and ingroups and outgroups are compared in terms of their prototypicality for higher-order, superordinate self-categories that include both the ingroup and the outgroup. Since superordinate categories are usually positively valued ingroups, subgroups obtain positive value from prototypicality. According to this theory, "ethnocentrism, attraction to one's own group as a whole, depends upon the perceived prototypicality of the ingroup in comparison with relevant outgroups (relative prototypicality) in terms of the valued superordinate self-category that provides the basis of the intergroup comparison" (Turner, 1987, p. 61). Group membership gives people important orientations and helps them to define their own position in a social context and to understand and evaluate what is going on and what they are supposed to do (Turner, Oakes, Haslam, & McGarty, 1994). Being prototypical is a source of esteem, a positive identity (Tajfel & Turner, 1979). People have more positive attitudes toward groups that they consider to be more prototypical (Waldzus, Mummendey, Wenzel, & Weber, 2003; Wenzel et al., 2003; see Wenzel, Mummendey, & Waldzus, 2007, for a meta-analysis). Prototypicality is also related to entitlements to all the good things that the superordinate category (e.g., Europeans, teachers, Americans, humans) has to offer (Wenzel, 2000, 2004) and higher-status positions are seen as more legitimate if the higher-status group is more prototypical (Weber, Mummendey, & Waldzus, 2002). Outgroups that are not yet included but intend to join the more inclusive group (e.g., Turkey trying to join the European Union) are the more welcome, the more similar they are to the superordinate category's prototype (Waldzus, Schubert, & Raimundo, 2009, see also Ullrich, Christ, & Schlüter, 2006).

Mummendey and Wenzel (1999) proposed that a process that they call *ingroup projection* is the reason why ethnocentrism and biased attraction toward the own group are so prevalent. Ingroup projection means that the representations that people have of their ingroup and of relevant superordinate categories overlap. The projection metaphor, and particularly Mummendey and Wenzel's (1999) claim that the attributes that are projected are the ones that render an ingroup distinct in comparison with the outgroup, suggests a unidirectional bottom-up generalization of ingroup features to the superordinate category. Indeed, Waldzus, Mummendey, & Wenzel (2005) found that experimentally induced changes in the self-stereotype of Germans were reflected in parallel changes in participants' stereotypes of Europeans, a result that was replicated with implicit measures by Bianchi et al. (in press). However, as was clarified by Wenzel et al. (2007):

> group members may also claim relative prototypicality for their group by assimilating the perception of their ingroup to the prototype of the superordinate group ... In fact, in our research we cannot always distinguish between these two possibilities; rather, we use the term *ingroup projection* as a short general label for *the perception, or claim, of the ingroup's greater relative prototypicality for the superordinate group* [italics added].
>
> (p. 337)

Thus, what is important in ingroup projection is that what people think of their ingroup and what they think of superordinate categories that provide comparison standards and norms is often the same. Groups confuse their ingroup with the superordinate category; they take it as *pars-pro-toto,* as a part that stands for the whole (Wenzel et al., 2003). Outgroups that are different from an ingroup are not only seen as different, but also as deviating from the prototype of the superordinate category. They are less representative and, accordingly, what is different in them is wrong, bad, or unattractive, non-normative, and inferior.

It seems that, apart from ingroup projection, there are other sources of ethnocentrism in intergroup relations that do not necessarily involve generalizations to the superordinate category (e.g., Hegarty & Chryssochoou, 2005). However, intergroup attitudes are reliably related to the perception of prototypicality (Wenzel et al., 2007), and the evidence presented here suggests that ingroup projection explains at least part of the phenomenon.

As a final note before moving on to factors that reduce ingroup projection, a similar phenomenon on the individual level has to be mentioned: the false consensus effect. It has been studied for a long time in social psychology (Ross, Greene, & House, 1977), and researchers identified social projection (Allport, 1924), the tendency to expect similarity between oneself and others, particularly ingroup members (Clement & Krueger, 2002; Mullen, Dovidio, Johnson, & Cooper, 1992) as underlying process (see Krueger, 2007; Robbins & Krueger, 2005 for reviews). Although a similar phenomenon, ingroup projection is empirically and theoretically distinct from social projection (Bianchi, Machunsky, Steffens, & Mummendey, 2009; Machunsky & Meiser, 2009). In social projection we generalize from our "self" to others. In contrast, in ingroup projection we generalize from a particular self-category (the ingroup) to another particular self-category, namely the superordinate category, which is an ingroup on a more inclusive level. Ingroup projection is particularly important in intergroup contexts, when we compare people of our own kind with others that are different. It provides our group with positive distinctiveness, because the ingroup is seen as more similar to the (positive) prototype of the superordinate category than the outgroup. With that it contributes to a positive social identity (Tajfel & Turner, 1979), but also legitimizes the negative treatment of outgroups to the extent that we perceive them as deviating from what we consider normal, or even as questioning our way of being (Mummendey & Wenzel, 1999). It leads to psychologically produced intolerance, as we judge others by our own measures; we apply norms and expectations that they would not apply themselves, and often they do the same with us.

Reducing Ingroup Projection

What can be done about such psychologically based intolerance? Mummendey and Wenzel (1999) suggested two major predictors of ingroup projection: Dual identification, that is, the simultaneous identification with the ingroup and the superordinate category, and the definition of a clear prototype of the superordinate category. These two predictors will be discussed in more detail in the following pages. Before that, it should also be mentioned that recently, more general conditions of information processing (Machunsky & Meiser, 2009, Rosa & Waldzus, 2009), more specific strategic group goals (Sindic & Reicher, 2008), and intergroup threat (Finley, 2006; Ullrich et al., 2006) have been studied as predictors for ingroup projection as well, but they will not be discussed further in this chapter.

Group members that simultaneously identify with the ingroup and the superordinate category have been found to show higher levels of ingroup projection (Wenzel et al., 2003; Waldzus et al., 2003). It seems that these people have a particular interest in viewing their ingroup as prototypical, as they take the standards provided by the superordinate category more seriously and they have a stronger interest in seeing the ingroup in a positive light. Such dual identification, combined with ingroup projection, that is, a large overlap between these two identities, can also be considered as part of a self-concept typical for persons with low social identity complexity (Brewer, this volume; Brewer & Pierce, 2005; Roccas & Brewer, 2002). Reducing intolerance by changing people's identifications is difficult. Identifications have particular functions (see Riketta, 2008 for an overview). Moreover, inducing a more inclusive ingroup while at the same time maintaining one's subgroup identification has been proposed as a way to reduce prejudice (Crisp, Stone, & Hall, 2006; Gaertner & Dovidio, 2000; Hornsey & Hogg, (2000a, 2000b). As dual identifiers have also a stronger tendency for ingroup projection, however, there seems to be a trade-off in the effects of dual identity. On the one hand it might reduce intergroup discrimination because outgroup members are partly seen as ingroup members of the more inclusive common ingroup. On the other hand, the more inclusive ingroup might be represented as a superordinate category, providing ethnocentric standards for subgroup evaluations via ingroup projection. That is why it is important to search for conditions that can reduce ingroup projection without necessarily undermining dual identification.

The present chapter focuses on such a condition discussed by Mummendey and Wenzel (1999), namely the definition of the prototype of the superordinate category. Representations of social categories can differ, for instance in terms of their entitativity (e.g., Brewer & Harasty, 1996; Lickel et al., 2000; McGarty, Haslam, Hutchinson, & Grace, 1995) or variability (e.g., Linville & Fischer, 1993; Park, Judd, & Carey, 1991), and these variations can have implications for processing information about members of these categories (e.g., Ryan, Bogart, & Vender, 2000).

Mummendey and Wenzel (1999) emphasize the role of varying the representations of superordinate categories rather than the representations of the target groups in changing intergroup attitudes. They hypothesise that ingroup projection will be attenuated if the prototype of the superordinate category is less well defined, and they distinguish between four structural properties that make up a prototype's degree of definition. Only three of them have been studied so far: The prototype (1) may be represented clearly or unclearly, (2) it may have a small or broad scope, and (3) it may be simple or complex.

(Un)Clarity

The idea that the prototype may be represented with different degrees of clarity was inspired by a similar proposal by Hogg, Cooper-Shaw, and Holzworth (1993) for the intra-group level. They had found that perceived clarity of the ingroup prototype was positively related with perceived self-prototypicality in terms of the group norm and with the use of prototypicality as the basis for judgments on social attraction amongst group members. In a similar vein, Mummendey and Wenzel (1999) propose that if the notions on the prototype of the superordinate category are not clear, no group can claim to be more prototypic than the others.

Waldzus et al. (2003, Study 1) measured the prototypicality of Germans and Poles for Europeans as perceived by German participants. The clarity of the European prototype was manipulated by false feedback on ingroup consensus. Participants had to rate Europe on several attributes (culture, tradition, sense of community, etc.) and received information about the alleged responses of German participants in five other studies. The information was presented as profiles, that is, lines connecting attribute ratings in a graph. In one condition the presented profiles of ratings in other studies were very similar to each other and to the participants' own responses, suggesting a clear profile of the European prototype shared within the German ingroup. In the other condition all profiles were very different from each other and from the participants' own responses, so that it seemed to be completely unclear how Europe is, as there was obviously no consensus about it. Relative ingroup prototypicality was measured by asking participants to type in typical attributes of Germans in comparison to Polish people and of Polish in comparison to German people, and then rate how much they thought these attributes apply to Europeans. The more the German attributes and the less the Polish attributes applied to Europeans, the higher the relative ingroup prototypicality. Critically and, as predicted, relative ingroup prototypicality was higher in the condition with a clearly defined prototype of Europeans than in the condition where this definition was unclear. It seems that convincing people that the proto- type of superordinate categories is unclear can indeed reduce ingroup projection. However, one result of this study was rather discouraging: The manipulation had no effect for participants who simultaneously identified with both Germans and Europeans (see Figure 10.1). Prob- ably they were highly motivated to see their group as prototypic, or they held strong convictions on the German and European self-stereotypes so that they still projected their German ingroup attributes to Euro- peans. This is one of the reasons why subsequent research focused more on complexity of the representation of the superordinate cate- gory rather than on variation in clarity, although the latter is at least of equal theoretical relevance.

Scope

The second property is the variation between broad or narrow scope of the prototype of the superordinate category. Note that the variation between narrow and broad refers here to the number of dimensions on which a prototype is defined. For instance, if a prototypical posi- tion is only defined on one dimension (e.g., everyone who is born in America is a prototypical American) the prototype has a narrower scope than if prototypical positions are defined on four dimensions (e.g., to be a prototypical American, one has to be born in America, but also to be white, Christian and male). A narrow scope prototype is similar to an unclear prototype, but it does not leave the prototype of the superordinate category completely undefined. Prototypic posi- tions within the superordinate category *are* defined, but only on very

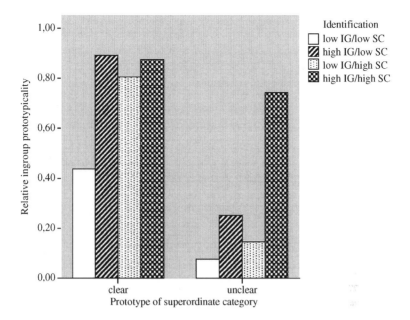

Figure 10.1 Relative ingroup prototypicality in the conditions with a clear or unclear prototype of the superordinate category (SC) for participants with different levels of identification with the ingroup (IG) and the SC (data from Waldzus et al., 2003, study 1).

few dimensions, leaving prototypic positions on many other dimensions open. Compared to a broader scope prototype, a narrow-scope prototype should reduce ingroup projection. The reason is that any subgroup (e.g., African American, Asian American, White American, Native American) can be seen as potentially prototypical as long as it fits the defined typical positions on the few prescriptive dimensions (e.g., being born in America). One advantage of a narrow-scope prototype compared to an unclear prototype is that it might be easier to accept for people for whom the superordinate category is relevant. Although in Waldzus et al. (2003, Study 1) the manipulation had no effect on the identification with Europeans, in the long run completely undefined categories might become useless and people may resist or have difficulties to implement unclear category definitions into their self-concept. Narrow-scope representations (e.g., everyone with German citizenship is a German) might be easier to accept, as they provide at least some meaning. There has been little research on the effect of narrow-scope prototypes of the superordinate category (Waldzus, Meireles, Dumont, & O'Sullivan, 2009), and for reasons of clarity I will return to discuss research on narrow-scope prototypes later on when I discuss the role of cognitive mindsets in ingroup projection.

Complexity

Probably the most interesting, but also most challenging way of reducing ingroup projection by modifying the representation of super-ordinate categories is to make them more complex or diverse. A complex representation of a superordinate category implies that there is no single prototype that best represents that category. Mummendey and Wenzel (1999) define it as a representation in which "the distribution of representative members on the prototypical dimension is . . . multimodal" (p. 167). That means that "various distinctive positions on the underlying dimension may be perceived as prototypical and normative" (p. 168). To give an example, a representation of Americans by a white, male, Christian prototype is simple in comparison to the more complex representation of Americans as White American, African American, Asian American, Latino American, Native American and "racially" mixed, such as Protestant, Catholic, Mormon, Amish, Muslim, Jewish, Buddhist, Bahai, Atheist, Agnostic, etc.; male, female, or transgender; young, middle-aged, old; rich or poor; liberal or conservative.

Some Terminology

Complexity or diversity of the superordinate category should not be confused with mere heterogeneity, that is, with the idea that many differences between subgroups can be identified within it. It should also not be confused with diversity as it is used in organizational psychology or management science, namely as meaning that an organization or team includes members that have different category membership in terms of affiliation, age, sex, professional background, ethnicity or "any attribute which may lead people to the perception that: *that person is different from me*" (Triandis, Kurowski, & Gelfand, 1994, p. 772, quoted in De Abreu Dos Reis, Sastre Castillo, & Roig Dobón, 2007; see also Rink & Jehn, this volume; van Knippenberg & van Ginkel, this volume, and Williams & O'Reilly, 1998 for a review). Diversity perceptions in this sense can be even an instantiation of ingroup projection, namely when one distinguishes between more or less prototypical subgroups. In contrast, a complex representation of the superordinate category is a representation of this category *as being diverse*, that is, diversity is seen as one of its characteristics. It goes beyond, and does not even depend on the knowledge about the existence of particular subgroups. For example, someone might be aware that there are Muslim and Buddhist believers in the United States, but still consider America as a predominantly Christian country (simple representation). In contrast, someone might think of America as a country with a great diversity of religious beliefs and institutions. Only in the latter case we would talk of a complex representation. If the superordinate category representation is complex, for instance if someone reads about a "multi-professional team," differences between subgroups or members are not only factual: they are expected. The inclusive group would not be what it is without them.

Another terminological clarification is necessary in terms of the use of the combinations "complex prototype" or "complex representation." Although some previous publications (e.g., Waldzus et al., 2003) and some researchers on ingroup projection have been using the term "complex prototype," I agree with some critique by others (e.g. Manuela Barreto, personal communication) that the notion of complexity is not entirely compatible with the definition of a prototype. Instead, I prefer to talk about a complex representation that allows for multiple prototypes. For instance, both a robin and an eagle can be considered as two different prototypes of the moderately complex category of birds. The world of birds would be poorer if one of the two prototypes were missing.

Some Data

The first evidence that inducing a complex representation of the superordinate category can reduce ingroup projection comes from Waldzus et al. (2003, Study 2). The study was basically the same as the one reported in the section on clarity (Study 1) with the exception that not the clarity but the complexity of the superordinate category was manipulated. Participants were asked to imagine that they had to describe to another person either the diversity (complex condition) or the unity (simple condition) of Europe, and to type in their ideas into an open text field. Results showed that in the simple condition the German participants expressed a higher prototypicality of Germans than of Poles for Europeans and this tendency was increased for those who simultaneously identified with Germans and Europeans. In the condition in which a complex representation of Europe was primed, however, participants expressed equal prototypicality of Germans and Poles. This was even the case for dual identifiers (see Figure 10.2).

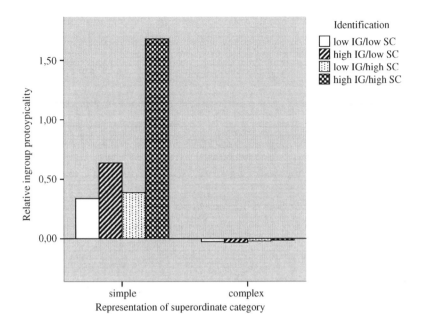

Figure 10.2   Relative ingroup prototypicality in the conditions with a simple or complex representation of the superordinate category (SC) for participants with different levels of identification with the ingroup (IG) and the SC (data from Waldzus et al., 2003, study 2).

The reduction of ingroup projection by a complex superordinate category was replicated by Waldzus et al. (2005) with the same manipulation and again with Germans as ingroup and Europeans as superordinate category, but with different outgroups and using a different indicator of ingroup projection. Apart from the representation of Europeans as either complex or simple, the self-stereotype of Germans was manipulated by presenting participants with either the Italians or the British as an outgroup. Ingroup, outgroup, and the European superordinate category had to be rated on a list of attributes. As expected, Germans scored higher on different attributes, depending on which outgroup was involved. Germans were seen, for instance, as more "reserved" and "stiff" when the outgroup was the Italians, but as "having tastier meals" and "being more companionable" when the outgroup was the British. Ingroup projection was indicated by the fact that the same manipulation led to similar shifts in the attribution of the same characteristics to the superordinate category. Not only Germans, but also Europeans were seen as "having tastier meals," being less "reserved," etc., when the British as compared to the Italian outgroup was involved. Most importantly, this tendency was only shown by participants primed with a simple representation, but not by those primed with a complex representation of Europeans (see Figure 10.3). Again, priming a complex representation of the superordinate category reduced ingroup projection and indirectly led to more positive attitudes toward the respective outgroup.

Complexity and Prototypicality in Asymmetric Status Relations

Not all groups consider themselves to be more prototypic than the outgroup. Asian Americans, for instance, have stronger associations between White Americans and America than between Asian Americans and America (Devos & Banaji, 2005). East Germans agreed that West Germans are more prototypical Germans than themselves (Waldzus et al., 2004). Scottish participants who had separatist political goals saw the Scottish as less prototypic than the English for Britain when the independence of Scotland was made salient (Sindic & Reicher, 2008). There are several explanations for such low prototypicality of some groups. On the one hand, there might be strategic reasons for people to consider lower prototypicality of their group as more desirable, as with the Scots aspiring for independence. On the other hand, lower-status groups or minorities may face so-called reality constraints (e.g., Ellemers, van Rijswijk, Roefs, & Simons, 1997). Numerical minority/majority ratios, but also social status (e.g., Weber et al., 2002) are often used as prototypicality cues. Moreover, powerful groups may dominate social discourse in a way that suggests that what they are is more representative than what the others are, and less dominating groups may after a while accept this idea, something that might also contribute to what Major and Schmader (2001) call "legitimacy appraisals." Whatever the reason, some groups are low-prototypicality groups, that is, they feel less prototypic within the superordinate category than the outgroup.

What would be the effect of a complex representation of the superordinate category for low prototypicality groups, such as low-status minorities? For instance, if complexity had the opposite effect, namely to increase the prototypicality of groups that normally consider themselves as non-prototypic, both groups in such an asymmetric context would end up with perception of more equal prototypicality of the two

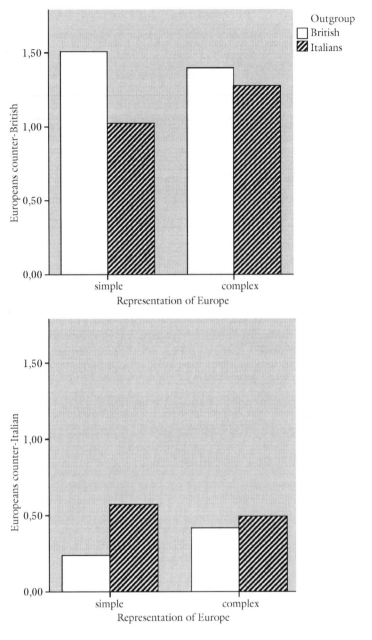

Figure 10.3 Ratings of Europeans on attributes distinctive for Germans in comparison to the British (counter-British) and to Italians (counter-Italian), depending on the salient outgroup of Germans and complexity of the super-ordinate category representation (data from Waldzus et al., 2005).

involved groups, which may contribute to intergroup consensus and, in the long run, higher equality.

In an online experiment, Alexandre, Waldzus, and Esteves (2009) categorized people into artificial groups in an intergroup context. After participating in an alleged test of emotional intelligence, participants received false feedback that they were a member of the group of people with either Inductive or Deductive emotional intelligence. Relative ingroup status and the complexity of the superordinate category were manipulated. In the higher-status condition participants were told that members of their particular group were the majority of emotionally intelligent people, socially more valued, more often selected in job interviews, and more often achieving leadership positions. In the lower-status condition participants were told the opposite. Complexity was manipulated in a similar way as in the other studies: participants were asked to imagine that they had to describe to another person either the diversity of the group of people with high emotional intelligence (complex condition) or simply how highly emotionally intelligent people are, that is, which characteristics would describe this group (simple condition). Relative ingroup prototypicality was measured by ratings of the ingroup, the outgroup, and the superordinate category on a list of attributes (Wenzel et al., 2003) and with two other prototypicality measures using geometrical pictures (Waldzus & Mummendey, 2004). For participants who identified themselves with both the superordinate category and their subgroup the result was a significant interaction between the status and the complexity manipulation. Complexity decreased relative prototypicality, though not significantly, in the higher-status condition, but increased it significantly in the lower-status condition. Moreover, in the simple condition relative ingroup prototypicality was lower for the lower-status minority than for the higher-status majority, but in the complex condition both groups perceived equal prototypicality of the ingroup and the outgroup. It seems that a complex representation helps lower-status minority groups to detach their prototypicality judgments from reality constraints.

In another correlational study, Alexandre, Waldzus, and Esteves (2009) found that White Portuguese (higher-status majority) were seen as more prototypical for people living in Portugal than Cape Verdean or Brazilian immigrants. More importantly, perceived complexity of the superordinate category was negatively correlated with relative ingroup prototypicality for the White Portuguese participants, but positively for Cape Verdean and Brazilian participants.

To sum up, in asymmetric status relations in which social and numerical status shapes the perception of prototypicality, a complex representation of the superordinate category can lead to a consensus between the two groups on more equal prototypicality. This result is very encouraging, as it opens a way to social change that does not necessarily depend on escalation of conflicts between groups (e.g., Subasic, Reynolds, & Turner, 2008). What was still confounded in these studies was numerical status (membership in the majority vs. minority) and social status, two variables that are not always correlated in real-life contexts (e.g., organizations). More research is necessary to disentangle these two variables and also to test whether the relation between complexity, status, and relative prototypicality is shaped by the formal structure of more or less legitimate status relations.

Complexity of Negatively Valued Superordinate Categories and Prototypicality

Sometimes being prototypic is something that one should better avoid, namely if the category for which one is potentially prototypic is a negative reference group (e.g., criminals). Although people have in general a preference to see their ingroups in a positive light, comparisons between subgroups can also be made with reference to negative superordinate categories. In such a case, relative ingroup prototypicality is negatively related to ingroup identification and legitimacy of high ingroup status, and positively related to attitudes toward the outgroup (Weber et al., 2002; Wenzel et al., 2003).

What can be expected from a complex representation of a negative superordinate category? Lower-status groups (e.g., African immigrants in Europe) are often seen as prototypical for negative reference groups (e.g., criminals), although the base-rates make them a minority within that group (e.g., Fiske, 1998; Hamilton, 1981). Negative reference groups can be ingroups or not, but even if they are outgroups they can still be superordinate categories for self-relevant subgroup comparisons, as they include members of subgroups (e.g., Black and White criminals) that potentially share group membership with the perceiver. Would complexity reduce prototypicality of lower-status groups and increase prototypicality of members of the higher-status group? In that case, complexity of superordinate categories would offer a way to change negative stereotypes.

These questions were examined in an experiment by Alexandre, Waldzus, and Esteves (2009) with Social Sciences students (lower-status group, mainly from Sociology and Psychology) and Exact

Sciences students (higher-status group, mainly from Engineering, Physics, and Applied Mathematic). Complexity and the valence of the superordinate category (undergraduate students) were manipulated. The results showed the expected three-way interaction: For the positive superordinate category the pattern was the same as in the studies by Alexandre et al. (2009) reported above. For the negative superordinate category the pattern was, as expected, reversed: The lower-status group was seen as more prototypic than the higher-status group, but only in the simple condition. Making the superordinate category more complex eliminated this pattern as well. A complex representation seems to reduce the prototypicality of lower-status groups for negative superordinate categories, that is, negative stereotypes.

A similar effect was observed in a relevant real life context in which Black and White Portuguese were compared with reference to a negative superordinate category (criminals) that is often used for such comparisons although the two compared groups are not entirely nested within this group. In June 2005, the Portuguese and international media reported on a collective mugging, allegedly committed by about 500 adolescents at Carcavelos beach near Lisbon, a beach often frequented by immigrants with African descent. In fact, this mugging never occurred, but the myth was spread by usually serious newspapers and television channels (e.g., BBC World: http://news.bbc.co.uk/ 2/hi/europe/4083030.stm, downloaded June 7, 2009). Using this event as a backdrop, Alexandre et al. (2009) asked White and Black undergraduate students at Lisbon universities about their perception of the prototypicality of Black and White Portuguese for the superordinate category of criminals in Portugal. The complexity of the representation of criminals in Portugal was manipulated. When left–right political orientation was statistically controlled as a covariate, Black participants saw their own group as being more similar to the prototypical criminal in Portugal than did White participants, but only in the simple, not in the complex condition. Moreover, the complexity manipulation had consistent effects on several other variables of the intergroup context, such as attributions, feelings of threat, and behavioral intentions toward the outgroup. That is, in the complex condition the alleged event was interpreted less as an intergroup conflict than in the simple condition.

How Does It Work?

As a summary of the research reported so far (for a summary see Table 10.1), one can conclude that making representations of superordinate

Table 10.1 Effects of a Complex Representation of the Superordinate Category on Perceived Relative Ingroup Prototypicality for Higher- and Lower-status Groups in Positive and Negative Contexts Found in the Reported Studies

Relative ingroup status study	Positive superordinate category		Negative superordinate category	
	High	Low	High	Low
Waldzus et al., 2003	Decrease			
Waldzus et al., 2005	Decrease			
Alexandre et al., 2009, Study 1	Increase	Decrease		
Alexandre et al., 2009, Study 2	Increase	Decrease		
Alexandre et al., 2009, Study 1	Increase	Increase	Decrease	
Alexandre et al., 2009, Study 2	Increase	Decrease	Increase	Decrease

categories more complex is a promising way to reduce ingroup projection, and thus to overcome intolerance, to reduce intergroup conflicts and to achieve more equality in judgments on the prototypicality of the ingroup and the outgroup. This effect generalizes even to asymmetric status relations where complexity leads to more consensus between high and low prototypicality groups and to contexts in which lower-status groups are seen as prototypic for negatively evaluated reference groups. The results follow the logic of the extended version of the ingroup projection model that takes into account moderations by relative status of subgroups and valence of the superordinate category (Wenzel et al., 2007). They open a promising line for interventions in intergroup tensions and conflicts without necessarily altering the salience of categorizations into ingroup and outgroup, unlike other approaches that propose to reduce prejudice by fostering a more individualized perception of outgroup members (Brewer & Miller, 1984), cross-categorization or multiple categorization in general (Crisp & Hewstone, 2007; Deschamps & Doise, 1978; Migdal, Hewstone, & Mullen, 1998; Miller, Spanovic, & Stenstrom, this volume) or by inducing more inclusive common ingroups (Gaertner & Dovidio, 2000; Gaertner, Dovidio, Anastasio, Bachman, & Rust, 1993). Complex superordinate categories can complement such approaches. For instance, they can prevent a common ingroup from triggering ingroup projection or they may support the development of mutual intergroup differentiation that takes into account the strengths and weaknesses of both groups involved (Brown & Hewstone, 2005; Hewstone & Brown, 1986).

One important issue, however, was not addressed by the research reported so far, namely which processes are involved in the reduction of ingroup projection by complex superordinate categories. On the one hand, superordinate categories can be seen as social construal, as an outcome and vehicle of social interaction, of negotiation and of discourse between and within groups, as general orientations that shape social relationships and social change. Indeed, ingroup projection can be seen as part of more general shared belief systems about social structure (Kessler and Mummendey, 2002, Kessler et al., in press; Tajfel & Turner, 1979). Complex superordinate categories have much in common with the idea of multiculturalism, that is, the appreciation of intergroup differences (e.g., Verkuyten, 2005, this volume). The propagation of complex superordinate categories, for instance of Canada as a country with different sociolinguistic groups that are equally representative, seems to be a constitutive part of a multiculturalism ideology, which has an effect on intergroup perceptions very similar to that of complex superordinate categories. For instance, when exposed to a multiculturalism ideology, White Americans expressed less ethnocentric bias (Wolsko, Park, Judd, & Wittenbrink, 2000), and preferences for a multiculturalism ideology over a colorblind, assimilationism, or separatism ideology have been found to moderate the usual correlation between intergroup differentiation and ingroup bias (Park & Judd, 2005).

On the other hand, the concept of a complex representation of a superordinate category is also distinct from the concept of a multicultural ideology. It is a cognitive representation of one social group rather than a fully fledged belief system about society as a whole. Moreover, differently from a multicultural ideology and from what are discussed by Ely and Thomas (2001) as "diversity perspectives," complex superordinate categories do not imply but rather explain the appreciation of intergroup differences. In this approach, diversity norms should be seen rather as the *explanandum* than the *explanans*. Intergroup differences become normative as a result of cognitive representations. They are appreciated *because* the superordinate category is seen as complex and as a relevant and usually positively evaluated self-category (Turner et al., 1987). Such a perspective does not exclude the possibility of strategic processes in which norms or attributions of prototypicality are accepted when they fit long-term goals (e.g., Sindic & Reicher, 2008). It also does not exclude the possibility that cognitive representations of superordinate categories develop as a response to normative prescriptions. However, to understand the effects of complex superordinate categories it is necessary to disentangle cognitive from normative or strategic processes analytically and empirically, even if they may be intertwined in social reality.

The manipulations and measures of complexity that have been discussed so far were too explicit for such a differentiation as they were openly referring to the intergroup context in which the prototypicality judgments were made and openly triggered the idea of diversity. The reported effects could partly be an effect of social desirability. Participants may have inferred that diversity is appreciated by the experimenter or the institution behind the study. Some evidence of social desirability effects in prototypicality judgments comes from the studies of Devos and Banaji (2005), who found a discrepancy between implicit and explicit measures of associations between America and Black and White Americans.

Another alternative explanation could be that the manipulations primed tolerance or diversity goals that then automatically guided cognition. For instance, multiculturalism ideology has been found to reduce ethnocentric bias even on the implicit level (Richeson & Nussbaum, 2004; Sibley & Liu, 2007).

A third and empirically more challenging explanation is that indeed the cognitive process of gathering prototypicality information was changed by the complex cognitive representations. Research has shown that certain cognitive mindsets can reduce ingroup bias even if they were induced by manipulations that do not make any reference to the intergroup context at stake. For instance, priming the consideration of multiple criteria for social categorization reduces intergroup bias (Hall & Crisp, 2005). Ingroup projection can, under some circumstances, be an outcome of cognitive biases in information processing (Machunsky & Meiser, 2009; Rosa & Waldzus, 2009). The use of complex categories might have led participants to end up with more balanced views on the prototypicality of the subgroups involved because they handled different dimensions of the superordinate category separately when searching for prototypicality cues instead of collapsing them in heuristic judgments.

Cognitive and Small-scope Mindsets Reduce Ingroup Projection

Waldzus et al. (2009) tested this cognitive hypothesis. The use of multiple orthogonal dimensions in information processing has been studied as an inter-individual difference variable (cognitive complexity, e.g., Goldstein & Blackman, 1978; Scott, Osgood, & Peterson, 1979), and as a situational variable. In social psychological research on category use in social perception, the complexity of knowledge structures is assumed to depend on the number of features or attribute dimensions and on the average correlation between these dimensions (Judd & Lusk, 1984; Linville, 1982; Linville & Jones, 1980). In the same vein, Waldzus et al. (2009) assumed that the representations of superordinate categories should depend on the number and the orthogonality of the dimensions that are used in these representations. They distinguish between representations using only few or many dimensions and between high or low orthogonality (that is, non-correlation) of these dimensions. Representations with only few dimensions—orthogonal or correlated—should lead to narrow-scope prototypes of the superordinate category and representations with many orthogonal dimensions should lead to more complex representations of superordinate categories. In both cases, ingroup projection should be reduced, because the prototype of the superordinate category is not clearly defined (Mummendey & Wenzel, 1999). Representations, however, that use many correlated dimensions should lead to a well-defined prototype of the superordinate category that contains many prototypical positions on the various dimensions and should trigger ingroup projection.

In a study with undergraduate psychology students of a South African university, Waldzus et al. (2009) manipulated the use of many versus few dimensions and the orthogonality of these dimensions by a mindset priming. After that, ingroup projection was measured by two indicators assessing relative prototypicality of the ingroup (psychology students) in comparison to the outgroup (law students) within the superordinate category (students of the university in general). The mindset priming made no reference to the intergroup context. Instead, participants were presented with descriptions of persons and had to select the best-fitting one out of a number of possible names. Each person description contained one or more attributes (e.g., a woman who is likable). The task was divided into six subtasks and, depending on whether participants had to switch to a new subtask after matching three or seven names to persons, the use of few versus many dimensions was primed, respectively. The use of orthogonal vs. correlated dimensions was manipulated by either cumulating attributes over the person descriptions within one block (e.g., a woman who is likable; a woman who is likable and bright; a woman who is likable, bright, and determined) or not (e.g., a woman who is likable; a woman who is bright; a woman who is determined), respectively. The assumption was that cumulating attributes would produce the tendency to interpret the cumulated attributes as non-redundant (Grice, 1975), thus priming the use of dimensions as orthogonal. The hypothesis was that relative ingroup prototypicality should be reduced in the conditions priming the use of many orthogonal dimensions (complex) or the use of only a few dimensions (narrow scope). Results confirmed the hypothesis, but only on the more subtle prototypicality measure using attribute ratings. There was no effect on the more blatant pictorial measure.

The same result was found in another study for Portuguese Business students (higher-status group), but not for Accountancy students (lower-status group). That is, although a cognitive process, the effect of the mindset priming on perceived prototypicality was adaptive to the social context (e.g., status). Moreover, in the latter study factor loadings of attribute ratings of the superordinate category in a factor analysis with forced one-factor solution was used as an indicator of the degree of definition of the prototype of the superordinate category, and this variable mediated the effect of the manipulation.

To conclude, although normative, strategic or ideological processes might be involved in the effects of complexity on relative ingroup prototypicality, the fact that priming mindsets that undermine a clear definition of the prototype of the superordinate category reduces ingroup projection supports the argument that indeed a cognitive process plays a mediating role.

And Cognitive Complexity?

Is it possible to conclude from this result that people with higher cognitive complexity are more tolerant, that is, less prone to ingroup projection? For instance, cognitive complexity has been found to be associated with less ingroup bias, less extreme ingroup and outgroup evaluations, and more perceived variability within the ingroup and the outgroup (Ben-Hari, Kedem, & Levy-Weiner, 1992). However, it seems that the relation between cognitive complexity and ingroup projection is less straightforward. Meireles (2007) found in a study with alumni of a Portuguese university that, although the manipulation of cognitive complexity had a similar, though weak, effect as manipulations of complex superordinate categories, cognitive complexity measured as an inter-individual difference variable (using Scott's H; Scott et al., 1979) was positively related to the relative prototypicality of participants' professional ingroup! One explanation can be that cognitively highly complex people use more dimensions but do not always represent social categories as more complex. When repeatedly processing information on the same social category, they may activate prototypical positions on many dimensions simultaneously, which leads in the long run to strong associations between them and to representations that use many correlated instead of many orthogonal dimensions. Thus, paradoxically, although having the cognitive capacity for complex representations, particularly when confronted with new categories, cognitively complex individuals may hold richer ingroup stereotypes, as more dimensions are involved. In most social contexts these more elaborated self-stereotypes may be functional, but they can also be responsible for ingroup projection triggering ethnocentric bias. More research is necessary to clarify these processes.

Implications for Policy and Practice

The overall conclusion from the accumulated research reported here is clear: Inducing a more complex representation of superordinate categories, positive or negative, can promote intergroup tolerance and attenuate negative self-evaluations of disadvantaged groups, as it contributes to judgments of equal prototypicality in intergroup contexts. Before going into detail, however, I would like to emphasize that this chapter does not advocate tolerance or complexity in every case. Sometimes, there is too much tolerance (e.g., toward corruption, domestic violence, human rights violations). Whether or not tolerance is desirable depends on political goals and cultural norms rather than on psychological principles. In our rapidly changing society, however, we face increasing diversity in many social contexts, globally (e.g., challenge of Western dominance in international relations) and locally (e.g., in families, schools, cities, organizations) for which ethnocentric intergroup comparisons due to simplified superordinate categories are dysfunctional as they can trigger unnecessary conflicts and hostility. Moreover, historical changes have made status differences between important social categories (e.g., Blacks and Whites, men and women) obsolete in most social contexts, but without eliminating the perception of status-related prototypicality differences by a large part of the population. What this research shows are some fundamental psychological principles that can eliminate perceptions of unequal prototypicality in cases in which tolerance and equality is desirable but difficult to achieve.

As these are fundamental processes, they are potentially relevant for all social contexts in which superordinate categories are used as sources of standards and norms that serve as reference for the evaluation of others and of one's own group. Politicians may emphasize in their rhetoric not only the unity, but also the complexity of superordinate categories when they attempt to mobilize several groups in society for an important common goal, just as that time Senator Barack Obama did in his legendary speech "A More Perfect Union" on March 18, 2008 (http://www.youtube.com/watch?v=pWe7wTVbLUU, retrieved September 22, 2009). The media, if they do not intend to blindly re-enforce resentment, dysfunctional stereotypes, and prejudice, might reflect on whether they pay the actual complexity of superordinate groups enough tribute when framing their messages (e.g., Seyle & Newman, 2006). Social workers, consultants, or leaders in public service and in the business world might use complex representations of superordinate categories as a means for conflict prevention and resolution. Finally, teachers may consider supporting children in the development of the ability to take on a complexity mindset if necessary.

Outlook

Social change processes that increase social and cultural diversity can be a challenge and a chance for a better life for everybody. The knowledge about how complex superordinate categories affect judgments on relative prototypicality is important for the understanding of how our psychological equipment deals with them, leading to desired or undesired outcomes. However, it should not be understood in isolation. The nested structure of intergroup contexts within superordinate categories is a particular case of more general constellations of multiple categorizations (Crisp & Hewstone, 2007). Superordinate categories play a key role in intergroup contact (Allport, 1954; Brown & Hewstone, 2005; Gaertner & Dovidio, 2000; Pettigrew, 1998). They affect people's social identity complexity (Miller, Brewer & Arbuckle, 2009; Roccas & Brewer, 2002), acculturation strategies (Berry, 1984, Bourhis, Moïse, Perreault, & Senecal, 1997), group-based emotions (e.g., Wohl & Branscombe, 2005), belief systems (Kessler et al., in press; Weber et al., 2002), justice perceptions (Wenzel, 2000, 2004), ideology (Park & Judd, 2005), power relations (Simon & Oakes, 2006; Turner, 2005), and many other important variables. Compared to this importance, research on characteristics of such superordinate categories is in a relatively early stage. For instance, more sophisticated measures have to be developed in order to disentangle the cognitive, normative, motivational, and strategic processes that are involved. Interventions have to be developed, implemented, and evaluated in longitudinal studies before we can be sure whether complex superordinate categories can hold what they promise: to provide the psychological conditions of tolerance and appreciation of intergroup difference.

Acknowledgments

Part of the research reported in this chapter was supported by the Deutsche Forschungsgemeinschaft (Mu551/18), the Fundação para a Ciência e a Tecnologia (FCT/POCI[0]/PSI/55088/2004[0]; FCT/POCI/PSI/61915/2004,FCT/SFRH/BSAB/868/2008), and by the Centro de Investigação e Intervenção Social (CIS/ISCTE-IUL), Portugal.

References

Alexandre, J. D., Waldzus, S., & Esteves, C. (2009). Consensus through complex inclusive categories: Ingroup projection in asymmetric relations.

Alexandre, J. D., Waldzus, S., & Esteves, C. (2009). To be or not to be: The role of valence and complexity of inclusive categories in prototypicality perceptions for higher and lower status groups.

Allport, F. H. (1924). *Social psychology*. Boston: Houghton Mifflin.

Allport, G. W. (1954). *The nature of prejudice*. Reading, MA: Addison-Wesley.

Ben-Hari, R., Kedem, P., & Levy-Weiner, N. (1992). Cognitive complexity and intergroup perception and evaluation. *Personality and Individual Differences, 13*(12), 1291–1298.

Berry, J. W. (1984). Cultural relations in plural societies: Alternatives to segregation and their sociopsychological implications. In N. Miller & M.B. Brewer (Eds.), *Groups in contact: The psychology of desegregation* (pp. 11–27). Orlando, FL: Academic Press.

Bianchi, M., Machunsky, M., Steffens, M. C., & Mummendey, A. (2009). Like me or like us: Is ingroup projection just social projection? *Experimental Psychology, 56*(3), 198–205.

Bianchi, M., Mummendey, A., Steffens, M. C., & Yzerbyt, V. Y.(in press). What do you mean by European? Spontaneous ingroup projection: Evidence from sequential priming.

Bourhis, R. Y., Moïse, L. C., Perreault, S., & Senecal, S. (1997). Toward an interactive acculturation model: A social psychological approach. *International Journal of Psychology, 32*(6), 269–386.

Brewer, M. B., & Harasty, A. S. (1996). Seeing groups as entities: The role of perceiver motivation. In R. M. Sorrentino & E.T. Higgins (Eds.), *Handbook of motivation and cognition, Vol. 3: The interpersonal context* (pp. 347–370). New York: Guilford Press.

Brewer, M. B., & Miller, N. (1984). Beyond the contact hypothesis: Theoretical perspectives on desegregation. In N. Miller & M.B. Brewer (Eds.), *Groups in contact: The psychology of desegregation* (pp. 281–302). New York: Academic Press.

Brewer, M. B., & Pierce, K. P. (2005). Social identity complexity and outgroup tolerance. *Personality and Social Psychology Bulletin, 31*(3), 428–437.

Brown, R., & Hewstone, M. (2005). An integrative theory of intergroup contact. In M. P. Zanna (Ed.), *Advances in experimental social psychology* (Vol. 37, pp. 255–343). San Diego, CA: Elsevier Academic Press.

Clement, R. W., & Krueger, J. (2002). Social categorization moderates social projection. *Journal of Experimental Social Psychology, 38*, 219–231.

Crisp, R. J., & Hewstone, M. (2007). Multiple social categorization. In M. P. Zanna (Ed.), *Advances in experimental social psychology* (pp. 163–254). San Diego, CA: Elsevier Academic Press.

Crisp, R. J., Stone, C. H., & Hall, N. R. (2006). Recategorization and subgroup identification: Predicting and preventing threats from common ingroups. *Personality and Social Psychology Bulletin, 32,* 230–243.

De Abreu Dos Reis, C. R., Sastre Castillo, M. A., & Roig Dobón, S. R. (2007). Diversity and business performance: 50 years of research. *Service Business, 1,* 257–274.

Deschamps, J. C., & Doise, W. (1978). Crossed category memberships in intergroup relations. In H. Tajfel (Ed.), *Differentiation between social groups* (pp. 141–158). London: Academic Press.

Devos, T., & Banaji, M. R. (2005). American = White? *Journal of Personality and Social Psychology, 88,* 447–466.

Ellemers, N., Van Rijswijk, W., Roefs, M., & Simons, C. (1997). Bias in intergroup perceptions: Balancing group identity with social reality. *Personality and Social Psychology Bulletin, 23*(2), 186–198.

Ely, R. J., & Thomas, D. A. (2001). Cultural diversity at work: The effects of diversity perspectives on work group processes and outcomes. *Administrative Science Quarterly, 46*(2), 229–73.

Finley, S. (2006). *Social groups in times of change: The impact of a threatened identity.* Unpublished doctoral thesis, Australian National University, Canberra, Australia.

Fiske, S. T. (1998). Stereotyping, prejudice, and discrimination. In D. T. Gilbert, S.T. Fiske, & G. Lindzey (Eds.), *The handbook of social psychology* (4th ed., Vol. 2, pp. 357–411). New York: McGraw-Hill.

Gaertner, S. L., & Dovidio, J. F. (2000). *Reducing intergroup bias: The common ingroup identity model.* Philadelphia, PA: Psychology Press.

Gaertner, S. L., Dovidio, J. F., Anastasio, P. A., Bachman, B. A., & Rust, M. C. (1993). The common ingroup identity model: Recategorization and the reduction of intergroup bias. In W. Stroebe & M. Hewstone (Eds.), *European review of social psychology* (Vol. 4, pp. 1–26). Chichester, UK: Wiley.

Goldstein, K. M., & Blackman, S. (1978). *Cognitive style: Five approaches and relevant research.* New York: Wiley.

Grice, H. P. (1975). Logic and conversation. In: Peter Cole & Jerry L. Morgan (Eds.), *Syntax and semantics: Vol. 3. Speech acts* (pp. 41–58). New York: Academic Press.

Hall, N. R., & Crisp, R. J. (2005). Considering multiple criteria for social categorization can reduce intergroup bias. *Personality and Social Psychology Bulletin, 31*(10), 1435–1444.

Hamilton, D. L. (1981). *Cognitive processes in stereotyping and intergroup behaviour.* Hillsdale, NJ: Erlbaum.

Hegarty, P., & Chryssochoou, X. (2005). Why "our" policies set the standard more than "theirs": Category norms and generalization between European Union countries. *Social Cognition, 23*(6), 491–528.

Hewstone, M., & Brown, R. (1986). Contact is not enough: An intergroup perspective on the "contact hypothesis". In M. Hewstone & R. Brown

(Eds.), *Contact and conflict in intergroup encounters* (pp. 1–44). Oxford, UK: Blackwell.

Hogg, M. A., Cooper-Shaw, L., & Holzworth, D. W. (1993). Group prototypicality and depersonalized attraction in small interactive groups. *Personality and Social Psychology Bulletin, 19,* 452–465.

Hornsey, M. J., & Hogg, M. A. (2000a). Subgroup relations: A comparison of mutual intergroup differentiation and common ingroup identity models of prejudice reduction. *Personality and Social Psychology Bulletin, 26,* 242–256.

Hornsey, M. J., & Hogg, M. A. (2000b). Assimilation and diversity: An integrative model of subgroup relations. *Personality and Social Psychology Review, 4,* 143–156.

Judd, C. M., & Lusk, C. M. (1984). Knowledge structures and evaluative judgments: Effects of structural variables on judgmental extremity. *Journal of Personality and Social Psychology, 46*(6), 1193–1207.

Kessler, T., & Mummendey, A. (2002). Sequential or parallel processes? A longitudinal field study concerning determinants of identity management strategies. *Journal of Personality and Social Psychology, 82,* 75–88.

Kessler, T., Mummendey, A., Funke, F., Brown, R., Binder, J., Zagefka, H., Leyens, J. P., Demoulin, S., & Maquil, A.(in press). We all live in Germany, but...: Ingroup projection, intergroup emotions, and prejudice against immigrants. *European Journal of Social Psychology.*

Krueger, J. (2007). From social projection to social behaviour. In W. Stroebe & M. Hewstone (Eds.), *European review of social psychology* (Vol. 18, pp. 1–35). Hove, UK: Psychology Press.

Lickel, B., Hamilton, D. L., Wieczorkowska, G., Lewis, A., Sherman, S. J., & Uhles, A. N. (2000). Varieties of groups and the perception of group entitativity. *Journal of Personality and Social Psychology, 78,* 223–246.

Linville, P. W. (1982). The complexity-extremity effect and age-based stereotyping. *Journal of Personality and Social Psychology, 42*(2), 193–211.

Linville, P. W., & Fischer, G. W. (1993). Exemplar and abstraction models of perceived group variability and stereotypicality. *Social Cognition, 11,* 92–125.

Linville, P. W., & Jones, E. E. (1980). Polarized appraisals of out-group members. *Journal of Personality and Social Psychology, 38*(5), 689–703.

Machunsky, M., & Meiser, T. (2009). Ingroup projection as a means to define the superordinate category efficiently: Response time evidence. *Social Cognition, 27*(1), 57–76.

Major, B., & Schmader, T. (2001). Legitimacy and the construal of social disadvantage. In J. Jost & B. Major (Eds.), *The psychology of legitimacy: Emerging perspectives on ideology, justice, and intergroup relationships* (pp. 176–204). New York: Cambridge University Press.

Marques, J., Abrams, D., & Serôdio, R. G. (2001). Being better by being right: Subjective group dynamics and derogation of in-group deviants when generic norms are undermined. *Journal of Personality and Social Psychology, 81*(3), 436–447.

McGarty, C., Haslam, S. A., Hutchinson, K. J., & Grace, D. M. (1995). Determinants of perceived consistency: The relationship between group entitativity and the meaningfulness of categories. *British Journal of Social Psychology, 34,* 237–256.

Meireles, C. (2007). *Tolerance in intergroup relations: cognitive representations reducing ingroup projection.* Unpublished master's thesis, Lisbon: Lisbon University Institute (ISCTE).

Migdal, M. J., Hewstone, M., & Mullen, B. (1998). The effects of crossed categorization on intergroup evaluations: A meta-analysis. *British Journal of Social Psychology, 37,* 303–324.

Miller, K. P., Brewer, M. B., & Arbuckle, N. L. (2009). Social identity complexity: Its correlates and antecedents. *Group Processes & Intergroup Relations, 12*(1), 79–94.

Mullen, B., Dovidio, J. F., Johnson, C., & Cooper, C. (1992). In-group–out-group differences in social projection. *Journal of Experimental Social Psychology, 28,* 422–440.

Mummendey, A., & Wenzel, M. (1999). Social discrimination and tolerance in intergroup relations: Reactions to intergroup difference. *Personality and Social Psychology Review, 3,* 158–174.

Paladino, M. P., & Vaes, J. (2009). Ours is human: On the pervasiveness of infra-humanization in intergroup relations. *British Journal of Social Psychology, 48*(2), 237–251.

Park, B., & Judd, C. M. (2005). Rethinking the link between categorization and prejudice within the social cognition perspective. *Personality and Social Psychology Review, 9,* 108–130.

Park, B., Judd, C. M., & Carey, S. R. (1991). Social categorization and the representation of variability information. In W. Stroebe & M. Hewstone (Eds.), *European review of social psychology* (Vol. 2, pp. 211–245). Chichester, UK: Wiley.

Pettigrew, T. F. (1998). Intergroup contact theory. *Annual Review of Psychology, 49,* 65–85.

Richeson, J. A., & Nussbaum, R. J. (2004). The impact of multiculturalism versus color-blindness on racial bias. *Journal of Experimental Social Psychology, 40,* 417–423.

Riketta, M. (2008). "Who identifies with which group?" The motive-feature match principle and its limitations. *European Journal of Social Psychology, 38*(4), 715–735.

Robbins, J. M., & Krueger, J. I. (2005). Social projection to ingroups and outgroups: A review and meta-analysis. *Personality and Social Psychology Review, 9*(1), 32–47.

Roccas, S., & Brewer, M. B. (2002). Social identity complexity. *Personality and Social Psychology Review, 6*(2), 88–106.

Rosa, M., & Waldzus, S. (2009). Hot and Cold Ingroup Projection: Sources of Prototypicality in Secure and Insecure Intergroup Relations.

Ross, L., Greene, D., & House, P. (1977). The "false consensus effect": An egocentric bias in social perception and attribution processes. *Journal of Experimental Social Psychology, 13,* 279–301.

Ryan, C. S., Bogart, L. M., & Vender, J. P. (2000). Effects of perceived group variability on the gathering of information about individual group members. *Journal of Experimental Social Psychology, 36,* 90–101.

Scott, W. A., Osgood, D. W., & Peterson, C. (1979). *Cognitive structure: The theory and measurement of individual differences.* Washington, DC: V. H. Winston & Sons.

Seyle, D. C., & Newman, M. L. (2006). A house divided? The psychology of Red and Blue America. *American Psychologist, 61*(6), 571–580.

Sibley, C. G., & Liu, J. H. (2007). New Zealand = bicultural? Implicit and explicit associations between ethnicity and nationhood in the New Zealand context. *European Journal of Social Psychology, 37*(6), 1222–1243.

Simon, B., & Oakes, P. (2006). Beyond dependence: An identity approach to social power and domination. *Human Relations, 59,* 105–139.

Sindic, D., & Reicher, S. (2008). The instrumental use of group prototypicality judgements. *Journal of Experimental Social Psychology, 44,* 1425–1435.

Subasic, E., Reynolds, K. J., & Turner, J. (2008). The political solidarity model of social change: Dynamics of self-categorization in intergroup power relations. *Personality and Social Psychology Review, 12,* 330–352.

Tajfel, H., & Turner, J. C. (1979). An integrative theory of intergroup conflict. In W. G. Austin & S. Worchel (Eds.), *The social psychology of intergroup relations* (pp. 33–47). Monterey, CA: Brooks/Cole.

Triandis, H. C., Kurowski, L. L., & Gelfand, M. J. (1994). Workplace diversity. In: H. C. Triandis, M.P. Dunnette, & L. M. Hough (Eds.), *Handbook of industrial and organizational psychology* (2nd ed., Vol. 4, pp. 769–827). Palo Alto, CA: Consulting Psychologists Press.

Turner, J. C. (1987). A self-categorization theory. In J. C. Turner, M.A. Hogg, P. J. Oakes, S. D. Reicher, & M. Wetherell (Eds.), *Rediscovering the social group: A self-categorization theory* (pp. 42–67). New York: Basil Blackwell.

Turner, J. C. (2005). Explaining the nature of power: A three-process theory. *European Journal of Social Psychology, 35,* 1–22.

Turner, J. C., Hogg, M. A., Oakes, P. J., Reicher, S. D., & Wetherell, M. S. (1987). *Rediscovering the social group: A self-categorization theory.* New York: Basil Blackwell.

Turner, J. C., Oakes, P. J., Haslam, S. A., & McGarty, C. (1994). Self and collective: Cognition and social context. Special Issue: The self and the collective. *Personality and Social Psychology Bulletin, 20*(5), 454–463.

Ullrich, J., Christ, O., & Schlüter, E. (2006). Merging on Mayday: Subgroup and superordinate identification as joint moderators of threat effects in the context of European Union's expansion. *European Journal of Social Psychology, 36,* 857–875.

Verkuyten, M. (2005). Ethnic group identification and group evaluation among minority and majority groups: Testing the multiculturalism
hypothesis. *Journal of Personality and Social Psychology*, 88, 121–
138.

Waldzus, S., Meireles, C., Dumont, K., & O'Sullivan, C. (2009). Open your
mind: Reduction of ingroup projection by priming complexity and narrow
scope mindsets.

Waldzus, S., & Mummendey, A. (2004). Inclusion in a superordinate category, ingroup prototypicality, and attitudes toward outgroup. *Journal of
Experimental Social Psychology*, 40(4), 466–477.

Waldzus, S., Mummendey, A., & Wenzel, M. (2005). When "different" means
"worse": Ingroup prototypicality in changing intergroup contexts. *Journal
of Experimental Social Psychology*, 41(1), 76–83.

Waldzus, S., Mummendey, A., Wenzel, M., & Boettcher, F. (2004). Of bikers,
teachers and Germans: Groups' diverging views about their prototypicality.
British Journal of Social Psychology, 43, 385–400.

Waldzus, S., Mummendey, A., Wenzel, M., & Weber, U. (2003). Toward
tolerance: Representations of superordinate categories and perceived
ingroup prototypicality. *Journal of Experimental Social Psychology*, 39, 31–
47.

Waldzus, S., Schubert, T., & Raimundo, A. (2009). Better close the door:
Minimal-goal mindset and relative prototypicality as predictors of preventive
exclusion or inclusion of outgroups.

Weber, U., Mummendey, A., & Waldzus, S. (2002). Perceived legitimacy of
intergroup status differences: Its prediction by relative ingroup prototypicality. *European Journal of Social Psychology*, 32, 449–470.

Wenzel, M. (2000). Justice and identity: The significance of inclusion for
perceptions of entitlement and the justice motive. *Personality and Social
Psychology Bulletin*, 26, 157–176.

Wenzel, M. (2004). A social categorisation approach to distributive justice.
In W. Stroebe & M. Hewstone (Eds.), *European Review of Social Psychology*
(Vol. 15, pp. 219–257). Hove, UK: Psychology Press.

Wenzel, M., Mummendey, A., & Waldzus, S. (2007). Superordinate identities
and intergroup conflict: The ingroup projection model. In W. Stroebe &
M. Hewstone (Eds.), *European Review of Social Psychology* (Vol. 18, pp.
331–372). Hove, UK: Psychology Press.

Wenzel, M., Mummendey, A., Weber, U., & Waldzus, S. (2003). The ingroup
as pars pro toto: Projection from the ingroup onto the inclusive category as a
precursor to social discrimination. *Personality and Social Psychology Bulletin*,
29(4), 461–473.

Williams, K., & O'Reilly, C. (1998). The complexity of diversity: a review
of forty years of research. *Research in Organizational Behavior*, 20, 77–
140.

Wohl, M. J. A., & Branscombe, N. R. (2005). Forgiveness and collective
guilt assignment to historical perpetrator groups depend on level of social

category inclusiveness. *Journal of Personality and Social Psychology, 88*, 288–303.

Wolsko, C., Park, B., Judd, C. M., & Wittenbrink, B. (2000). Framing interethnic ideology: Effects of multicultural and color-blind perspectives on judgments of groups and individuals. *Journal of Personality and Social Psychology, 78*, 635–654.

Part V

Group Processes

11

The Categorization-Elaboration Model of Work Group Diversity

Wielding the Double-Edged Sword

Daan van Knippenberg and
Wendy P. van Ginkel

As organizations are increasingly shifting to team-based work and societies and organizations are becoming increasingly diverse, work group diversity has become a fact of organizational life. More than fifty years of research in work group diversity provides abundant evidence that diversity is not without consequence for day-to-day life in organizations. Work group diversity may have positive effects as well as negative effects on group process and group performance, and in addition may affect group member well-being (van Knippenberg & Schippers, 2007; Williams & O'Reilly, 1998). Not surprisingly, then, key questions for research and practice in organizational behavior is how work group diversity affects group functioning and performance and how these processes may be managed to turn diversity into an asset rather than a liability.

The abundance of research in work group diversity has also illustrated, however, that the effects of diversity are elusive. There are no simple answers as to whether diversity is helpful or harmful or as to whether some dimensions of diversity may have more positive effects than others. Rather, the key conclusion from diversity research seems to be that "it depends." Diversity's effects are highly contingent on other factors and key to the study and management of diversity is the identification and understanding of variables that moderate the effects of diversity (van Knippenberg & Schippers, 2007). In this chapter, we outline a model that was developed to address this very issue—the Categorization-Elaboration Model of work group diversity and group performance (van Knippenberg, De Dreu, & Homan, 2004). The Categorization-Elaboration Model identifies the processes underlying the positive and negative effects of work group diversity and working from this understanding of these processes identifies a range of contingencies of these effects. To introduce and contextualize the model, we first provide a brief introduction and review of the field of work group diversity. Then we present the model and review the empirical evidence in support of the model that has been accumulating since its publication. Subsequently, we outline the implications for organizational practice—what does all this mean for the management of work group diversity?

Diversity and Performance: A Rough Review

Diversity is a characteristic of a social group that "reflects the degree to which there are objective or subjective differences between people within the group" (van Knippenberg & Schippers, 2007, p. 519; cf. Jackson, 1992;Williams & O'Reilly, 1998). In principle, diversity thus refers to any dimension of differentiation, from age and ethnicity to functional and educational background to attitudes and values, and from obvious ones like gender and nationality to highly idiosyncratic ones like preference for local sports clubs or "rival" pop bands. In academic and organizational practice, however, the study of diversity is heavily dominated by a limited set of dimensions: age, ethnicity, gender, tenure, and functional background (van Dijk, van Engen, & van Knippenberg, 2009; Williams & O'Reilly, 1998). Age, ethnicity, gender, and related variables such as nationality are often clustered as demographic diversity, on the assumption that the characteristics they share in common may imply they have similar effects. In a similar vein, functional background is often grouped with variables like educational background under a heading like job-related diversity (e.g., Jehn, Northcraft, & Neale, 1999; Pelled, Eisenhardt, & Xin, 1999). More recently, there is also increasing attention to so called deep-level diversity (Bell, 2007; Harrison, Price, & Bell, 1998), diversity in more psychological variables that are typically not easily discernable like personality, attitudes, and values.

Whether the interest in diversity is defined in terms of such category labels as demographic and job-related, and deep-level diversity, or rather in reference to specific dimensions of diversity such as gender, functional background, and extraversion, the key question for research and practice remains the same: how does diversity affect group process and performance, and how can this be managed? Two theoretical perspectives have dominated diversity research in the pursuit of answers to this question: the social categorization (and similarity/attraction) perspective and the information/decision making (or informational resource) perspective (van Knippenberg & Schippers, 2007; Williams & O'Reilly, 1998).

The social categorization perspective has firm roots in the social psychology of intergroup relations (Brewer & Brown, 1998; Tajfel & Turner, 1986; Turner, Hogg, Oakes, Reicher, & Wetherell, 1987; cf. van Knippenberg, 2003). The basic premise in this perspective is that differences between people provide the basis for social categorization, the distinction between self and others similar to self—ingroup—and others different from self—outgroup. Such "us–them" subgroupings (cf. diversity as separation; Harrison & Klein, 2007) within work groups are potentially problematic, because people are prone to like ingroup more than outgroup, to trust ingroup more than outgroup, and to be more willing to cooperate and communicate with ingroup than with outgroup. As a consequence, diverse work groups as compared with more homogeneous groups may experience more problematic group process, for instance in terms of disrupted communication, lowered cooperation, or relational conflicts. Moreover, group cohesion and group member identification with and commitment to the group may be lower (also see Chattopadhyay, Tluchowska, & George, 2004). As a result of these disruptive influences, diverse groups would perform more poorly than homogeneous groups.

The similarity/attraction perspective (cf. Byrne, 1971)—with a lighter footprint in diversity research—focuses on interpersonal attraction rather than on social categorization, but essentially arrives at the same basic prediction as the social categorization perspective: people are more attracted to similar others, and as a consequence homogeneous groups function more smoothly than diverse groups.

In sharp contrast, the informational resource perspective does not view diversity as a liability, but rather as an asset. In this perspective, the emphasis is on diversity as a source of information, knowledge, and expertise (cf. diversity as variety; Harrison & Klein, 2007) that may benefit the team. The basic premise here is that differences between people are associated valuable differences in task-relevant knowledge, insight, and expertise. Accordingly, the more diverse a group is, the larger the pool of task-relevant information and perspectives available to the group, and the better able the group will be to address the challenges and problems encountered in task performance. Indeed, the differences of expertise and insights should lead diverse groups to be more creative and innovative, better problem solvers and decision makers, and overall to perform better than more homogeneous groups (e.g., Ancona & Caldwell, 1992).

Both the positive perspective on diversity and performance—the informational resource perspective—and the negative perspective on diversity and performance—the social categorization (and similarity/attraction) perspective—make intuitive sense, and indeed they are both rooted in well-grounded social psychological research traditions. Yet they arrive at sharply opposing predictions. Perhaps not surprisingly, then, while there is both evidence that diversity may disrupt performance (e.g., Simons, Pelled, & Smith, 1999) and that diversity may stimulate performance (e.g., Bantel & Jackson, 1989), neither perspective is reliably supported. Narrative reviews (Jackson, Joshi, & Erhardt, 2003; Milliken & Martins, 1996; van Knippenberg & Schippers, 2007; Williams & O'Reilly, 1998) and meta-analyses (Bowers, Pharmer, & Salas, 2000; Horwitz & Horwitz, 2007; Joshi & Roh, 2009; van Dijk et al., 2009; Webber & Donahue, 2001) alike show that the effects of diversity are highly variable and range from the positive to the negative. This has invited Milliken and Martins's (1996) often-quoted conclusion that diversity is a double-edged sword, and points to the need to identify the contingencies of the effects of diversity—to find out how to wield the double-edged sword.

For many, the most obvious answer has been to point to the type of diversity involved, and to argue that the positive effects of diversity are linked to job-related diversity while the negative effects of diversity are associated with demographic diversity (Jehn et al., 1999; Pelled et al., 1999). The reasoning behind this proposition is that social categorization processes would be more easily elicited by demographic categories that are more readily associated with stereotypes (Fiske, 1998) than job-related categories, while on the other hand, task-relevant information and perspectives that would turn diversity into an informational resource would be more strongly associated with job-related differences. Despite the great variety in findings for both demographic diversity and job-related diversity, recent meta-analyses have indeed yielded some support for this proposition (Horwitz & Horwitz, 2007; Joshi & Roh, 2009). A more recent meta-analysis by van Dijk et al. (2009) involving a substantially larger number of studies and effect sizes, however, calls these conclusions into question and shows they can be attributed to biases against demographic diversity in subjective ratings of performance—objective performance indicators show no overall differences between the effects of demographic and job-related diversity. This can at least in part be explained by the notions that demographic diversity too can be associated with important differences in task-relevant information and perspectives (Tsui & O'Reilly, 1989), whereas job-related diversity too may engender social categorization processes (van Knippenberg et al., 2004). What van Dijk et al.'s meta-analysis does highlight is the heterogeneity of relationships observed for both demographic and job-related diversity. Again, but this time meta-analytically, this points to the need to identify moderators of the diversity–performance relationship. To this end van Knippenberg et al. (2004) proposed the Categorization-Elaboration Model of work group diversity and performance. In the following section, we outline the model.

The Categorization-Elaboration Model

Neither the social categorization perspective nor the informational resource perspective are supported in their basic form—as a main effect of diversity. Indeed, the striking lack of support for main-effects approaches to diversity has even invited van Knippenberg and Schippers (2007) to propose that "it is time to declare the bankruptcy of the main effects approach" (p. 518). This is not to say, however, that the social categorization perspective and the informational resource perspective are fundamentally flawed in predicting and explaining the influence of work group diversity. Rather, van Knippenberg et al. (2004) argued, what is required is a more sophisticated and integrated reading of theory and research in social categorization and group information processing to make sense of diversity's effects. This was the point of departure for the Categorization-Elaboration Model.

Group Information Elaboration Processes

Consistent with earlier approaches to work group diversity, the Categorization-Elaboration Model proposes that the relationship between diversity and performance is governed by social categorization and group information elaboration processes. In contrast to these earlier approaches, however, in which the social categorization and informational resource perspectives were studied more or less in isolation, the Categorization-Elaboration Model emphasizes the interaction between social categorization and group information elaboration processes. Moreover, by working from a more sophisticated reading of these processes that is more commensurate with the state of the science in social categorization and group information processing outside the diversity domain, the Categorization-Elaboration Model is able to identify key moderators of these processes.

The starting point for the Categorization-Elaboration Model is the observation that diversity as an informational resource does not automatically benefit group performance. Rather, groups need to mobilize this informational resource. Members' unique knowledge and perspectives need to be shared within the group—a process that cannot be taken for granted (Stasser, 1999). Moreover, exchange of diverse information and perspectives is not enough. This information needs to be discussed and integrated into a group product (e.g., decision, problem, solution)—again, something that cannot be assumed to happen as an inevitable consequence of information sharing (Gigone & Hastie, 1993; Winquist & Larson, 1998). In short, what is required to benefit from diversity as an informational resource is a process of what van Knippenberg et al. (2004) defined as group information elaboration—the exchange, discussion, and integration of task-relevant information and perspectives. Indeed, consistent with a conceptualization of groups as information-processing systems (De Dreu, Nijstad, & van Knippenberg, 2008; Hinsz, Tindale, & Vollrath, 1997), the Categorization-Elaboration Model proposes that group information elaboration is the key mediating process explaining the positive effects of diversity on performance.

An experimental study by van Ginkel and van Knippenberg (2008) illustrates this. Van Ginkel and van Knippenberg studied decision-making groups' use of distributed information—information that is uniquely available to one of the members and that thus needs to be exchanged and integrated to benefit group decision-making (Stasser, 1999). From an informational resource perspective, distributed information captures the essence of diversity: different members know different things and the group as a whole may benefit by mobilizing this informational resource. While the importance of group information elaboration may seem shockingly obvious to those understanding the principle of distributed information, the equally shocking reality is that groups typically are poor users of their distributed information and rather focus on the information group members have in common from the start (Stasser, 1999). Indeed, the very point van Ginkel and van Knippenberg set out to make was that groups typically have a poor understanding of the information elaboration requirements of their job, and that this helps explain groups' poor use of their distributed informational resources. In providing evidence for their analysis, they demonstrated the importance of information elaboration in two ways. First, they developed a behavioral coding scheme to assess information elaboration through the observation of group interaction and showed that elaboration mediated the effects of experimental manipulations on performance. Second, they experimentally varied groups' understanding of the need for information elaboration (i.e., group members' task representations), and showed that groups made better decisions the more they had a shared understanding of the importance of information elaboration.

The mediating role of information elaboration in the diversity–performance relationship has now been supported by a series of studies in the laboratory as well as the field, and focusing on a range of diversity dimensions including demographic as well as job-related diversity (Homan et al., 2008; Homan, van Knippenberg, van Kleef, & De Dreu, 2007a, 2007b; Kearney & Gebert, 2009; Kearney, Gebert, & Voelpel, 2009; Kooij-de Bode, van Knippenberg, & van Ginkel, 2008; van Ginkel, Tindale, & van Knippenberg, in press; van Ginkel & van Knippenberg, 2008, 2009; van Knippenberg, Kooij-de Bode, & van Ginkel, in press). Equally important, the focus on elaboration as following from a conceptualization of groups as information-processing systems also allows the Categorization-Elaboration Model to identify key moderators of the relationship between diversity and information elaboration, and thus between diversity and performance.

Moderators of the Relationship between Diversity and Elaboration

Models of social information-processing span a variety of types of information, judgments, and decisions, from the perception of individuals and groups to the processing of persuasive communication. What these models tend to have in common, however, is their identification of processing motivation and ability as key drivers of the extent to which information is systematically and thoroughly processed (Chaiken & Trope, 1999). Only to the extent that individuals are motivated and able to do so will they systematically scrutinize the available information in forming an impression, making a decision, etc. In the Categorization-Elaboration Model van Knippenberg et al. (2004) extended these insights from the individual domain to the group domain, and proposed that processing motivation and ability are key moderators of the diversity–elaboration (and therefore diversity–performance) relationship. Diverse groups will only utilize their diverse informational resources to the extent that they are motivated and able to do so.

Scholten, van Knippenberg, Nijstad, and De Dreu (2007) illustrated this principle for motivation in an experimental study of the role of process accountability in groups with distributed information (cf. van Ginkel & van Knippenberg, 2008). Process accountability, the requirement to justify the way in which a task is performed, has been identified as a determinant of processing motivation (Lerner & Tetlock, 1999). Accordingly, based on the Categorization-Elaboration Model we would expect that groups make better use of their diversity of information when they are process-accountable than when they are not. This is exactly what Scholten et al. found. Moreover, they found this effect to be mediated by a process measure that can be interpreted as a proxy for group information elaboration. Complementing this study with evidence from the field, in a study of diversity in age and educational background, Kearney et al. (2009) similarly found that diversity was more positively related to performance in groups with members higher in need for cognition—a dispositional determinant of processing motivation. The moderating role of processing ability in diverse groups still awaits an empirical test, however.

Viewing the same issue from a different angle, van Knippenberg et al. (2004) also considered the moderating role of the task itself. Diversity as an informational resource can boost task performance because it may stimulate a more in-depth understanding of the issues at hand and may lead to more creative and higher-quality solutions to problems, superior decisions, and more innovative products. What this in fact implies is that diversity should be more positively related to performance the more task performance is contingent on in-depth understanding of the task and creative and innovative solutions, decisions, and outcomes. That is, tasks may differ in the extent to which they are complex and non-routine and have clear information elaboration requirements or rather are simple and routine and require little in terms of extensive information-processing to deal with issues that cannot be included in task routines. In short, task complexity should moderate the diversity–performance relationship (Bowers et al., 2000; Jehn et al., 1999).

Recent meta-analytical evidence suggests that this in fact may be where the distinction between demographic and job-related diversity does come in. In a sense addressing the lack of support for the moderating role of task complexity in the Horwitz and Horwitz (2007) meta-analysis, van Dijk et al. (2009) proposed and found that task complexity moderated the influence of job-related diversity but not of demographic diversity. The argument here is that job-related diversity typically revolves around differences in formal training and education (i.e., functional background), and these are more likely to be important and have added value the more complex the task is. Differences in demographic background, in contrast, may be associated with differences in information and perspectives that are potentially important to task performance (e.g., differences in cultural background may be related to differences in knowledge about certain consumer groups that is valuable from a marketing perspective), but these would typically be less likely to be the kind of "technical" information and perspectives that may be relevant primarily to more complex tasks (e.g., specialized biomedical expertise relevant to the development of new drugs).

In sum, the Categorization-Elaboration Model's group information-processing perspective identifies group information elaboration as the core process involved in harvesting the informational benefits of diversity. Building on this proposition, it also points to group member task motivation and ability as well as to task complexity as important moderators of the diversity–performance relationship. The Categorization-Elaboration Model thus develops and extends the informational resource perspective both in terms of its understanding of the mediating process involved (i.e., information elaboration) and in terms of the moderator variables it identifies (i.e., motivation, ability, and task requirements). In addition, the model should and does address the role of social categorization processes.

Social Categorization Processes

In considering the role of social categorization processes in diversity research, van Knippenberg et al. (2004) identified a somewhat simplified understanding of theory and research in social identity and self-categorization (Tajfel & Turner, 1986; Turner et al., 1987) as a key problem in the modest support for social categorization analysis in at least the first 40 years of diversity research or so. In short, diversity research seemed to implicitly work from two flawed assumptions. First, the notion that differences between people drive social categorization and that therefore the greater the differences on a dimension of diversity, the stronger the social categorization processes. Second, the tendency to implicitly equate social categorization and intergroup bias. A state-of-the-science reading of research in intergroup relations shows that both these assumptions are at least partly incorrect, and this is the jumping off point for the Categorization-Elaboration Model's analysis of the role of social categorization in the diversity–performance relationship.

When it comes to the relationship between interpersonal differences and social categorization, self-categorization theory points to the key role of the salience of social categorizations, that is, the extent to which a categorization is cognitively activated (Oakes, Haslam, & Turner, 1994; Turner et al., 1987; cf. Crisp & Hewstone, 2007). The notion of categorization salience is critical to understanding that differences between people do not translate one-on-one to social categorization. For instance, whether the male and female members of a work group will view the other gender as outgroup, as "them," and the own gender as ingroup, as "us," is not just a function of being similar or different—indeed, otherwise the only outcome that could ever obtain in mixed-gender groups is gender-based subgroupings. Rather, it is a matter of categorization salience: only to the extent that a given categorization is salient will it influence group member attitudes and behavior. Therefore, a better understanding of the factors governing categorization salience would give us a better understanding of why and when diversity will engender social categorization processes.

This, then, gives rise to the question of what determines category salience. This, according to self-categorization theory and its application in the Categorization-Elaboration Model, revolves around three issues: comparative fit, normative fit, and cognitive accessibility. Comparative fit refers to the extent to which a categorization captures similarities and differences between people. The more a categorization adequately captures similarities and differences between people, the more likely it is to be salient. Normative fit indicates the extent to which the categorization makes sense within the individual's cognitive frame of reference. The more a categorization matches individuals' beliefs system (e.g., in terms of stereotypes associated with the categorization), the more likely the categorization is to be salient. Cognitive accessibility refers to the ease with which the categorization can be retrieved from memory and activated. The more easily a categorization can come to mind, the more likely it is to be salient.

To date, research in the role of categorization salience in diversity has more or less exclusively revolved around the principle of comparative fit, and we will therefore largely limit our discussion here to comparative fit. We do note, however, that the categorization salience analysis provides no reason to prioritize comparative fit over normative fit in diversity research (the cognitive accessibility of categorizations based on differences in demographic characteristics such as gender, age, and ethnicity may be more or less a given, and therefore less inviting of research attention when the goal is to identify important moderator variables), and we would advocate greater research attention to the role of normative fit in diversity research.

The principle of comparative fit refers to the extent to which a given categorization would result in groupings of people that capture similarities and differences between these people. The more a categorization leads to categories with high within-group similarity and high between-group differences (i.e., the so-called meta-contrast ratio; Turner et al., 1987), that is, the more it adequately captures similarities and differences between people, the higher its comparative fit. Because an important function of categorizations is to make sense of the world—to capture communalities and differences—a categorization is more likely to be salient the higher its comparative fit. The great importance of the notion of comparative fit lies in the fact that it points to the influence of different dimensions of diversity in combination, because the comparative fit of a categorization based on any dimension of differentiation (e.g., gender) is greater when it also captures differences on other dimensions (e.g., age). When, for instance, the male members of a gender-diverse work group also are the older members of the group, the comparative fit of the gender categorization (i.e., capturing subgroups of young women and old men) is higher than when gender and age differences are unrelated (i.e., a situation also referred to as cross-categorization of gender and age; Crisp & Hewstone, 2007; Miller et al., this volume).

Lau and Murnighan (1998) introduced the term "faultlines" to diversity research to refer to such combinations of diversity dimensions that would render subgroupings salient. There is a longer tradition in the study of intergroup relations to study the principles involved in faultline effects by reference to the reverse of faultlines, i.e., cross-categorization, which reduces comparative fit and thus renders categorizations less salient (e.g., Deschamps, 1977), as opposed to convergent categorization (cf. faultlines; Crisp & Hewstone, 2007). The faultline concept stuck, however, and is the going term to capture the principle of comparative fit in diversity research. The value of the concept of diversity faultlines to diversity research is that it points to the need to not just study dimensions of diversity in isolation or in additive models (the traditional approach in diversity research), but to consider the influence of different dimensions of diversity in combination in terms of the extent to which positions on the dimensions converge to form a faultline or rather, crosscut each other.

Working from this perspective, an experimental study by Homan et al. (2007b) nicely illustrates how the exact same diversity on two dimensions may have markedly different effects contingent on whether differences on the dimensions combine to form a diversity faultline or rather to cut across differences on the other dimension. They introduced two manipulations to a four-person group task context, a manipulation of gender diversity (homogeneity vs. diversity, enforced by bogus personality feedback suggesting gender differences and thus in fact creating a gender/personality faultline) and a manipulation of informational diversity, contrasting a situation where all group members had the exact same task background information with a situation in which members shared some information that the other half of the group did not possess (cf. distributed information). Of critical importance was the way in which these two manipulations were combined when the group was both gender-diverse and informationally diverse. For half the double-diverse groups, informational differences were aligned with gender differences to form a faultline: the male members of the group both had the same information unknown to the female members and vice versa. In the other half of the double-diverse groups, gender and informational differences crosscut each other: one male member had information only known to one of the female members, whereas the other male member had information only known to the other female member before group interaction.

Behavioral observation of group interaction confirmed the social benefits of cross-categorization as opposed to faultlines in diverse groups. Observation of team climate (i.e., behavioral patterns that capture the way in which team members typically interact) showed that team climate in the cross-categorization condition was markedly better in terms of interpersonal relations than in the faultline condition, and in fact at least as good as in the homogeneous and informational diversity conditions (see Figure 11.1). In line with the faultline perspective, the weaker gender/personality faultline by itself also resulted in poorer team climate. For observations of task conflict and relationship conflict, similar patterns of results were obtained. Of critical importance to diversity research, this pattern of results would never have been uncovered by the traditional approach to diversity considering diversity on different dimensions in additive models, as the cross-categorization and faultline groups are identical in terms of gender and informational diversity.

The Categorization-Elaboration Model thus identifies (the determinants of) categorization salience as key moderator(s) of the extent to which diversity engenders social categorization processes. In another important development of the social categorization perspective on diversity, it also introduces a second consideration: social

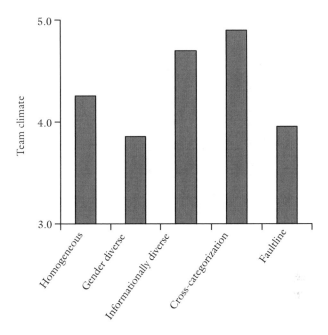

Figure 11.1 Cross-categorization versus faultlines: team climate (interpersonal relations) as a function of gender and informational diversity (based on Homan et al., 2007b).

categorization, the perception of individuals in terms of their membership in ingroup or outgroup, and intergroup bias, the preference for and favoring of ingroup over outgroup, should not be equated. Social categorization is a necessary precondition for intergroup bias, but this should not be taken to mean that social categorization inevitably engenders intergroup bias. Indeed, it is perfectly possible to perceive intergroup differences and not be biased against the other group. Research in intergroup relations suggests that social categorizations mainly result in intergroup biases to the extent that the intergroup context is perceived as a threat to the group's identity or status, and that sometimes explicit acknowledgement of subgroups in that sense is even preferable to downplaying intergroup differences, which may be perceived as negating group identity (Gaertner & Dovidio, 2000; Hewstone & Brown, 1986; Hornsey & Hogg, 2000; van Leeuwen & van Knippenberg, 2003). Thus, the Categorization-Elaboration Model proposes that social categorization in diverse groups does only result in intergroup biases to the extent that the intergroup context

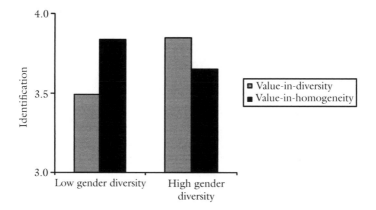

Figure 11.2   Diversity belief as moderator of the diversity—identification relationship (adapted from van Knippenberg et al., 2007).

is perceived as threatening to ingroup identity (cf. Amiot & de la Sablonnière, this volume; Verkuyten, this volume).

While a direct test of this proposition relying on an operationalization of identity threat in diverse groups has to date not been conducted, research in diversity beliefs (van Knippenberg & Haslam, 2003) may be interpreted as indirect evidence in support of this proposition. Diversity beliefs refer to people's beliefs about the value in diversity (versus homogeneity) on a given dimension to group performance. Building on the Categorization-Elaboration Model, van Knippenberg, Haslam, and Platow (2007) proposed that group members' diversity beliefs moderate the effects of diversity such that diversity is more likely to have positive effects and less likely to have negative effects the more group members believe in the value of diversity rather than homogeneity (also see Cameron & Turner, this volume; Verkkuyten, this volume). Testing this prediction for diversity's effects on group identification, which arguably is related to the issue of diversity's relationship with identity threats, van Knippenberg et al. conducted a survey of team identification in organizations as a function of the interaction of team gender diversity and team member gender diversity beliefs. As illustrated in Figure 11.2, gender diversity was positively related to team identification for group members believing in the value of diversity, whereas it was negatively related to identification for group members believing in the value of homogeneity. Establishing causality in these relationships, van Knippenberg et al. obtained a similar pattern of results in a second, experimental study, and Homan et al. (2007a) showed that these findings extend to the relationship with elaboration and performance (also see van Dick, van Knippenberg, Hägele, Guillaume, & Brodbeck, 2008).

In sum, the Categorization-Elaboration Model points to the fact that differences between people do not automatically elicit social categorizations and that social categorization does not inevitably engender intergroup bias, and identifies moderators of both these relationships. In doing so, it offers an account of the role of social categorization processes in diverse groups that is more commensurate with the state of the science in research in social categorization and intergroup relations outside of the diversity domain as well as more consistent with the evidence regarding the diversity–performance relationship. Another issue in diversity research is that social categorization and informational resource analyses have largely developed in isolation, and the model makes a final and important step in understanding the role of elaboration and social categorization processes in diverse groups in integrating the informational resource and social categorization perspectives through an understanding of the interactive effects of these processes.

The Interaction of Social Categorization and Elaboration Processes

Research in the role of social categorization in the processing of persuasive communication has shown that categorization of a source of communication as outgroup leads to a closing of the mind against that communication (e.g., Mackie, Worth, & Asuncion, 1990; for a review, see van Knippenberg, 1999), a communication-specific expression of intergroup biases rooted in the greater trust in ingroup as a source of information about social reality (Turner et al., 1987). Building on these findings, van Knippenberg et al. (2004) proposed in the Categorization-Elaboration Model that the intergroup biases that may follow from diversity-based social categorization may express themselves in intragroup conflict, poorer team climate, and ultimately disrupted communication, expressing itself in both a closing of the mind against communication from diverse others and a lowered willingness to share information and perspectives with diverse others. In short, intergroup bias in diverse groups disrupts information elaboration—the very process on which the positive influence of diversity as an informational resource is contingent.

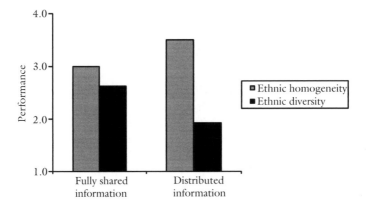

Figure 11.3   The interactive effect of ethnic diversity x distribution of information on group performance (adapted from Kooij-de Bode et al., 2008).

These processes are illustrated as part of an experimental study by Kooij-de Bode et al. (2008; for the sake of brevity, we are ignoring another part of this study's design with additional task instructions that yielded additional evidence for the current proposition). Kooij-de Bode and colleagues studied group decision-making in groups that were either diverse or homogenous in terms of ethnicity and worked under conditions of either distributed information or information that was already fully shared before group interaction (i.e., fully available to all group members). The rationale for this design was that when ethnic diversity would be associated with intergroup biases disrupting elaboration, this should be more evident in groups with distributed information than in groups with fully shared information. Distributed information as compared with fully shared information makes groups much more dependent on the exchange and integration of information (i.e., elaboration), and threats to elaboration thus more problematic for group performance. Results confirmed exactly this prediction (see Figure 11.3). Decision quality was unaffected by ethnic diversity when information was fully shared, but when information was distributed homogeneous groups reached better decisions than diverse groups, and this effect was mediated by group information elaboration.

While these findings perfectly illustrate that diversity may disrupt information elaboration and therefore performance, in view of the Categorization-Elaboration Model's other propositions regarding social categorization processes, one may also raise the question of

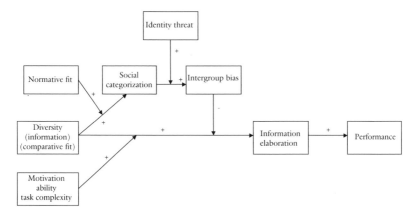

Figure 11.4   The Categorization–Elaboration Model of work group diversity and group performance (adapted from van Knippenberg et al., 2004).

whether this influence should not be contingent on (a) the salience of social categorizations and (b) identity threat. Indeed, it is. Homan et al.'s (2007b) study of faultlines and cross-categorization also included a measure of information elaboration, and showed, as would be expected on the basis of the current discussion, that gender diversity only disrupted the elaboration of information distributed under fault-line conditions and not under cross-categorization conditions. That is, diversity only disrupted information elaboration when salient. Likewise, Homan et al.'s (2007a) study of diversity beliefs focused on faultline conditions (i.e., presumably conditions of salient diversity), and showed that these were only associated with lower information elaboration and performance when group members believed in the value of homogeneity rather than diversity (also see Homan et al., 2008). That is, when diversity presumably was not a threat to identity, group members did not respond negatively to salient diversity.

The Categorization-Elaboration Model's propositions regarding the interactive effects of categorization and elaboration processes are particularly important, because they directly speak to the disparate findings in diversity research. When diversity does not elicit intergroup biases, it may benefit group performance through a process of information elaboration, but when diversity does result in intergroup biases, group information elaboration suffers at the expense of group performance. To summarize the discussion so far, the Categorization-Elaboration Model is displayed in Figure 11.4.

Managing Diversity

The Categorization-Elaboration Model offers a more sophisticated understanding of the diversity–performance relationship than previous perspective, and moreover one that is more consistent with the available empirical evidence (van Dijk et al., 2009; van Knippenberg & Schippers, 2007). An obvious question therefore is what the implications of the Categorization-Elaboration Model are for practice— for the management of diverse work groups and teams in organizations. Obviously, these implications revolve around the management of categorization and elaboration processes. Importantly, the Categorization-Elaboration Model also points to the fact that the management of only categorization or only elaboration processes in and of itself is not enough to harvest the potential benefits inherent in diversity. First, social categorization-based intergroup biases disrupt elaboration, and the in-depth elaboration of diverse information can only be realized without intergroup bias. Second, preventing intergroup bias in and of itself is not enough to engender elaboration—elaboration is a process that needs to be actively managed (van Ginkel, van Knippenberg, & de Kroes, 2008).

Managing elaboration requires the management of team motivation and ability. To a certain extent, this may be no different than other efforts to manage team member motivation and ability (for a discussion, see Kozlowski & Bell, 2003). In at least two respects, these efforts may be more specific for the diversity–elaboration relationship. First, as van Ginkel and van Knippenberg (2008) outline, groups' understanding of the importance of information elaboration is often underdeveloped, and specific efforts may be required to develop this understanding. Motivation for certain behavior in part follows from the understanding of the effects and importance of the behavior, and efforts to build this understanding may thus specifically build the motivation for information elaboration. Van Ginkel and colleagues have shown that such understanding can be built through a process of team reflexivity (i.e., collectively reflecting on the team task and team process) as well as through building awareness of the groups' distributed expertise—its diversity as an informational resource (van Ginkel et al., in press; van Ginkel & van Knippenberg, 2009). Second, organizations may also build diversity-specific motivation by fostering group members' beliefs in the value of diversity—indeed, by fostering a climate that puts a premium on learning from diversity (Ely & Thomas, 2001). Leadership may play an important role in this respect (van Ginkel, van Knippenberg, & de Kroes, 2008).

From the perspective of team design, organizations may want to actively compose teams to be (functionally; van Dijk et al., 2009) diverse when teams face highly complex tasks. However, we would be much more hesitant to argue for team design interventions when it comes to preventing intergroup biases. One reading of the diversity faultline analysis would be that one way to manage diversity is to prevent faultlines in group composition. Whereas this may be sound advice in theory, it may produce undesirable side effects in practice. Given that certain groups (e.g., women and ethnic minorities) are typically underrepresented in organizations, attempts to prevent faultlines could easily translate in de facto hiring biases against underrepresented groups. Accordingly, we would advocate addressing the issue of social category salience through different routes. First, addressing the issue of normative fit is an option: when a given categorization does not seem relevant to the individuals involved, it is less likely to be salient. In effect, this revolves around, for instance, combating negative stereotypes. While obviously this is easier said than done, it is not a priori impossible (cf. Gaertner & Dovidio, 2000).

Second, organizations may actively aim to manage responses to salient social categorizations. Research on diversity beliefs and related constructs (e.g., Ely & Thomas, 2001; van Knippenberg & Schippers, 2007) suggests that the management of diversity beliefs and climates may also have important benefits in this respect. Van Knippenberg et al.'s (2007) finding that diversity was associated with higher identification than homogeneity for people believing in the value of diversity—a finding that could not obtain without people's awareness of the group's diversity—is illustrative in this respect. Van Ginkel et al's leadership study also made a conscious effort to make differences salient, and showed that leaders can be trained to build group members' belief in the value of diversity in such contexts. Clearly, work in this area is only emerging, but these findings hold a clear promise for the further development of this perspective.

In Conclusion

Over fifty years of diversity research show that the relationship between work group diversity and performance is far from straightforward. Accordingly, when it comes to managing diversity to help realize its potential as an important asset to organizations rather than letting it turn into a liability, there still is a lot of progress to be made. In view of the ever-increasing diversity of societies and of organizations as integral part of these societies, developments thus increasingly put a premium on our ability to understand, predict, and manage diversity's effects. While far from perfect, we would like to believe that the Categorization-Elaboration Model represents an important step forward in this respect. The challenge now is to push both diversity research and its application in organizational practice further, and the Categorization-Elaboration Model may provide a useful guiding framework in these efforts.

Acknowledgment

Wendy van Ginkel is grateful to S. Bob Vierkantbroek for his inspirational influence.

References

Ancona, D. G., & Caldwell, D. F. (1992). Demography and design: Predictors of new product team performance. *Organization Science, 3*, 321–341.

Bantel, K., & Jackson, S. (1989). Top management and innovations in banking: Does the composition of the team make a difference? *Strategic Management Journal, 10*, 107–124.

Bell, S. T. (2007). Deep-level composition variables as predictors of team performance: A meta-analysis. *Journal of Applied Psychology, 92*, 595–615.

Bowers, C., Pharmer, J. A., & Salas, E. (2000). When member homogeneity is needed in work teams: A meta-analysis. *Small Group Research, 31*, 305–327.

Brewer, M. B., & Brown, R. J. (1998). Intergroup relations. In D. T. Gilbert & S.T. Fiske (Eds.), *Handbook of social psychology* (4th ed., pp. 554–594). Boston: McGraw-Hill.

Byrne, D. (1971). *The Attraction Paradigm.* New York: Academic Press.

Chaiken, S., & Trope, Y. (1999). *Dual process theories in social psychology.* New York: Guilford Press.

Chattopadhyay, P., Tluchowska, M., & George, E. (2004). Identifying the ingroup: A closer look at the influence of demographic dissimilarity on employee social identity. *Academy of Management Review, 29*, 180–202.

Crisp, R. J., & Hewstone, M. (2007). Multiple social categorization. In M. P. Zanna (Ed.), *Advances in Experimental Social Psychology* (Vol. 39, pp. 163–254). Orlando, FL: Academic Press.

De Dreu, C. K. W., Nijstad, B. A., & van Knippenberg, D. (2008). Motivated information processing in group judgment and decision making. *Personality and Social Psychology Review, 12*, 22–49.

Deschamps, J. C. (1977). Effect of crossing category membership on quantitative judgment. *European Journal of Social Psychology, 7*, 517–521.

Ely, R. J., & Thomas, D. A. (2001). Cultural diversity at work: The effects of diversity perspectives on work group processes and outcomes. *Administrative Science Quarterly, 46*, 229–273.

Fiske, S. T. (1998). Stereotyping, prejudice, and discrimination. In D. T. Gilbert, S.T. Fiske, & G. Lindzey (Eds.), *Handbook of social psychology* (4th ed., pp. 357–411). Boston: McGraw-Hill.

Gaertner, S. L., & Dovidio, J. F. (2000). *Reducing intergroup bias. The common ingroup identity model.* Philadelphia, PA: Psychology Press.

Gigone, D., & Hastie, R. (1993). The common knowledge effect: Information sharing and group judgment. *Journal of Personality and Social Psychology, 65*, 959–974.

Harrison, D., & Klein, K. J. (2007). What's the difference? Diversity constructs as separation, variety, or disparity in organizations. *Academy of Management Review, 32*, 1199–1228.

Harrison, D. A., Price, K. H., & Bell, M. P. (1998). Beyond relational demography: Time and the effects of surface- and deep-level diversity on work group cohesion. *Academy of Management Journal, 41*, 96–107.

Hewstone, M., & Brown, R. (1986). Contact is not enough: An intergroup perspective on the "contact hypothesis". In M. Hewstone & R. Brown (Eds.), *Contact and conflict in intergroup encounters* (pp. 1–44). Cambridge, MA: Blackwell.

Hinsz, V. B., Tindale, R. S., & Vollrath, D. A. (1997). The emerging conceptualization of groups as information processors. *Psychological Bulletin, 121*, 43–64.

Homan, A. C., Hollenbeck, J. R., Humphrey, S. E., van Knippenberg, D., Van Kleef, G. A., & Ilgen, D. R. (2008). Facing differences with an open mind: Openness to experience, salience of intra-group differences, and performance of diverse work groups. *Academy of Management Journal, 51*, 1204–1222.

Homan, A. C., van Knippenberg, D., van Kleef, G. A., & De Dreu, C. K. W. (2007a). Bridging faultlines by valuing diversity: Diversity beliefs, information elaboration, and performance in diverse work groups. *Journal of Applied Psychology, 92*, 1189–1199.

Homan, A. C., van Knippenberg, D., van Kleef, G. A., & De Dreu, C. K. W. (2007b). Interacting dimensions of diversity: Cross-categorization and the functioning of diverse work groups. *Group Dynamics, 11*, 79–94.

Hornsey, M. J., & Hogg, M. A. (2000). Assimilation and diversity: An integrative model of subgroup relations. *Personality and Social Psychology Review, 4*, 143–156.

Horwitz, S. K., & Horwitz, I. B. (2007). The effects of team diversity on team outcomes: A meta-analytic review of team demography. *Journal of Management, 33,* 987–1015.

Jackson, S. E. (1992). Team composition in organizational settings: Issues in managing an increasingly diverse workforce. In S. Worchel, W. Wood, & J. A. Simpson (Eds.), *Group processes and productivity* (pp. 136–180). Newbury Park, CA: Sage.

Jackson, S. E., Joshi, A., & Erhardt, N. L. (2003). Recent research on team and organizational diversity: SWOT analysis and implications. *Journal of Management, 29,* 801–830.

Jehn, K. A., Northcraft, G. B., & Neale, M. A. (1999). Why differences make a difference: A field study of diversity, conflict, and performance in workgroups. *Administrative Science Quarterly, 44,* 741–763.

Joshi, A. A., & Roh, H. (2009). The role of context in work team diversity research: A meta-analytic review. *Academy of Management Journal, 52,* 599–627.

Kearney, E., & Gebert, D. (2009). Managing diversity and enhancing team outcomes: The promise of transformational leadership. *Journal of Applied Psychology, 94,* 77–89.

Kearney, E., Gebert, D., & Voelpel, S. C. (2009). When and how diversity benefits teams: The importance of team members' need for cognition. *Academy of Management Journal, 52,* 581–598.

Kooij-de Bode, H. J. M., van Knippenberg, D., & van Ginkel, W. P. (2008). Ethnic diversity and distributed information in group decision making: The importance of information elaboration. *Group Dynamics, 12,* 307–320.

Kozlowski, S. W. J., & Bell, B. S. (2003). Work groups and teams in organizations. In W. C. Borman & D.R. Ilgen (Eds.), *Handbook of psychology: Industrial and organizational psychology* (Vol. 12, pp. 333–375). New York: Wiley.

Lau, D. C., & Murnighan, J. K. (1998). Demographic diversity and faultlines: The compositional dynamics of organizational groups. *Academy of Management Review, 23,* 325–340.

Lerner, J. S., & Tetlock, P. E. (1999). Accounting for the effects of accountability. *Psychological Bulletin, 125,* 255–275.

Mackie, D. M., Worth, L. T., & Asuncion, A. G. (1990). Processing of persuasive in-group messages. *Journal of Personality and Social Psychology, 58,* 812–822.

Milliken, F., & Martins, L. (1996). Searching for common threads: Understanding the multiple effects of diversity in organizational groups. *Academy of Management Review, 21,* 402–433.

Oakes, P. J., Haslam, S. A., & Turner, J. C. (1994). *Stereotyping and social reality.* Malden, MA: Blackwell.

Pelled, L. H., Eisenhardt, K. M., & Xin, K. R. (1999). Exploring the black box: An analysis of work group diversity, conflict, and performance. *Administrative Science Quarterly, 44,* 1–28.

Scholten, L., van Knippenberg, D., Nijstad, B. A., & De Dreu, C. K. W. (2007). Motivated information processing and group decision making: Effects of process accountability on information sharing and decision quality. *Journal of Experimental Social Psychology, 43*, 539–552.

Simons, T., Pelled, L. H., & Smith, K. A. (1999). Making use of difference: Diversity, debate, and decision comprehensiveness in top management teams. *Academy of Management Journal, 42*, 662–673.

Stasser, G. (1999). The uncertain role of unshared information in collective choice. In L. L. Thompson, J.M. Levine, & D. M. Messick (Eds.), *Shared cognition in organizations* (pp. 49–69). Mahwah, NJ: Erlbaum.

Tajfel, H., & Turner, J. (1986). The social identity of intergroup behavior. In W. A. S. Worchel (Ed.), *Psychology and intergroup relations* (pp. 15–40). Chicago: Nelson-Hall.

Tsui, A. S., & O'Reilly, C. A. (1989). Beyond simple demographic effects: The importance of relational demography in superior-subordinate dyads. *Academy of Management Journal, 32*, 402–423.

Turner, J. C., Hogg, M. A., Oakes, P. J., Reicher, S. D., & Wetherell, M. S. (1987). *Rediscovering the social group. A self-categorization theory.* Oxford, UK: Blackwell.

van Dick, R., van Knippenberg, D., Hägele, S., Guillaume, Y. R. F., & Brodbeck, F. C. (2008). Group diversity and group identification: The moderating role of diversity beliefs. *Human Relations, 61*, 1463–1492.

van Dijk, H., van Engen, M. L., & van Knippenberg, D. (2009, August). *Work group diversity and performance: A meta-analysis.* Paper presented at the Academy of Management Annual Meeting, Chicago.

van Ginkel, W. P., Tindale, R. S., & van Knippenberg, D.(in press). Team reflexivity, development of shared task representations, and the use of distributed information in group decision making. *Group Dynamics.*

van Ginkel, W. P., & van Knippenberg, D. (2008). Group information elaboration and group decision making: The role of shared task representations. *Organizational Behavior and Human Decision Processes, 105*, 82–97.

van Ginkel, W. P., & van Knippenberg, D. (2009). Knowledge about the distribution of information and group decision making: When and why does it work? *Organizational Behavior and Human Decision Processes, 108*, 218–229.

van Ginkel, W. P., van Knippenberg, D., & de Kroes, S. (2008, April). *Leadership, diversity mindsets, and group performance.* Paper presented at the 23rd Annual Conference of the Society for Industrial and Organizational Psychology, San Francisco.

van Knippenberg, D. (1999). Social identity and persuasion: Reconsidering the role of group membership. In D. Abrams & M.A. Hogg (Eds.), *Social identity and social cognition* (pp. 315–331). Oxford, UK: Blackwell.

van Knippenberg, D. (2003). Intergroup relations in organizations. In M. West, D. Tjosvold, & K. G. Smith (Eds.), *International handbook of organizational teamwork and cooperative working* (pp. 381–399). Chichester, UK: Wiley.

van Knippenberg, D., De Dreu, C. K. W., & Homan, A. C. (2004). Work group diversity and group performance: An integrative model and research agenda. *Journal of Applied Psychology, 89,* 1008–1022.

van Knippenberg, D., & Haslam, S. A. (2003). Realizing the diversity dividend: Exploring the subtle interplay between identity, ideology, and reality. In S. A. Haslam, D. van Knippenberg, M. J. Platow, & N. Ellemers (Eds.), *Social identity at work: Developing theory for organizational practice* (pp. 61–77). New York and Hove, UK: Psychology Press.

van Knippenberg, D., Haslam, S. A., & Platow, M. J. (2007). Unity through diversity: Value-in-diversity beliefs as moderator of the relationship between work group diversity and group identification. *Group Dynamics, 11,* 207–222.

van Knippenberg, D., Kooij-de Bode, H. J. M., & van Ginkel, W. P. (in press). The interactive effects of mood and trait negative affect in group decision making. *Organization Science.*

van Knippenberg, D., & Schippers, M. C. (2007). Work group diversity. *Annual Review of Psychology, 58,* 515–541.

van Leeuwen, E., & van Knippenberg, D. (2003). Organizational identification following a merger: The importance of agreeing to differ. In S. A. Haslam, D. van Knippenberg, M. J. Platow, & N. Ellemers (Eds.), *Social identity at work: Developing theory for organizational practice* (pp. 205–221). New York and Hove: Psychology Press.

Webber, S. S., & Donahue, L. M. (2001). Impact of highly and less job-related diversity on work group cohesion and performance: A meta-analysis. *Journal of Management, 27,* 141–162.

Williams, K. Y., & O'Reilly, C. A. (1998). Demography and diversity in organizations: A review of 40 years of research. *Research in Organizational Behavior, 20,* 77–140.

Winquist, J. R., & Larson, J. R., Jr. (1998). Information pooling: When it impacts group decision making. *Journal of Personality and Social Psychology, 74,* 371–377.

12

Divided We Fall, or United We Stand?

How Identity Processes Affect Faultline Perceptions and the Functioning of Diverse Teams

Floor A. Rink and Karen A. Jehn

Nowadays, the nature of the workforce is changing rapidly. An aging workforce and the participation of women and ethnic minorities cause cracks in the glass ceiling, resulting in an increasingly diverse work environment (Ryan & Haslam, 2007). In this chapter we will discuss the key issues that inform diversity research today. After presenting an overview of the two most influential traditional theoretical paradigms in this area, we will concentrate on one important, but relatively neglected phenomenon that can occur within diverse teams and is expected to have a strong influence on team cooperation and team innovation. This is the presence of faultlines and the consequent formation of subgroups. Our goal is to connect the use of the faultlines concept to the social identity and cross-categorization perspectives in explaining the mixed and complex effects of diversity in teams.

Even though it is generally acknowledged that diversity has a large impact on people's initial responses toward others (e.g. stereotyping, ingroup bias; identification, van Knippenberg & Schippers, 2007), previous research in the area of organizational behavior/psychology has mainly focused on the effects of diversity at the *work-group level*. In this chapter, when we refer to diversity, we refer specifically to work-group or organizational diversity. In organizations, work groups or teams generally consist of two or more people who each have specific roles or functions to fulfill, and have to work interdependently on a collective task (Rink & Ellemers, 2007). The primary aim of this chapter is to show that the individual *and* work group level effects of diversity are interrelated, and mutually influence each other. That is, we argue that social identity processes can inform us under which conditions faultline perceptions will devolve into actual subgroups, and how these subgroups will consequently affect the ability of teams to be innovative. Based on existing literature, we propose that members of diverse teams will only perceive dividing lines (i.e. faultlines) among them on the basis of demographic characteristics, e.g., gender, ethnicity, or functional background when they identify highly with these characteristics. The resulting subgroups will in turn only have a negative effect on the cooperation within, and innovation of, diverse teams when members start valuing their subgroup membership over their overarching team membership. Based on this proposition, we will end this chapter with several practical implementations of diversity policies that foster cohesion within diverse teams that have to cope with distinct subgroups.

Overview of Diversity Findings

In diversity research, the concept of diversity is broadly defined and generally refers to many kinds of individual differences that can exist within a group, ranging from demographic differences between the group members in race, gender, or age to differences concerning their functional expertise, or work norms and values (Bunderson & Sutcliffe, 2002; Harrison, Price, & Bell, 1998; Jehn, Northcraft, & Neale, 1999; Pelled, Eisenhardt, & Xin, 1999; Rink & Ellemers, 2007).

With diversity becoming an increasingly familiar part of work teams, research in this area has proliferated (for reviews see van Knippenberg & Schippers, 2007; Williams & O'Reilly, 1998; see also van Knippenberg & van Ginkel, this volume). However, the way in which diversity impacts on organizational life and team functioning reveals an interesting paradox for researchers and practitioners alike. On the one hand, there are still challenges that those who differ from the majority need to face in order to become fully integrated and worthy team members (Prislin & Christensen, 2002). Research shows that teams generally prefer to focus on the features (e.g., demographic attributes, expert knowledge) that all members have in common, and find it difficult to cope with the conflict that may arise when they are confronted with different others (Wittenbaum, Hollingshead, & Botero, 2004). As a result, teams often oppose an increasing amount of diversity, believing that the presence of differences among team members will undermine a sense of cohesiveness or mutual understanding, and threaten the attainment of common goals (Rink & Ellemers, 2008).

Yet, at the same time, research suggests that a diverse workforce can enhance innovation and creativity. Especially in this time of international economic crisis, innovation is crucially important in order for organizations to remain competitive. Innovation—defined as the origination and implementation of new ideas, products, services, or processes in management—not only refers to technical improvements, but also to advances in the effective use of human capital. Within teams, demographic differences, such as those based on gender or ethnicity, can indeed lead to more variability in the means and insights that group members possess and in the values and beliefs they have. These "underlying" differences can, in turn, positively influence team decisions and team outcomes (see the "value-in-diversity" perspective; Cox, Lobel, & McLeod, 1991; Hambrick & Mason, 1984; Jackson, May, & Whitney, 1995; Milliken & Martins, 1996; see also Fiske & Taylor, 1991; Lawrence, 1997). Indeed, a diverse workforce can potentially be a key source of new skills and knowledge and can thus have a profound influence on both organizational productivity and organizational success. As such, organizations need to be able to retain the unique talents of all their employees.

The paradoxical findings of diversity are a concern to organizations, as they suggest that one must choose between having a cohesive team or an innovative one. In order to better understand such findings, a social identity approach is useful (e.g., Haslam, Ryan, Postmes, Jetten, & Webley, 2006). This approach proposes that people's self-concept, and thus their attitudes and behaviors, are largely determined by the groups to which they belong, that is, their social identities (Tajfel & Turner, 1979; Turner, Oakes, Haslam, & McGarty, 1994). In addition, self-categorization theory developed by Turner and colleagues (Turner, 1985; Turner, Hogg, Oakes, Reicher, & Wetherell, 1987) proposes that people cognitively categorize themselves into social groups (self-categorization) when they feel that they share relevant features with others from these (in)groups. As a result, people use the norms of their groups to infer how they should behave, generally perceive themselves to be similar to fellow team members, and expect them to possess similar skills, knowledge, and abilities (Haslam, 2004). Such inferences give team members the ability to derive meaning from a situation, and provide the motivation to allow them to work toward the attainment of group goals (Ellemers, De Gilder, & Haslam, 2004).

In sum, because of the importance that people attach to the groups to which they belong, diversity can represent a source of conflict and result in reduced group cohesiveness (Prislin & Christensen, 2002). However, while homogeneity may facilitate acceptance and group cohesion, such a strategy may threaten the potential for enhanced performance and innovation. Researchers have therefore acknowledged that it is important to examine more complex and dynamic team processes and potential moderators in order to gain a better understanding of the varied effects of diversity on teams.

Faultline Theory and Subgroup Formation

The concept of group faultlines was first introduced by Lau and Murnighan (1998, 2005). They stressed the importance of group dynamics and the *composition* of multiple demographic differences among group members, in addition to the extent to which group members perceive dissimilarity among them. They defined group faultlines as hypothetical dividing lines that may split a group into subgroups based on one or more converging diversity attributes (p. 328). In this paradigm, subgroupings typically consist of two or more members separate from other group members based on demographics characteristics, expertise, skills, or work values (Thatcher, Jehn, & Zanutto, 2003). It is argued that the extent to which faultlines actually cause a group to split into homogeneous subgroups (the strength of a faultline) is dependent upon the number of diversity attributes in a group and the extent to which individual group members are able to classify themselves into categories based on these attributes. For instance, a group of four people consisting of two female Psychology students and two male Law students (converging differences) will have a stronger faultline (based on gender *and* study major) than a group of four people consisting of one female and one male Psychology student and one female and one male Law student (where the same number of differences emerge but cross-cut each other). This reasoning implies that two groups that may seem identical in terms of the number of diversity attributes present are not necessarily similarly affected by these attributes. Rather, the argument is that this depends on the potential for faultlines within each group; or put another way, the extent to which faultlines converge or diverge.

Based on literature on coalition formation (see, e.g., Murnighan & Brass, 1991), faultline scholars argue that when subgroups emerge (along, for example, demographic or expertise faultlines), members are likely to experience more conflict within the team as a whole and are less inclined to use their different knowledge and backgrounds to enhance team performance (Jehn & Bezrukova, in press). Indeed, there is a large body of literature showing that people tend to form coalitions on the basis of agreement on issues, or similar definitions of their task situation, or on the basis of initial similarity and attraction (Eisenhardt & Bourgeois, 1988; Murnighan & Brass, 1991). As a result, they tend to band together, actively pursue subgroup goals, and try to favorably influence their own outcomes at the expense of the other team members, creating intergroup distrust and conflict (Insko & Schopler, 1998; Jehn & Bezrukova, in press; Stevenson, Pearce, & Porter, 1985). A high level of conflict can in turn cause extreme negative process problems within teams, such as lack of cohesion and performance (for a meta-analysis see De Dreu & Weingart, 2003; see also LaBianca, Brass, & Gray, 1998).

It is important to note that the concept of faultlines and its consequences for teams is closely related to the work on cross-categorization (Crisp & Hewstone, 1999; Miller, Spanovic, & Stenstrom, this volume). This line of work also shows that when people are different from each other on multiple dimensions (e.g., constitute a "double outgroup" for each other), they display more intergroup bias and are less identified with their superordinate group than under conditions of diverged cross-categorization (i.e., when they differ in just one respect; cf. Vanbeselaere, 1991). Admittedly, cross-categorization research specifically examines group-level differences, reflecting *intergroup relations*, whereas faultline theory applies these processes to investigate individual differences within a team, representing an *intragroup* context. Nevertheless, this line of research also suggests that it can be harmful for teams when members are able to align into subgroups on the basis of diversity dimensions.

Importantly, even though it is generally assumed that the presence of faultlines within a team—or converging cross-categorizations—should have negative consequences for team processes and team outcomes, this relationship does not always seem to hold. Recent findings in this domain in fact sometimes report that the existence of subgroups within a team on the basis of diversity attributes does not necessarily undermine feelings of trust or team cohesion (e.g., Lau & Murnighan, 2005; Pearsall, Ellis, & Evans, 2008; Sawyer, Houlette, & Yeagley, 2006). For instance, past research has demonstrated that the type of task that a team has to perform is a key moderator of the relationship between faultlines in teams and team innovation or performance (Jehn et al., 1999). In fact, the more relevant the diversity characteristics on which the faultlines are based are to the task, the more likely the task will elicit conflict between the different subgroups. For instance, if a team's task is to determine the marketing strategy for selling their product to African Americans, the racial composition within the team and the faultlines that arise from it will most likely have a negative effect on conflict and performance. Indeed, findings on cross-categorization have shown that bias is related to whether crossed categories converge (and reinforce each other) or diverge (and cut across each other; e.g., a female, part-time employee vs. a male, full-time employee both being a member of the same team; Crisp, Hewstone, & Rubin 2001; Mullen, Migdal, & Hewstone, 2001). In the next two sections, we will discuss one important, but relatively neglected factor that to our opinion can also determine whether faultlines will in fact lead to actual subgroup formation, and whether the presence of these subgroups will in turn lead to conflict and poor team innovation, namely; the role of (personal and social) identity processes within the team.

From Faultlines to Subgroups

While Lau and Murnighan's (1998) initial conceptualization of fault-lines infers activation, much of this past work on faultlines did not examine whether the members actually *perceive* these subgroup distinctions to exist, and thus, whether subgroup formation indeed takes place. Similar to the geological concept of faults in the Earth's crust, we argue that faultlines in groups can be inactive and go unnoticed for years without any changes in group processes (Lau & Murnighan, 1998; Wiprut & Zoback, 2000). We therefore distinguish between dormant faultlines and active group faultlines (see Figure 12.1). We define

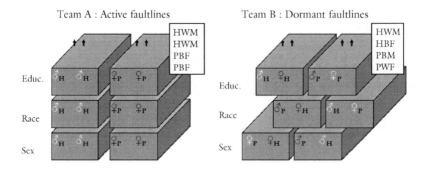

H = High school, P=PhD, W=White, B=Black, M=Male, F=Female

Figure 12.1   Dormant vs. active faultlines.

dormant faultlines as the demographic alignment across members that may (or may not) divide a group into subgroups based on objective demographic alignment across members (Jehn & Bezrukova, in press). This objective alignment is what most past faultline research has studied (for an exception see Earley & Mosakowski, 2000). *Active group fault-lines* occur in groups when members actually perceive these divisions into subgroups based on demographic attributes. While dormant fault-lines are based on the objective demographics of group members, active group faultlines only exist when the members perceive two separate (and potentially even opposed) subgroups. In the geological literature, to continue with the metaphor, there are certain things that lead to the likelihood of a dormant fault being activated: (1) the predisposition of the fault orientation (i.e., the alignment exists, the dormant fault); and (2) an increase in stress or pressure that pushes on the sides of the faults (Wiprut & Zoback, 2000). Most past organizational and team research has assumed that the first criterion is enough, but we focus on the second, the faultline *activation process*, and propose that dormant faultlines do not necessarily turn into active group divisions, but that certain group configurations activate potential dormant alignments.

Thus, the first question that we focus on is: when do team members actually perceive these objective alignments (dormant faultlines)? We propose that the extent to which individual team members attach value to, or personally *identify* with the individual characteristics they possess (e.g., their gender, race, educational background, or work strategies they use) will determine whether faultlines become activated and elicit subgroup formation within a team (Harrison & Klein, 2007; Li & Hambrick, 2005).

It is generally agreed that diversity has a greater effect—either positive or negative—on the interactions between team members when they are well aware of their mutual differences (c.f., Rink & Ellemers, 2007; Riordan, 2000; Strauss, Barrick, & Connerley, 2001; Turban & Jones, 1988). Yet, relatively little diversity research has examined the processes by which a specific individual characteristic of a team member becomes salient in a workgroup (c.f., Harrison & Klein, 2007; Rink & Ellemers, 2006). Importantly, this research is based on notions derived from identity and self theories, suggesting an activation process within individuals based on the salience of social categories (c.f., Oakes, 1987; Pearsall et al., 2008). For instance, theories of the social self state that different selves can be activated at different times or in different contexts. That is, from the perspective of multiple identities or identity complexity, Roccas and Brewer (2002) indicate that objective identities (what the person is: White, Christian, young, female) are not always decisive for how people see themselves and others at a specific time. Based on this reasoning, we argue that the salience of diversity characteristics—and the activation of faultlines into subgroups—within a team is dependent on the extent to which individual team members apply a *category-based* account of identification in order to define the self and secure one's self-esteem (Brewer, 1991; Jackson & Smith, 1999). This means that team members tend to attach more value to the individual characteristics that they possess, or the categories that they represent—their personal identity (e.g., being female or a psychologist)—than to the other team members who belong to different categories (males, economists). In this situation, team members try to balance their need for personal distinctiveness with their need to belong (Brewer, 1991; Hornsey & Jetten, 2004). However, within teams, members can also use a *prototype-based* account of identification, meaning that they primarily develop a view of the self on the basis of how their team can be distinguished from other teams in that context (c.f., meta-contrast in *inter-group* comparisons; Turner, 1985). We argue that, for these team members, diversity attributes within the team are less likely to become salient, nor will dormant faultlines lead to the formation of subgroups.

In the final section of this chapter, we will discuss the situation in which individual team members identify highly with their individual characteristics, and as a consequence, perceive alignment on the basis of diversity attributes among the members of their team. As we described above, we propose that identification processes can also explain under which conditions the resulting subgroups will be harmful for team performance and innovation or not.

Subgroup Formation and the Performance of Diverse Teams

Recent work based on the social identity perspective by Hornsey and Hogg (2000) shows that under certain conditions, the emergence of subgroups is not necessarily detrimental (and can even be beneficial) for groups. Subcategorization only reduces group cohesiveness and causes subgroup resistance when members identify more strongly with their subgroup than with the group as a whole (Brewer, 1991). Indeed, research exists which shows that if there is a strong superordinate identity within diverse teams, members are more willing to deal with their differences (Kane, Argote, & Levine, 2005). A strong team identity is expected to act as "social glue," or a common uniting force through which the members remain committed to each other and focused on the team's goals. This mechanism could in principle prevent subgroups from eliciting negative group processes (such as conflict) based on stereotyping and outgroup biases.

However, it is important to note that there is also a downside to a strong superordinate team identity. Findings have been mixed so far, as too much focus on the overall team identity can also threaten the distinctiveness of the subgroups within a team. As a result, the members of those subgroups tend to resist inclusion in the larger group (e.g. Brown & Wade, 1987; Gonzalez & Brown, 2006; Hewstone, 1996). So, whereas sole identification with the subgroup most likely has the result that subgroup members no longer consider themselves to be a part of the superordinate team and will be less likely to place effort for the benefit of the collective, too much emphasis on the superordinate team identity may cause these same high subgroup identifiers to obstruct the common goals as well (e.g. van Leeuwen, van Knippenberg, & Ellemers, 2003).

In line with the dual-categorization model, we argue that these potential negative effects of identification processes do not necessarily have to occur when the more inclusive and binding identity of the superordinate team is equally salient for members as the identity of their subgroup (see also the common ingroup identity model; Gaertner, Dovidio, & Bachman, 1996). This can be achieved by mutually acknowledging and respecting the overall group goals *and* distinctions between the subgroups (Barreto & Ellemers, 2002). Indeed, Crisp, Stone, and Hall (2006) even showed that presenting a dual identity to those members who highly identify with their subgroup counteracted their distinctiveness concerns and led to reduced bias. Thus, these perspectives seem to suggest that the *balance* between subgroup and superordinate group identification determines whether group members show subgroup biases, and lose their motivation to work for the team as a whole.

How can this balance between subgroup and superordinate team identification be achieved? We believe that this can be done during the formation phase of more general identity-relevant aims and norms within the team. The development of specific norms has the capacity to influence the extent to which teams are open to diversity, and can thus counteract tendencies to exclude minorities or subgroups from the overall team (Rink & Ellemers, 2007). This is the case when teams learn how to develop norms that maintain the importance of all subgroup identities within the superordinate whole, hereby satisfying subgroup members' distinctiveness motivations while at the same time positively

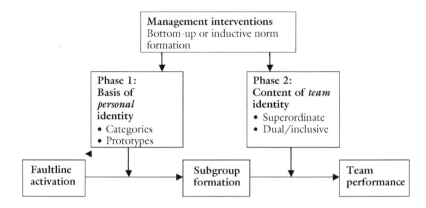

Figure 12.2   Two-phase model explaining how faultlines affect team performance.

orienting them toward accepting the inclusive team (see Waldzus, this volume).

Literature shows that one can make a distinction between *top-down* and *bottom-up* norm development. That is, whether norms have been forced upon teams by management (top-down) compared to when teams have been able to develop norms themselves (bottom-up; see the ASPIRe model by Reynolds, Eggins, & Haslam, 2003). Reynolds et al. (2003) argue that if organizations wish to facilitate the acceptance of diversity they should utilize a bottom-up approach. Such an approach allows team members to play an active role in the definition of themselves as a team, in contrast to a top-down approach where norms are imposed upon teams. Indeed, research has shown that teams who are allowed to actively form their own identity and norms are more likely to create clear expectations about the presence of differences or subgroups among the members. As a result, such teams are more likely to internalize diversity as a feature of their team, and develop a more inclusive superordinate identity in which subgroups are acknowledged (Postmes, Spears, Lee, & Novak, 2005). In contrast, organizations that use a top-down approach to induce certain norms in teams often exclusively rely on features at the superordinate team level, hereby undermining and threatening the existent subgroups. For an overview of our theoretical model see Figure 12.2.

Conclusions

In this chapter, we argued in favor of a social-cognitive analysis of subgroup relations to provide a good understanding of the conditions under which potential faultlines become activated or when they might instead remain *passive* and not lead to subgroup formation. We distinguished between dormant versus active faultlines, theorizing that the objective diversity or individual characteristics that members may align on, while present, are not automatically noticed by group members and thus do not necessarily become activated such that team members perceive this alignment.

In fact, we propose when people are primarily inclined to define the personal self in terms of the characteristics or categories to which they belong (i.e., use a category-based account), dormant faultlines are likely to turn into activated faultlines, or actual subgroup formation based on diversity characteristics. This is less likely to be the case when members develop a view of their personal self on the basis of meta-contrast principles (use a prototype-based account), and focus on the distinction between their team versus other teams in that context.

Once activated, faultlines can lead to negative group behaviors (outgroup bias, coalition formation, and conflict) that hinder team innovation and performance. However, the news is not all bad. Importantly, identification processes can be regulated by interventions within organizations. Our theoretical argument can thus inform management practices aimed at improving the acceptance of diversity in teams in order to enhance innovation. For instance, our reasoning above suggests that organizations should implement reward systems that emphasize inclusive team norms, or could install bottom-up team identity development training. Such interventions will make sure that intragroup differences constitute an essential part of the overall team identity and make it clearer to the team members that diversity can in fact even help them to obtain common group goals (see Rink & Ellemers, 2007). At the same time, subgroup members can then preserve their distinctiveness, and feel accepted by the team as a whole. In this way, active faultline alignment based on diversity attributes will be least detrimental for team processes and outcomes, and team members are able to cherish both identities simultaneously.

References

Barreto, M., & Ellemers, N. (2002). The impact of respect versus neglect of self identities on identification and group loyalty. *Personality and Social Psychology Bulletin, 28*, 629–639.

Brewer, M. B. (1991). The social self: On being the same and different at the same time. *Personality and Social Psychology Bulletin, 17*, 472–482.

Brown, R. J., & Wade, G. (1987). Superordinate goals and intergroup behaviour: The effect of role ambiguity and status on intergroup attitudes and task performance. *European Journal of Social Psychology, 17*, 131–142.

Bunderson, J. S., & Sutcliffe, K. M. (2002). Comparing alternative conceptualizations of functional diversity in management teams: Process and performance effects. *Academy of Management Journal, 45*, 875–893.

Cox, T., Lobel, S., & McLeod, P. (1991). Effects of ethnic group cultural differences on cooperative and competitive behavior on a group task. *Academy of Management Journal, 34*, 827–847.

Crisp, R. J., & Hewstone, M. (1999). Subcategorization of physical stimuli: category differentiation and decategorization processes. *European Journal of Social Psychology, 29*, 665–671.

Crisp, R. J., Hewstone, M., & Rubin, M. (2001). Does multiple categorization reduce intergroup bias?. *Personality and Social Psychology Bulletin, 27*, 76–89.

Crisp, R. J., Stone, C. H., & Hall, N. R. (2006). Recategorization and subgroup identification: Predicting and preventing threats from common ingroups. *Personality and Social Psychology Bulletin, 32*, 230–243.

De Dreu, C. K. W., & Weingart, L. R. (2003). Task versus Relationship conflict, team performance and team member satisfaction: A meta-analysis. *Journal of Applied Psychology, 88*, 741–749.

Earley, P. C., & Mosakowski, E. (2000). Creating hybrid team cultures: An empirical test of transnational team functioning. *Academy of Management Journal, 43*(1), 26–49.

Eisenhardt, K., & Bourgeois, L. (1988). Politics of strategic decision making in high-velocity environments: Toward a midrange theory. *Academy of Management Journal, 31*, 737–770.

Ellemers, N., De Gilder, D., & Haslam, S. A. (2004). Motivating individuals and groups at work: A social identity perspective on leadership and group performance. *Academy of Management Review, 29*, 459–478.

Fiske, S. T., & Taylor, S. E. (1991). *Social cognition* (2nd. Ed). New York: McGraw-Hill.

Gaertner, S. L., Dovidio, J. F., & Bachman, B. A. (1996). Revisiting the contact hypothesis: The induction of a common inteam identity. *International Journal of Intercultural Relations, 20*, 271–290.

Gonzalez, R., & Brown, R. (2006). Dual identities in intergroup contact: Group status and size moderate the generalization of positive attitude change. *Journal of Experimental Social Psychology, 42*, 753–767.

Hambrick, D. C., & Mason, P. A. (1984). Upper echelons: The organization as a reflection of its top managers. *Academy of Management Review, 9*, 193–206.

Harrison, D. A., & Klein, K. J. (2007). What's the difference? Diversity constructs as separation, variety, or disparity in organizations. *Academy of Management Review, 32*(4), 1199–1228.

Harrison, D. A., Price, K. H., & Bell, M. P. (1998). Beyond relational demography: Time and the effects of surface- and deep-level diversity on work group cohesion. *Academy of Management Journal*, *41*(1), 96–107.

Haslam, S. A. (2004). *Psychology in Organizations: The social identity approach.* London: Sage.

Haslam, S. A., Ryan, M. K., Postmes, T., Jetten, J., & Webley, P. (2006). Sticking to our guns: Social identity as a basis for the maintenance of commitment to faltering organizational projects. *Journal of Organizational Behaviour*, *27*, 607–628.

Hewstone, M. R. (1996). Contact and categorization: Social psychological interventions to change intergroup relations. In C. N. Macrae, C. Stangor, M. R. C. Hewstone (Eds.), *Stereotypes and stereotyping* (pp. 323–368). London: Guilford Press.

Hornsey, M. J., & Hogg, M. A. (2000). Assimilation and diversity: An integrative model of subgroup relations. *Personality and Social Psychology Review*, *4*, 143–156.

Hornsey, M. J., & Jetten, J. (2004). The individual within the group: Balancing the need to belong with the need to be different. *Personality and Social Psychology Review*, *8*, 248–264.

Insko, C. A., & Schopler, J. (1998). Differential distrust of groups and individuals. In C. Sedikides, J. Schopler, C. A. Insko (Eds.), *Intergroup cognition and intergroup behavior* (pp. 75–108). Mahwah, NJ: Erlbaum.

Jackson, J. W., & Smith, E. R. (1999). Conceptualizing social identity: A new framework and evidence for the impact of different dimensions. *Personality and Social Psychology Bulletin*, *1*, 120–135.

Jackson, S. E., May, K. E., & Whitney, K. (1995). Under the dynamics of diversity in decision-making teams. In R. A. Guzzo & E. Salas (Eds.), *Team effectiveness and decision making in organizations* (pp. 204–261). San Francisco: Jossey-Bass.

Jehn, K. A., & Bezrukova, K. (in press). The faultline activation process and the effects of activated faultlines on coalition formation, conflict, and group outcomes. *Organizational Behavior and Human Decision Processes*.

Jehn, K. A., Northcraft, G., & Neale, M. (1999). Why differences make a difference: A field study of diversity, conflict, and performance in workgroups. *Administrative Science Quarterly*, *44*, 741–763.

Kane, A. A., Argote, L., & Levine, J. M. (2005). Knowledge transfer between groups via personnel rotation: Effects of social identity and knowledge quality. *Organizational Behavior and Human Decision Processes*, *96*, 56–71.

LaBianca, G., Brass, D. J., & Gray, B. (1998). Social networks and perceptions of intergroup conflict: The role of negative relationships and third parties. *Academy of Management Journal*, *41*, 55–67.

Lau, D., & Murnighan, J. K. (1998). Demographic diversity and faultlines: The compositional dynamics of organizational groups. *Academy of Management Review*, *23*, 325–340.

Lau, D., & Murnighan, J. K. (2005). Interactions within groups and subgroups: The dynamic effects of demographic faultlines. *Academy of Management Journal, 48*(4), 645–659.

Lawrence, B. S. (1997). The black box of organizational demography. *Organizational Science, 8*, 1–22.

Li, J. T., & Hambrick, D. C. (2005). Factional groups: A new vantage on demographic faultlines, conflict, and disintegration in work teams. *Academy of Management Journal, 48*(5), 794–813.

Milliken, F. J., & Martins, L. L. (1996). Searching for common threads: Understanding the multiple effects of diversity in organizational groups. *Academy of Management Review, 21*, 402–433.

Mullen, B., Migdal, M. J., & Hewstone, M. (2001). Crossed categorization versus simple categorization and intergroup evaluations: a meta-analysis. *European Journal of Social Psychology, 31*, 721–736.

Murnighan, J. K., & Brass, D. J. (1991). Intraorganizational coalitions. In M. H. Bazerman, R.J. Lewicki, & B. H. Sheppard (Eds.), *Research on negotiation in organizations: The handbook of negotiation research* (pp. 283–306). Greenwich, CT: JAI Press.

Oakes, P. J. (1987). The salience of social categories. In: J. C. Turner, M.A. Hogg, P. J. Oakes, S. Reicher, & M. S. Wetherell, *Rediscovering the social group: A self-categorization theory* (117–141). Oxford, UK: Basil Blackwell.

Pearsall, M. J., Ellis, A. P., & Evans, J. M. (2008). Unlocking the effects of gender faultlines on team creativity: Is activation the key? *Journal of Applied Psychology, 93*(1), 225–234.

Pelled, L. H., Eisenhardt, K. M., & Xin, K. R. (1999). Exploring the black box: An analysis of work group diversity, conflict, and performance. *Administrative Science Quarterly, 44*, 1–28.

Postmes, T., Spears, R., Lee, A. T., & Novak, R. J. (2005). Individuality and social influence in groups: Inductive and deductive routes to group identity. *Journal of Personality and Social Psychology, 89*, 747–763.

Prislin, R., & Christensen, P. N. (2002). Group conversion versus group expansion as modes of change in majority and minority positions: All losses hurt but only some gains gratify. *Journal of Personality and Social Psychology, 83*, 1095–1102.

Reynolds, K., Eggins, R., & Haslam, A. (2003). How best to address issues arising from a diverse workforce: The role of fitting social identities in subgroup-superordinate group relations. *Australian Journal of Psychology, 55*, 59–70.

Rink, F., & Ellemers, N. (2006). What can you expect? The influence of gender diversity in dyads on work goal expectancies and subsequent work commitment. *Group Processes and Intergroup Relations, 9*, 577–588.

Rink, F., & Ellemers, N. (2007). Diversity as a basis for shared organizational identity: The norm congruity principle. *British Journal of Management, 18*, 17–27.

Rink, F., & Ellemers, N. (2008). Managing diversity in organizations: How identity processes affect work groups. In M. Barreto, M. Ryan, & M. Schmitt. *Barriers to diversity: The Glass Ceiling 20 years on* (pp. 204–221). Washington, DC: American Psychological Association.

Riordan, C. M. (2000). Relational demography within groups: Past developments, contradictions, and new directions. *Research in Personnel and Human Resource Management, 19,* 131–173.

Roccas, S., & Brewer, M. B. (2002). Social identity complex. *Personality and Social Psychological Review, 6*(2), 88–106.

Ryan, M. K., & Haslam, S. A. (2007). The glass cliff: Exploring the dynamics surrounding the appointment of women to precarious leadership positions. *Academy of Management Review, 32,* 549–572.

Sawyer, J. E., Houlette, M. A., & Yeagley, E. L. (2006). Decision performance and diversity structure: Comparing faultlines in convergent, crosscut, and racially homogeneous groups. *Organizational Behavior and Human Decision Processes, 99*(1), 1–15.

Stevenson, W. B., Pearce, J. L., & Porter, L. W. (1985). The concept of "coalition" in organizational theory and research. *Academy of Management Review, 10,* 256–268.

Strauss, J. P., Barrick, M. R., & Connerley, M. L. (2001). An investigation of relational personality effects on peer and supervisor ratings and the impact of familiarity. *Journal of Occupational and Organizational Psychology, 74,* 637–57.

Tajfel, H., & Turner, J. C. (1979). An integrative theory of intergroup conflict. In W. Austin & S. Worchel (Eds.), *The social psychology of intergroup relations* (pp. 33–47). Monterey, CA: Brooks/Cole.

Thatcher, S. M. B., Jehn, K. A., & Zanutto, E. (2003). Cracks in diversity research: The effects of diversity faultlines on conflict and performance. *Group Decision and Negotiation, 12*(3), 217–241.

Turban, D. B., & Jones, A. P. (1988). Supervisor-subordinate similarity: Types, effects and mechanisms. *Journal of Applied Psychology, 73,* 28–234.

Turner, J. C. (1985). Social categorization and the self-concept: A social cognitive theory of group behaviour. In E. J. Lawjer (Ed.), *Advances in group processes: Theory and Research* (Vol. 2, pp. 77–122). Greenwich, CT: JAI.

Turner, J. C., Hogg, M. A., Oakes, P. J., Reicher, S., & Wetherell, M. S. (1987). *Rediscovering the social group: A self-categorization theory.* Oxford, UK: Basil Blackwell.

Turner, J. C., Oakes, P. J., Haslam, S. A., & McGarty, C. (1994). Self and collective: Cognition and social context. *Personality and Social Psychology Bulletin, 20,* 454–463.

Vanbeselaere, N. (1991). The different effects of simple and crossed categorizations. In W. Stroebe & M. Hewstone (Eds.), *European Review of Social Psychology* (Vol. 2, pp. 247–278). Chichester, UK: Wiley.

van Knippenberg, D., & Schippers, M. C. (2007). Work group diversity. *Annual Review of Psychology, 58,* 515–541.

van Leeuwen, E., van Knippenberg, D., & Ellemers, N. (2003). Continuing and changing team identities: The effects of merging on social identification and ingroup bias. *Personality and Social Psychology Bulletin, 29*, 679–690.

Williams, K., & O'Reilly, C. (1998). Demography and Diversity in Organizations: A Review of 40 Years of Research. *Research in Organizational Behavior, 20*, 77–140.

Wiprut, D., & Zoback, M. D. (2000). Fault reactivation and fluid flow along a previously dormant fault. *Geology, 28*, 595–598.

Wittenbaum, G. M., Hollingshead, A. B., & Botero, I. C. (2004). From cooperative to motivated information sharing in groups: Moving beyond the hidden profile paradigm. *Communication Monographs, 71*, 286–310.

Part VI

Interventions

13

Combined Effects of Intergroup Contact and Multiple Categorization

Consequences for Intergroup Attitudes in Diverse Social Contexts

Katharina Schmid and Miles Hewstone

As societies are growing ever more ethnically, racially and religiously diverse, recurrent questions are being asked as to whether such increased diversity fosters or hinders positive intergroup relations. One long-established social-scientific perspective on ethnic, racial or religious diversity argues that it poses a threat, particularly (but not exclusively) to the majority group, and thus inevitably leads to heightened intergroup tensions and prejudice (e.g., Blalock, 1967; see more recently, Putnam, 2007). A more recent, and somewhat more optimistic view on the consequences of such diversity can, however, be found in social psychological thinking. In this chapter, we draw upon two key social psychological approaches to improving intergroup relations and reducing prejudice: intergroup contact and self-categorization, in particular, multiple categorization. We do so with particular reference to ethnic, racial or religious diversity, by discussing specifically how both these approaches, in isolation or in combination, are centrally important to understanding how exposure to diversity at the macro-level, such as in residential or educational settings, may positively affect intergroup attitudes.

This chapter is organized into four main sections. In part one, we describe the theoretical background to intergroup contact approaches, with particular reference to diverse social contexts. Specifically, we delineate different types of contact, and describe briefly the conditions and mechanisms that explain when and how contact has positive consequences for intergroup attitudes. In part two, we briefly describe the theoretical background of multiple categorization processes and address the relationship between multiple categorization and intergroup attitudes, focusing in particular on social identity complexity and common ingroup/dual identification perspectives. We then proceed, in part three, with a discussion of the combined consequences of contact and multiple categorization. We first discuss the extent to which multiple categorization processes may be conceived of as moderators of intergroup contact, before we draw attention to a central research question that, in our opinion, has received insufficient attention in the literature to date. Namely, we evaluate the extent to which contact may not only lead to more differentiated outgroup, but also more differentiated ingroup, or rather multiple ingroup, perceptions. We thus argue that multiple categorization processes may be important mediators of contact effects, whereby contact may lead to more differentiated outgroup perceptions *by virtue of* promoting more differentiated multiple ingroup perceptions. We focus especially on how contact, and indeed diversity, may lead to increased social identity complexity, i.e. more complex, inclusive and differentiated cognitive representations of one's multiple ingroups. We end, in part four, by discussing how these two key social psychological approaches, intergroup contact and multiple categorization, may usefully inform social interventions and policy initiatives, as well as drawing general conclusions about the theoretical relevance of considering the combined consequences of contact and multiple categorization on outgroup differentiation and intergroup attitudes in diverse social contexts.

Diversity, Intergroup Contact and Outgroup Attitudes

Intergroup Contact Theory

Since its earliest articulations in the 1940s and 1950s (Allport, 1954; Williams, 1947), intergroup contact theory has been one of the most commonly invoked social psychological approaches to prejudice reduction and the promotion of positive intergroup relations. Contact theory rests upon the notion that direct, face-to-face contact with individual outgroup members may reduce negative, and promote positive, intergroup attitudes via processes of generalization of positive attitudes from the encountered individual to the wider outgroup. Such positive effects are said to be maximized (yet do not occur exclusively; see Pettigrew & Tropp, 2006) if the contact between group members is cooperative, if group members meet under equal status conditions, if there is some pursuit of common goals, and if the contact is in some form institutionally supported, as well as if the contact situation holds the potential for the development of friendships (see Pettigrew, 1998).

Over the years intergroup contact researchers have not only accumulated widespread empirical support for contact theory in many different contexts and under many different conditions, but, more significantly, have furthered a more in-depth understanding of the extent to which different *types* of contact are effective, and *when* and *how* they are (for detailed reviews see Brown & Hewstone, 2005; Hewstone, 2009; for meta-analytic support see Pettigrew & Tropp, 2006). It is now well established that not only the frequency of contact, but, importantly, the quality of contact determines the extent to which contact positively affects outgroup attitudes. Not surprising therefore is that direct contact in the form of cross-group friendship has been found to be a particularly strong antecedent of positive intergroup relations (e.g., Paolini, Hewstone, Cairns, & Voci, 2004).

Extending the initial formulations of the theory, research over the last decade has also demonstrated that direct, face-to-face contact is not the only form of contact that brings about such positive generalization effects. Indirect, or extended, contact, is also typically associated with positive intergroup effects—and particularly so for individuals who have no direct contact (see Christ, Hewstone, Tausch, Wagner, Hughes, & Cairns, 2009). Indirect or extended contact refers to the (mere) knowledge of a fellow ingroup member's contact with outgroup members and thus does not necessitate direct contact (typically, but not necessarily, the fellow ingroup members are ones to whom one is close, e.g., family members or friends; Wright, Aron, McLaughlin-Volpe, & Ropp, 1997; see Turner, Hewstone, Voci, Paolini, & Christ, 2008, for a review), Moreover, extended contact appears to be an important antecedent of direct contact (Tausch et al., 2009). There now also exists evidence to show that imagined contact (Turner, Crisp, & Lambert, 2007), as well as parasocial contact via mass media exposure (e.g., Schiappa, Gregg, & Hewes, 2005) can exert positive effects on outgroup attitudes.

Significant advances have also been made in understanding both moderating and mediating factors of contact effects, that is, the "when" and "how" of contact effects, respectively. For example, contact has been found to be particularly effective when group membership salience is high (e.g., Voci & Hewstone, 2003). Contact is also known to exert positive effects on intergroup attitudes by reducing intergroup anxiety and group-based threat perceptions (e.g., Islam & Hewstone, 1993; Tausch, Hewstone, Kenworthy, Cairns, & Christ, 2007), or by fostering empathy, perspective taking and positive emotions (see e.g., Miller, Smith, & Mackie, 2004). Although we do not have space to elaborate on this in detail (but see Brown & Hewstone, 2005, for a detailed review), we return to a discussion of moderators and mediators of contact effects at a later point in this chapter, where we focus explicitly on the extent to which multiple categorization processes may both moderate and mediate the effects of contact on attitudinal and other outcomes.

One finding in intergroup contact research that is particularly relevant for the study of diversity pertains to so-called *secondary transfer effects* (Pettigrew, 2009), whereby contact with a member of one particular outgroup has positive consequences for attitudes not only towards this group in general, but also towards other, even unrelated outgroups that were not involved in the initial contact situation. Among seven national probability samples in Europe, Pettigrew (1997) observed that contact effects with one outgroup generalized to a range of other groups, and also led to more support for more tolerant immigration policy preferences. Since this earliest documentation this phenomenon has been replicated in a set of studies in a number of different contexts, including Cyprus, Northern Ireland and the US (Tausch et al., 2009).

Intergroup Contact: Implications for Diverse Contexts

How does contact theory contribute to a more differentiated understanding of the consequences of ethnic, racial or religious diversity on intergroup attitudes? Diverse contexts, whether residential, educational or other, offer opportunities for contact. Research has moreover repeatedly shown that the *opportunity* for contact, while itself not typically a direct predictor of attitudes, tends to be a central predictor of *actual* contact (e.g., Wagner, Hewstone, & Machleit, 1989), which tends to exert positive effects on intergroup relations. Extending this thought further, one may thus argue that more diverse social environments, by virtue of affording more opportunities for engaging in multiple outgroup interaction, should also be predictive of actual contact, a consequence of which should then be (if contact is positive) a reduction of intergroup tensions (see Schmid, Tausch, Hewstone, Cairns, & Hughes, 2008).

There is some support for this assertion. In Germany, for example, Wagner, Christ, Pettigrew, Stellmacher, and Wolf (2006) showed that increased percentages of foreigners in a population district were associated with more frequent and positive contact with ethnic minorities, which in turn had a positive effect on perceptions of foreigners. Similarly, in Northern Ireland, living in mixed as opposed to segregated neighbourhoods was associated with more contact, which positively mediated the effects of context on outgroup attitudes (Schmid et al., 2008). However, this general conjecture seemingly contradicts social scientific theoretical perspectives rooted in group threat or conflict theory, which contend that diversity increases threat perceptions, and thus should be negatively associated with intergroup attitudes (e.g., Quillian, 1996), as well as outgroup, and even ingroup, trust (Putnam, 2007).

The discrepancy in viewpoints between threat and contact theory arises, in our opinion, due to the fact that many studies in support of group threat theory are methodologically flawed when they implicitly infer a linear relationship between *macro*-level diversity and *individual*-level threat perceptions, without directly measuring individual level threat. It is undisputed, of course, that increased threat perceptions tend to predict negative intergroup attitudes and prejudice (see e.g., Schlueter, Schmidt, & Wagner, 2008; Stephan & Stephan, 2000), and diversity may, of course, pose competitive threat under negative conditions. However, it is imperative that threat perceptions be measured at the individual level to be able to confirm any theoretical conjecture that diversity poses threat.

More importantly, however, many empirical examinations of group threat theory fail to take into account additional, centrally important variables when examining the relationship between diversity and intergroup attitudes. Specifically, *macro*-level phenomena, e.g. percentage diversity in a contextual unit, are often correlated or compared with *individual*-level attitude variables, without considering or clearly defining additional moderating or mediating processes that also occur at the individual level. Such individual-level moderators and mediators may explain when and how diversity (as a macro-level phenomenon) may affect people's intergroup attitudes. For example, any examination of the contextual, *macro*-level effects of diversity needs to consider how such contextual diversity is subjectively experienced and encountered. Thus one needs to take into account individuals' contact experiences with members of various outgroups that co-inhabit one's diverse social environment when seeking to draw inferences on the impact of diversity. Moreover, since research on mediators of contact effects has shown that contact may reduce group-based threat perceptions, intergroup contact needs to be accounted for as a mediating variable between diversity and threat, hence as an antecedent of group based threat perceptions at the individual level (see Schmid et al., 2008). Importantly, such combined effects of macro- and individual-level variables are best explored in empirical research that allows for the hierarchical nature of such effects. Specifically, one needs to keep in mind that individuals are, in essence, *nested* within social contexts, i.e., within macro-level contextual units, so in order to take account of the contextual effects of diversity, multilevel (or hierarchical) regression modeling techniques need to be employed (see, e.g., Wagner et al., 2006).

In sum, we consider group threat and contact theory not to be opposing, but complementary approaches to understanding the effects of ethnic, racial or religious diversity on intergroup relations. In the presence of intergroup tensions, marked by an absence of positive intergroup contact experiences, diversity may of course pose threat, yet macro-level diversity that is positively experienced and encountered should be associated with reduced threat perceptions, and more positive intergroup attitudes.

Diversity, Multiple Categorization and Intergroup Attitudes

The social identity approach, encompassing both Social Identity Theory (e.g., Tajfel & Turner, 1979) and Self-Categorization Theory (Turner, Hogg, Oakes, Reicher, & Wetherell, 1987), rests upon the assumption that individuals tend to categorize their social world into discrete social categories, some of which they are part of, which then gives rise to categorization of self and others into ingroups ("we") and outgroups ("they"), respectively. In recent years, significant advances have been made in fostering understanding of *multiple* categorization processes and the consequences thereof for intergroup perception. Theoretical and empirical examinations of, for example, crossed-categorization phenomena (see Crisp & Hewstone, 2007, for a detailed review; see also Miller, Spanovic, & Stenstrom, this volume), have highlighted that multiple group identities can become salient at the same time, to the extent that individuals are able to attend to and process information along multiple categories simultaneously. Of particular merit in multiple categorization research is a growing body of empirical evidence demonstrating that self-definition in terms of multiple social categories is more often than not associated with more positive evaluation of outgroups (Crisp & Hewstone, 2000; Crisp, Hewstone, & Cairns, 2001; see Brewer, Ho, Lee, & Miller, 1987). We discuss here only two multiple categorization approaches that become relevant for a discussion of combined effects of contact and multiple categorization that we address in subsequent parts of this chapter: the common-ingroup/dual identity approach, and the social identity complexity perspective (but see Crisp & Hewstone, 2007, for a comprehensive review of multiple categorization processes).

Subgroup vs. Superordinate Identification

Most social categories may be thought of as subgroup categories nested within more inclusive, superordinate groups. Thus individuals may categorize themselves and others either as part of subordinate ingroups and outgroups ("us" and "them") or as part of superordinate, common ingroups ("we"), or both. Categorization that does not occur (exclusively) at the subgroup level is then thought to yield positive consequences for intergroup perception and attitudes. It is this basic reasoning upon which the common ingroup identity model of recategorization (Gaertner, Dovidio, Anastasio, Bachman, & Rust, 1993), and the dual-identity model (Gaertner & Dovidio, 2000), rest. Specifically, the common ingroup identity model argues that a process of recategorization, whereby subordinate categories are replaced with superordinate categories, may lead to a reduction in intergroup bias and prejudice. There is an impressive body of (mainly experimental) empirical evidence supporting this model, showing that, as predicted, bias is reduced primarily by improving attitudes towards former outgroup members (for a review see Gaertner & Dovidio, 2000).

However, a number of problems surround the common ingroup identity model (Brewer & Gaertner, 2001). For one, many categorizations are long-established, making recategorization an unrealistic possibility. Moreover, in situations of intergroup conflict where groups are engaged in hostilities, or in clearly-defined minority-majority contexts, where groups differ in size, power or status, recategorization may be perceived as threatening, and instead of reducing may in fact exacerbate negative intergroup relations (see, e.g., Hewstone, Rubin, & Willis, 2002). Thus the common ingroup identity model holds the risk of depriving individuals of valued social categories (Brewer & Gaertner, 2001), a concern that is particularly relevant for minority group members, who tend to identify much more strongly with their in-group than do members of majority groups (see Simon, Aufderheide, & Kampmeier, 2001).

Responding to these concerns, Gaertner and Dovidio (2000) subsequently developed the so-called "dual identity model", which recognizes both different and common group memberships and thereby emphasizes a more complex form of common ingroup identity. This model suggests that if individuals simultaneously identify with nested subgroup identities *and* identities at a superordinate level, this may be particularly beneficial for intergroup attitudes. Empirical evidence has confirmed positive consequences for intergroup attitudes when both subgroup and superordinate groups are equally salient (e.g., Gaertner, Dovidio, & Bachman, 1996). Moreover, a dual identity may lead to more positive out-group attitudes than a superordinate identity alone when the superordinate category is too inclusive to provide individuals with adequate distinctiveness (Hornsey & Hogg, 2000).

Social Identity Complexity

The social identity complexity model (Roccas & Brewer, 2002; see also Brewer, this volume) underlies the notion that individuals may hold more or less complex self-descriptions in terms of multiple social categories and are able to subjectively combine their multiple in-group identities in a more or less exclusive manner, with complexity ranging on a continuum from high to low. The model thus deals much more explicitly with individuals' multiple *self*-categorization processes, unlike the common ingroup/dual identity models which refer to the categorization of others in functional relation to the ingroup. Social identity complexity refers to an individual's subjective representation of the interrelationships among his or her multiple identities (Roccas & Brewer, 2002). Social categories may thus be subjectively perceived as largely overlapping so that only individuals who share membership on the sum of these identities are regarded as fellow ingroup members, while people who share none or only a few of these identities are regarded as outgroup members. Individuals may, however, be aware that others do not always share in-group membership on all of these self-descriptive categories, i.e. that not all their multiple ingroups overlap (Brewer & Pierce, 2005; Roccas & Brewer, 2002). The case of overlapping identities reflects relatively lower, whereas non-overlapping identities reflect relatively higher social identity complexity.

Significantly, social identity complexity tends to positively covary with intergroup attitudes. For example, research has shown that higher social identity complexity was associated with greater tolerance, reduced intergroup bias and greater support for affirmative action and multiculturalism in data based on a public opinion survey in the US (Brewer & Pierce, 2005; Roccas & Brewer, 2002). Similar results were reported in two studies in Northern Ireland, where higher social identity complexity was associated with more tolerance and less ingroup bias (Schmid, Hewstone, Tausch, Cairns, & Hughes, 2009a).

Multiple Categorization: Implications for Diverse Contexts

One may assume that if individuals depend less on a single ingroup to satisfy the psychological need of "belonging" they will be less likely to polarize their loyalties along any specific ingroup category (see Brewer, 1993). This should then reduce the likelihood of intergroup tensions. Analogously, it has long been argued that more complex societies, where loyalty structures cut across groups (e.g., through intermarriage), hold reduced potential for intergroup conflict compared with more polarized societies, characterized by a singular, hierarchical structure (see Murphy, 1957; see also Brewer & Gaertner, 2001). According to Brewer and Pierce (2005), exposure to socially diverse environments should increase awareness of the non-overlapping nature of social categories, in other words, diversity may be associated with greater social identity complexity. Indeed in the US, Miller, Brewer and Arbuckle (2009) found that people who reported living in residential areas with a greater proportion of residents from different ethnic backgrounds had higher social identity complexity. Similarly, in Northern Ireland, where residential segregation between Catholics and Protestants is still a pervasive problem, living in mixed as opposed to segregated neighbourhoods was associated with higher social identity complexity (see Schmid et al., in press).

There is also some evidence to suggest that exposure to diversity encourages identification with superordinate categories. In Northern Ireland, we found that individuals living in mixed neighbourhoods (co-inhabited by both Catholics and Protestants) were more inclined to self-categorize in terms of the common ingroup category, Northern Irish, than were respondents living in ethno-religiously segregated neighbourhoods (Schmid et al., in press). Moreover, it has been argued that dual identity models may be appropriate models for multiethnic societies since they allow individuals to preserve their ethnic subgroups, while also integrating at the national, superordinate level (Berry, 1997; Brewer, 2000; Huo, Smith, Tyler, & Lind, 1996; see also Nguyen &

Benet-Martinez, this volume; Tadmor, Hong, Chiu, & No, this volume; Verkuyten, this volume). However, it is questionable whether such a dual identity model works equally well for majority and minority members in diverse, multi-ethnic societies. In essence, the dual identity model is inherently reflective of integration approaches, whereas the common ingroup model is more in line with assimilation perspectives; the former of course being generally favoured by minority group members, the latter by majority group members (see Berry, 1997). A dual identity model may thus be effective primarily for members of minority groups, while for members of majority groups a common in-group representation may be more likely to lead to more positive effects. González and Brown (2006), for example, have shown that creating a dual identity during a cooperative task was associated with more positive intergroup attitudes for members of a numerical minority, but not for the majority (see also Berry, Kim, Minde, & Mok, 1987).

Two further limitations of positive attitude generalization effects surround the dual identity model, and indeed also the common ingroup identity model, particularly so in diverse social contexts. One problem with these perspectives is that ingroup projection might occur (see Wenzel, Mummendey, Weber, & Waldzus, 2003; Waldzus, this volume), which refers to situations in which the defining, typically positive, characteristics of the common ingroup are perceived as reflecting those of the former subordinate ingroup only. Since the subgroup outgroup category is then not equally included in the common ingroup, positive attitudes towards outgroup members may not be observed. Moreover, Brewer (2008) pursues an interesting conjecture on the relationship between social identity complexity and common ingroup perspectives. Specifically, she argues that for common ingroup identification to yield positive effects on intergroup attitudes, the superordinate group needs not only to be perceived as inclusive of both former ingroups and outgroups on a single dimension of categorization, but also to be perceived as a complex category that can encompass a range of subgroups that do not need to overlap. If the superordinate category is perceived as consisting of a range of mostly convergent social categories, then identification with the superordinate group will not be sufficient to promote positive intergroup relations in cases where individuals deviate from a less complex common ingroup. This argumentation relies on implicit assumptions about intrinsic differences between the two perspectives.

Common ingroup and dual identity perspectives reflect the inherent hierarchy of single dimensions of categorization, where individuals may categorise and perceive self and others in terms of subgroup categories nested, at different levels of inclusiveness, within a superordinate, common ingroup. Similar to the crossed-categorization perspective, the social identity complexity perspective (Roccas & Brewer, 2002) takes into account even orthogonal, unrelated categories, which may or may not be hierarchically structured, and which may or may not overlap. Thus, to come back to the points raised by Brewer (2008), it may be that individuals perceive a common ingroup as inclusive of a former outgroup member on a single, yet hierarchically structured dimension of categorization, yet the common ingroup may be perceived as low in complexity with regard to the *range* of one's multiple categories. Thus, in diverse societies, it becomes questionable whether identification with a common ingroup for individuals low in social identity complexity is a sufficient means for generating positive intergroup relations.

Combined Effects of Intergroup Contact and Multiple Categorization

Although intergroup contact and multiple categorization research have independently much to offer, an even more comprehensive understanding of the nature of intergroup relations in ethnically, racially or religiously diverse environments becomes attainable when these two key social psychological approaches are considered in combination with each other. In the following we thus examine the combined effects of intergroup contact and multiple categorization on intergroup attitudes in diverse social contexts. In particular, we discuss pertinent social psychological literature that has examined both the moderating and mediating effects of multiple categorization on the relationship between intergroup contact and outgroup attitudes.

Multiple Categorization as a Moderator of Contact Effects

As mentioned earlier, contact between groups tends to be particularly effective for prejudice reduction if certain moderating conditions are met, one of which pertains to the salience of group membership and group boundaries. Specifically, it has been argued that for contact to be effective it should be structured in ways that allow for a change in the cognitive representations of self and others, as well as more inclusive conditions for ingroup membership, although the exact nature of such changes in the structure of social categorization remains disputed.

Table 13.1 Overview of Key Theoretical Models Describing the Conditions under which Contact Should be Maximally Effective

Perspectives and originators	Salience of group boundaries	Key stipulations on the nature of contact
Decategorization (Brewer & Miller, 1984)	Low subgroup salience	Contact should be personalised, deemphasizing subgroup boundaries
Mutual differentiation (Hewstone & Brown, 1986)	High subgroup salience	Contact should be depersonalized, emphasizing subgroup boundaries
Recategorization – common ingroup identity model (Gaertner et al., 1993)	Low subgroup, high superordinate group salience	Contact should deemphasize subgroup, but emphasize superordinate group boundaries
Recategorization – dual identity model (Gaertner & Dovidio, 2000)	High subgroup, high superordinate group salience	Contact should emphasize both subgroup and superordinate group boundaries

Three diverging theoretical approaches are of relevance here and are summarised in Table 13.1: the decategorization perspective (Brewer & Miller, 1984), the mutual differentiation perspective (Hewstone & Brown, 1986), and the recategorization perspective (Gaertner et al., 1993), all of which have been tested extensively in both experimental and field research.

In short, the decategorization perspective (Brewer & Miller, 1984) contends that contact should be structured in ways that de-emphasize social categorizations. By reducing the salience of social categories, and inducing cognitive processes of "differentiation" and "personalization", individuals should be less likely to attend to category-based stereotypical information (Brewer & Gaertner, 2001). Consequently, they should be less likely to hold negative intergroup attitudes, an assumption supported by a number of experimental studies (e.g., Bettencourt, Brewer, Croak, & Miller, 1992).

In sharp contrast, the mutual differentiation perspective advocates that group membership salience should be *retained* during intergroup encounters if contact is to be maximally effective. In particular, Hewstone and Brown (1986) argue that a de-emphasis of social category based information may prevent generalization effects from the encountered individual to the outgroup as a whole, particularly if the encountered individual is perceived as atypical of the wider outgroup. Indeed, both experimental and correlational evidence has shown that the relationship between contact and intergroup attitudes is stronger when group membership salience is high or when the encountered outgroup members are perceived as highly typical (see Brown & Hewstone, 2005). Nonetheless, keeping intergroup boundaries salient risks reinforcement of negative intergroup perceptions (see Islam & Hewstone, 1993), for which reason more recent lines of research have sought to integrate the decategorization and mutual differentiation perspectives (Brown & Hewstone, 2005; Ensari & Miller, 2002). This integrative approach demonstrates that contact is particularly effective when the intergroup encounter is personalized (e.g., involves self-disclosure) *and* when social categories are salient or the encountered out-group member is perceived as typical. Such a combined approach may also explain why contact in the form of cross-group friendship is a particularly strong predictor of intergroup attitudes.

Strictly speaking, however, neither the decategorization nor the mutual differentiation approach inherently need to involve *multiple* categorization processes, i.e., both approaches can refer to situations where ingroup-outgroup comparisons are made based on a single category. The recategorization approach however draws upon the common ingroup identity model and the dual identity model described above, and thus by necessity involves multiple categories. Specifically, the recategorization perspective (Gaertner et al., 1993) argues that intergroup contact should be maximally effective in yielding positive intergroup effects if the encountered individual is cognitively included in a common, superordinate ingroup. It assumes that a contact situation should be structured so that individuals conceive of group boundaries in a more differentiated, inclusive manner. Contact that takes place under the premise of a common ingroup may then be such that only the common ingroup is salient (as suggested by the common ingroup identity model, Gaertner et al., 1993), or to the extent that both former subgroup and the recategorized common ingroup are salient (as suggested by the dual identity model, Gaertner & Dovidio, 2000). Both experimental studies using artifical groups, as well as a number of field studies involving real groups (see e.g., Gaertner & Dovidio, 2000; González & Brown, 2006), have demonstrated that a superordinate categorization during contact yielded particularly positive effects on intergroup attitudes.

Multiple Categorization as a Mediator of Contact Effects

As mentioned above, combined effects of contact and multiple categorization may be such that contact is mainly, or particularly, effective *if* multiple categorization occurs at different levels of inclusiveness. It is, however, possible to conceive of the combined effects of contact and multiple categorization on intergroup attitudes in a different way, so that contact effects are not only moderated but also *mediated* by multiple categorization processes. Specifically, intergroup contact may exert positive effects on attitudes as a consequence of changing people's multiple ingroup perceptions, in particular, social identity complexity.

According to Pettigrew (1997), intergroup contact may prompt individuals to re-assess their views of their ingroup, and should attune them to the fact that the ingroup's norms, customs and lifestyles may not be the only acceptable ways to manage the social world, a process he refers to as "deprovincialization". Confirming these general predictions, he found that contact with minority groups was related to less positive views of the ingroup (Pettigrew, 1997). It should however be noted that in this study the focus rested on categorization and identification processes surrounding a single category. Allowing for the possibility that contact may even influence *multiple* categorization processes, Gaertner et al. (1996) argued that contact should yield positive outgroup differentiation effects by changing people's cognitive representations of ingroup and outgroup from two separate subgroups to one common, more inclusive superordinate ingroup.

Intergroup contact may also affect much more explicitly the cognitive representation of one's multiple ingroups, i.e., it may influence social identity complexity, and it may be this change in cognitive representation that explains *how* contact may positively influence intergroup attitudes. As alluded to above, living in more diverse social environments and being subjected to more diverse social experiences, such as engaging in intergroup contact, should predispose people to hold more inclusive and differentiated perceptions of their multiple ingroups (see Brewer, 2008; Brewer & Pierce, 2005; Miller, Brewer, & Arbuckle, 2009). In two recent studies in Northern Ireland, we tested not only whether intergroup contact was associated with social identity complexity, but also whether the effects of contact on attitudes were mediated by social identity complexity (Schmid et al., 2009a). Our results showed that contact was indeed associated with greater social identity complexity surrounding individuals' religious and national categories, which positively mediated the effects of contact on ingroup bias and tolerance towards the *other* ethno-religious group.

Interestingly, Brewer (2008) suggested that even extended contact, mere vicarious contact experiences, may also explain in part why social identity complexity is typically associated with more positive intergroup attitudes. This proposition has not been empirically tested to date, but appears worthy of research attention. Brewer argues that the awareness of other ingroup members' contact with outgroup members inevitably enhances awareness that not each and every ingroup category can overlap entirely with every other. Hence, individuals who are ingroup members on some dimensions of social categorization may be outgroup members on others. Since extended contact involves the knowledge of fellow ingroup members' contact with a diverse group of others (with whom the individual may *not* be friends him or herself), the individual becomes attuned to the fact that not all of his or her own ingroups fully overlap. Thus the recognition that not all of one's acquaintances and friendship circles overlap should enhance awareness of the complexity of others' multiple group membership, and thus translate into more differentiated multiple ingroup perceptions.

Both direct and extended contact should thus positively affect social identity complexity, since they highlight the complexity and non-overlapping nature of social environments. Coming into contact with diverse others, who may be ingroup members on some categories (e.g., gender, profession), but outgroup members on others (e.g., religion, ethnicity) should prompt individuals to engage in increased cognitive differentiation processes, and thus lead to increased social identity complexity.

There is also evidence to suggest that social identity complexity may be involved in secondary transfer effects. As mentioned above, the secondary transfer effect (Pettigrew, 2009) refers to situations in which contact with one outgroup may positively affect attitudes towards secondary outgroups. We hypothesize that intergroup contact may be positively associated with intergroup attitudes, also towards secondary outgroups, via positively influencing one's cognitive perceptions of one's multiple ingroups, i.e., via higher social identity complexity. We illustrate the hypothesized direction and nature of relationships in Figure 13.1. Social identity complexity may thus not only mediate the effects of intergroup contact on attitudes towards the contacted outgroup, but also towards secondary outgroups (since social identity

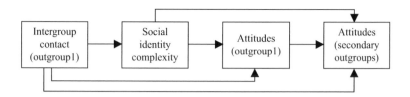

Figure 13.1 Hypothesized *"secondary transfer effects,"* mediated by social identity complexity.

complexity should be associated with a more inclusive representation of a multitude of outgroups).

We have confirmed this set of relationships empirically (Schmid, Hewstone, Tausch, Cairns, & Hughes, 2009b). Specifically, we found that social identity complexity mediated the effects of contact in the form of cross-group friendship between Catholics and Protestants in Northern Ireland on a range of secondary outgroups (e.g., racial minorities, and male homosexuals), even after controlling for individuals' direct contact with these other groups (Schmid et al., 2009b). Thus, we found that cross-group friendship was associated with secondary transfer effects indirectly, via increased social identity complexity. Arguably, such secondary transfer effects are of particular relevance for a discussion of the effects of diversity on intergroup relations, since they highlight the potential multiplicative effects of encountering diversity. But also, they may explain how individuals who live, work or socialize in more or less diverse environments may still display favourable intergroup perceptions of diverse groups even in the absence of direct contact with a wide range of outgroups.

In sum, it seems that the combined effects of contact and multiple categorization are centrally important to understanding the nature of intergroup attitudes, and especially so in diverse social contexts. So far, social psychological research has paid insufficient attention to the idea that contact may affect multiple categorization and identification processes, and that this might *explain* the positive effects of contact on intergroup attitudes. Of particular importance, we argue, is the social identity complexity perspective, in that contact and indeed macro-social diversity itself may be a central predictor of identity complexity, which might then positively mediate the effects of contact and diversity on intergroup attitudes. Social identity complexity may also be a central individual level variable missing in group threat theory accounts that aim to explain the absolute effects of diversity on intergroup attitudes referred to above. Specifically, Roccas and Brewer (2002) argued that group based threat should be associated with reduced social identity complexity.

In our recent studies, we found that group based threat, in the form of distinctiveness threat, was indeed associated with lower social identity complexity scores (Schmid et al., 2009a). However, in these studies we also tested the extent to which intergroup contact was associated with reduced threat, and, as a consequence, increased social identity complexity, thereby placing intergroup threat as an intermediate link in the relationship between contact and complexity, and attitudes. Our results confirmed our predictions, namely that more positive intergroup contact was associated with lower threat perceptions and higher social identity complexity, and that both threat and complexity mediated the effects of contact on ingroup bias and tolerance. This suggests that any examination of the effects of macro-level diversity on intergroup attitudes that aims to be comprehensive needs to take a more complex set of relationships into account. Specifically, any analyses should allow for a range of individual level variables, such as intergroup contact experiences, identity based threat perceptions, and of course multiple categorization processes, in particular social identity complexity.

Policy Implications

Although diversity offers opportunities for contact and holds increased potential for multiple categorization, both of which may positively influence intergroup relations, experience of diversity is not a realistic possibility for everyone. Many individuals live, work, socialise or are educated in relatively homogenous social environments, preventing them from engaging in contact with diverse others or creating awareness of the multiplicity of social categories. Moreover, institutional or residential segregation remains a pervasive feature not only of conflict-ridden societies (e.g., segregation between Israelis and Palestinians, Greek-Cypriots and Turkish-Cypriots, or Catholics and Protestants in Northern Ireland), but of many non-conflict societies (e.g., between Blacks and Whites in the US).

Aforementioned research thus has important implications for government policy aiming to implement interventions to improve intergroup relations. In educational contexts, intergroup contact interventions, e.g., in the form of twinning, are a particularly useful means of positively affecting children's attitudes towards others from different backgrounds than their own (see also Cameron & Turner, this volume). Moreover, given the powerful effects of extended contact, such interventions need not take place on a large scale. Interventions involving small numbers of students may be beneficial even on a larger scale if children are made aware of and are thus able to reap the benefits of their peers' cross-group encounters via extended contact. Contact interventions that attune children to the multiplicity of social identities and the complexity of their social world should thereby be particularly effective.

However, one also needs to keep in mind that exposure to diversity in and of itself is not always sufficient to encourage the uptake of contact, or to prompt complex and inclusive categorization and identification processes. Individuals are typically confronted with and influenced by prevailing norms of family or fellow ingroup members surrounding, for example, the desirability of intergroup friendships or the acceptability of negative intergroup behaviour. Societal norms regarding multiculturalism, as well as diverging perspectives of majority and minority members on assimilation versus integration preferences may also pose obstacles to differentiated intergroup perceptions, and may prevent positive intergroup relations (see Brewer, 2008; Hornsey & Hogg, 2000). In the absence of positive intergroup contact experiences, and under conditions that prevent differentiated, complex and inclusive multiple identity perceptions, macro-level diversity may indeed hold the risk of intergroup tensions and negative intergroup relations, as predicted by group threat theory. Often, environments that are seemingly diverse hold risks of re-segregation. Schools and classrooms may, for example, be classified as ethnically, racially or religiously diverse, yet their students may only sit with or spend time with members of their own group. It thus is imperative that policy initiatives aiming to maintain and promote positive intergroup relations, whether in educational, institutional or residential settings or at the societal level, are attuned to these risks. In such contexts, policy makers need to actively encourage positive interaction between members of different groups and positively highlight the complexity of individuals' social environments.

Conclusion

In contrast to the notion that diversity inevitably leads to intergroup tensions, social psychological approaches to prejudice reduction and attitude change allow for a much more optimistic outlook, namely that diversity holds the potential for positive intergroup relations. In this short contribution we have discussed how two key social psychological approaches, intergroup contact and multiple categorization, may enhance understanding of the nature of intergroup relations in diverse social contexts. We have argued that ethnically, racially or religiously diverse contexts and societies offer opportunities for contact with diverse others and also have the potential to encourage more differentiated multiple ingroup perceptions. We have paid particular attention to the combined effects of contact and multiple categorization on intergroup relations, since the relationship between diversity, intergroup contact and multiple categorization, and the consequences thereof, remain surprisingly under-researched in social psychological and indeed social scientific research in general. This chapter thus highlighted that multiple categorization processes may be usefully perceived as both moderators and particularly mediators (in the form of social identity complexity) of contact effects. In our opinion such a conceptualisation holds unique potential for enhancing the social psychological understanding of intergroup attitudes as well as practically informing policy initiatives aimed at improving intergroup relations in more or less diverse social environments.

Acknowledgements

We gratefully acknowledge support from the Leverhulme Trust (to Miles Hewstone, Anthony Heath, Ceri Peach, Sarah Spencer, and Steven Vertovec).

References

Allport, G. W. (1954). *The nature of prejudice*. Reading, MA: Addison-Wesley.

Berry, J. K., Kim, V., Minde, T., & Mok, D. (1987). Comparative studies of acculturative stress. *International Migration Review, 21*, 491–511.

Berry, J. W. (1997). Immigration, acculturation, and adaptation. *Applied Psychology: An International Review, 46*, 5–68.

Bettencourt, B. A., Brewer, M., Croak, R., & Miller, N. (1992). Cooperation and the reduction of intergroup bias: the role of reward structure and social orientation. *Journal of Experimental Social Psychology, 28*, 301–319.

Blalock, H. M. (1967). Percent non-white and discrimination in the south. *American Sociological Review, 22*, 677–682.

Brewer, M. (2000). Reducing prejudice through cross-categorization: Effects of multiple social identities. In S. Oskamp (Ed.), *Reducing prejudice and discrimination* (pp. 165–183). Hillsdale, NJ: Lawrence Erlbaum.

Brewer, M. (2008). Deprovincialization: Social identity complexity and out-group acceptance. In U. Wagner, C. Tredoux, G. Finchilescu, & L. Tropp (Eds.), *Improving intergroup relations* (pp. 160–176). Oxford, UK & Malden, MA: Blackwell.

Brewer, M., & Gaertner, S. L. (2001). Toward reduction of prejudice: Inter-group contact and social categorization. In R. Brown & S.L. Gaertner (Eds.), *Blackwell handbook of social psychology: Intergroup processes* (pp. 451–474). Oxford: Blackwell.

Brewer, M. B. (1993). The role of distinctiveness in social identity and group behavior. In M. Hogg & D. Abrams (Eds.), *Group motivation: Social psycho-logical perspectives* (pp. 1–16). London: Harvester Wheatsheaf.

Brewer, M. B., Ho, H.-K., Lee, J., & Miller, N. (1987). Social identity and social distance among Hong Kong school children. *Personality and Social Psychology Bulletin, 13*, 156–165.

Brewer, M. B., & Miller, N. (1984). Beyond the contact hypothesis: Theo-retical perspectives on desegregation. In N. Miller & M.B. Brewer (Eds.), *Groups in contact: The psychology of desegregation* (pp. 281–302). Orlando, FL: Academic Press.

Brewer, M. B., & Pierce, K. P. (2005). Social identity complexity and outgroup tolerance. *Personality and Social Psychology Bulletin, 31*, 428–437.

Brown, R. J., & Hewstone, M. (2005). An integrative theory of intergroup contact. In M. Zanna (Ed.), *Advances in experimental social psychology* (Vol. 37, pp. 255–331). San Diego, CA: Academic Press.

Christ, O., Hewstone, M., Tausch, N., Wagner, U., Hughes, J., & Cairns, E. (2009). The benefits and limitations of direct and indirect intergroup contact.

Crisp, R. J., & Hewstone, M. (2000). Crossed categorization and intergroup bias: The moderating role of intergroup and affective context. *Journal of Experimental Social Psychology, 36*, 357–383.

Crisp, R. J., Hewstone, M., & Cairns, E. (2001). Multiple identities in Northern Ireland: Hierarchical ordering in the representation of group membership. *British Journal of Social Psychology, 40*, 501–514.

Crisp, R. J., & Hewstone, M. (2007). Multiple social categorization. In M. Zanna (Eds.), *Advances in experimental social psychology* (Vol. 39, pp. 163–254). San Diego, CA: Academic Press.

Ensari, N., & Miller, N. (2002). The out-group must not be so bad after all: The effects of disclosure, typicality, and salience on intergroup bias. *Journal of Personality and Social Psychology, 83*, 313–329.

Gaertner, S. L., & Dovidio, J. F. (2000). *Reducing intergroup bias: The com-mon ingroup identity model.* Philadelphia, PA: Psychology Press/Taylor & Francis.

Gaertner, S. L., Dovidio, J. F., Anastasio, P. A., Bachman, B. A., & Rust, M. C. (1993). The common ingroup identity model: Recategorization and the reduction of intergroup bias. In W. Stroebe & M. Hewstone (Eds.), *European review of social psychology* (Vol. 4, pp. 1–26). Chichester, UK: Wiley.

Gaertner, S. L., Dovidio, J. F., & Bachman, B. A. (1996). Revisiting the contact hypothesis: the induction of a common ingroup identity. *International Journal of Intercultural Relations*, *20*, 271–290.

González, R., & Brown, R. (2006). Dual identities in intergroup contact: Group status and size moderate the generalization of positive attitude change. *Journal of Experimental Social Psychology*, *42*, 753–767.

Hewstone, M. (2009). Living apart, living together? The role of intergroup contact in social integration. *Proceedings of the British Academy*, *162*, 243–300.

Hewstone, M., & Brown, R. (1986). Contact is not enough: An intergroup perspective on the "contact hypothesis". In M. Hewstone & R. Brown (Eds.), *Contact and conflict in intergroup encounters* (pp. 1–44). Oxford: Blackwell.

Hewstone, M., Rubin, M., & Willis, H. (2002). Intergroup bias. *Annual Review of Psychology*, *53*, 575–604.

Hornsey, M. J., & Hogg, M. A. (2000). Assimilation and diversity: An integrative model of subgroup relations. *Personality and Social Psychology Review*, *4*, 143–156.

Huo, Y. J., Smith, H. J., Tyler, T. R., & Lind, E. A. (1996). Superordinate identification, subgroup identification and social justice concerns: Is separatism the problem; is assimilation the answer? *Psychological Science*, *7*, 40–45.

Islam, M. R., & Hewstone, M. (1993). Dimensions of contact as predictors of intergroup anxiety, perceived out-group variability, and out-group attitudes: An integrative model. *Personality and Social Psychology Bulletin*, *19*, 700–710.

Miller, D. A., Smith, E. R., & Mackie, D. M. (2004). Effects of intergroup contact and political predispositions on prejudice: Role of intergroup emotions. *Group Processes and Intergroup Relations*, *7*, 221–237.

Miller, K. P., Brewer, M., & Arbuckle, N. L. (2009). Social identity complexity: Its correlates and antecedents. *Group Processes and Intergroup Relations*, *12*, 79–94.

Murphy, R. F. (1957). Intergroup hostility and social cohesion. *American Anthropologist*, *59*, 1018–1035.

Paolini, S., Hewstone, M., Cairns, E., & Voci, A. (2004). Effects of direct and indirect cross-group friendships on judgments of Catholics and Protestants in Northern Ireland: The mediating role of an anxiety-reduction mechanism. *Personality and Social Psychology Bulletin*, *30*, 770–786.

Pettigrew, T. F. (1997). Generalized intergroup contact effects on prejudice. *Personality and Social Psychology Bulletin*, *23*, 173–185.

Pettigrew, T. F. (1998). Intergroup contact theory. *Annual Review of Psychology*, *49*, 65–85.

Pettigrew, T. F. (2009). Secondary transfer effects of contact: Do intergroup contact effects spread to noncontacted outgroups?. *Social Psychology*, *40*, 55–65.

Pettigrew, T. F., & Tropp, L. T. (2006). A meta-analytic test of intergroup contact theory. *Journal of Personality and Social Psychology, 90,* 751–783.

Putnam, R. (2007). E Pluribus unum: Diversity and community in the twenty-first century. The 2006 Jonathan Skytte prize lecture. *Scandinavian Political Studies, 30,* 137–174.

Quillian, L. (1996). Group threat and regional change in attitudes toward African Americans. *American Journal of Sociology, 102,* 816–860.

Roccas, S., & Brewer, M. B. (2002). Social identity complexity. *Personality and Social Psychology Review, 6,* 88–106.

Schiappa, E., Gregg, P. B., & Hewes, D. E. (2005). The parasocial contact hypothesis. *Communication Monographs, 72,* 92–115.

Schmid, K., Hewstone, M., Tausch, N., Cairns, E., & Hughes, J. (2009a). Antecedents and consequences of social identity complexity: Intergroup contact, distinctiveness threat and outgroup attitudes. *Personality and Social Psychology Bulletin, 35,* 1085–1098.

Schmid, K., Hewstone, M., Tausch, N., Cairns, E., & Hughes, J. (2009b). Mediators of generalized contact effects to non-target outgroups: Social identity complexity or generalized attitude effects?

Schmid, K., Hewstone, M., Tausch, N., Jenkins, R., Hughes, J., & Cairns, E. (in press). Identities, groups and communities: The case of Northern Ireland. To appear in M. Wetherell & C.T. Mohanty (Eds.), *The Sage handbook of identities.* London: Sage.

Schmid, K., Tausch, N., Hewstone, M., Cairns, E. and Hughes, J. (2008). The effects of living in segregated vs. mixed areas in Northern Ireland: A simultaneous analysis of contact and threat effects in the context of micro-level neighbourhoods. *International Journal of Conflict and Violence, 2,* 56–71.

Simon, B., Aufderheide, B., & Kampmeier, C. (2001). The social psychology of minority-majority relations. In R. Brown & S. Gaertner (Eds.), *Blackwell handbook of social psychology: Intergroup processes* (pp. 303–323). Oxford: Blackwell.

Stephan, W. G., & Stephan, C. W. (2000). An integrated threat theory of prejudice. In S. Oskamp (Ed.), *Reducing prejudice and discrimination* (pp. 23–46). Hillsdale, NJ: Lawrence Erlbaum.

Schlueter, E., Schmidt, P., & Wagner, U. (2008). Disentangling the causal relations of perceived group threat and outgroup derogation: Cross-national evidence from German and Russian panels. *European Sociological Review, 24,* 567–581.

Tajfel, H., & Turner, J. C. (1979). An integrative theory of intergroup conflict. In W. G. Austin & S. Worchel (Eds.), *The psychology of intergroup relations* (pp. 33–48). Monterey, CA: Brooks/Cole.

Tausch, N., Hewstone, M., Kenworthy, J., Cairns, E., & Christ, O. (2007). Cross-community contact, perceived status differences and intergroup attitudes in Northern Ireland: The mediating roles of individual-level vs.

group level threats and the moderating role of social identification. *Political Psychology*, *28*, 53–68.

Tausch, N., Hewstone, M., Kenworthy, J., Psaltis, C., Schmid, K., Popan, J., Cairns, E., Hughes, J. (2009). Generalized effects of intergroup contact on attitudes towards uninvolved outgroups: Attitude generalization or ingroup reappraisal?

Tausch, N., Hewstone, M., Schmid, K., Christ, O., Cairns, E., & Hughes, J. (2009). Extended contact effects: A longitudinal investigation.

Turner, J. C., Hogg, M. A., Oakes, P. J., Reicher, S. D., & Wetherell, M. S. (1987). *Rediscovering the social group: A self-categorization theory.* Cambridge, MA: Blackwell.

Turner, R. N., Crisp, R. J., & Lambert, E. (2007). Imagining intergroup contact can improve intergroup attitudes. *Group Processes and Intergroup Relations*, *10*, 427–441.

Turner, R. N., Hewstone, M., Voci, A., Paolini, S., & Christ, O. (2008). Reducing prejudice via direct and extended cross-group friendship. In W. Stroebe & M. Hewstone (Eds.), *European Review of Social Psychology* (Vol. 18, pp. 212–255). Hove, UK: Psychology Press.

Voci, A., & Hewstone, M. (2003). Intergroup contact and prejudice toward immigrants in Italy: The mediational role of anxiety and the moderational role of group salience. *Group Processes and Intergroup Relations*, *6*, 37–54.

Wagner, U., Christ, O., Pettigrew, T. F., Stellmacher, J., & Wolf, C. (2006). Prejudice and minority proportion: Contact instead of threat effects. *Social Psychology Quarterly*, *69*, 380–390.

Wagner, U., Hewstone, M., & Machleit, U. (1989). Contact and prejudice between Germans and Turks: A correlational study. *Human Relations*, *42*, 561–74.

Wenzel, M., Mummendey, A., Weber, U., & Waldzus, S. (2003). The ingroup as pars pro toto: Projection from the ingroup onto the inclusive category as a precursor to social discrimination. *Personality and Social Psychology Bulletin*, *29*, 461–473.

Williams, R. M., Jr. (1947). *The reduction of intergroup tensions.* New York: Social Science Research Council.

Wright, S. C., Aron, A., McLaughlin-Volpe, T., & Ropp, S. A. (1997). The extended contact effect: Knowledge of cross-group friendships and prejudice. *Journal of Personality and Social Psychology*, *73*, 73–90.

14

The Application of Diversity-based Interventions to Policy and Practice

Lindsey Cameron and Rhiannon N. Turner

The pursuit of positive intergroup relations has captured the attention and imagination of educators, policy-makers, and academics. This challenge has inspired extensive psychological research in the area, and has also led to the development and implementation of diversity-based interventions to promote positive relations between members of different communities. These interventions have been developed primarily by educators and policy makers. They are typically highly practical and well suited to the school or organization context, and are often based on practitioners' intuition, knowledge, and experience in applied settings. The goal of such interventions is often to increase knowledge of other cultures, challenge stereotypes and myths, and instill in participants an appreciation of diversity. Psychologists have typically focused on developing psychological theories concerning factors that contribute to prejudice in adults and children, and have rarely tested theoretical predictions in the field in the form of prejudice-reduction interventions (Oskamp, 2000). However, in recent years academics too have developed theoretically based prejudice-reduction interventions that are derived from the concept of diversity, and aim to induce social psychological processes associated with more positive intergroup relations. In this chapter we will argue that practitioners and academics have much to learn from one another, and closer collaboration will allow both groups to capitalize on each other's strengths. We believe such a partnership is essential in order to develop prejudice-reduction interventions and strategies that are both effective *and* practical.

This chapter will evaluate the effectiveness of diversity-based interventions in generating positive intergroup attitudes and increasing appreciation for diversity. We begin by explaining why diversity-based interventions are so important. We will then outline and critically evaluate four types of interventions designed by educators: multicultural education, anti-racism education, diversity training, and dual language schooling. Three interventions, developed by psychologists, and based explicitly on social psychological theory and research on prejudice and prejudice reduction, will also be outlined and critically evaluated: multiple classification training, intergroup contact, and indirect contact. The strengths and limitations of both academics' and practitioners' approaches to the development of diversity based interventions will be outlined. Techniques developed by practitioners are highly practical, but psychological theories and findings are rarely incorporated and the impact on intergroup relations or attitudes is rarely evaluated in a systematic way. Meanwhile, academics rarely translate psychological theories into interventions, and those interventions that are developed are often impractical and unsustainable. The mutual benefits of closer collaboration between practitioners and academics will then be explored and some recommendations will be made for how closer collaboration between practitioners and academics could be brought about.

Why Are Diversity-Based Interventions Important?

Experience of diversity has a broad range of benefits. Research has, for example, shown that attending an ethnically diverse school is associated with more positive intergroup attitudes from 3 years of age to adolescence (e.g., Aboud, Mendelson, & Purdy, 2003; Feddes, Noack, & Rutland, 2009; Jackson, Barth, Powell, & Lochman, 2006; Rutland, Cameron, Bennett, & Ferrell, 2005; Tropp & Prenovost, 2008; Wagner, van Dick, Pettigrew, & Christ, 2003). Children in settings with high ethnic diversity are less likely to exhibit ingroup bias (Rutland et al., 2005; Feddes et al., 2009), more likely to nominate outgroup peers as close friends (Jackson et al., 2006), more likely to interpret outgroup members' behavior positively and be more inclusive in their friendships (McGlothlin & Killen, 2005). Among adults, there is also evidence that thinking about the diverse groups that people belong to can promote greater intergroup tolerance (see Crisp & Hewstone, 2007, for a review). In sum, experience of diversity is associated with numerous benefits for intergroup relations, so it is perhaps unsurprising that diversity-focused interventions have been developed to promote more tolerant outgroup attitudes. We begin below by discussing interventions developed by educators before considering the contributions made in this domain by academics. In doing so, we will demonstrate their respective strengths and weaknesses, highlighting the potential benefit of integrating these two approaches.

Interventions Developed by Educators

Interventions developed by educators try to increase appreciation for diversity and encourage tolerance toward members of diverse social groups. In non-diverse settings, these interventions allow individuals to learn about diversity and thereby experience the same benefits as people in more diverse settings, in terms of knowledge of other groups, appreciation of diversity, and intergroup tolerance. But even where the opportunities to experience diversity are present, individuals do not always take full advantage of them. Diversity-based interventions can help individuals to overcome this, by maximizing the impact of living in a diverse community on positive outcomes for intergroup relations. We will consider four types of intervention developed by educators: multicultural education, anti-racism education, diversity training, and dual language schooling.

Multicultural and Anti-racism Education   Multicultural education programs and anti-racism education will be considered together, as the techniques have similar strengths and weaknesses. Furthermore, in practice there is often overlap between the two approaches: multicultural education programs often incorporate anti-racism techniques. Multicultural curricula programs involve teaching children about the culture and lifestyle of minority groups. This perspective is based on two key assumptions: that prejudice is caused by ignorance, so teaching children about the outgroup should reduce prejudice (see Bigler, 1999) and that children tend to tailor their public behavior, if not their private thoughts (Gavin & Furman, 1989), to fit acceptable norms. If multicultural materials can be used to establish a norm of tolerance and respect toward an outgroup, through a process of cognitive dissonance (Festinger, 1957), attitudes should eventually fall in line with behavior, leading to better intergroup relations. Some multicultural programs simply present information about the outgroup to participants in order to reduce ignorance (Hill & Augoustinos, 2001), while others explicitly provide counter-stereotypic information about the outgroup (e.g., Litcher & Johnson, 1969).

These interventions use a variety of different media sources, including books, videos, games, and activities. Some interventions involve slight changes to the curriculum, for instance the use of stories featuring outgroup members (Bigler, 1999; see Litcher & Johnson, 1969). Others adopt a more transformative approach to prejudice-reduction (Banks, 1995), involving extensive changes to the curriculum (Bigler, 1999). Transformative interventions tend to be more intensive and structured, and use a number of media and activities such as art, games, and drama to tackle different aspects of prejudice (e.g. Salzman & D'Andrea, 2001; see Bigler, 1999 for review). Others have recommended that multicultural education should follow a 'whole school' approach, whereby the entire school adopts a multicultural ethos, and multiculturalism is evident in all aspects of school life, for instance in wall displays, games, and all lessons including geography and social studies as well as other subjects such as maths and domestic science (Knowles & Ridley, 2006).

Several studies have evaluated multicultural education, with some finding evidence for a positive impact. Salzman & D'Andrea (2001) examined a multicultural prejudice-reduction intervention program that was administered to a fourth-grade class in Hawaii, and consisted of weekly sessions designed specifically to address the issue of multicultural awareness. Classes were held once a week for 10 weeks, and incorporated several activities, some based on psychological concepts associated with prejudice-reduction and others on the intuition of the program designers. A number of activities aimed to encourage children to identify their own and others' cultural and ethnic group and highlighted the differences and similarities between different cultures (e.g. 'Multicultural Bingo' and the 'Hands Activity'). One session employed the Blue-eyes/Brown-eyes approach (e.g., Weiner & Wright, 1973), which allows children to experience at first hand the emotions that occur as a consequence of discrimination and prejudice. Children were also introduced to the concepts of "prejudice" and "stereotyping," and were invited to examine their own prejudice and bias. Teachers observed a significant improvement in children's cooperative social skills, compared to a control group that did not receive the intervention. Cole et al. (2003) evaluated an intervention in which Israeli and Palestinian children watched a TV series, *Rechov-Sumsum/Shara'a Simsim*, which presented messages of mutual respect and understanding. This led to more positive attitudes toward the relevant outgroup.

Findings regarding the benefits of multicultural education interventions are, however, mixed. A number of researchers have shown that multicultural interventions are ineffective and may even have a detrimental effect on intergroup attitudes (see Aboud & Levy, 2000 for review; Katz & Zalk, 1978). Koeller (1977), for instance, found that reading 11–year-olds stories about Mexican Americans did not lead to more positive racial attitudes. Moreover, some reviews of the literature have been rather pessimistic about the benefits of multicultural education (Bigler, 1999; Williams & Morland, 1976), while others have concluded that multicultural interventions can change intergroup attitudes and behavior: In their meta-analysis, Stephan, Renfro, and Stephan (2004) concluded that multicultural interventions improved intergroup attitudes and behaviors, although the effect sizes were not as strong as expected.

The contradictory findings regarding the impact of multicultural interventions may reflect a problem with the basic premise on which multicultural teaching is based: the idea that children are *passive* recipients of information (Bigler, 1999). Children are in fact thought to actively construct schemas, based on their own observations, which they then use to understand and interpret their social world (Piaget, 1970). When children are presented with attitude-incongruent information which challenges an existing schema they have a tendency to forget, distort, or ignore that information, leaving the original attitude intact (Bigler & Liben, 1993; Neuberg, 1996; Rothbart & John, 1985). Bigler and Liben demonstrated how children's memory for multicultural materials depends on their cognitive ability. Children were presented stories that featured an African American and Euro-American child. Embedded in these stories were either counter-stereotypic or stereotypic information. Children with more advanced cognitive abilities had better memory for counter-stereotypic information, whereas children with less advanced cognitive abilities mis-remembered the counter-stereotypic information (Bigler & Liben, 1993). This has implications for the development of multicultural materials: children may not remember the counter-stereotypic information presented, and instead focus on differences between the ingroup and outgroup rather than what they share in common. This may therefore contribute to a stereotyped knowledge of a group rather than counteracting it (Bigler, 1999).

A related approach, anti-racism education, involves encouraging children to discuss racism and teaching them to recognise and confront racism and discrimination, for example the "Teaching Tolerance" program (see Aboud & Levy, 2000 for review; Derman-Sparks & Phillips, 1997; Hughes, Bigler, & Levy, 2007). Programs are typically more interactive than multicultural education, involving group discussion and role-play to explore the concepts of prejudice, discrimination, and tolerance (Spencer, 1998). When an individual is forced to face up to their prejudiced attitudes and behavior, the subsequent guilt they feel is likely to result in increased vigilance in the presence of outgroup members, and therefore more positive behavior toward them (Devine, Monteith, Zuwernick, & Elliot, 1991).

Slavin and Madden (1979) found that while the racial attitudes and degree of reported cross-racial friendships among White American teenagers were not significantly affected by multicultural education, they were significantly improved by discussions about race. Aboud and Fenwick (1999) found that highly prejudiced elementary school children who discussed their intergroup attitudes with an unprejudiced friend subsequently showed lower levels of prejudice. In addition, a review of anti-racist teaching programs revealed a moderately positive effect of such programs on outgroup attitudes (McGregor, 1993). Research with young adults also suggests that alerting individuals to the need for improved interracial relations and increased harmony between racial groups leads to a reduction in ingroup favoritism (Wolsko, Park, Judd, & Wittenbrink, 2000).

But despite these findings, there is inadequate research into the effects of anti-racist programs, a fact that is concerning in light of the frequency with which they are used (Aboud & Levy, 2000). Anti-racist programs also have the potential to increase rather than decrease prejudice because insight into the prejudiced attitudes of the ingroup may arouse feelings of self-righteousness rather than guilt, resulting in anger directed toward the target ethnic group (Glasberg & Aboud, 1981; McGregor, 1993). Furthermore, the effect of anti-racism interventions may be limited to majority groups or groups with high societal status. Hughes et al. (2007) found that learning about historical racism did not affect intergroup attitudes of African American children.

An additional concern when considering delivery of both anti-racism and multicultural education is the provision of adequate teacher training. A recent British report illustrated that teachers lack confidence and training in order to deal with diversity issues in the classroom (Department for Education and Skills, 2007). In their review, Stephan and colleagues also highlighted the importance of teacher training, confidence and preparation for the success of multicultural education programs in changing intergroup attitudes and behaviors (Stephan et al., 2004). Meanwhile there is evidence that the process of learning to teach children about multicultural issues can change teachers' preconceptions about ethnic groups other than their own (Cameron, 2009). Further research is required in order to explore the effect of teaching multicultural and anti-racism lessons on teachers' own attitudes.

Diversity Training   Diversity training refers to programs run by organizations for employees which aim to increase cultural awareness, knowledge, and skills. Their ultimate goal is to protect the organization against civil rights violations, increase the inclusion of different groups at work, and to promote better teamwork and better performance. The use of these programs is now highly popular, with an estimated $8 billion dollars spent on corporate diversity training in the United States alone (Paluck & Green, 2009).

Gurin, Peng, Lopez, and Nagda (1999) evaluated a social justice educational program which focused on dialogue and hands-on experience with outgroup members. Participants completed a pre-test, and on the basis of this were matched up to a control group with similar demographic characteristics. Four years later, students who had taken part in the scheme were more likely than control students to perceive commonalities in interests and values with a variety of other groups. Hanover and Cellar (1998) evaluated white managers in the human resources department of a company who took part in diversity training which involved watching videos, and taking part in role-plays and discussions about diversity. Participants were subsequently more likely to rate diversity practices as important and to report that they discourage prejudiced comments among employees, when compared to control managers who had not yet taken part in diversity training. However, only self-report measures were taken, and it may be the case that success was exaggerated in order to ensure positive evaluation by their bosses.

Other studies show that diversity training can lead to an *increase* in prejudice. Business students who were instructed via diversity training videos to suppress negative thoughts about the elderly subsequently evaluated older job candidates less favorably (Kulik, Perry, & Bourhis, 2000). This is in line with social psychological research which shows that suppressing a thought can lead to an ironic increase in the accessibility of that thought in our mind, as we try to monitor our mind to ensure that it does not appear (Macrae, Bodenhausen, & Milne, 1995). Another concern is that many of the studies used to evaluate training are methodologically flawed (Paluck & Green, 2009). First, many involve participants who have volunteered to take part and are thus more likely to have positive outgroup attitudes to begin with. Moreover, the control conditions used are often inadequate. Ellis and Sonnenfield (1994), for example, reported that participants who had volunteered to take part in a seminar on 'valuing diversity' were more culturally tolerant than participants who had chosen not to attend the seminar. Such methodological problems make it difficult to be fully confident about the effects of such programs.

Bilingual Schooling One type of bilingual education, 'immersion', aims to change the intergroup attitudes of members of the ethno-linguistic majority, for example English-speaking Canadians, in non-diverse contexts where they have little opportunity for direct contact with the ethno-linguistic minority (e.g., French-speaking Canadians). Staying with the French-Canadian example, children are taught in the minority language, French, and are taught using French materials and are immersed in French-Canadian culture, but they do not have any direct contact with members of the linguistic outgroup (French-speaking Canadians). Research has shown that immersion students are more positive toward French Canadians, see English-Canadians and French-Canadians as more similar and see *themselves* as more similar to French-Canadians than non-immersion students do (Genesee & Gandara, 1999). This could be due to increased experience of French Canadian culture through school materials, or as a consequence of a shared identity with French-Canadians (Genesee & Gandara, 1999).

More recently, Wright and Tropp (2005) investigated the effect of English—Spanish bilingual instruction on outgroup attitude among children with varying degrees of opportunity to interact with the ethnic out-group. They found that European American children in ethnically mixed schools who received bilingual education were more positive toward Latino children than those in English only ethnically mixed schools, and non-mixed schools. That is, bilingual education had a beneficial effect over and above exposure to diversity in school. Wright and Tropp argue that bilingual education promotes respect for the outgroup because it signals the value and status of the minority language: both groups are given equal status and value through use of both languages in the classroom.

Strength and Limitations of Educator-Designed Interventions

Educator-designed interventions have three main advantages. Firstly, educator-designed interventions can be administered in non-diverse and diverse contexts, where real-life experience of other groups is likely to differ. In non-diverse settings, interventions may prepare people for diversity, and ensure that when they do meet people from diverse social groups, they behave positively. In diverse contexts, these interventions have the potential to improve existing intergroup relations: increased awareness of prejudice and stereotyping could cause individuals to be more vigilant in their own behaviors to ensure they are not being discriminatory. In both diverse and non-diverse settings, the resultant positive attitudes toward diversity and other groups, and reduced stereotyping could facilitate future friendship behavior toward members of other groups (Genesee & Gandara, 1999). Importantly, these interventions do not rely on the presence of outgroup members, and so they are both practical and flexible.

Secondly, interventions developed by educators and practitioners are usually highly practical and user-friendly. Practitioners are usually more experienced at working in the field and consequently they are more likely to know what types of interventions are practical and would be used by fellow education professionals. Furthermore, they are likely to know whether intervention techniques will engage the audience (e.g. young children).

Finally, educator-designed interventions are often more responsive to changes in intergroup relations in particular communities. Educators and practitioners are arguably more aware of the changing challenges and social issues that are affecting the communities they work in. For instance, teachers and educators with an 'ear to the ground' are more aware of the particular intergroup conflicts evident in their communities and schools: they know the social groups who are most likely to be stereotyped and stigmatized. This information is particularly useful in communities where the changing patterns of immigration mean different intergroup conflicts arise from year to year. Practitioners and educators can use this knowledge to create interventions that tackle prejudice and dispel myths that are actually found on the street and in the playground. In this way, interventions created by practitioners and educators can be responsive to changes in society, and therefore more useful in tackling negative intergroup attitudes as they emerge.

Unfortunately, interventions designed by practitioners and educators also have limitations, the main one being lack of rigorous, systematic evaluation (Connolly, 2009). According to Paluck & Green (2009) it is essential that interventions are reliably evaluated so that we understand *whether* an intervention has the desired impact, *when* prejudice reduction interventions work, *why* they have an effect and *with whom* they have the biggest impact. Therefore it is essential that the proper conditions and controls are put in place in order to evaluate interventions reliably. One characteristic of educator-developed interventions is that they are often additive in nature, utilizing a diverse range of methods and tasks within one intervention (Banks, 1995; Duckitt, 1992; Salzman & D'Andrea, 2001). This makes it difficult to isolate the effect of each technique used (Hill & Augoustinos, 2001). In addition, there are frequently inadequate control conditions, no pre-test measure of attitude, and no validated measures of intergroup attitudes (Bigler, 1999).

In order to reliably evaluate an intervention, the intervention evaluation must have four characteristics. First, randomised controlled experimental designs should be employed, whereby participants are randomly assigned to either the intervention or control condition, with participants receiving no intervention training in the control condition (Paluck & Green, 2009). This allows for more reliable conclusions to be drawn from the findings. Second, while additive interventions are recommended *after* the effect of the individual components of the intervention program have been determined, when intervention techniques are initially developed, it is necessary to avoid multiple techniques within one intervention.

Third, evaluations should identify the underlying mechanisms that drive the effects of the intervention: for example, does the intervention work by increasing empathy or reducing anxiety toward other groups? This information can then be used to inform the development of future prejudice-reduction interventions. Fourth, in order to accurately gauge the impact of interventions such as multicultural education programs, evaluations must include suitable, reliable and pre-tested outcome indicators that encompass the different components of the intervention and the expected outcomes (Stephan et al., 2004). Indeed, it is these methodological weaknesses in intervention evaluations that could account for the mixed findings in previous research, for instance in multicultural education programs (Bigler, 1999; Stephan et al., 2004).

Importantly, academics and researchers have expertise in methodological design and statistical analysis that can help to develop reliable and rigorous evaluations that can incorporate the above requirements and allow reliable conclusions to be drawn regarding the impact of interventions on intergroup attitudes. Closer collaboration between psychologists and educators is essential and could improve intervention design and assessment so that more reliable conclusions can be drawn.

Interventions Based on Psychological Theories and Principles

Academics' main focus has been on the development of theories concerning prejudice and its reduction, which are often based on laboratory experiments. In terms of developing effective interventions, diversity-based interventions that are derived from psychological theories and research have two clear strengths. First, the techniques are subject to rigorous psychological evaluation and careful manipulation in order to reliably evaluate their effect on intergroup attitudes. It is therefore possible to accurately ascertain the extent of their impact on intergroup attitudes and behaviors. This also allows researchers to understand how the intervention works and with whom it is most effective. This information is essential for tailoring interventions to suit particular groups of people, for example the young, minority groups, and groups with high social status. Second, psychological interventions are evidence-based, rather than relying on intuition and experience. Social and developmental psychologists have shown that flexible thinking (Bigler & Liben, 1992), positive intergroup contact (Allport, 1954; Pettigrew & Tropp, 2006), low levels of intergroup anxiety (Stephan & Stephan, 1985), intergroup empathy (Batson et al., 1997), and intergroup trust (Turner, Hewstone, & Voci, 2007b) are all associated with positive outcomes for intergroup relations. Interventions developed by academics attempt to induce these processes. Below we review three types of intervention that have recently been developed and tested by academics: multiple classification training, intergroup contact and indirect contact.

Multiple Classification Training

A social-cognitive ability that has been linked to reduced prejudice is multiple classification skill (Bigler & Liben, 1992; Aboud, 1988; Bigler, 1995; Bigler, Jones, & Lobliner, 1997). This is the ability to attend to more than one dimension of an object and classify it along multiple categories simultaneously. Up to around the age of 3, children are able to sort objects along one dimension only, but as they get older they develop the ability to classify objects, including people, along multiple dimensions (Piaget, 1965). So for instance older, but not younger, children understand that people can belong to two or more social categories simultaneously and sometimes these categories will not match traditional stereotypes, for example a woman who is also an engineer (Bigler & Liben, 1992). Research with adults has also shown that individuals with greater experience of diversity think in a more flexible way. Compared to monocultural individuals, bicultural individuals who have experience of two different cultures simultaneously have higher 'integrative complexity', an enhanced capacity to construe people, objects, and ideas in a multidimensional way (e.g., Tadmor & Tetlock, 2006). Similarly, bicultural individuals are more 'perspectivist' than monoculturals when analyzing the behavior of others: they are more likely to explain behaviors by identifying the interacting role of environmental, constitutional, and psychological influences rather than identifying a singular cause (e.g., environmental factors). This research suggests that exposure to diversity can lead to more flexible thinking (see Nguyen & Benet-Martínez, this volume; Tadmor, Hong, Chiu, & No, this volume).

Bigler and colleagues developed an intervention to increase perceptions of diversity among primary school children, known as 'multiple classification skills training'. The intervention attempts to accelerate children's ability to engage in multiple classification (e.g., Bigler & Liben, 1992; see Pfeifer, Brown, & Juvonen, 2007, for a review) and involves training children to classify stimuli along more than one dimension simultaneously. Bigler and Liben (1992) found that following a multiple classification intervention, in which 5 to 10 year old children were trained to classify objects and people along multiple cross-cutting dimensions (i.e., classify men and women according to gender and occupation), children were less likely to stereotype, or generalize across, the outgroup. The effect of multiple classification training on stereotypes has been replicated in a number of studies (Bigler, 1995; Bigler, Jones, & Lobliner, 1997). Accelerated multiple classification training may also lead to fast development of complex social identities (Brewer, this volume; Amiot & de la Sablonnière, this volume).

Research among adults has also shown that getting people to think about others along multiple dimensions can reduce intergroup bias. Crisp, Hewstone, and Rubin (2001) asked Cardiff University students to think about outgroup members (Bristol University students).

Participants were asked to think about five other ways that Bristol University students could be classified (for example, according to age, subject of study, gender). It emerged that compared to a baseline condition, in which participants simply thought about the outgroup, participants showed less intergroup bias, less of a preference for Cardiff students over Bristol students intergroup bias. They were also less likely to see Bristol students as one group, and more likely to see them as individuals, suggesting that such an intervention should break down stereotypes (see also Hall & Crisp, 2005; Miller et al., this volume).

Crisp and Hewstone (2007) argue that this effect can be explained by decategorization. When participants are required to use multiple group criteria to form an impression of another person, the increase in task complexity prompts a shift in focus away from using categories to the adoption of a more systematic processing style, consistent with the processes outlined by Fiske & Neuberg's (1990) continuum model. This process is associated with a reduction in intergroup bias (because categories become less salient as guides to impression formation). It is important to note that these are lab-based studies rather than applied interventions. They do, however, demonstrate the potential benefits of encouraging diversity among adults.

Intergroup Contact

One of the most influential social psychological theories of prejudice and intergroup relations is Allport's intergroup contact hypothesis (Allport, 1954). According to this theory, interactions between members of different groups will produce more harmonious intergroup relations, provided that those interactions are characterized by equal status, cooperation in order to achieve common goals, and institutional support. Thus living in a diverse community with high opportunity to interact with members of other groups is likely to lead to more positive intergroup relations and attitudes (see Schmid & Hewstone, this volume). The intergroup contact effect is highly robust amongst both children and adults (Pettigrew & Tropp, 2006; Tropp & Prenovost, 2008). Diversity-based interventions involving contact have taken various forms, including integrated schooling (Tropp & Prenovost, 2008; Wright & Tropp, 2005; Maras & Brown, 1996, 2000), and two forms of types of indirect or 'vicarious' contact: extended contact (Wright, Aron, McLaughlin-Volpe, & Ropp, 1997), and imagined contact (Crisp & Turner, 2009; Turner, Crisp, & Lambert, 2007a).

Generating Cross-Group Friendship Through Integrated Schooling

While academics themselves did not conceive of and implement 'integrated schooling', psychological research has highlighted the impact of integrated schooling on intergroup attitudes, the mechanisms by which this diversity-based intervention operates and the type of direct contact interventions that is most successful. In this way, psychological research on direct contact informs the *content* of future direct contact interventions.

Research over the past decade has shown that one particularly effective form of intergroup contact is cross-group friendship (Levin, van Laar, & Sidanius, 2003; Pettigrew, 1998; Turner, Hewstone, Voci, Paolini, & Christ, 2007c). Pettigrew (1997) found friendship with members of minority groups to result not only in reduced blatant and subtle prejudice toward those groups, but also in more liberal attitudes to immigration policy and more positive attitudes toward a variety of other minority groups. The effects of co-worker and neighborhood contact were considerably weaker. Moreover, Pettigrew and Tropp's (2006) meta-analysis compared studies looking at the effect of cross-group friendship to those looking at other types of contact (e.g., acquaintance and workplace contact). They found that cross-group friendships yielded a substantially stronger effect in reducing prejudice than other types of contact. Cross-group friendship has also been shown to predict more positive outgroup attitudes amongst young people, from 6 years to adolescence, and in multiple contexts (e.g. Aboud et al., 2003; Jackson et al., 2006; Wagner et al., 2003; Turner et al., 2007c; Turner, Hewstone, Voci, & Vonofakou, 2008).

Previous research on intergroup contact has shown that higher quality contact, contact that is comfortable and pleasant, is associated with more positive outgroup attitudes (Voci & Hewstone, 2003). As cross-group friendship implies contact of a high quality, it is perhaps not surprising that friendship is particularly effective at reducing prejudice. Thus, the potential for friendship has been added to Allport's (1954) key facilitating conditions in recent reformulations of the contact hypothesis (Pettigrew, 1998). Friendships that cross group boundaries may be instrumental in explaining the benefits of attending an ethnically diverse school. Children in diverse schools tend to be more inclusive in their friendships and are more likely to believe that intergroup friendships are likely (McGlothlin & Killen, 2005; Rutland et al., 2005).

Two of the processes underlying the positive effect of cross-group friendship have been identified as reduced intergroup anxiety and self-disclosure. *Intergroup anxiety* is the negative emotional arousal that can characterize intergroup encounters (Stephan & Stephan, 1985). It can arise as a consequence of expectations of rejection or discrimination during cross-group interactions, or fears that the interaction partner, or the respondents themselves, may behave in an incompetent or offensive manner. When individuals have had a successful interaction with an outgroup member, however, their level of intergroup anxiety is reduced, as they come to realize they have nothing to fear from the outgroup. Accordingly, research has shown that intergroup contact, especially friendship, improves intergroup attitudes by reducing intergroup anxiety (Paolini, Hewstone, Cairns & Voci, 2004; Turner et al., 2007c). *Self-disclosure*, the sharing of personal information with another person, is also an important process in cross-group friendships. Children and adults with outgroup friends engage in more mutual self-disclosure with outgroup members. This generates intergroup empathy and trust, which in turn are associated with more positive outgroup attitudes (Turner et al., 2007c).

While exposure to diversity through schooling can improve intergroup attitudes, the development of cross-group friendships in this setting may be particularly important in encouraging intergroup tolerance. But unfortunately, although children in diverse settings have the *opportunity* to form cross-group friendships, these opportunities are not always pursued. Specifically, research has shown that children's friendship groups often do not reflect the ethnic make-up of the school: cross-race friendships have been shown to be relatively uncommon (Aboud & Sankar, 2007), are less durable, and decline with age (Aboud et al., 2003). For instance, Graham & Cohen (1997) found that, in a setting in which half the children enrolled in the school were African American, older African American children (approximately 12 years) were significantly more likely to form same-race and less likely to form cross-race friendships, than younger African American children. Thus, as children get older, they are more likely to 'self-segregate' and have more same-group friends than cross-group friends. It is therefore essential that children are not only exposed to diversity, but are also encouraged to *take up* opportunities to form cross-group friendships in these diverse settings. Below we identify some of the barriers and promoters of cross-group friendship, before discussing other contact-based interventions—cooperative learning, extended contact and imagined contact—which may help to encourage the development of cross-group friendship. The potential barriers and promoters we will discuss are (i) *opportunity to interact in multiple contexts*, (ii) *intergroup anxiety*,

(iii) *perceived ingroup norms,* (iv) *perceived outgroup norms,* and (v) *shared identities.*

Opportunity to interact in multiple contexts: An important require-ment for the development of cross-group friendships is opportunity to interact with that potential friend in multiple contexts. Aboud & Sankar (2007) examined the qualities of friendships amongst children and found that most children spent less time playing alone with out-group friends than with ingroup friends. Moreover, when they did spend time with outgroup friends, play tended to occur only in the school playground. In order to encourage cross-group friendships, con-tact interventions must therefore provide children with the opportunity to engage in multiple activities with outgroup peers, and in multiple settings, for example sports clubs, youth groups, and at home.

Intergroup anxiety: When levels of intergroup anxiety are very high, people tend to avoid intergroup contact. There is evidence that white participants who have negative expectations about interacting with black people avoid encounters with them (Plant & Devine, 2003), while people often explain their failure to initiate intergroup contact in terms of their fear of being rejected by outgroup members (Shelton & Richeson, 2005). Intergroup anxiety is therefore a barrier that must be overcome if cross-group friendships are to develop. Two potential sources of anxiety arise from the norms we perceive ingroup members and outgroup members to hold.

Ingroup norms: According to social identity development theory (see Nesdale, 2008), ingroup members are viewed by children as a source of information about what behaviors are acceptable. Nesdale argues that if ethnic ingroup members express prejudice, then this is likely to be accepted as normative ingroup behavior and children may be more likely to express prejudice themselves. It would therefore follow that perceived peer norms about the outgroup can influence children's intergroup attitudes and friendship choices. Supporting this premise, there is evidence that if children believe their fellow ingroup mem-bers dislike outgroup members and disapprove of cross-race friendships, they are more likely to have a negative outgroup attitude (Cameron & Rutland, 2008; Turner et al., 2008). Moreover, a longitudinal study among adolescents showed that social norms for cross-group friend-ship at the start of the school year predicted cross-group friendships at the end of the school year (Feddes et al., 2009). Children also prefer members of their own group who hold same-race friendships. Castelli, De Amicis, and Sherman (2007) found that children aged 4 to 7 years preferred same-group friends who are 'loyal' to their ingroup and are friends with other ingroup members rather than outgroup members. It is therefore imperative to encourage the perception that other ingroup members have positive norms about outgroup members if cross-group friendships are to arise.

Outgroup norms: Perceived outgroup norms for cross-group friendship may also influence friendship choices. If people believe that members of other social groups are against cross-group friendship (i.e. 'they' do not want to be friends with 'us'), they may fear rejection by outgroup members and then avoid them, leading to a reduction in cross-race friendships (e.g., Turner et al., 2008). Research with adults suggests that fear of discrimination may reduce the frequency of subsequent cross-group friendships (Levin et al., 2003). Interventions that can demonstrate that the outgroup *are* friendly and interested in positive intergroup relations may be instrumental in overcoming this barrier to friendship.

Emphasising shared identities: According to the common ingroup identity model (Gaertner & Dovidio, 2000) categorizing people into distinct groups can be a *cause* of intergroup bias. Verkuyten and Steenhuis (2005) found that one of the reasons for not forming cross-group friendships most often cited by teenagers was perceived differences between the ingroup and outgroup. Thus, emphasising a common group to which members of two different groups all belong to, for example a sports team or being in the same class at school, may reduce intergroup bias and increase a desire to form cross-group friendships (see Gaertner et al., 2008, for review). In their evaluation of the 'Green Circle' intervention, Houlette et al. (2004) found that children became more inclusive in their friendship choices when a common category or identity, shared by ingroup and outgroup members, was evoked, while McGlothlin, Killen, and Edmonds (2005) found that shared activity preference was the most important determinant of whether children believed dyads could be friends.

It is, however, important to acknowledge that shared identities do not always reduce intergroup bias. Hornsey and Hogg (2000) found that merging category boundaries led to an increase in intergroup bias, because group members' are motivated to achieve positive distinctiveness from other groups, particularly among those who highly identify with their ingroup (e.g., Crisp, Stone, & Hall, 2006). But according to the dual identity approach (Gaertner & Dovidio, 2000), provided that when a shared identity is introduced, initial group categories are also retained. This will help to avoid any threat to distinctiveness, while enabling the benefits of holding a shared group identity.

In sum, there are a number of factors that impede or, in the case of shared identities, help to promote cross-group friendship. These barriers can be overcome and the promoters can be emphasized through three types of intervention, which we outline below: cooperative learning, extended contact, and indirect contact.

Cooperative Learning

Cooperative learning interventions have been found to improve intergroup attitudes in majority group adults and children (e.g. Desforges et al., 1991; Maras & Brown, 1996). One of the most popular cooperative learning interventions is the Jigsaw Classroom technique (Aronson & Bridgeman, 1979). This involves arranging students into groups which are evenly balanced according to race, ethnicity, sex, and academic ability. This essentially creates a "crossed categorization" context, in which people from diverse groups have the opportunity to interact with one another. Each student learns a unique segment of information which they teach to other group members; they are therefore dependent on one another to acquire the composite parts which constitute the entire lesson. Tests of the Jigsaw Classroom generally reveal improved academic performance and liking for outgroup peers, in part due to the cooperation necessary for the tasks involved (Miller & Harrington, 1990; Walker & Crogan, 1998).

Cooperative learning interventions have been found to improve intergroup attitudes in majority group adults (see Slavin & Cooper, 1999 for review; Desforges et al., 1991) and children. Maras and Brown (1996), for example, evaluated a cooperative learning intervention that involved mainstream children taking part in regular activities with disabled children. These activities were carefully structured so that children had to collaborate in order to complete the tasks. Compared to children in a control condition, those who took part expressed greater liking for the outgroup. Cooperative learning also allows a positive, successful interaction between members of different groups at school which improves intergroup attitudes. We also know from other studies that positive contact is associated with reduced intergroup anxiety (e.g., Voci & Hewstone, 2003). So by generating more positive attitudes and reducing anxiety, children should be more comfortable about developing relationships with outgroup acquaintances they have met into friendships.

Indirect Contact

Two interventions which might help encourage the development of cross-group friendships are extended contact and imagined contact.

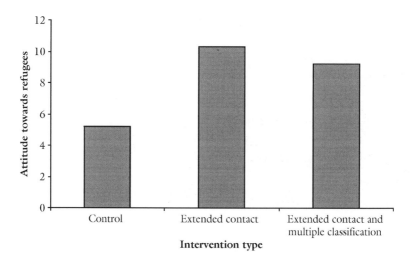

Figure 14.1 Attitude toward refugees as a function of intervention type (Cameron et al., 2007, Study 2).

These are both indirect forms of contact, because they are derived from the contact hypothesis, but need not involve any face-to-face interaction with an outgroup member.

Extended contact is the idea that knowledge of intergroup friendships between members of one's own group and another group can improve intergroup attitudes (Wright et al., 1997). There is evidence to support the extended contact hypothesis in adult populations (see Turner et al., 2007c for review), in adolescents (Liebkind & McAlister, 1999; Turner et al., 2007b, 2008), and in young children (Cameron, Rutland, Brown, & Douch, 2006; Cameron & Rutland, 2006; Cameron, Rutland, & Brown, 2007; Turner et al., 2007c). Interventions based on extended contact have been implemented and evaluated by researchers in schools. Cameron and colleagues developed extended contact interventions for children as young as 5 years (see Cameron & Rutland, 2008, for a review). They exposed children to intergroup friendships by reading them illustrated stories that portrayed friendships between ingroup and outgroup members. In each of the programs, children took part in around six sessions, where they would read and discuss the stories.

The intervention was effective in improving children's attitudes toward outgroups across a number of different stigmatized outgroups, including the disabled (Cameron & Rutland, 2006), refugees (Cameron et al., 2006, 2007), and Asian people (Cameron et al., 2007;

see Figure 14.1). Liebkind & McAlister (1999) designed and evaluated an extended contact intervention that was administered to Finnish adolescents aged 13 to 15 years. Participants were exposed to an extended contact intervention in the form of printed stories of ingroup members in close friendships with members of the outgroup. Compared to a control group who received no intervention, participants who received the extended contact intervention were more positive toward the outgroup and were more tolerant of them.

A number of mediators of the extended contact effect have been established. Cameron and colleagues found among children that extended contact changed norms for intergroup friendship, reduced anxiety and increased 'inclusion of the other in the self' (IOS; see Cameron & Rutland, 2008 for review), whereas Turner et al. (2008) found among adolescents and adults that positive ingroup norms about the outgroup, positive outgroup norms about the ingroup, reduced intergroup anxiety, and IOS mediated the positive relationship between extended contact and outgroup attitude among South Asians and Whites in the UK.

Imagined contact is "the mental simulation of social interaction with a member or members of an outgroup category" (Crisp & Turner, 2009, p. 234). Mental imagery has been found to elicit similar emotional and motivational responses as the real experience (Dadds, Bovbjerg, Redd, & Cutmore, 1997) and neuropsychological studies have shown that it shares the same neurological basis as perception and employs similar neurological mechanisms as memory, emotion and motor control (Kosslyn, Ganis, & Thompson, 2001). Accordingly, imagining oneself interacting positively with an outgroup member should automatically activate thoughts and feelings similar to those experienced in real-life intergroup interactions, for example feeling more comfortable and less apprehensive about interacting with outgroup members. Imagined contact may also generate deliberative thought processes similar to those experienced in real-life contact, for example thinking about what might be learned from the outgroup member and what emotions might be experienced during the interaction. By activating these automatic and deliberative processes that occur during *actual* contact, imagined contact should have the same positive effects on outgroup evaluations (Turner et al., 2007a).

Recent research with minority and majority adults supports this theory. Two initial studies showed that young participants who were asked to imagine having a positive interaction with an elderly stranger showed less ingroup bias than participants in a control condition (Turner et al., 2007b; Studies 1 & 2). Subsequently, imagined contact has been shown to change straight men's attitudes toward gay men (Turner et al., 2007b; Study 3), Mexicans' attitudes toward Mestizos in Mexico (Stathi & Crisp, 2008), and non-Muslims' implicit attitudes toward Muslims (Turner & Crisp, 2009).

One of the main advantages of indirect forms of contact is that they might be used as a means of *preparing* people for face-to-face contact, and more specifically, cross-group friendships (Crisp & Turner, 2009; Turner et al., 2007a, 2007c). Extended contact involves observing the successful behavior of another person. This reduces fears and inhibitions (e.g., Paolini et al., 2004; Turner et al., 2007a, 2007b; Vonofakou, Hewstone, & Voci, 2007) and should therefore increase self-efficacy about performing the same behavior ourselves (Bandura, 1977). Imagined contact has also been shown to reduce intergroup anxiety (Turner et al., 2007a). Moreover, both extended and imagined contact are associated with more positive outgroup attitudes. Given that, following these interventions, participants should feel more positive and comfortable about the prospect of actual contact, indirect contact should increase the likelihood that intergroup contact will be instigated. Moreover, when an encounter occurs, the interaction is likely to run more smoothly, be more successful, and therefore improve intergroup attitudes further. This should increase the likelihood that acquaintance contact will develop into long-lasting friendships.

Mutual Benefits of Collaboration between Academics and Educators

In this review, we have considered diversity-based interventions developed by educators and practitioners, and interventions developed by psychologists. Both types of interventions have been shown to be successful in generating more positive intergroup attitudes and behaviors. However, each has limitations and strengths. On the one hand, interventions developed by educators are highly practical, and have been implemented extensively and across a number of contexts. However, they are often not subject to rigorous evaluation. This can led to mixed findings, and means that it is difficult to determine the impact such interventions have, their underlying mechanisms and the groups with whom they are most effective. This information is essential for the development of effective diversity-based intervention strategies that are tailored to suit their recipients (Paluck & Green, 2009; Bigler, 1999).

On the other hand, academic-developed interventions benefit in terms of 1) their rigorous evaluation, which provides information on the mechanisms by which interventions work, and the contexts and groups of people with whom they are most effective and 2) their basis in psychological research and findings, which leads to more effective interventions which have a greater impact on intergroup attitudes. But one weakness of these interventions is that the resultant technique is often impractical. In many cases, in order to achieve the level of control required in order to reliably test a technique, the intervention is often delivered by an additional member of staff, or the research assistant themselves. While this ensures that the intervention can be evaluated reliably, and that the intervention follows the main tenets of the psychological theory upon which it is based, this can lead to interventions which in practice are impractical, and are unlikely to be used following the research project.

We argue that increased collaboration between educators and psychologists allows both parties to capitalise on the others' strengths and overcome their respective limitations, resulting in interventions that are both practical *and* effective. More specifically, collaborations with researchers allow practitioners to capitalise on academics' empirical expertise and determine whether their intervention is having the desired impact on intergroup attitudes, determine with whom the intervention is effective and also allow them to test different versions of the interventions in order to develop the most effective intervention type. Furthermore, theoretical perspectives on and research findings concerning prejudice in children could potentially inform the *content* of prejudice-reduction interventions, improving their effectiveness. Meanwhile, academics would benefit from practitioners' extensive practical expertise and experience in the field: they know what works practically and the crucial social issues and conflicts that should be addressed through diversity-interventions. Such collaboration would result in diversity-based interventions that have a significant impact on intergroup attitudes, and are user-friendly and responsive to emerging intergroup conflicts.

Route to Collaboration

There are a number of ways in which a partnership between academics and educators could operate, but here we describe two potential routes to successful collaborations. Firstly, intervention programs can be designed that combine educator-and academic-developed interventions for maximal impact. An advantage of diversity-based interventions developed by educators is that they can often be used in contexts in which the recipients have little opportunity to experience diversity directly. Such interventions could be used to prepare individuals for experience of diversity in the next stage of the intervention program, in which individuals experience direct contact, for instance, through cooperative learning groups. Such a combination of techniques would ensure that the direct contact ran smoothly and had maximal impact on intergroup attitudes. The second approach would involve drawing on the expertise of both groups to devise completely new diversity-based interventions that are both practical, and theoretically-based. For example, an intervention for use in non-diverse schools might be developed that involves successful elements of anti-racist programs with indirect contact techniques, such as imagining interactions with outgroup members, or learning through stories about friendships between ingroup and outgroup members. Moreover, teachers could be trained to ensure that practitioner and academic-developed components are delivered effectively.

In both cases, the partnership would benefit from academics' expertise in experimental design and methodology, which would facilitate rigorous evaluation to determine the impact of the techniques on intergroup attitudes. In our experience, such collaborations are most beneficial when both parties are equally involved in the development and design of the diversity-based intervention from the outset. In order to ensure adequate restrictions are in place and that reliable evaluations can be conducted, academics should be involved from the design stage of the intervention in order to advise on appropriate measures and to ensure there is a large enough sample and adequate control groups in order to test the effectiveness of the intervention reliably. This increases the likelihood that conditions and controls are put in place that allow systematic evaluation of the intervention impact, and ensures the intervention is practical and sustainable. However, both parties should be prepared to recognise and value the other's expertise, make compromises and be flexible and realistic in their requirements.

In this chapter, we have reviewed the respective strengths and weaknesses of academic- and educator-developed diversity-based interventions. The expertises of both parties are highly complementary and a partnership which draws on their respective contributions would allow each to overcome their limitations. Accordingly, we are optimistic that through greater collaboration, practical *and* effective diversity-based interventions can be developed.

References

Aboud, F. (1988). *Children and prejudice*. Oxford: Blackwell.

Aboud, F. E., & Fenwick, V. (1999). Exploring and evaluating school-based interventions to reduce prejudice. *Journal of Social Issues, 55*, 767–785.

Aboud, F. E., & Levy, S. R. (2000). Interventions to reduce prejudice and discrimination in children and adolescents. In Stuart Oskamp (Ed.), *Reducing prejudice and discrimination* (pp. 269–293). Mahwah, NJ: Erlbaum.

Aboud, F. E., Mendelson, M. J., & Purdy, K. T. (2003). Cross-race peer relations and friendship quality. *International Journal of Behavioral Development, 27*, 165–173.

Aboud, F. E., & Sankar, J. (2007). Friendship and identity in a language-integrated school. *International Journal of Behavioral Development, 31*, 445–453.

Allport, G. W. (1954). *The nature of prejudice*. New York: Doubleday Anchor.

Aronson, E., & Bridgeman, D. (1979). Jigsaw groups and the desegregated classroom: in pursuit of common goals. *Personality and Social Psychology Bulletin, 5*, 438–446.

Bandura, A. (1977). Self-efficacy: Towards a unifying theory of behavioral change. *Psychological Review, 84*, 191–215.

Banks, J. A. (1995). Multicultural education: Its effects on students' racial and gender role attitudes. In J. A. Banks & C. M. Banks (Eds.), *Handbook of research on multicultural education* (pp. 617–727). New York: Macmillan.

Batson, C. D., Polycarpou, M. P., Harmon-Jones, E., Imhoff, H. J., Mitchener, E. C., Bednar, L. L., Klein, T. R., & Highberger, L. (1997). Empathy and attitudes: can feelings for a member of a stigmatized group improve feelings toward the group? *Journal of Personality and Social Psychology, 72*, 105–118.

Bigler, R. S. (1995). The role of classification skill in moderating environmental influences on children's gender stereotyping: A study of the functional use of gender in the classroom. *Child Development, 66*, 1072–1087.

Bigler, R. S. (1999). The use of multicultural curricula and materials to counter racism in children. *Journal of Social Issues, 55*, 687–705.

Bigler, R. S., Jones, L. C., & Lobliner, D. B. (1997). Social categorization and the formation of intergroup attitudes in children. *Child Development, 68*, 530–543.

Bigler, R. S., & Liben, L. S. (1992). Cognitive mechanisms in children's gender stereotyping: Theoretical and educational implications of a cognitive-based intervention. *Child Development, 63*, 1351–1363.

Bigler, R. S., & Liben, L. S. (1993). A cognitive developmental approach to racial stereotyping and reconstructive memory in Euro-American children. *Child Development, 64*, 1507–1518.

Cameron, D. (2009). *Attitude is Everything: Final Report*. Report of research findings to World Education Development Group.

Cameron, L., & Rutland, A. (2006). Extended contact through story reading in school: Reducing children's prejudice towards the disabled. *Journal of Social Issues, 62,* 469–488.

Cameron, L., & Rutland, A. (2008). Comparing theoretical models of prejudice reduction among different age groups. In S. Levy & M. Killen (Eds.), *Intergroup relations: An integrative developmental and social psychological perspective.* Oxford: Oxford University Press.

Cameron, L., Rutland, A., & Brown, R. (2007). Promoting children's positive intergroup attitudes towards stigmatized groups: Extended contact and multiple classification skills training. *International Journal of Behavioral Development, 31,* 454–466.

Cameron, L., Rutland, A., Brown, R. J., & Douch, R. (2006). Changing children's intergroup attitudes towards refugees: Testing different models of extended contact. *Child Development, 77,* 1208–1219.

Castelli, L., De Amicis, L., & Sherman, S. J. (2007). The loyal member effect: On the preference for ingroup members who engage in exclusive relations with the ingroup. *Developmental Psychology, 43*(6), 1347–1359.

Cole, C., Arafat, C., Tidhar, C., Zidan, W. T., Fox, N. A., Killen, M., Leavitt, L., Lesser, G., Richman, B. A., Ardila-Rey, A., & Yung, F. (2003). The educational impact of Rechov Sumsum/Shara'a Simsim, a television series for Israeli and Palestinian children. *International Journal of Behavioral Development, 27,* 409–422.

Connolly, P. (2009). Developing programmes to promote ethnic diversity in early childhood: Lessons from Northern Ireland. Working Paper No. 52. The Hague, The Netherlands: Bernard van Leer Foundation.

Crisp, R. J., & Hewstone, M. (2007). Multiple social categorization. In M. P. Zanna (Ed.), *Advances in Experimental Social Psychology* (Vol. 39, pp. 163–254). Orlando, FL: Academic Press.

Crisp, R. J., Hewstone, M., & Rubin, M. (2001). Does multiple categorization reduce intergroup bias? *Personality and Social Psychology Bulletin, 27,* 76–89.

Crisp, R. J., Stone, C. H., & Hall, N. R. (2006). Recategorization and subgroup identification: Predicting and preventing threats from common ingroups. *Personality and Social Psychology Bulletin, 32,* 230–243.

Crisp, R. J., & Turner, R. N. (2009). Can imagined interactions produce positive perceptions? Reducing prejudice through simulated social contact. *American Psychologist, 64,* 231–240.

Dadds, M. R., Bovbjerg, D. H., Redd, W. H., & Cutmore, T. R. (1997). Imagery in human classical conditioning. *Psychological Bulletin, 122,* 89–103.

Department for Education and Skills (2007). *Diversity and Citizenship Curriculum Review.* London: HMSO.

Derman-Sparks, L., & Phillips, C. B. (1997). *Teaching/learning anti-racism: A developmental approach.* New York: Teachers College, Columbia University Press.

Desforges, D. M., Lord, C. G., Ramsey, S. L., Mason, J. A., Van Leeuwen, M. D., West, S. C., & Lepper, M. (1991). Effects of structured cooperative contact on changing negative attitudes toward stigmatized social groups. *Journal of Personality and Social Psychology*, 60, 531–544.

Devine, P. G., Monteith, M. J., Zuwernick, J. R., & Elliot, A. J. (1991). Prejudice with and without compunction. *Journal of Personality and Social Psychology*, 60, 817–830.

Duckitt, J. (1992). *The social psychology of prejudice*. New York: Praeger.

Ellis, C., & Sonnenfield, J. A. (1994). Diverse approaches to managing diversity. *Human Resources Management*, 33, 77–109.

Feddes, A. R., Noack, P., & Rutland, A. (2009). Direct and extended friendship effects on minority and majority children's interethnic attitudes: A longitudinal study. *Child Development*, 80, 377–390.

Festinger, L. (1957). *A theory of cognitive dissonance*. Stanford, CA: Stanford University Press.

Fiske, S. T., & Neuberg, S. L. (1990). A continuum of impression formation, from category-based to individuating processes: Influences of information and motivation on attention and interpretation. In L. Berkowitz (Ed.), *Advances in experimental social psychology* (Vol. 23, pp. 1–74). New York: Academic Press.

Gaertner, S. L., & Dovidio, J. F. (2000). *Reducing intergroup bias: The common in-group identity model*. Hove, East Sussex: Psychology Press.

Gaertner, S. L., Dovidio, J. F., Guerra, R., Rebelo, M., Riek, B. M., & Houlette, M. A. (2008). The Common Ingroup Identity Model: Applications to children and adults. In S. Levy & M. Killen (Eds.), *Intergroup Relations: An Integrative Developmental and Social Psychological Perspective*. Oxford University Press: Oxford.

Gavin, L. A., & Furman, W. (1989). Age differences in adolescents' perceptions of their peer groups. *Developmental Psychology*, 25, 827–834.

Genesee, F., & Gandara, P. (1999). Bilingual education programs: A cross-national perspective. *Journal of Social Issues*, 55, 665–686.

Glasberg, R., & Aboud, F. E. (1981). A developmental perspective on the study of depression: Children's evaluative reactions to sadness. *Developmental Psychology*, 17, 195–202.

Graham, J. A., & Cohen, R. (1997). Race and sex as factors in children's sociometric ratings and friendship choices. *Social Development*, 6, 355–372.

Gurin, P., Peng, T., Lopez, G., & Nagda, B. R. (1999). Context identity and intergroup relations. In D. Prentice & D. Miller (Eds.), *Cultural divides: The social psychology of intergroup contact* (pp. 133–170). New York: Sage.

Hall, N. R., & Crisp, R. J. (2005). Considering multiple criteria for social categorization can reduce intergroup bias. *Personality and Social Psychology Bulletin*, 31, 1435–1444.

Hanover, J. M. B., & Cellar, D. F. (1998). Environmental factors and the effectiveness of workforce diversity training. *Human Resources Development Quarterly*, 9, 105–124.

Hill, M. E., & Augoustinos, M. (2001). Stereotype change and prejudice reduction: Short- and long-term evaluation of a cross-cultural awareness programme. *Journal of Community and Applied Social Psychology, 11*, 243–262.

Hornsey, M. J., & Hogg, M. A. (2000). Subgroup relations: A comparison of mutual intergroup differentiation and common ingroup identity models of prejudice reduction. *Personality and Social Psychology Bulletin, 26*, 242–256.

Houlette, M., Gaertner, S. L., Johnson, K. M., Banker, B. S., Riek, B. M., & Dovidio, J. F. (2004). Developing a more inclusive social identity: An elementary school intervention. *Journal of Social Issues, 60*, 35–55.

Hughes, J. M., Bigler, R. S., & Levy, S. R. (2007). Consequences of learning about historical racism among European American and African American adolescents. *Child Development, 78*, 1689–1705.

Jackson, M. F., Barth, J. M., Powell, N., & Lochman, J. E. (2006). Classroom Contextual Effects of Race on Children's Peer Nominations. *Child Development, 77*, 1325–1337.

Katz, P. A., & Zalk, S. R. (1978). Modification of children's racial attitudes. *Developmental Psychology, 14*, 447–461.

Knowles, E., & Ridley, W. (2006). *Another spanner in the works*. Stoke-on-Trent, UK: Trentham Books.

Koeller, S. (1977). The effects of listening to excerpts from children's stories about Mexican-Americans on the attitudes of sixth graders. *Journal of Educational Research, 70*, 329–334.

Kosslyn, S. M., Ganis, G., & Thompson, W. L. (2001). Neural foundations of imagery. *Nature Reviews Neuroscience, 2*, 635–642.

Kulik, C. T., Perry, E. L., & Bourhis, A. C. (2000). Ironic evaluation processes: effects of thought suppression on evaluation of older job applicants. *Journal of Organizational Behavior, 21*, 689–711.

Levin, S., van Laar, C., & Sidanius, J. (2003). The effects of ingroup and outgroup friendships on ethnic attitudes in college: A longitudinal study. *Group Processes and Intergroup Relations, 6*, 76–92.

Liebkind, K., & McAlister, A. (1999). Extended contact through peer modelling to promote tolerance in Finland. *European Journal of Social Psychology, 29*, 765–780.

Litcher, J. H., & Johnson, D. W. (1969). Changes in attitudes towards Negroes of White elementary school students after of multiethnic readers. *Journal of Educational Psychology, 60*, 148–152.

Macrae, C. N., Bodenhausen, G. V., & Milne, A. B. (1995). The dissection of selection in person perception: Inhibitory processes in social stereotyping. *Journal of Personality & Social Psychology, 69*, 397–407.

Maras, P., & Brown, R. (1996). Effects of contact on children's attitudes towards disability: A longitudinal study. *Journal of Applied Social Psychology, 26*, 2113–2134.

Maras, P., & Brown, R. (2000). Effects of different forms of school contact on children's attitudes toward disabled and non-disabled peers. *British Journal of Educational Psychology, 70*, 337–351.

McGlothlin, H., & Killen, M. (2005). Children's perceptions of intergroup and intragroup similarity and the role of social experience. *Journal of Applied Developmental Psychology, 26,* 680–698.

McGlothlin, H., Killen, M., & Edmonds, C. (2005). European-American children's intergroup attitudes about peer relationships. *British Journal of Developmental Psychology, 23,* 227–249.

McGregor, J. (1993). Effectiveness of role-playing antiracist teaching in reducing student prejudice. *Journal of Educational Research, 86,* 215–226.

Miller, N., & Harrington, H. J. (1990). A situational identity perspective on cultural diversity and teamwork in the classroom. In S. Sharon (Ed.), *Cooperative learning: Theory and research* (pp. 39–75). New York: Praeger.

Nesdale, D. (2008). Peer group rejection and children's intergroup prejudice. In S. Levy & M. Killen (Eds.), *Intergroup relations: An integrative developmental and social psychological perspective.* Oxford University Press: Oxford.

Neuberg, S. L. (1996). Expectancy influences in social interaction: The moderating role of social goals. In J. A. Bargh & P. M. Gollwitzer (Eds.), *The psychology of action: Linking cognition and motivation to behavior* (pp. 529–552). New York: Guilford Press.

Oskamp, S. (2000). *Reducing prejudice and discrimination.* Mahwah, NJ: Erlbaum.

Paluck, E. L., & Green, D. L. (2009). Prejudice reduction: What works? A review and assessment of research and practice. *Annual Review of Psychology, 60,* 339–367.

Paolini, S., Hewstone, M., Cairns, E., & Voci, A. (2004). Effect of direct and indirect cross-group friendships on judgements of Catholics and Protestants in Northern Ireland: The mediating role of an anxiety-reduction mechanism. *Personality and Social Psychology Bulletin, 30,* 770–786.

Pettigrew, T. (1997). Generalized intergroup contact effects on prejudice. *Personality and Social Psychology Bulletin, 23,* 173–185.

Pettigrew, T. F. (1998). Intergroup contact: Theory, research and new perspectives. *Annual Review of Psychology, 49,* 65–85.

Pettigrew, T. F., & Tropp, L. R. (2006). A meta-analytic test of intergroup contact theory. *Journal of Personality and Social Psychology, 90,* 751–783.

Pfeifer, J. H., Brown, C. S., & Juvonen, J. (2007). Fifty years since Brown v. Board of Education: Lessons learned about the development and reduction of children's prejudice. *Social Policy Report. 21*(2).

Piaget, J. (1965). *The moral judgment of the child.* New York: Free Press.

Piaget, J. (1970). *The science of education and the psychology of the child.* New York: Grossman.

Plant, E. A., & Devine, P. G. (2003). The antecedents and implications of interracial anxiety. *Personality and Social Psychology Bulletin, 29,* 790–801.

Rothbart, M., & John, O. P. (1985). Social categorization and behavioral episodes: A cognitive analysis of the effects of intergroup contact. *Journal of Social Issues, 41,* 81–104.

Rutland, A., Cameron, L., Bennett, L., & Ferrell, J. (2005). Interracial contact and racial constancy: A multi-site study of racial intergroup bias in 3–5 year old Anglo-British children. *Journal of Applied Developmental Psychology, 26,* 699–713.

Salzman, M., & D'Andrea, M. (2001). Assessing the impact of a prejudice prevention project. *Journal of Counselling & Development, 79,* 341–347.

Shelton, J. N., & Richeson, J. A. (2005). Intergroup contact and pluralistic ignorance. *Journal of Personality and Social Psychology, 88,* 91–107.

Slavin, R. E., & Madden, N. A. (1979). School practices that improve race relations. *American Educational Research Journal, 16,* 169–180.

Slavin, R. E., & Cooper, R. (1999). Improving intergroup relations: Lessons learned from cooperative learning programmes. *Journal of Social Issues, 55,* 647–664.

Spencer, M. S. (1998). Reducing racism in schools: Moving beyond the rhetoric. *Social Work in Education, 20,* 25–36.

Stathi, S., & Crisp, R. J. (2008). Imagining intergroup contact promotes projection to outgroups. *Journal of Experimental Social Psychology, 44,* 943–957.

Stephan, C. W., Renfro, L., & Stephan, W. G. (2004). The evaluation of multicultural education programs: Techniques and a meta-analysis. In W. G. Stephan & W. P. Vogt (Eds.), *Education programs for improving intergroup relations: Theory, research and practice* (pp. 227–242). New York: Teachers College Press.

Stephan, W. G., & Stephan, C. W. (1985). Intergroup anxiety. *Journal of Social Issues, 41,* 157–176.

Tadmor, C. T., & Tetlock, P. E. (2006). Biculturalism: A model of the effects of second-culture exposure on acculturation and integrative complexity. *Journal of Cross-Cultural Psychology, 37,* 173–190.

Tropp, L. R., & Prenovost, M. (2008). The role of intergroup contact in predicting interethnic attitudes: Evidence from meta-analytic and field studies. In S. Levy & M. Killen (Eds.), *Intergroup attitudes and relations in childhood through adulthood* (pp. 236–248). Oxford: Oxford University Press.

Turner, R. N., & Crisp, R. J. (2009). Imagining intergroup contact reduces implicit prejudice. *British Journal of Social Psychology.* DOI: 10.1348/014466609X419901 .

Turner, R. N., Crisp, R. J., & Lambert, E. (2007a). Imagining intergroup contact can improve intergroup attitudes. *Group Processes and Intergroup Relations, 10,* 427–441.

Turner, R. N., Hewstone, M., & Voci, A. (2007b). Reducing explicit and implicit prejudice via direct and extended contact: The mediating role of self-disclosure and intergroup anxiety. *Journal of Personality and Social Psychology, 93,* 369–388.

Turner, R. N., Hewstone, M., Voci, A., Paolini, S., & Christ, O. (2007c). Reducing prejudice via direct and extended cross-group friendship. *European Review of Social Psychology, 18,* 212–255.

Turner, R. N., Hewstone, M., Voci, A., & Vonofakou, C. (2008). A test of the extended contact hypothesis: The mediating role of intergroup anxiety, perceived ingroup and outgroup norms, and inclusion of the outgroup in the self. *Journal of Personality and Social Psychology*, 95, 843–860.

Verkuyten, M., & Steenhuis, A. (2005). Preadolescents' understanding and reasoning about asylum seeker peers and friendships. *Journal of Applied Developmental Psychology*, 26, 652–667.

Voci, A., & Hewstone, M. (2003). Intergroup contact and prejudice towards immigrants in Italy: The mediational role of anxiety and the moderational role of group salience. *Group Processes and Intergroup Relations*, 6, 37–54.

Vonofakou, C., Hewstone, M., & Voci, A. (2007). Contact with outgroup friends as a predictor of meta-attitudinal strength and accessibility of attitudes towards gay men. *Journal of Personality and Social Psychology*, 92, 804–820.

Wagner, U., van Dick, R., Pettigrew, T. F., & Christ, O. (2003). Ethnic prejudice in East and West Germany: The explanatory power of intergroup contact. *Group Processes and Intergroup Relations*, 6, 22–36.

Walker, I., & Crogan, M. (1998). Academic performance, prejudice, and the jigsaw classroom: New pieces to the puzzle. *Journal of Community and Applied Social Psychology*, 8, 381–393.

Weiner, M. J., & Wright, F. E. (1973). Effects of undergoing arbitrary discrimination upon subsequent attitudes toward a minority group. *Journal of Applied Social Psychology*, 3, 94–102.

Williams, J. E., & Morland, J. K. (1976). *Race, color and the young child*. Chapel Hill: University of North Carolina Press.

Wolsko, C., Park, B., Judd, C. M., & Wittenbrink, B. (2000). Framing interethnic ideology: Effects of multicultural and colour-blind perspectives on judgements of groups and individuals. *Journal of Personality and Social Psychology*, 78, 635–654.

Wright, S. C., & Tropp, L. R. (2005). Language and intergroup contact: Investigating the impact of bilingual instruction on children's intergroup attitudes. *Group Processes and Intergroup Relations*, 8, 309–328.

Wright, S. C., Aron, A., McLaughlin-Volpe, T., & Ropp, S. A. (1997). The extended contact effect: Knowledge of cross-group friendships and prejudice. *Journal of Personality and Social Psychology*, 73, 73–90.

Index

Note: page numbers in italics denote tables or figures